Practical PHP and MySQL Web Site Databases

A Simplified Approach

Adrian W. West

Apress®

Practical PHP and MySQL Web Site Databases: A Simplified Approach

ISBN-13 (pbk): 978-1-4302-6076-9

ISBN-13 (electronic): 978-1-4302-6077-6

President and Publisher: Paul Manning
Lead Editor: Ben Renow-Clarke
Technical Reviewer: Andrew Zack
Editorial Board: Steve Anglin, Ewan Buckingham, Gary Cornell, Louise Corrigan, James DeWolf, Jonathan Gennick, Jonathan Hassell, Robert Hutchinson, Michelle Lowman, James Markham, Matthew Moodie, Jeff Olson, Jeffrey Pepper, Douglas Pundick, Ben Renow-Clarke, Dominic Shakeshaft, Gwenan Spearing, Matt Wade, Steve Weiss, Tom Welsh
Coordinating Editor: Kevin Shea
Copy Editor: Roger LeBlanc
Compositor: SPi Global
Indexer: SPi Global
Artist: SPi Global
Cover Designer: Anna Ishchenko

Distributed to the book trade worldwide by Springer Science+Business Media New York, 233 Spring Street, 6th Floor, New York, NY 10013. Phone 1-800-SPRINGER, fax (201) 348-4505, e-mail orders-ny@springer-sbm.com, or visit www.springeronline.com.

For information on translations, please e-mail rights@apress.com, or visit www.apress.com.

Apress and friends of ED books may be purchased in bulk for academic, corporate, or promotional use. eBook versions and licenses are also available for most titles. For more information, reference our Special Bulk Sales–eBook Licensing web page at www.apress.com/bulk-sales.

Any source code or other supplementary materials referenced by the author in this text is available to readers at www.apress.com. For detailed information about how to locate your book's source code, go to www.apress.com/source-code.

I dedicate this book to the open source community, without which there would be no Apache, PHP, MySQL, XAMPP, MAMPP, EASYPHP or phpMyAdmin to write about. Because the software is free and supported by many forums and lists run by knowledgeable enthusiasts, there is no obstacle preventing me (or my readers) from learning how to produce database-driven websites.

—Adrian W. West

Contents at a Glance

Contents

About the Author

Adrian West resigned as a chartered engineer to become the UK director of a correspondence school. He has been teaching in one form or another since 1982. He introduced computers into his workplace in 1987 and taught the staff how to use them. For four years, he taught undergraduates computer skills at a college in Cheshire in the United Kingdom.

Adrian lives in Colyton, a town in Devon, England, and for the last 14 years, he has designed and produced web sites for local businesses and charities. For a time, he also served as a computer technician and teacher to about 100 people in his community. Then he decided to concentrate on his favorite occupation, designing web sites. To avoid disappointing his former clients, he launched a free computer-help web site at `http://www.colycomputerhelp.co.uk`.

Adrian also writes monthly computer-help articles for two local magazines.

Adrian is the author of *Practical HTML5 Projects* (`Apress.com`, 2012), a book dedicated to improving the design of web sites. That book was prompted by the lack of information on certain aspects of web design. He researched, tested, and developed solutions for these useful but otherwise poorly documented techniques.

About the Technical Reviewer

Andrew Zack is the CEO of ZTMC, Inc. (ztmc.com) specializing in Search Engine Optimization (SEO) and Internet marketing strategies. His project background includes almost 20 years of site development and project management experience and over 15 years as a SEO and Internet marketing expert.

Mr. Zack has also been very active in the publishing industry, having co-authored *Flash 5 Studio* and served as a technical reviewer on over ten books and industry publications.

Acknowledgments

I thank my wife, Janice, for her love and support, for taking over my share of the chores so that I could concentrate on this book, for her encouragement, and for putting up with my absence as I hunched over the keyboard. I could never have managed without her meticulous proofreading, which she patiently repeated four times per chapter as each editorial stage was reached.

My thanks also go to the magnificent team at Apress: Ben Renow-Clarke for his encouragement and for his advice on the layout and content of the chapters; Kevin Shea, who coordinated everybody and ensured that I sent chapters and files on time; and Roger LeBlanc, the copy editor, who polished my chapters and helped me conform to the Apress house style. I thank Andrew Zack, the technical reviewer, who checked my code and suggested several useful resources for inclusion in the book. I thank the Apress production team and SPi Global for promptly and efficiently dealing with tweaks and revisions to the page proofs.

And my thanks go to all the people in forums who helped me and replied to my queries and to all those who placed information on the Internet, from which I learned so much.

—Adrian W. West

Introduction

The Teaching Method

I am a web site designer rather than a programmer. My choice of a book is based on how much practical application it contains, not on how much a book concentrates on the syntax of a language as an end in itself. This book follows my preference; therefore, *Practical PHP and MySQL Web Site Databases - A Simplified Approach* uses a different way of teaching web site database design than the majority of manuals. The usual layout starts with several lessons on PHP followed by snippets of command-line code, and it may eventually conclude with a project or two. This book abandons that approach. The primary focus is on fully worked, practical MySQL database projects built into real-world web pages.

In this book, practical databases and interactive web pages are presented as early as possible; in fact, you will create a database and a table in the first chapter. In the second chapter, you will embed a database into an interactive (dynamic) web page and test it. Each subsequent chapter will introduce you to increasingly sophisticated and useful database-driven web site pages.

To a busy web designer who is unfamiliar with PHP and databases, the requirements in order of importance are as follows:

- How to embed PHP and interactive databases into real-world web pages. This is the primary theme throughout the book.

- How to create a free environment for testing database-driven web pages.

- How to create a user-friendly interface so that an administrator with minimum computer skills can monitor the database.

- To understand how PHP, HTML, and MySQL work together to create and maintain a database and its data.

Instead of presenting PHP, SQL, and MYSQL as completely separate topics, these are explained in context as the projects unfold. However, when you eventually become proficient in these languages, a quick PHP/MySQL reference would be helpful; therefore, you will find this in the Appendix.

Because databases can only be viewed and tested on a server, the first part of Chapter 1 has instructions for using a free server that can be downloaded and installed on the reader's computer. This ensures that readers will have a safe development platform for learning and testing as they explore the book's practical projects.

A study of the theory and syntax can deter learners and prolong the time until they get their hands on a practical application. The history and development of the car and a study of the internal combustion engine will not help a would-be driver. However, jumping into a car and driving it will produce quicker results, and learners are enthused when they achieve something. This book jumps into the database driving seat right from the beginning. Essential PHP and MySQL techniques are presented in context within each tutorial, where they are most relevant.

Some database text books advocate using a framework; they suggest that this facilitates the development of a database-driven web site. I find frameworks utterly confusing, even though I have experience programming databases using raw code. If you are a beginner, I suggest you steer clear of frameworks until you have gained some more experience and understand the fundamentals of how a database-driven website works.

Who Is This Book For?

The book assumes that the reader is thoroughly familiar with HTML and CSS. However, concerning MySQL, PHP, and phpMyAdmin, the book starts from an absolute beginner's point of view. As the chapters unfold, they progress towards intermediate level. Because command-line programming would not be welcomed by the modern generation of readers, the book concentrates on mouse-operated Graphical User Interfaces (GUIs) and PHP files for creating and managing databases.

You do not need to acquire an extensive knowledge of PHP to create interactive databases. I introduce all the PHP you will need in the appropriate place within each project. Each piece of PHP code is explained fully in plain English. The step-by-step, fully-worked examples will show you what MySQL and PHP can do and how to do it. *Practical PHP and MySQL Web Site Databases - A Simplified Approach* is for web designers who wish to begin developing database-driven web sites. Like the author, they may have struggled with the current manuals and despaired. They may also have been frustrated by the limitations of paint-by-numbers content management systems such as Joomla and Wordpress.

With this in mind, *Practical PHP and MySQL Web Site Databases - A Simplified Approach* uses a highly motivational, step-by-step approach. The author recognizes fully that a sense of achievement encourages the reader to look forward eagerly to the next step. For readers who have little or no knowledge of PHP, the book will teach enough PHP to complete all the projects in the book. Web developers who are ready to move beyond the MySQL basics, or who have not kept up to date with their MySQL and PHP, will also benefit from *Practical PHP and MySQL Web Site Databases - A Simplified Approach*.

College and university IT teachers will find that the book provides an excellent set text; the projects can form a basis for students to adapt for their course work.

The "Quick and Easy-to-Learn" Myth

Manuals frequently state that PHP and MySQL databases are easily and quickly learned. This discourages beginners, because when they are confronted with the inevitable difficulties (and error messages), they begin to think that they will never grasp even the basic principles.

Beginners should not be discouraged if they remember the following fact: authors claiming that PHP and MySQL are easily and quickly learned are not being deceptive; they have probably been using PHP and MySQL for more than a decade and have forgotten the difficulties they encountered when they first began.

If you accept that some time and effort is required to learn PHP and MySQL, then as time passes, it will become increasingly apparent that you are learning something very worthwhile. The task will become progressively easier, so have patience and persevere. You will then begin to enjoy mastering this valuable new discipline.

The Origin of This Book

I was asked to enhance one of my client's web sites by adding a membership database and a members' registration form. Although I have designed, developed, and maintained web sites for many years, I had no knowledge of MySQL databases. I bought and borrowed a boatload of books and searched the Internet for tutorials. I was very disappointed with the majority of the books.

Most of the MySQL manuals tended to demonstrate the author's deep and extensive knowledge of PHP and MySQL instead of teaching how to embed MySQL databases into web pages. In contrast , this book uses fully worked examples to demonstrate how to integrate databases into a web site.

PHP/MySQL manuals can have up to 800 pages, which would deter any beginner. I once bought such a manual. It contained hardly any practical worked examples. This meant that I could only use the book to stand on when changing a light bulb. (The manual was almost 2 inches thick.)

The many MySQL database manuals that I own (or borrowed) were unnecessarily complicated. The authors had become used to using neat tricks and shortcuts that were second nature to them. These cluttered the code, making it difficult for beginners to discern the basic structure.

Practical PHP and MySQL Web Site Databases - A Simplified Approach avoids this mistake. A few useful tricks are introduced gradually and are fully explained in plain English. I based the book on a quote from the composer Brahms, who said:

It is easy to compose but wonderfully hard to let the superfluous notes fall under the table.

MySQL manuals are nearly always written assuming that the web designer will administer the databases. Smaller e-commerce web sites, clubs, and societies cannot afford to do this and would prefer that their membership secretary was able to administer the database using a user-friendly interface. Of course, the web designer should always be available for major administrative jobs, such as adding a new column or a table. The majority of the databases created in this book can be administered by both an unskilled membership secretary and the web designer.

Some manuals provide instructions using only MS-DOS style command-lines. Having used a GUI (mouse-operated system) from the start of their computing experience, anyone under the age of 40 would not know what an MS-DOS command line was. Some manuals published in 2012 still use command-line listings. What would a beginner make of the sort of code shown in Figure 1?

```
C:\mysql\bin>mysql -u root
Welcome to the MYSQL monitor. Commands ends with ; or/g.
Your MYSQL connection id is 10 to server version 4.0.18.nt

Type 'help;' or '\h' for help. Type '\c' to clear the buffer.

Mysql> grant all privileges on *.* to fredbloggs@localhost
     Identified by "ringtone7" with grant option;
Query Ok, 0 rows affected (0.03 secs)
|
mysql>
```

Figure 1. *An example of the command-line code that would frighten most beginners*

Sometimes I had as many as seven MySQL/PHP manuals open at the same time to piece together enough information to complete a simple task. In parallel, I ran Internet searches to supplement the most obscure manuals; sadly, some forums tended to deal more with paint-by-numbers (CMS) web sites rather than HTML web sites. Only two of the seven manuals took the trouble to embed its databases into real-world web pages.

Eventually, I concluded that I must write my own manual based on what I could learn by concatenating snippets of information from multiple resources. I also based the manual on my own trial-and-error approach as a raw beginner. This automatically ensured that the manual's content was presented in simple, logical, and progressive steps without suddenly introducing unexplained items.

My home-grown manual was so useful that I decided that it should be shared with other web site designers. This book is the result of that decision.

Computer software and database techniques are constantly improving and being updated. Because of this, most of the available manuals and Internet tutorials were obsolescent, so I had to research the latest versions of the scripts, tools, and the available software. This ensured that my content and illustrations would remain relevant for as long as possible.

To follow the tutorials in this book requires an absolute minimum of software. Some manuals ask readers to download and learn a new piece of software before they can proceed to each new chapter. I came across one book that required readers to download MySQL, Apache, PHP, phpMyAdmin, Prototype 1.5, Scriptaculous, Zend Framework, Smarty Template Engine, FCK editor, Jquery, and Ajax. In this book, in addition to a code editor, I have limited the software to one item as described next.

What Equipment Is Required

The book assumes that, as a web designer, you will already have an HTML editor such as Dreamweaver, MS Expression Web (now free), Kompozer (free), or NotePad++ (free). I used MS Expression Web because it was about one third of the price of Dreamweaver and it used an interface similar to MS Word. I was considering an update to my Expression Web, but it would cost about £199, which deterred me. Then, suddenly, Microsoft decided to discontinue the development and maintenance of Expression Web and offered it free of charge. Naturally, I was delighted and promptly downloaded the latest version of Expression Web Version 4; I can thoroughly recommend it.

In addition you will need:

- A notebook for recording the passwords and file names for your databases and table entries. DON'T RELY ON MEMORY; WRITE EVERYTHING DOWN

You will need to download:

- The sample code from the book's page, available at www.apress.com.

- XAMPP, a free, all-in-one package for testing your work.

- The latest browsers (all free): Internet Explorer, Mozilla Firefox, Safari, Chrome, and Opera.

The Conventions Used in This Book

Care has been taken to relate every listing to its screenshot. For instance, Figure 3-6 will be described by Listing 3-6. If two listings are needed, such as the HTML code and the CSS, both will relate to the screenshot by using Listing 3-6a and Listing 3-6b. If a screenshot such as Figure 4-6 does not need a listing, the next screenshot and listing will use Figure 4-7 and Listing 4-7.

Special tips, notes, and warnings are shown in the following format:

■ **Note**   Security is very important when dealing with databases, especially if they contain personal data. The technique for making your work secure is woven into each step of the instructions.

All code listings use HTML5 and PHP. The meta description and meta keywords have been omitted from each <head></head> section to save space.

Code listings are shown as follows:

```
<div id='container'>
<?php include('header.php'); ?><!--include the new header file-->
```

Code shown in bold type indicates either a new feature or a change from a previous version of the code.

Code lines are sometimes numbered to help with the explanations as follows:

```
if (empty($errors)) { // If no problems occured, register the user in the database  #1
```

The line numbers are for explanation only and must not be included in your own code.

Interactive vs. Dynamic

Most manuals use the term "dynamic" web pages when referring to interactive pages. The words *dynamic* and *interactive* both describe pages that provide a live link between a user and a database. For instance, a user can register for membership and view his/her account details. A membership secretary can view a table of members, but the table is hidden from ordinary members. Because the word *dynamic* can have so many connotations and meanings, I have chosen to use the more precise term *interactive* in this book.

CHAPTER 1

■ ■ ■

Create and Test a MySQL Database and Table

This chapter introduces the concept of a database and a practical way of testing it. Using the projects, you will create a MySQL database and a table. As you work through the projects, you will become familiar with the phpMyAdmin interface.

This chapter has the following main sections:

- Definitions

- The free tool for developing and maintaining interactive databases

- Using phpMyAdmin to create a database and a table

- Exploring SQL

- Deleting databases, tables, and rows.

Defining the Term Database

Databases can be used to store products, details of customers, records of members of a society or a club, and much more. They can store names, passwords, addresses, e-mail addresses, registration dates, blog entries, and telephone numbers. Databases can be regarded as folders containing tables of data. The table of data, like all tables, has columns and rows; however, the rows in database tables are called records. A typical database table is shown in Table 1-1.

Table 1-1. *A typical database*

user_id	fname	lname	email	psword	phone
1	Kevin	Kettle	kev@kettle.co.uk	kettlefur	01111 111 1111
2	Susan	Saucepan	sue@kitchen.org.uk	nasus5	01111 222 1111
3	Oliver	Oven	oliver@cooker.co.uk	hotstove	03333 111 4444

Defining Developer, Administrator, and User

In this book, the term "developer" (a.k.a. "webmaster") means the person who designs and produces the database; he or she will integrate the database into a web site. Sometimes I will use the term "webmaster" or "web designer." When I do, it usually means the same thing as "developer." The words "administrator" and "membership secretary" have the same meaning in some of the book's tutorials, which are based on building a database for a club. The word "administrator" means the person responsible for monitoring and maintaining the content of the database tables. Clearly, one person can be both a developer and an administrator. However, most developers will maintain the structure of a database but will not want the hassle of amending and deleting records; that should be the role of an administrator (a club or society's membership secretary, say).

The "user" is any member of the general public viewing and possibly interacting with a web site database. For security reasons, users have extremely limited access to the database; however, they will be allowed to register for membership, log in to a special section, or change their password.

■ **Caution** The organization commissioning a database must conform to the Data Protection Act for the territory in which the database is developed. This is especially important if that data is going to be used for profit. Conformance usually means obtaining a license. In addition the developer and administrator must normally sign a document confirming that they will never disclose the details of persons recorded in the database. In the UK, the Information Commissioner's Office (ICO) requires an annual license fee based on the revenues of the organization that owns the database. Currently, there is no equivalent in the USA, but privacy laws differ between states. It is essential that you understand and obey the data-protection laws for your client's territory.However, you do not have to apply for a license if you use fictitious data in a database for the purpose of learning and experimenting with databases.

Defining Interactive Web Sites

Interactive web sites are often called dynamic web sites; however, I prefer to use the word interactive because dynamic can signify so many things. For instance, it can mean moving, powerful, eye catching, flashy, exciting. To a beginner, none of those meanings define a web page that interacts with a user.

Dynamic is so often used to mean exciting, but there is little excitement to be seen in an interactive registration form. Dynamic is also a musical term meaning changes or variations in loudness or speed. If dynamic can refer to change, why were dynamic templates designed to provide consistency from one web page to another? The term interactive has one clear meaning and will be used from now on in this book.

MySQL (with PHP) allows users and administrators to interact with a database using web site pages. For instance, users can register as members of an organization via a registration page on a web site. Users will be able to supply their personal data for the membership tables. MySQL then enters the users' input into the administrator's tables automatically; this lightens the workload of the administrator. The web site's registration page can be programmed to filter users' data input and verify it. From an interactive page, users may even be allowed to update their own records in a database.

Interactivity means that the administrator's workload is greatly reduced, but not completely. For instance, if the database is for a bookshop, the administrator will still have to enter any new titles and prices. On the other hand, an interactive database can be programmed to alert the administrator when the stock of a certain book needs replenishing.

In Chapter 2, you will learn to develop a simple interactive web site.

Only Use MySQL for Interactive Database Tables

A non-interactive database table means that only the administrator can enter or amend the table's data.
A non-interactive database would be more easily created and administered using a spreadsheet or database program, such as Microsoft Excel or Microsoft Access. Web site users cannot interact with such a database. Employing MySQL to create a non-interactive (static) version of the database would be like using a sledgehammer to crack a nut. A static database such as Excel or Access has one advantage, it cannot be easily accessed online by hackers; however, it has to be maintained by an administrator and is very labor intensive. Website users have no input, and they cannot search or update their data.

Using MySQL for a non-interactive version would not reduce the workload of an administrator, he would have to enter all the members' data and verify that the data is genuine.

■ **Note** A few interactive web pages do not need a database in order to function. For instance, a Contact Us form can be regarded as interactive because it takes a user's input and transmits it to the web site's owner in the form of an e-mail; this can be achieved easily without a database. In this book, the term "interactive" always means the user can interact with a database.

Methods for Developing and Maintaining Databases

The four methods for managing databases are as follows (with the easiest method on the left and hardest on the right):

PhpMyAdmin — PHP —SQL command line — MS-DOS style command line.

In this book, we will be mainly using the first two methods, but not the MS-DOS-style command line. For interactive databases, you will need some PHP files. You do not need an extensive knowledge of PHP before you can create interactive databases. I introduce the PHP you require in the appropriate place in each project—that is, in context. The step-by-step, fully-worked examples will show you what MySQL and PHP can do and how to do it.

Because of its popularity, GUIs (mouse operated Graphical User Interfaces) have been developed to facilitate the task of developing databases. These are known as development platforms, and the platform used throughout this book is XAMPP.

A Brief Look Inside the Machinery

Databases need a server, a database program, and a PHP processor as shown in Figure 1-1. These can be downloaded as an all-in-one, ready-configured package. The testing and development of the projects in this book are based on the free XAMPP package that is available for all operating systems.

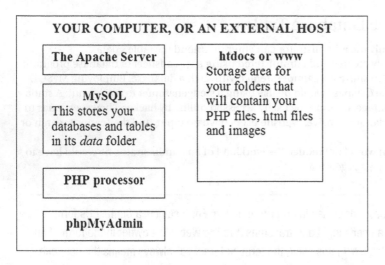

Figure 1-1. A diagram of the machinery for passing database information to and from users

Figure 1-1 shows the main components built into the XAMPP development platform. They are as follows:

- Apache is the web page server used by the great majority of hosts and on local computers for developing databases. PHP files and databases need a server in order to work.

- MySQL is the database, and it provides management tools.

- The PHP processor checks for errors and processes the PHP files that are needed to make databases interact with users.

- phpMyAdmin is a mouse-operated program for creating and maintaining databases and their tables.

A single all-in-one package such as XAMPP contains the four programs and is called a WAMP (Windows, Apache, MySQL, and PHP). In WAMPs such as XAMPP, the main components are preconfigured so that they can talk to each other. The equivalent on a Mac computer is MAMP, and on a Linux computer it is LAMP.

The folder htdocs is part of XAMPP and is the storage area for your web pages. Apache and MySQL, by default, look in htdocs for your web pages. These pages may be designed to allow users to interact with the database. Other pages will operate unseen as they transmit information back and forth between user and database. The pages are usually HTML and PHP files or a combination of both.

■ **Caution** Everything inside the envelope in the diagram shown in Figure 1-1 will be already installed on a remote host, but you should never use a remote host to create a database while you are learning. For security reasons, do not use a remote host until you have become proficient. Always learn and develop a database using a WAMP on your own computer. Note that a WAMP installed on your own computer is purely a development tool. The database, when developed and thoroughly tested, can eventually be uploaded to a host to make it available to users. Uploading a data base is covered in Chapter 7.

A Free Development Platform for Testing

You will not be able to test your work in the normal way—that is, by using a browser to view a database and PHP files located on your hard drive. However, you can develop, test, and view your database and PHP files by using a WAMP on your computer. This book assumes that you will use XAMPP on your own computer while you are learning, and for developing future database-driven websites.

I have omitted instruction on the EASYPHP and WAMPServer programs to save space; they are very similar and are as effective as XAMPP. I use XAMPP because I am used to it, and I think the interface is slightly better than the others (my opinion only).

■ **Caution**   The earlier projects in this book are necessarily simple and are not secure enough to be uploaded to a host. When you have gained experience and confidence, and you are sure that you understand the security issues, you could adapt the book's later projects for use in your own websites and then upload them to a remote host.

Using XAMPP on Your Own Computer

The XAMPP package is free and is preconfigured so that the components will talk to each other. This eliminates the hassle of the usual practice of downloading several individual components and then configuring them to work together.

At the time of writing, the most recent version of XAMPP is version 1.8.1. This version is used throughout the book. It has component versions as follows: Apache 2.4.3, MySQL 5.5.27, PHP 5.4.7, and phpMyAdmin 3.5.2.2. The package and its components are improved with each release, but the processes described in this book are rarely affected because the updates are usually backward compatible.

■ **Caution**   Make sure that the package you intend to use contains version 3.5.2.2 of phpMyAdmin or later. All the instructions that follow do not relate to earlier versions; they had a few minor flaws, such as the interface column headings not lining up properly with the content, and also there was some occasional odd behavior. The new version seems slick and flawless.

Before I give you the instructions for downloading XAMPP, I need to settle a question that bothers every beginner concerning the transferring of a developed database from XAMPP to the remote host. If you use XAMPP on your own computer, a question will arise, as stated in the title of the next section.

Will I Be Able to Transfer the Database from XAMPP to a Remote Host?

The main thought that haunts a beginner is "If I develop a database on a local WAMP, will I be able to move it easily to a remote host?" Beginners have every reason to be worried because most manuals rarely give even a hint on this topic. However, the answer is "Yes, you will be able to move the database." You will find full instructions in Chapter 7.

Now I will provide the information for downloading and installing XAMPP.

■ **Caution**   Should you wish to explore other free WAMPs, it is possible to install both EASYPHP and XAMPP on the same computer. However, make sure one of them is shut down before opening the other; otherwise, they will fight for the same ports and cause annoying problems.

Download and Install XAMPP

XAMP is free and needs no configuring. To download the package, go to:

`http://www.apachefriends.org/en/xampp-windows.html`

The home page varies from time to time, so you may have to explore the buttons on the tool bar a little to load the screen shown in Figure 1-2.

XAMPP for Windows 1.8.1, 30.9.2012		
Version	Size	Content
XAMPP Windows 1.8.1		Apache 2.4.2, MySQL 5.5.27, PHP 5.4.7, OpenSSL 1.0.1c, phpMyAdmin 3.5.2.2, XAMPP Control Panel 3.1.0, Webalizer 2.23-04, Mercury Mail Transport System v4.62, FileZilla FTP Server 0.9.41, Tomcat 7.0.30 (with mod_proxy_ajp as connector), Strawberry Perl 5.16.0.1 Portable For Windows 2000, XP, Vista, 7.
⊡ Installer	97 MB	Installer MD5 checksum: e682e5f791c26eff70e7c6151235abce
⊡ ZIP	184 MB	ZIP archive MD5 checksum: 924e9cdc0fc49984e0c4916aa8f31c18
⊡ 7zip	84 MB	7zip archive MD5 checksum: 462f6bc3c9e96a8c9228927ff8e0d217

Figure 1-2. *Installing XAMPP*

The download page will state that you must have C++ MS VC 2008 runtime libraries installed. These are normally already installed in modern versions of Windows; however, the XAMPP installation page provides a URL where you can download the libraries if necessary.

Scroll right down the download page until you see the section illustrated in Figure 1-2.

I chose the zip version for Windows, and this installed in 32-bit and 64-bit computers without any problems. I also used the installer version on another computer and found no difference in operation or appearance.

Download the file into your Downloads folder and then double-click it to unzip it into a new folder named xampp on the root of the hard drive; to avoid security issues, don't install it in the Program Files folder. If your main hard drive is C:, the default folder for the installation will then be C:\xampp. During the installation, you may see some black screens with white text—just keep going until the installation is completely finished. You may see a window named XAMPP Options. The installation may demand a restart; my installations did not. You will be asked if you want to load the XAMPP control panel; click Yes. If XAMPP is running, you will see an icon in the Notification area like the one shown in Figure 1-3.

Figure 1-3. *The XAMPP icon*

The items on the XAMPP control panel labeled *Running* usually appear automatically, and you will then be able to stop the various modules. If they do not start automatically, click the start buttons on the XAMPP control panel for Apache and MySQL. If a button says Stop, that module is already running. What next? When the interface appears, change the language to your version of English. If you are asked about running the modules as services, choose to run Apache and MySQL as services, and then those modules will automatically start when you double-click the XAMPP desktop icon.

■ **Caution** The XAMPP icon in the Notification area is the same color and shape as the Java update icon.

Create a shortcut on your Desktop for XAMPP's htdocs folder, and place it alongside the XAMPP icon as shown in Figure 1-4. Use this shortcut for loading your PHP files into the C:\xampp\htdocs folder.

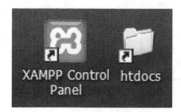

Figure 1-4. *Time-saving shortcuts*

If a desktop icon was not created during the installation, I recommend that you go to the C:\xampp folder, and then create a Desktop shortcut for the xampp-*control.exe* file.

For maximum convenience, put the two Desktop items side by side as shown in Figure 1-4. One icon starts and stops XAMPP, and the other allows you to create and modify pages directly in the XAMPP htdocs folder.

One common problem is that Skype uses the same port as Apache. So if users have Skype running, Apache won't start. You can change the ports in Skype's advanced options screen. If you have web deployment Agent Services running, you will have to stop that to enable Apache to run.

Starting XAMPP

From here onward, to test your pages in XAMPP, double-click the desktop icon and check that Apache and MySQL have started. If they have not started, click the start buttons for each and then minimize the control panel.

The XAMPP control panel is shown in Figure 1-5.

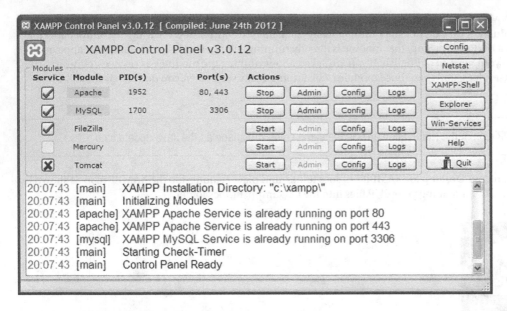

Figure 1-5. *The XAMPP control panel*

Note that, under Service, I have shown that the first three modules are running as services, as indicated by the selected boxes. This ensures that those modules will run as soon as you start XAMPP.

Always minimize the control panel so that you have a clear desktop for starting work on your databases.

After starting Apache and MySQL, you can test your installation and examine all of the XAMPP examples and tools; to do this, enter the following address in your browser.

`http://localhost/` or `http://127.0.0.1/`

Closing XAMPP

Close XAMPP when you have finished testing your database and PHP files. This will free up memory for tasks other than database development. To close down, click the minimized XAMPP control panel on the task bar and then click the Quit button on the control panel as shown in Figure 1-6. Alternatively, you can right-click the icon in the Notification area and then click Quit.

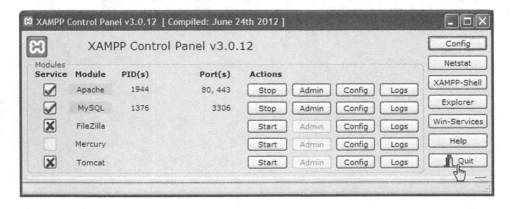

Figure 1-6. *Closing down the XAMPP program*

The security of a database and its data is extremely important. XAMPP provides an interface for making the database and tables on your computer safe from harmful interference, this is described next.

The XAMPP Security Console

The initial installation of XAMPP has the username root, and there is no password. If you use those settings on your own computer, there is a security risk when connected to the Internet. If you work in the same room with other people, the password will protect against interference as long as the password is not divulged to the other people. As a best practice, you should password-protect your working environment, and XAMPP has a Security Console that simplifies this task.

Start XAMPP by double-clicking the desktop icon. Then enter the following URL in the address field of a browser:

http://localhost/security/

A page will appear as shown in Figure 1-7. Select your language in the left panel.

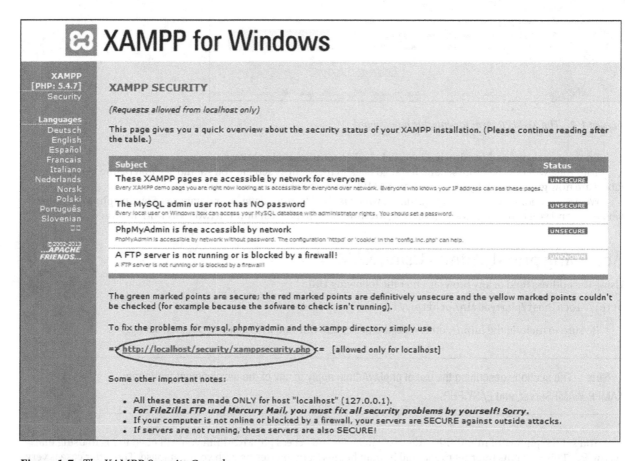

Figure 1-7. *The XAMPP Security Console*

The unprotected components are indicated by boxes with a red background. Click the URL that is circled in Figure 1-7 and you will be taken to the page shown in Figure 1-8. Only the top half of the page is shown because the password is sufficient protection; the rest of the page can be ignored.

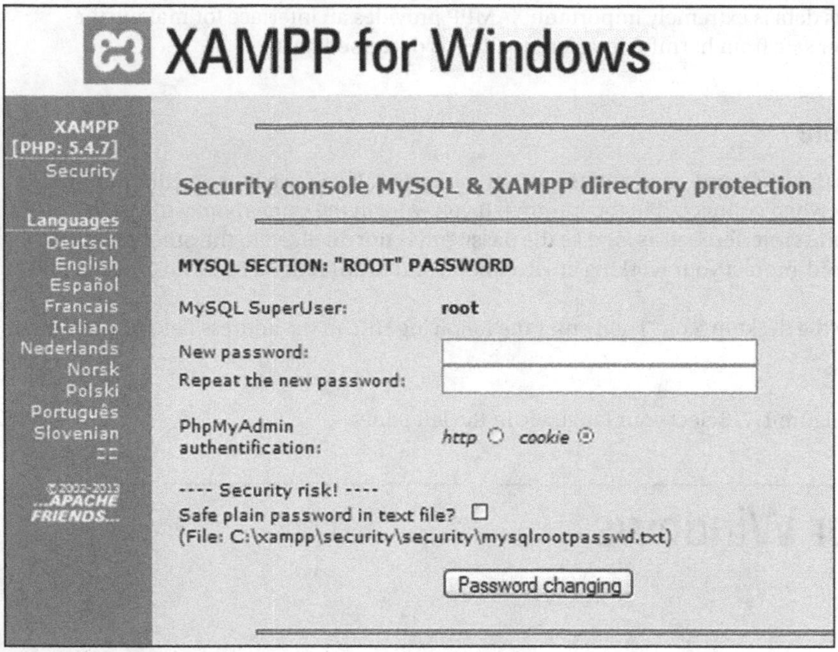

Figure 1-8. The XAMPP form for entering a password

Enter a password and confirm it. Then click the Password changing button.

Your data will now be more secure. If you go back to the security screen, you should see that (some of) those red labels are now green. You may have to restart XAMPP to see the changes.

We are now going to look at phpMyAdmin, which is used to administer your databases. Starting phpMyAdmin is very easy, and you can start it without running XAMPP. Let's first look at how the two tools work together.

Accessing phpMyAdmin Using XAMPP

Using the address field of any browser, enter the following URL:

`http://localhost/phpmyadmin/` or `http://127.0.01/phpmyadmin/`

Be sure to include the http://; otherwise, a browser like Chrome will treat it as a search string.

■ **Note** The sections describing the use of phpMyAdmin apply to any of the development platforms: XAMPP, WAMPServer, and EASY PHP.

You set the password in XAMPP earlier, so whenever you access phpMyAdmin you will need to log in using that password. This prevents Internet robots and human beings from interfering with your database. The latter case is very important if you work in an office with others—you could have a spy or mischievous meddler in the place where you work. When you access phpMyAdmin, a dialog box will appear as shown in Figure 1-9.

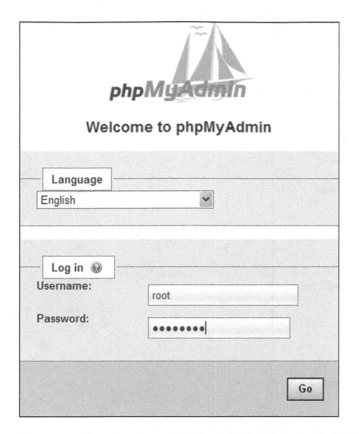

Figure 1-9. Enter the password in the dialog box to access phpMyAdmin

Enter your username (usually "root") and password, and then click the button labeled Go. phpMyAdmin loads rather slowly, but it will eventually appear.

Note that open source programs are continually being improved and upgraded, and you may find that you have a newer version of phpMyAdmin in your XAMPP package than that used in this book. You may also see upgrade messages alerting you to a new version in the phpMyAdmin main window. Where personal data is concerned, security is paramount, so these incremental updates are a good thing for you, though they do mean that some of the screenshots in the book no longer accurately reflect what you see on screen. Don't worry if an interface looks a little different from the ones shown in this book, the usage will normally be similar.

The phpMyAdmin interface may look a little daunting at first, but we'll cover the relevant parts of it when we need to use them. For the moment, you can close the phpMyAdmin window and we'll return to XAMPP.

You now know how to install and secure XAMPP, and you also learned how to start and stop XAMPP. Most of what you have just read will probably be very new, but there are some parts of XAMPP that you will recognize because they follow the normal Windows organization of files and folders.

The Familiar Bits

Within the XAMPP package, the structure of the folders and files will be familiar to Windows users, although their names may not be recognizable.

The XAMPP folders are shown in Figure 1-10.

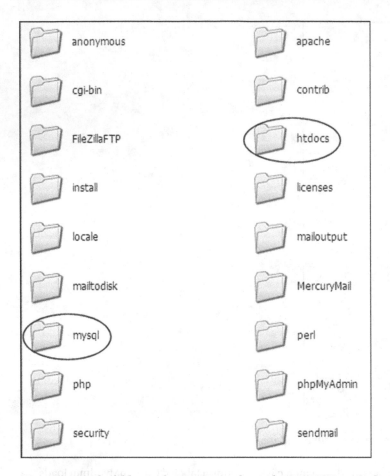

Figure 1-10. *The folders in the XAMPP package; the EASYPHP equivalent of htdocs is www*

In Figure 1-10, note the htdocs folder. This is where you will place all your PHP files and the html pages for your website and databases.

Within the XAMPP folder, you will find a folder called MySQL. This folder contains a folder called data where the databases and tables will reside. Regard a database as a folder; a database must have a unique name. A file within the data folder contains all the information about the database, and it has the file type *.opt.

Tables are files; when you have created any tables, these will also live inside the folder named data and they will have the file type *.frm.

Now that you're familiar with the look and feel of the tools you'll be using, you're ready to move ahead. The next section will take you nearer to creating your first database and table.

Planning a Database: The Essential First Step

The first and most important stage is to plan the database so that you have something practical to play with. Let's assume we need to plan a database for the membership of an organization. Follow these steps:

1. Decide on a name for the database. We will give this database the name simpleIdb. Remember that the database is like an empty folder that will eventually contain one or more tables. The last part of the name, …Idb, stands for Interactive Database.

2. Assemble the data items into a table. I have given this table the name *users*. Decide what information you want in the table; your decision is not binding because you can change any part of the database during development. Let's suppose we need five pieces of information about the users. I have set out some typical data in Table 1-1 earlier in the chapter and in Table 1-2.

Table 1-2. *My draft plan for the database table named "users"*

user_id	fname	lname	email	psword	registration_date
	Kevin	Kettle	kev@kettle.co.uk	kettlefur	
	Susan	Saucepan	sue@kitchen.org.uk	nasus5	
	Oliver	Oven	oliver@cooker.co.uk	hotstove	

Each row in a table is called a record, and each cell is called a field. A database can contain more than one table. I have used some fictitious names to help plan the table. The first column is labeled user_id, and this column is additional to the five columns of data. The column user_id will be explained later; just accept it for the moment and be sure to leave it empty. Also, leave the registration dates empty because this is an automatic entry; it does not need examples, nor does it need allocated space.

3. Now we must allocate some space for the data. Table 1-3 shows the number of characters I have allocated for each item.

Table 1-3. *The number of characters to allow for each piece of data in the table named "users"*

User_id	fname	lname	email	psword	registration_date
6	30	40	50	40	

4. Write down or print the two tables, and keep them close at hand because you will be referring to them in the next stages.

5. Now decide on a username and password for the database, and enter that information in your notebook. Four pieces of information are required: the name of the database, the host, the password, and the username. In this project, these are as follows:

Name: simpleIdb

Host: localhost

Password: hmsvictory

User: horatio

Next we will create our first database using phpMyAdmin.

Create a Database Using phpMyAdmin

There is no need to start XAMPP to access phpMyAdmin, although you can if you wish. Note that you will need to have MySQL running, though. If, for some reason, you previously stopped this service, you will need to open up XAMPP to start it again. Open a browser, and then access phpMyAdmin by typing the following in the address field:

```
http://localhost/phpmyadmin
```

Click the Databases tab in the top menu. You will then see the interface shown in Figure 1-11.

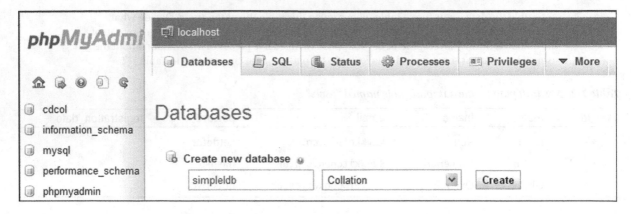

Figure 1-11. *The phpMyAdmin interface for creating the database*

Type a name for the database. For this example, it will be simpleIdb, all in lowercase except for the uppercase letter I (for Interactive) in the last three letters. Then click the Create button (ignore the Collation field). After you click the Create button, the top part of the interface does not change. However, lower down you will see a list of items with check boxes. Figure 1-12 shows the lower part of the page and a list with check boxes.

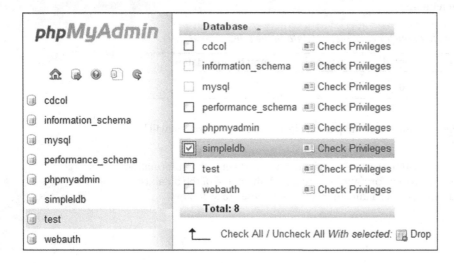

Figure 1-12. *In the lower part of the page, select the box next to the name of your new database*

When you select the box next to your new database as shown in Figure 1-12, click Check Privileges and you will be taken to a screen where you will see a list of users that have access to the database. To make the database secure, you must add a username and password. Click the words Add User as shown in Figure 1-13.

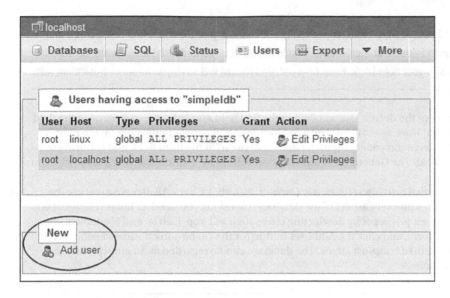

Figure 1-13. *The Add user icon is circled in this screenshot*

Clicking Add User will load the *Add a new User* screen, shown next in Figure 1-14.

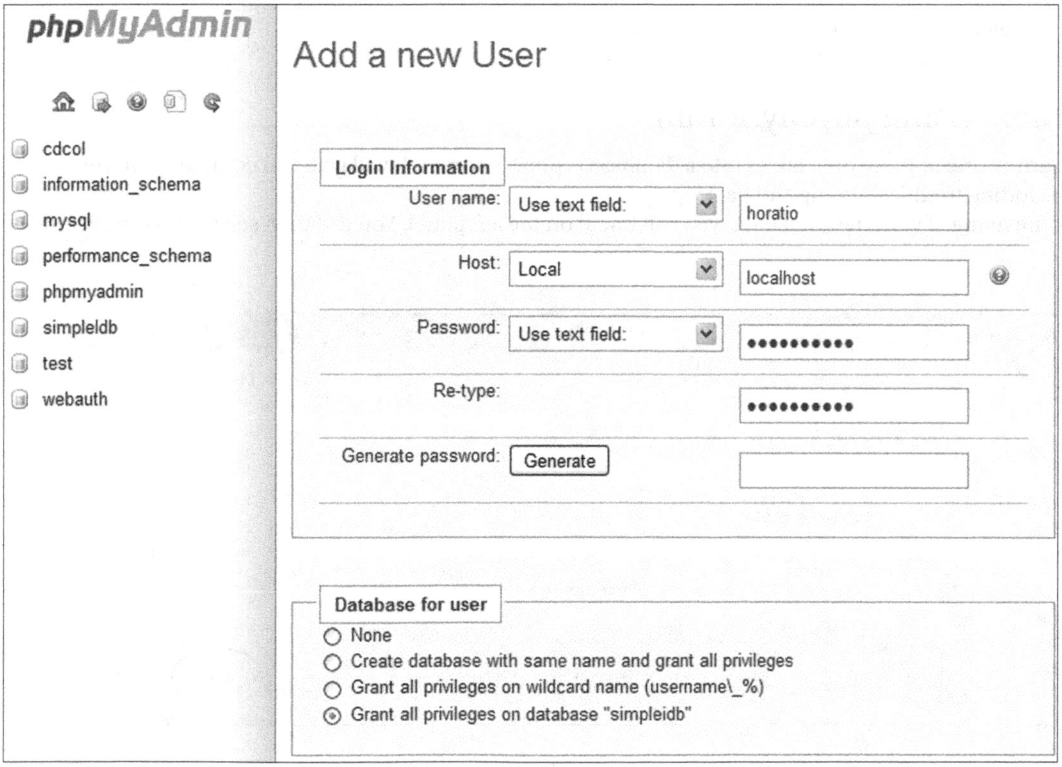

Figure 1-14. *This screen enables you to add a user and a password*

■ **Caution**   Adding a username and password is absolutely essential; otherwise, your database will be insecure and vulnerable to attack by unscrupulous individuals or their robots. This is the most important habit to cultivate. Be sure to record the user and password details in your note book. Keeping a detailed record will save you hours of frustration later.

Using the pull-down menus, accept the default Use text field in the first field and enter the username in the field to right of it. In the second field labeled Host, select local. The word localhost will appear in the field on the right. Localhost is the default name for the server on your computer. Enter a password in the third field, and confirm your password by retyping it in the lower field. The Generate Password button will create a random strong password if you want something unique.

Scroll down, and where it says *Global privileges (Check All/Uncheck All)*, click Check All. Because you are the webmaster, you need to be able to deal with every aspect of the database; therefore, you need all the privileges. If you add other users, you need to restrict their privileges by deselecting boxes such as Drop, Delete, and Shutdown.

Scroll down to the bottom of the form, and click the Add User button (or the Go button on some versions). You have now created the database and secured it against attack. The database can be regarded as an empty folder that will eventually contain one or more tables.

■ **Note**   If you get lost when using phpMyAdmin and can't see what you should do next, always click the little house at the top of the left panel. Hover over the icon to ensure that it is the Home button.

Now we will create our first table.

Create a Table Using phpMyAdmin

The GUI for inserting one or more data tables into a database is phpMyAdmin. It will give you complete control over your table(s), including troubleshooting and backing up.

Next, click the name of your new database; you will find it on the left panel. You will then see the screen shown in Figure 1-15.

Figure 1-15. *Click the Go button, shown circled, to create the table*

Enter a name for the table, and specify the number of columns. Then click the Go button (shown circled in Figure 1-15). You will be taken to a screen showing the columns flipped 90 degrees so that columns look like rows; this is shown in Figure 1-16. The fields are empty and waiting for you to define the table.

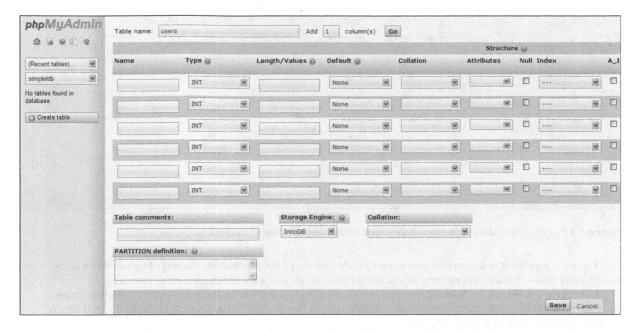

Figure 1-16. *The six rows represent six columns. The column titles will be entered in the fields on the left*

Use the data from Tables 1-2 and 1-3 that we planned earlier, and enter the column name, data type, and number of characters. The details for creating the users table are given in Table 1-4.

Table 1-4. *The attributes for the users table*

Column name	Type	Length/Values	Default	Attributes	NULL	Index	A_I
user_id	MEDIUMINT	6	None	UNSIGNED	☐	PRIMARY	☑
fname	VARCHAR	30	None		☐		☐
lname	VARCHAR	40	None		☐		☐
email	VARCHAR	50	None		☐		☐
psword	CHAR	40	None		☐		☐
registration_date	DATETIME		None		☐		☐

Accept all the default settings for each item except for the user_id. Here, you will need to select UNSIGNED, PRIMARY, and the type; also select the A_I box.

The various categories under the heading Type will be explained later; the heading Length/Values refers to the maximum number of characters. The Length/Values for the registration_date is left blank because the length is predetermined. Do not enter anything under the headings Default and NULL. The attribute UNSIGNED means that the user_id integer cannot be a negative quantity. The Index for the user_id is the primary index, and A_I means

Automatically Increment the id number; as each user is registered to the database, he or she is given a unique number. The number is increased by one as each new user is added. The screen for specifying the attributes is shown in Figure 1-17.

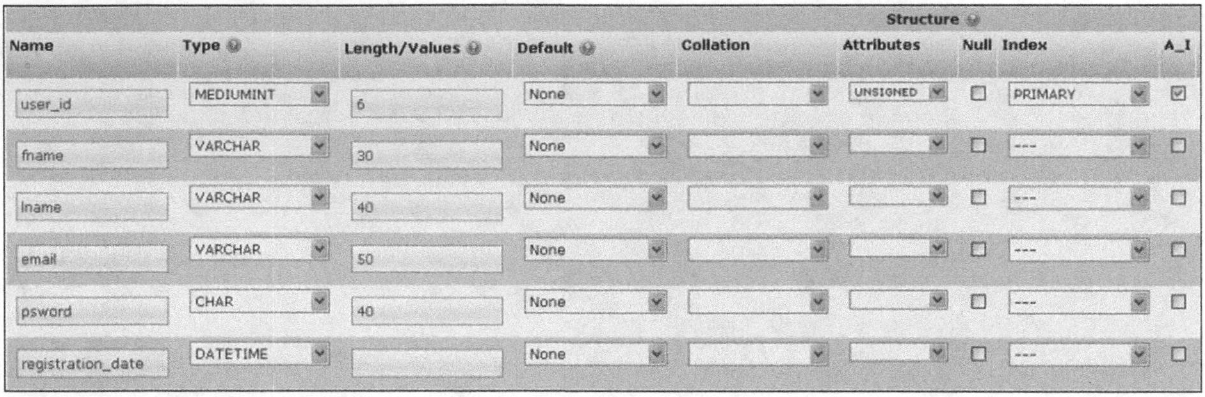

Name	Type	Length/Values	Default	Collation	Structure Attributes	Null	Index	A_I
user_id	MEDIUMINT	6	None		UNSIGNED	☐	PRIMARY	☑
fname	VARCHAR	30	None			☐	---	☐
lname	VARCHAR	40	None			☐	---	☐
email	VARCHAR	50	None			☐	---	☐
psword	CHAR	40	None			☐	---	☐
registration_date	DATETIME		None			☐	---	☐

Figure 1-17. *This screen allows you to specify column titles and the type of content*

The rows represent columns and they are very wide; you may have to scroll horizontally to enter some of the information. You will find more options as you scroll right, but we will not need them for this tutorial.

So how do you fill out the fields? Enter the six column titles in the fields on the left under the heading Name. Enter the type of column in the second column of fields under the heading Type. Select them from the Pull-down menus. The types used in this table are as follows:

- MEDIUMINT can store integers ranging from minus 8,388,608 to plus 8,388,607. You could choose the next smallest category SMALLINT if the number of users will never exceed 65,535.

- VARCHAR specifies a variable-length string of characters from 1 to 255 long.

- CHAR is a string of characters traditionally used for passwords. Be sure to give this 40 characters so that your database is able to encrypt the password using the function SHA1('$p'). MySQL then converts a password into an encrypted string of 40 characters. A user's password can be, say, 6 to 12 characters long, but it will still be stored in the database as an encrypted 40-character string. This will be discussed further in Chapter 2, together with an alternative encrypted function md5(). Incidentally, SHA stands for Secure Hash Algorithm.

- DATETIME stores the date and time in the format YYYY-MM-DD-HH:MM:SS.

Enter the number of characters in the fourth column of fields under the heading Length/Values. Refer to Table 1-4 for these numbers.

Under the heading Default, accept the default *None*. This field is where you can enter a default value if you wish.

Now scroll right. Under the heading *Attributes*, use the drop-down menu to select UNSIGNED for user_id. This ensures that the integer range becomes zero to 16,777,215. This is because a negative quantity is not applicable for the user_id.

The next two entries concern only the user_id. Scroll right so that you can see the headings shown in Figure 1-18.

Structure ⓘ							
Default ⓘ	Collation	Attributes	Null	Index		A_I	Comments
None ⌄	⌄	UNSIGNED ⌄	☐	PRIMARY ⌄		☑	

Figure 1-18. *Two extra entries for the user_id column*

For the user_id, under the heading Index, click the drop-down menu to enter PRIMARY. The user_id should always be a primary index.

Under the heading *A_I*, select the topmost check box so that the user_id number is automatically incremented when each new record is added to the database.

Now scroll to the bottom and click the SAVE button.

■ **Caution**   If you forget to select the A_I box for user_id, you will receive an error message when you later try to enter the second record. The message will say that you are trying to create a duplicate value "0" for id_user.

Some people prefer a blend of GUI and command-line for programming a table, phpMyAdmin allows you to do this by means of SQL. However, this book will mainly use the phpMyAdmin GUI. The SQL alternative is described next. You can skip this section if you wish, but I recommend that you come back to it at some future date because you will undoubtedly come across SQL in other more advanced manuals.

The SQL Alternative

The next section describes a slightly quicker way of using phpMyAdmin for creating a database and a table. The SQL part of MySQL stands for Structured Query Language; it is the official language for MySQL databases, and you will be pleased to read that it uses plain English commands. The only problem is that it is easier to create typographical errors or spelling mistakes in the SQL window than in the phpMyAdmin interface shown earlier in Figure 1-17.

Using SQL, a database can be created complete with a password and username. This saves several steps.

I assume you have created the database simpleIdb, so we cannot use that name again. Let's assume that an administrator (Adrian) wishes to create a database called members using the following information:

Database name: members;

Privileges: all

Username: adrian

Password: stapler12

Figure 1-19 shows the details entered into an SQL window.

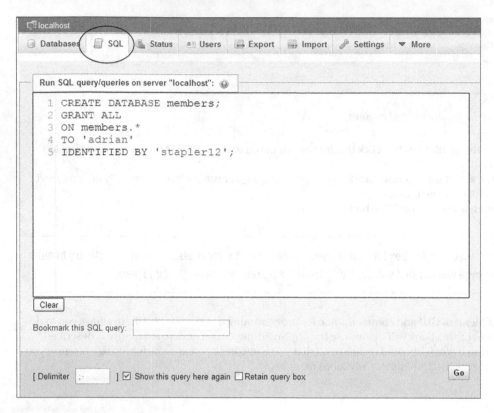

Figure 1-19. *The SQL window*

In phpMyAdmin, return to the home page so that you are no longer dealing with simpleIdb. Click the SQL tab (shown circled) to reveal an SQL window.

The details shown in Figure 1-19 must be entered in the following format:

```
CREATE DATABASE members;
GRANT ALL
ON members.*
TO 'adrian'
IDENTIFIED BY 'stapler12';
```

Enter each item on a separate line by pressing Enter after a line. The SQL keywords (like CREATE DATABASE) are traditionally in uppercase. Other items are normally entered in lowercase. Note the semicolons and the single quotes—these are important. When you are satisfied with the entries, click the Go button.

Figure 1-20 shows the screen confirming that the database was successfully created, including its security features.

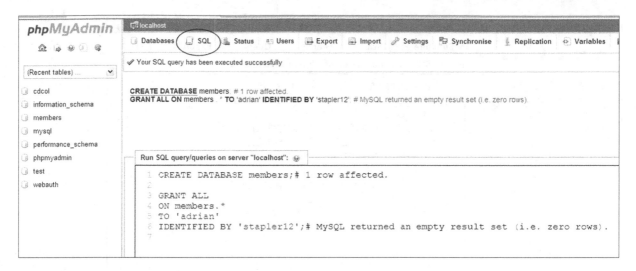

Figure 1-20. *Showing confirmation that the database was created (which might not be dsiplayed in later versions of phpMyAdmin)*

Now we will create a table named `users` in the `members` database using the SQL window.

Click the `members` database in the left panel of phpMyAdmin. If the `members` database does not show, refresh the page so that it does appear. Open the SQL window, and enter this:

```
CREATE TABLE users (
user_id MEDIUMINT (6) UNSIGNED
AUTO_INCREMENT,
fname VARCHAR(30) NOT NULL,
lname VARCHAR(40) NOT NULL,
email VARCHAR(50) NOT NULL,
psword CHAR(40) NOT NULL,
registration_date DATETIME,
PRIMARY KEY (user_id)
);
```

Figure 1-21 shows the details entered into the SQL window.

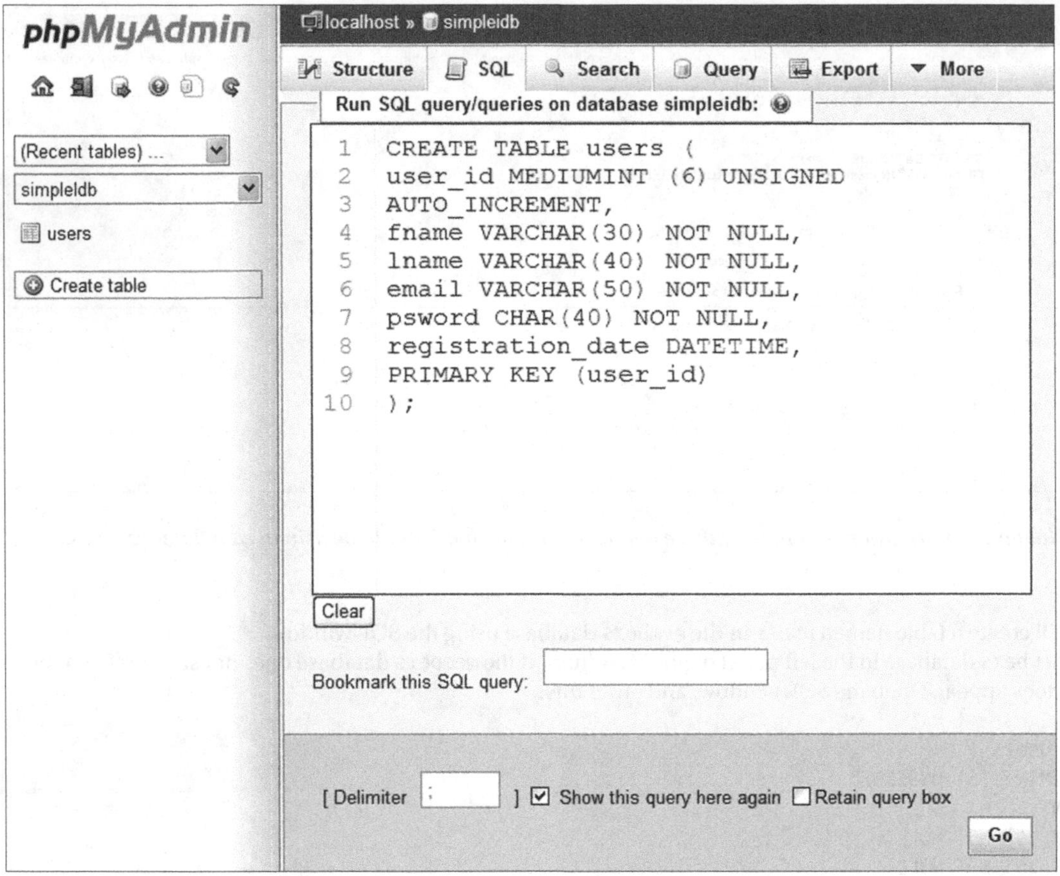

Figure 1-21. *Creating a table in the SQL window of phpMyAdmin*

Note that the brackets are all normal brackets, not curly brackets. Press the Enter key after each line, and remember to put the closing bracket and the semicolon at the end of the last line. Each item is separated by a closing comma (lines 3 through 8); if your table has six columns, you should have six commas. Click the Go button, and the table will be created.

■ **Tip**   I encourage you to explore the SQL topic just described. The ability to work with SQL will be a very useful alternative sometime in the future. You may wish to refer to the tutorial on:

`http://dev.mysql.com/doc/refman/5.0/en/tutorial.html`

Deleting Databases and Tables

When learning, beginners often need to start over after creating a database or a table. The learner may wish to delete earlier attempts. When I first used phpMyAdmin, I got carried away and created several databases and tables. I then decided to clear up the mess and delete some of them.

First you will learn how to delete a database. Run XAMPP, and then load phpMyAdmin by entering the following into a browser's address field:

```
http://localhost/phpmyadmin/
```

or

```
http://127.0.01/phpmyadmin/
```

Select the Databases tab (shown circled in Figure 1-22), and then select the box next to the database to be deleted. In this example, the members2 database was selected for deletion.

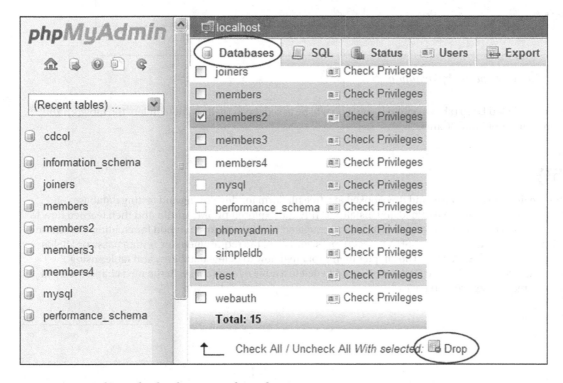

Figure 1-22. *Deleting the database named members2*

When you have selected the database to be deleted, click the icon labeled Drop (shown circled at the bottom right). You will be asked if you really want to delete the database; go ahead and complete the deletion. Everything associated with that database will be deleted, including its tables.

You may wish to preserve a database but delete all or one of its tables. In phpMyAdmin, in the left panel, find the database containing the table(s) to be deleted; click the database. In the next screen, you will see the table(s) and select the box next to the table(s) you wish to delete. Figure 1-23 shows that I chose to delete a table called dingdongs in the database called members4.

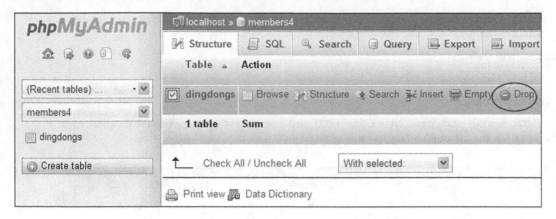

Figure 1-23. *Deleting a table in phpMyAdmin*

Click the icon labeled Drop (shown circled), and you will be asked if you really want to delete the table(s). You can choose between "Drop" and "Cancel."

Summary

In this chapter, we defined a database and then looked at a free platform for developing and testing databases and PHP files. I hope you were able to download and install XAMPP. You explored phpMyAdmin and then learned how to use it to create your first database and a table. SQL was investigated as an alternative method for creating a database and a table. You also learned about using SHA to secure passwords and the requirement for setting password fields long enough to include a full SHA hash. The chapter then explained how to delete databases and tables using phpMyAdmin. You discovered that the Drop icon is used to delete a table or a database. In the next chapter, we will create and test simple interactive web pages.

CHAPTER 2

■ ■ ■

Create Web Pages That Interact with Users

This chapter will demonstrate how a simple database can be linked to a web page so that the page can interact with users. The general public will have access to the web site but will not have access to the database structure or the data contained in the tables. They will not be permitted to view the protected pages, such as a *members-only* page, because they have no password until they register. However, the web designer must provide a way for users to interact with the database in order to (i) register as a member, (ii) search the database, and (iii) change a password. The PHP language and MySQL code provide the solution.

This chapter covers the following main topics:

- Creating a folder for the database

- Creating the database and a template for the web site pages

- Introducing the PHP include function

- Creating the included pages

- How does the server process a PHP page?

- An interactive version of the template page

- Connecting to the database

- Creating a registration page for members

- The PHP keyword *echo()*

- Styling forms

- Sticky forms

- Using arrays

- Displaying members' records

- Changing a password

- Dealing with apostrophes

- Testing the tutorials' pages

- More about using arrays

We will use the *simpleIdb* database and the *users* table from the previous projects for our interactive web pages. Be aware that this tutorial is neither secure nor practical. It is a stepping stone to the more secure and ambitious projects described in subsequent chapters. In practice, you would never allow ordinary members to view a list of members. The interactive elements in this project are as follows:

- Users can register as members by inserting their details into a form displayed on the screen. The registration details would be entered into the database table and could be used by the administrator to send regular newsletters to members.

- Registered users can change their password.

- A user can view the list of members (for this project only). In later chapters, this facility would be available only to the webmaster and (to a limited extent) the membership secretary.

The features that make this example unsuitable for the real-world are as follows:

- No provision is made for registered members to subsequently log in to access a special section or page. This will be dealt with in Chapter 3.

- Users should never be able to access a table of members' details.

- At this early stage, for simplicity, no filtering of the users' information is provided. The table could therefore contain faulty data and bogus e-mail addresses.

- In this chapter only, any user who knows a member's e-mail address could change the member's password.

All these security issues will be dealt with in subsequent chapters. Despite the drawbacks, the project will provide you with valuable practice in using your XAMPP program to test the pages. You will also learn more database jargon and some basic PHP code.

Create the Folder for Holding the Database Pages

Within XAMPP's htdocs folder, create a new folder named simpleIdb.

■ **Note**   The upper case "I" between the letters "e" and "d" stands for Interactive.

All the pages created in this chapter will be placed within the *simpleIdb* folder. You have a choice between hand-coding the files from the listings supplied and loading the book's code into the simpleIdb folder in htdocs. (Download the code from the book's page at www.apress.com.) I recommend that you hand-code them for this chapter; the files are small and won't delay you too much. You will learn more and learn faster if you type and test the code, especially if you make mistakes and learn to correct them.

Create the Temporary Template

Obviously, some aspects of an interactive database must be accessible to users. That means incorporating it into a real-world web page. We will name our web page template.php, and this is shown in Figure 2-1. As you can see, there is a main header with a graphic running behind it, some body text, a navigation sidebar on the left, an information column on the right, and a footer at the bottom of the page.

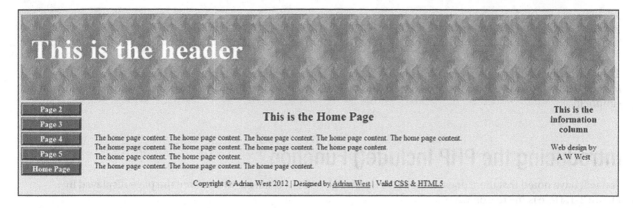

Figure 2-1. *The template*

The HTML5 Listing 2-1 for the template contains the DOCTYPE, a page title, and a link to a style sheet. The body of the page contains some PHP code, and this will be explained step by step at the end of the listing.

Because the file contains PHP code (no matter how little), the file is saved with the file type .php. The PHP code is indicated by bold type in Listing 2-1.

Listing 2-1. Creating a Template for the Project (template.php)

```
<!doctype html>
<html lang=en>
<head>
<title>Template for an interactive web page</title>
<meta charset=utf-8>
<link rel="stylesheet" type="text/css" href="includes.css">
</head>
<body>
<div id='container'>
<?php include('header-for-template.php'); ?>
<?php include('nav.php'); ?>
<?php include('info-col.php'); ?>
<div id='content'><!--Start of page content.-->
<h2>This is the Home Page</h2>
<p>The home page content. The home page content. The home page content. The home page ⏎
content. The home page content. <br>The home page content. The home page content. The ⏎
home page content. The home page content. <br>The home page content. The home page ⏎
content. <br>The home page content. The home page content. The home page content. </p>
<!--End of the home page content.-->
</div>
</div>
<?php include('footer.php'); ?>
</body>
</html>
```

■ **Note**   The <?php tag opens some PHP code, and the ?> closes the piece of PHP code.

The code in bold type uses the PHP *include* function, and this will now be explained. (Strictly speaking, the *include()* function is a PHP language construct, but the difference is so small that I will continue to call it a function for simplicity.)

Introducing the PHP include() Function

You will have noted that there does not seem to be enough code in Listing 2-1a to create the page displayed in Figure 2-1. Here is the reason why.

The four pieces of PHP code shown in bold type in Listing 2-1a have each pulled an additional file into the page. The page is therefore a combination of five files: a main file plus four external files. The four external files are pulled into the template page using the PHP include() function.

For updating and maintaining a web site, the include() function is a wonderful time saver. Let's suppose you have a client web site with 40 pages, and each page needs the same block of menu buttons. If your client asks you to add or delete one menu button, normally you would have to amend 40 pages to add or delete the button on each page. Using the include() function, you would design the web site so that each page included the line of PHP code: **<?php include('menu.php'); ?>**. This would pull the block of menu buttons into to each web page. You would design the block of buttons in another file named, say, *menu.php*. To add a new button to all 40 pages, you would have to add the new button only to the one file called menu.php.

■ **Note**   A PHP function is a tiny program that will perform a particular task. The include() function takes whatever is inside the brackets and pulls it into the page at the place where the include() function is located. PHP has two similar functions *include()* and *require()*. They both pull a file into a page so that the file is included in the displayed page. The difference is in the way they react to a missing or faulty file. If the file to be included is missing or corrupt, include() will not halt the execution of a page. A warning will appear, but the page will continue to load. In contrast, a fatal error will occur if require() can't find the file or the file is faulty. In this case, the page will cease executing. Use include for most inclusions, but use require() for loading the details of a database because the page will be of little use if the database can't be opened. Also, this makes the database more secure.

The four elements to be pulled into the page are (i) the header, (ii) the block of menu buttons, (iii) the info panel on the right side, and (iv) the footer. Included files can be any type—for instance, a .txt file, a .php file, or an .html file. An include() statement can be placed anywhere within an HTML page as long as it is surrounded by the PHP tags; these start with the tag <?php and close with the tag ?>. Examine one of the include() statements in bold type; note the quote symbols and the semi-colon are all very important. The details of the four included external files are explained next.

The Included Header File

Figure 2-2 shows a display of the included header file.

This is the header

Figure 2-2. *The header for the template*

This header is temporary. When we create an interactive version of the template, the new header will contain an additional menu so that users can register and thereby insert their details into the *simpleIdb* database.

■ **Caution**   Don't be tempted to create the four non-interactive pages yet (page-2.php, page-3.php, page-4.php, and page-5.php) because, later in the chapter, these will require a new version of the header.

The internal style in Listing 2-2 refers to an image. You will find the image tile-pale.jpg in the images folder that you can download from the book's page at www.apress.com. Place it in an images folder within the htdocs folder.

Listing 2-2. Creating the Code for the Temporary Header (header-for-template.php)

```
<style type="text/css">
#header { margin:10px auto 0 auto; min-width:960px; max-width:1200px; height:175px; ↵
background-image: url('images/tile-pale.jpg'); background-repeat: repeat; padding:0; ↵
color:white;
}
h1 {position:relative; top:40px; font-size:350%; color:white; margin:auto 0 auto 20px; ↵
width: 487px;
}
</style>
<div id="header">
<h1>This is the header</h1>
</div>
```

■ **Note**   The styling for the header is temporarily located in the included files for simplicity. This will cause error messages when the page is run through the W3C Validator. The validator does not approve of styles placed within an included file because those included styles will appear within the <body></body> section of an HTML document; style tags must appear in the <head></head> section. Future chapters will remedy this by relocating the styles in either the main style sheet or in the head section of a page.

The Included Menu File

The included block of menu buttons is shown in Figure 2-3.

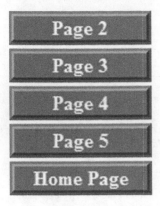

Figure 2-3. *The included menu buttons*

The listing contains an internal style for the layout of the menu block. This is not good practice because styling should never be included within an included file. It is bad because the included file will not validate using the w3.org validator. I used it here because it is easier to style this way to begin with. Later chapters will remove the style to the main style sheet thus allowing the included file to validate.

Some trial and error is usually required to position the included menu on the page. The code for the menu block is given in Listing 2-3.

Listing 2-3. Creating the Code for the Included Menu (nav.php)

```
<style type="text/css">
ul { position:absolute; top:190px; left:-10px; color:navy; ↵
width:135px; text-align:center; margin:0; }
/* set general side button styles */
li { width:115px; list-style-type :none; margin-bottom: 3px; text-align: center;
}
/* set general anchor styles */
li a { display: block; width:115px; color: white; font-weight: bold; text-decoration:none
}
/* specify state styles. */
/* mouseout (default) */
li a { background: #5B78BE; border: 4px outset #aabaff; }
}
/* mouseover */
li a:hover { display:block; background: #0a4adf; border: 4px outset #8abaff; width:115px;
}
/* onmousedown */
li a:active { background:#aecbff; border: 4px inset #aecbff;
</style>
<div id="nav"><!--The side menu column contains the vertical menu block-->
<ul>
<li><a href="page-2.php" title="Page two">Page 2</a></li>
<li><a href="page-3.php" title="Page three">Page 3</a></li>
<li><a href="page-4.php" title="Page four">Page 4</a></li>
<li><a href="page-5.php" title="Page five">Page 5</a></li>
```

```
<li><a href="index.php" title="Return to Home Page">Home Page</a></li>
</ul>
</div><!--end of side column and menu -->
```

The Included Information Column

The included information column sits on the right side of the page and is shown in Figure 2-4.

This is the information column

Web design by
A W West

Figure 2-4. *The information column for inclusion in the template*

Some trial and error is usually required to position the included info column on the page. The code for the information column is given in Listing 2-4.

Listing 2-4. Creating the Code for the Information Column (info-col.php)

```
<style type="text/css">
#info-col { position:absolute; top:190px; right:10px; color:navy; ↵
 width:135px; text-align:center; margin:5px 5px 0 0; }
</style>
<div id="info-col">
<h3>This is the information column</h3>
    <p>Web design by <br>A W West</p><p> </p>
</div>
```

Later chapters will remove the internal style to the main style sheet thus allowing the included file to validate.

The Included Footer File

The included footer is shown in Figure 2-5.

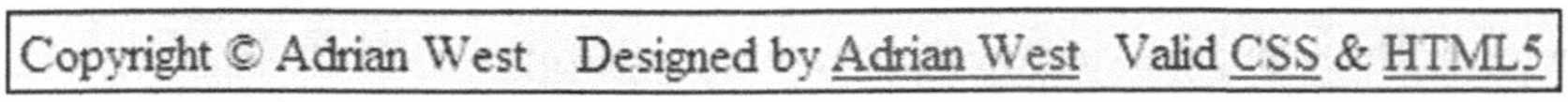

Copyright © Adrian West   Designed by Adrian West   Valid CSS & HTML5

Figure 2-5. *The footer for inclusion in the template*

The code for the footer is given in Listing 2-5a.

Listing 2-5a. Creating the Code for the Included Footer (footer.php)

```
<style type="text/css">
#footer { clear:both; margin:auto; height: 19px; text-align:center;
}
</style>
<div id="footer">
<p>Copyright &copy; Adrian West 2012  Designed by ↵
<a href="http://www.colycomputerhelp.co.uk/">Adrian West </a>  Valid ↵
<a href="http://jigsaw.w3.org/css-validator/">CSS</a> &amp; ↵
<a href="http://validator.w3.org/">HTML5</a></p>
</div>
```

Later chapters will remove the internal style to the main style sheet thus allowing the included file to validate.

How Does the Server Process the Page?

When an HTML file is saved as a PHP file, the .php extension alerts the server so that it processes the HTML as normal, but it also looks out for any PHP code. The server is in HTML mode by default, and any HTML code is sent to the browser as normal. When it finds a <?php tag, the server switches to PHP mode and executes the PHP code or echoes information to the browser. It continues in PHP mode until it encounters the PHP closing tag ?>; it then switches back to HTML mode. This cyclic behavior continues until the end of the page of code.

Styling the Temporary Template

Always try to put the majority of the styling into one main style sheet. In this tutorial, I named the CSS style sheet *includes.css*. However, during development some internal CSS styling may be needed within each included file. (See the internal styles in the code snippets for the four included files.) For instance, the only place where an <h1> heading is needed is in the header, so as a temporary measure, I put the styling for <h1> in the included header file.

Later, the separate internal styles will be placed in the main style sheet. Because several pages will eventually display a data table, the main style sheet includes styling for <table> and <td>. The main style sheet contains styling for the various user input forms associated with the registration process, such as the <label> and <input> elements. The code for the style sheet is given in Listing 2-5b.

Listing 2-5b. Creating the Template's Main Style Sheet (includes.css)

```
body {text-align:center; background-color:#D7FFEB; color:navy; ↵
font-family: "times new roman"; font-size: 100%; color: navy; margin: auto;
}
h2 { font-size:150%; color:navy; text-align:center;
}
h3 { font-size:110%; color:navy; text-align:center;
}
#container {position:relative; min-width:960px; max-width:1200px; margin:auto; ↵
text-align:left;
}
#midcol { margin-left:140px; margin-right:140px;
}
#content { margin-left:150px; margin-right:150px;
}
```

```
table { width:500px; border:1px navy solid; border-collapse:collapse; margin:auto;
}
td { border:1px navy solid; padding:1px 0 1px 4px; text-align:left;
}
form { margin-left:180px;
}
#footer { margin:auto; text-align:center;
}
p.error { color:red; font-size:105%; font-weight:bold;
}
.label { float:left; width:210px; text-align:right; clear:left; margin-right:5px;
}
#submit { margin-left:215px;
}
```

The temporary template is currently non-interactive. We will now modify the template so that it is ready to become interactive. To test the file, run XAMPP and then enter the file's URL in a browser using http://localhost/simpleIdb/template.php.

The Interactive Version of the Template

In this version of the template, we will introduce interactivity by creating a new header file with an additional menu. This menu will allow users to register and enter their details into the simpleIdb database. It will also allow users to change their password and view the table of members.

The new header is shown in Figure 2-6.

Figure 2-6. *A registration menu is added to the header*

The interactive element will be embedded in the header; therefore, the previous header is now modified to include a menu. The new header will be named *header.php*, and the code is shown in Listing 2-6. The interactive header menu is shown in bold type.

Listing 2-6. Placing a Registration Menu in the New Header (header.php)

```
<style type="text/css">
#header { margin:10px auto 0 auto; min-width:960px; max-width:1200px; ↵
height:175px; background-image: url('images/tile-pale.jpg'); background-repeat:repeat; ↵
padding:0; color:white;
}
h1 {position:relative; top:40px; font-size:350%; color:white; margin:auto 0 auto 20px; ↵
width: 487px;
}
```

```
#reg-navigation ul { float:right; font-size:medium; width:160px; ↵
margin:-150px 15px 0 88%;
</style>
<div id="header">
<h1>This is the header</h1>
<div id="reg-navigation">
    <ul>
        <li><a href="register-page.php">Register</a></li>
        <li><a href="register-view_users-page.php">View Users</a></li>
        <li><a href="register-password.php">New Password</a></li>
    </ul>
</div>
</div>
```

In the template file, swap the previous included header for the new header. The new template page will be named index.php, and it will now have two blocks of menu buttons as shown in Figure 2-7.

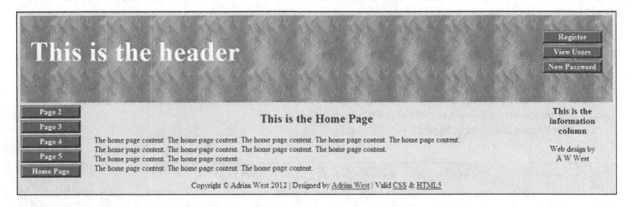

Figure 2-7. *The new home page template with two menus*

The only difference in the code between the old and new templates is that the new header is used. The name of the new header file is shown in bold type in the following snippet of code at the beginning of the new template. The snippet of code is given in Listing 2-7.

Listing 2-7. Including the New Header in the Home Page (index.php)

```
<!doctype html>
<html lang=en>
<head>
<title>Template for the home page of an interactive database</title>
<meta charset=utf-8>
<link rel="stylesheet" type="text/css" href="includes.css">
</head>
<body>
<div id='container'>
<?php include('header.php'); ?><!--include the new header file-->
<?php include('nav.php'); ?>
<?php include('info-col.php'); ?>
```

Now create the four ordinary web site pages, using the new template; save four copies of the file *index.php*, naming the copies page-2.php, page-3.php, page-4.php, and page-5.php. Change the content of those pages a little so that they differ from index.php and also to indicate which page the user is viewing. When this is done, you will have some pages to visit.

■ **Note**   The listing for the following interactive pages was inspired by code devised by Larry Ullman, who kindly gave me permission to adapt some of his code. His book PHP and MySQL for Dynamic Web Sites (Peachpit Press, 2011) is the most practical manual I have encountered so far. It is particularly good on database security. His web site and forum are always at the forefront of database development and can be seen at `http://www.LarryUllman.com`.

Connecting to the Database

Before we can do anything in the database, we must connect to it. This is achieved by creating a connection file that we will call *mysqli_connect.php*. The code for the connection file is given in the next snippet.

Listing for the Snippet of Code That Connects to the Database (mysqli_connect.php)

```php
<?php
// This file provides the information for accessing the database.and connecting ↵
to MySQL. It also sets the language coding to utf-8
// First we define the constants:                                          #1
DEFINE ('DB_USER', 'horatio');
DEFINE ('DB_PASSWORD', 'hmsvictory');
DEFINE ('DB_HOST', 'localhost');
DEFINE ('DB_NAME', 'simpleIdb');
// Next we assign the database connection to a variable that we will call $dbcon:   #2
$dbcon = @mysqli_connect (DB_HOST, DB_USER, DB_PASSWORD, DB_NAME) ↵
OR die ('Could not connect to MySQL: ' . mysqli_connect_error () );        #3
// Finally, we set the language encoding.as utf-8
mysqli_set_charset($dbcon, 'utf8');                                        #4
```

Save the file as mysqli_connect.php, and place it in the htdocs folder. When a database is set up on a remote host, this file is placed one level above the root folder for security. This is described in Chapter 7.

Explanation of the Code

The mysqli_connect.php file contains some code conventions that you may not be familiar with, so I'll briefly run through them here.

Single line comments begin with a double forward slash or with a hash symbol—for example:

> // we will set the language coding to utf-8

> Or # we will set the language coding to utf-8

> Constants are fixed definitions created by using the keyword `DEFINE`:

```php
DEFINE ('DB_USER', 'horatio');
```

Variables like $dbcon are storage devices for containing information that can be made to vary, they are preceded by a dollar symbol, like $dbcon shown next. Variables are created using the following format:

```
$var = some_information
```

The equals symbol means assign; the example assigns *some_information* to the variable $var. In other words, the item on the right of the equals symbol is assigned to the variable on the left.

We will now examine the code using the line numbers as references.

// First we define the constants: **#1**

```
DEFINE ('DB_USER', 'horatio');
DEFINE ('DB_PASSWORD', 'hmsvictory');
DEFINE ('DB_HOST', 'localhost');
DEFINE ('DB_NAME', 'simpleIdb');
// Next we assign the database connection to a variable that we will call $dbcon:    #2
$dbcon = @mysqli_connect (DB_HOST, DB_USER, DB_PASSWORD, DB_NAME) ↵
```

The text following the dollar sign can be anything as long as it is relevant to the information held in the memory. For instance, the variable for connecting to our database in the listing is named $dbcon. This was chosen to signify a connection to a database; it could be $db_c, $connect_db, or any other text that indicates a connection to the database. We use the host, username, password, and database name that we defined earlier to connect to the database. The @ symbol in our code suppresses error messages and prevents them from being shown to the user. Some error messages can help malevolent persons find their way around your database.

```
OR die ('Could not connect to MySQL: ' . mysqli_connect_error () );          #3
```

Normally, MySQL will display an explicit error message, but we have suppressed it completely by using the @ symbol. You will still want to notify users if something has gone wrong, though. The statement "OR die" provides an innocuous error message. If the file fails to connect to the database, the web site designer is alerted without a breach of security; however, the designer is warned so that the problem can be investigated and fixed.

```
mysqli_set_charset($dbcon, 'utf8');                                          #4
```

The final line in the code sets the encoding for the language to utf-8.

■ **Note**   The code is different from the code set in an HTML document because it does not include the hyphen as in utf-8.

Next, we need some pages for the header's new menu to work with. These pages will contain the interactive features. The pages will (i) allow users to register, (ii) allow users to view a table of the registered persons, and (iii) permit a password to be changed.

The Registration Page

■ **Caution**   When you finally migrate a database to a remote host, be sure to comply with the Data Protection Act for your territory, and state clearly on the registration page that the user's personal details will not be shared or sold to other organizations. The rules covering the protection of data vary from country to country, and it is essential that you read them and comply with them. Usually, any person within an organization who can access users' details must sign a document agreeing never to share personal information. An annual registration fee is payable to the government organization that regulates the data protection law. These precautions do not apply to experimental databases using fictitious data such as those described in this book.

The registration page allows users to enter their personal details directly into a table in the database. The interface is shown in Figure 2-8.

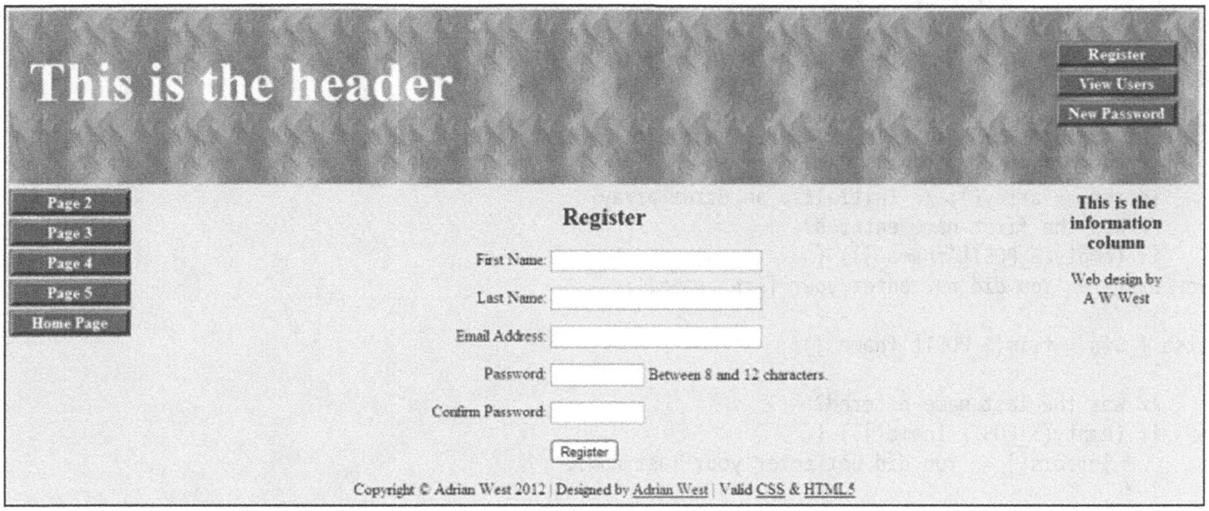

Figure 2-8. *The registration page*

When the user clicks the *Register* menu button on the new header, the page shown in Figure 2-8 is displayed. If the user fills out the form correctly and then clicks the Register button (below the entry fields), the user's entries are entered in the users table in the database. A *Thank you* page is then displayed.

Note that the Register and New Password buttons on the registration page are now redundant because the user has already accessed the registration page. Obviously, he or she does not yet have a password to change. The redundant buttons will be left in place for all the examples in this chapter to avoid complicating the instructions. The redundant buttons will be removed or changed in the next two chapters.

Now we will examine the code for the entire registration page. The new header is included in bold type in Listing 2-8.

■ **Caution**   If you type the listings in your text editor, do not include the line numbers (**#1**, **#2**, **#3**, and so on). These are provided to help you understand the explanation of the code given at the end of each listing. If you download the files from the book's web site page at www.apress.com, you will find that the line numbers are omitted from those files.

Listing 2-8. Creating the Complete Registration Page (register-page.php)

```
<!doctype html>
<html lang=en>
<head>
<title>Register page</title>
<meta charset=utf-8>
<link rel="stylesheet" type="text/css" href="includes.css">
<style type="text/css">
p.error { color:red; font-size:105%; font-weight:bold; text-align:center; }
</style>
</head>
```

```php
<body>
<div id="container">
<?php include("header.php"); ?>
<?php include("nav.php"); ?>
<?php include("info-col.php"); ?>
<div id="content"><!-- Start of the page content. -->
<p>
<?php
// This script performs an INSERT query that adds a record to the users table.
if ($_SERVER['REQUEST_METHOD'] == 'POST') {                                    #1
    $errors = array(); // Initialize an error array.
    // Was the first name entered?
    if (empty($_POST['fname'])) {
$errors[] = 'You did not enter your first name.';
    }
else { $fn = trim($_POST['fname']);
    }
    // Was the last name entered?
    if (empty($_POST['lname'])) {
        $errors[] = 'You did not enter your last name.';
    }
else { $ln = trim($_POST['lname']);
    }
    // Was an email address entered?
    if (empty($_POST['email'])) {
        $errors[] = 'You did not enter your email address.';
    }
else { $e = trim($_POST['email']);
    }
    // Did the two passwords match?                                            #2
    if (!empty($_POST['psword1'])) {
        if ($_POST['psword1'] != $_POST['psword2']) {
        $errors[] = 'Your passwords were not the same.';
    }
else { $p = trim($_POST['psword1']);
    }
    }
else { $errors[] = 'You did not enter your password.';
    }
//Start of the SUCCESSFUL SECTION. i.e all the fields were filled out
if (empty($errors)) { // If no problems encountered, register user in the database   #3
require ('mysqli_connect.php'); // Connect to the database.                    #4
// Make the query                                                             #5
$q = "INSERT INTO users (user_id, fname, lname, email, psword, registration_date)
VALUES (' ', '$fn', '$ln', '$e', SHA1('$p'), NOW() )";                        #6
$result = @mysqli_query ($dbcon, $q); // Run the query.                       #7
if ($result) { // If it ran OK.                                              #8
...header ("location: register-thanks.php");                                 #9
exit();                                                                      #10
//End of SUCCESSFUL SECTION
...}
```

```php
else { // If the form handler or database table contained errors            #11
// Display any error message
....echo '<h2>System Error</h2>
<p class="error">You could not be registered due to a system error. We apologize for any ↵
inconvenience.</p>';
// Debug the message:
....echo '<p>' . mysqli_error($dbcon) . '<br><br>Query: ' . $q . '</p>';
} // End of if clause ($result)
    mysqli_close($dbcon); // Close the database connection.
    // Include the footer and quit the script:
    include ('footer.php');
    exit();
    }
else { // Display the errors
        echo '<h2>Error!</h2>
        <p class="error">The following error(s) occurred:<br>';
        foreach ($errors as $msg) { // Print each error.                      #12
            echo " - $msg<br>\n";
    }
        echo '</p><h3>Please try again.</h3><p><br></p>';
    }// End of if (empty($errors)) IF.
    } // End of the main Submit conditional.
?>
<h2>Register</h2>                                                             #13
<!--display the form on the screen-->
<form action="register-page.php" method="post">

<p><label class="label" for="fname">First Name:</label>↵
<input id="fname" type="text" name="fname" size="30" maxlength="30" ↵
value="<?php if (isset($_POST['fname'])) echo $_POST['fname']; ?>"></p>

<p><label class="label" for="lname">Last Name:</label>↵
<input id="lname" type="text" name="lname" size="30" maxlength="40" ↵
value="<?php if (isset($_POST['lname'])) echo $_POST['lname']; ?>"></p>

<p><label class="label" for="email">Email Address:</label>↵
<input id="email" type="text" name="email" size="30" maxlength="60" ↵
value="<?php if (isset($_POST['email'])) echo $_POST['email']; ?>" > </p>

<p><label class="label" for="psword1">Password:</label>↵
<input id="psword1" type="password" name="psword1" size="12" maxlength="12" ↵
value="<?php if (isset($_POST['psword1'])) echo $_POST['psword1']; ?>" >  ↵
Between 8 and 12 characters.</p>

<p><label class="label" for="psword2">Confirm Password:</label>↵
<input id="psword2" type="password" name="psword2" size="12" maxlength="12" ↵
value="<?php if (isset($_POST['psword2'])) echo $_POST['psword2']; ?>" ></p>

<p><input id="submit" type="submit" name="submit" value="Register"></p>
</form><!-- End of the page content. -->
<?php include ('footer.php'); ?></p>
</div>
</div>
</body>
</html>
```

■ **Note** At this point, beginners may be mystified because they are more familiar with code that steps through a page from top to bottom. In the preceding example of interactive code, the beginner would expect the form fields to be at the top of the page of code. In fact, they come last in the listing. With a server-side script like PHP, the screen display is the last item to be actioned. The server scoops up the PHP code first and holds it in the server's memory. The HTML form fields are then displayed by the user's browser. When the user enters something into the fields, the input goes into the server's memory; there the PHP code checks it and deals with any problems. It then waits for the submit button to be clicked. When the submit button is clicked, the user's input (if it is correct) is inserted into the database table. If the input is incorrect, the server sends an error message to the user's browser.

Explanation of the Code

You can skip the fine details of the explanations if you would rather press on with creating and experimenting with the database tutorials. However, I strongly urge you to at least look for patterns in the explanations and make sure you grasp the logic of them.

For instance, one recurring pattern is the conditional that has the following format:

>   If a certain item has been set or if a certain condition exists

>   Do this

>   Or else (i.e., if the condition does not exist)

>   Do that

Later, when you want to adapt the tutorials for your own web sites, you will no doubt be motivated to discover the details of how the PHP code works.

Many of the PHP statements were explained by comments in the listings, but some items need further comment. The <form> section looks horribly complicated, but that will also be explained. For readers who wish to understand the code right now, the explanations are as follows:

```
if ($_SERVER['REQUEST_METHOD'] == 'POST') {                                    #1
$errors = array(); // Initialize an error array.
```

The array is initiated and given the name $errors. The array is a variable that can store multiple error messages. These multiple messages will be displayed by the file's subsequent code. Some additional information on arrays and their use is given at the end of this chapter.

```
// Was the first name entered?
if (empty($_POST['fname'])) {
```

If the first name fname field is empty, then...

```
$errors[] = 'You did not enter your first name.';
```

A suitable error message is inserted into the array. Note the square brackets:

```
} else {
```

Or else, if the field has been correctly filled out...

```
    $fn = trim($_POST['fname']);
}
```

An element in a global variable such as $_POST['fname'] is always enclosed in square brackets. This is a feature of global variables. The code beginning $fn = trim is an instruction to trim (remove) any spaces from the beginning and end of the user's fname entry. Spaces at the beginning and end of input data are unwanted characters. The trimmed fname is then assigned to the variable $fn.

■ **Note** Any variable taking the $_POST[] format, such as $_POST['fname'], is a global variable—it is accessible to any page on the web site. Ordinary variables have the format $fname, and they can be accessed only by loading the page in which they appear.

```
// Did the two passwords match?                                            #2
    if (!empty($_POST['psword1'])) {
        if ($_POST['psword1'] != $_POST['psword2']) {
            $errors[] = 'Your passwords were not the same.';
        }
else {
$p = trim($_POST['psword1']);
        }
    }
```

Note that the second line uses an exclamation mark and the equals character (!=) to denote not equal to. If the password in field 1 and the password in field 2 are not the same (not equal to), then the error message will be added to the errors array. This is shown in the earlier code in bold type:

```
if (empty($errors)) { // If no problems encountered, register user in the database  #3
```

This block of code is in the *successful* section. This section starts the registration process when all the fields have been filled out correctly—in which case, the $errors array is empty. The line is saying, "Because there are no errors, we can connect to the database and insert the user's data."

```
require ('mysqli_connect.php'); // Connect to the database.                 #4
```

In this line, the database connection is made with require() instead of include() so that the script will run if the connection is made, but it will not run if no connection is available. This is because there is no point continuing if the database is not accessible because data cannot be inserted into its table. We use require() when something vital is to be included and data needs to be protected from hackers.

```
// Make the query:                                                         #5
$q = "INSERT INTO users (user_id, fname, lname, email, psword, registration_date)
```

Assuming that a successful connection to the database is achieved, this line prepares the data for entry into the table called *users*. The word query sometimes means "query," but most often it means "Do something." In this case, it means "Insert a new record using the following data...." The line is saying, "Insert into the table named users, under the column headings labeled user_id, fname, and so on...." The query is assigned to a variable $q. Line #5 and line #6 are, in fact, SQL queries. This demonstrates how well HTML, PHP, and SQL work together.

```
VALUES (' ', '$fn', '$ln', '$e', SHA1('$p'), NOW() )";                     #6
```

This piece of SQL code describes the VALUES to be inserted. The user's entries in the registration form provide these values. Note that the first value is deliberately empty because it is the field that is automatically incremented and entered by MySQL, not by the user.

What are SHA1('$p') and NOW() in line #6 ? They are pieces of MySQL code; SHA1('$p') is a function for protecting a password. The acronym SHA stands for Secure Hash Algorithm, which is a security measure created by the US National Security Agency. It instructs MySQL to encode the password by converting it to a string 40 characters in length (no matter what length of password the user enters into the form). This explains why the password's attribute in the users table was set to CHAR(40). A hacker would have no idea which part of the 40-character string contains the password. In addition, the whole string would be thoroughly scrambled. The function NOW() instructs MySQL to automatically enter today's date into the registration date field:

```
$result = @mysqli_query ($dbc, $q); // Run the query.                           #7
```

This line runs the query. It puts the details into the specified columns. The result is assigned to the variable $result:

```
if ($result) { // If it ran without a problem                                   #8
header ("location: register-thanks.php");                                       #9
exit();                                                                          #10
```

Line #8 means, "If the operation was successful."
Lines #9 and #10 mean "Go to the page called register-thanks.php and quit the current page."
Or, in other words, "Quit the registration page, and display the Thank you page."

```
else { // If the form handler or database table contained errors               #11
    // Display an error message
        echo '<h2>System Error</h2>
<p class="error">You could not be registered due to a system error. ↵
We apologize for any inconvenience.</p>';
    // Debug information
        echo '<p>' . mysqli_error($dbcon) . '<br><br>Query: ' . $q . '</p>';
```

If an error in the database or table is encountered, display the error

```
foreach($errors as $msg) { // Echo each error                                   #12
        echo " - $msg<br>\n";
```

This line is a foreach loop. It cycles through the $errors array, and if it finds any error messages, each one is memorized and then displayed (echoed) on the screen (foreach is one word without a space).

The code following line #13 is explained in the "Styling the Forms" section later in the chapter.

The PHP Keyword echo

The keyword echo appears in code lines #11 and #12. It is the PHP way of telling a browser to "Display something on the screen." Some designers use the alternative keyword print, but this book will use echo because I have found that beginners confuse this with the command for sending something to an inkjet or laser printer; hard-copy printing is something that PHP cannot do.

■ **Note**　Any HTML code that you want can be placed in an echo statement. The echo writes the content into the HTML document (virtually, not literally) so that it can be displayed in a browser.

Beginners can be puzzled by the behavior of echo when a line space is required. For instance, the following code displays no line space:

```
echo "I found that PHP ";
echo "was much easier to learn than Perl";
```

Browsers display this as follows:

I found that PHP was much easier to learn than Perl

To push the second line down, you must insert the line-break tag <br> as follows:

```
echo "I found that PHP<br>";
echo "was much easier to learn than Perl";
```

Browsers display this as follows:

I found that PHP

was much easier to learn than Perl

■ **Tip**   Lines **#7** through **#9** show the standard PHP method for redirecting to a new page. Its format is as follows:

```
if($result) { // If it ran without a problem.
header ("location: register-thanks.php");
exit();
```

The thankyou.php page is shown and explained later in the chapter.

Styling the Form Fields

An unformatted registration form is neither attractive nor helpful, because the fields are not neatly arranged on the page. Figure 2-9 shows the raw form. Figure 2-10 shows the form when CSS formatting is applied.

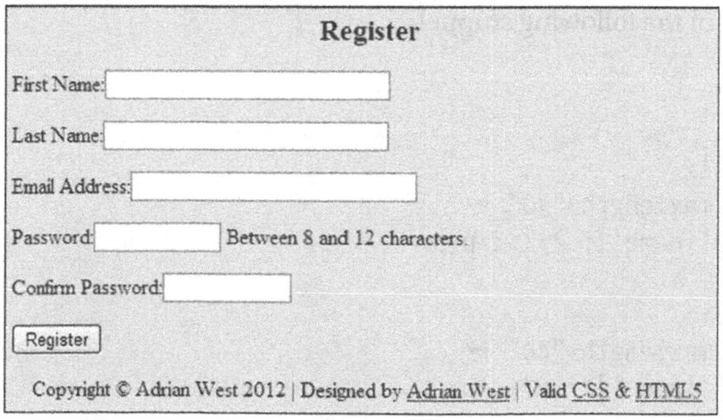

Figure 2-9. *The unformatted form*

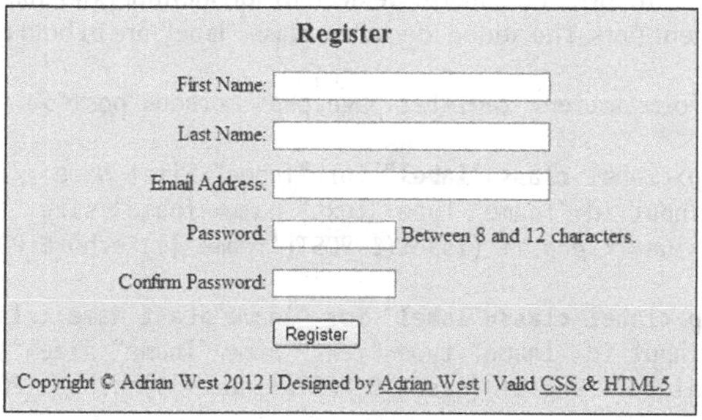

Figure 2-10. *The form when formatted*

The HTML code for labels and fields in HTML forms can be quite simple, something like this:

```
<p><label for="fname">First Name:</label>
<input id="fname" type="text" name="fname" size="30" maxlength="30"></p>
```

Our form fields are much more complicated. This will be explained later. (See the "Sticky Forms" section.) Meanwhile, we will concentrate on formatting the labels and fields using CSS.

The input fields in the unformatted version in Figure 2-9 were created by the following code:

```
<form action="register-page.php" method="post">

<p><label" for="fname">First Name:</label>
<input id="fname" type="text" name="fname" size="30" maxlength="30" ↵
value="<?php if (isset($_POST['fname'])) echo $_POST['fname']; ?>"></p>

<p><label for="lname">Last Name:</label>
<input id="lname" type="text" name="lname" size="30" maxlength="40" ↵
value="<?php if (isset($_POST['lname'])) echo $_POST['lname']; ?>"></p>

<p><label for="email">Email Address:</label>
<input id="email" type="text" name="email" size="30" maxlength="60" ↵
value="<?php if (isset($_POST['email'])) echo $_POST['email']; ?>" > </p>

<p><label for="psword1">Password:</label>
<input id="psword1" type="password" name="psword1" size="12" maxlength="12" ↵
value="<?php if (isset($_POST['psword1'])) echo $_POST['psword1']; ?>" >  ↵
Between 8 and 12 characters.</p>

<p><label for="psword2">Confirm Password:</label>
<input id="psword2" type="password" name="psword2" size="12" maxlength="12" ↵
value="<?php if (isset($_POST['psword2'])) echo $_POST['psword2']; ?>" ></p>

<p><input type="submit" name="submit" value="Register"></p>
</form>
```

To format the fields, we need to add identifiers so that the main CSS sheet called includes.css can target those identifiers. The added identifiers class="label" are in bold type in the following snippet:

```
<form action="register-page.php" method="post">

<p><label class="label" for="fname">First Name:</label>
<input id="fname" type="text" name="fname" size="30" maxlength="30" ↵
value="<?php if (isset($_POST['fname'])) echo $_POST['fname']; ?>"></p>

<p><label class="label" for="lname">Last Name:</label>
<input id="lname" type="text" name="lname" size="30" maxlength="40" ↵
value="<?php if (isset($_POST['lname'])) echo $_POST['lname']; ?>"></p>

<p><label class="label" for="email">Email Address:</label>
<input id="email" type="text" name="email" size="30" maxlength="60" ↵
value="<?php if (isset($_POST['email'])) echo $_POST['email']; ?>" > </p>
```

```
<p><label class="label" for="psword1">Password:</label>
<input id="psword1" type="password" name="psword1" size="12" maxlength="12" ↵
value="<?php if (isset($_POST['psword1'])) echo $_POST['psword1']; ?>" >  ↵
Between 8 and 12 characters.</p>

<p><label class="label" for="psword2">Confirm Password:</label>
<input id="psword2" type="password" name="psword2" size="12" maxlength="12" ↵
value="<?php if (isset($_POST['psword2'])) echo $_POST['psword2']; ?>" ></p>

<p><input id="submit" type="submit" name="submit" value="Register"></p>
</form>
```

If you look back at the main style sheet includes.css, you will see that the last two instructions style the form by using the class named label. The submit button is also styled using the id named submit in the HTML code and #submit in the style sheet. The two styles are as follows:

```
.label { float:left; width:210px; text-align:right; clear:left; margin-right:5px;
}
#submit { margin-left:215px;
}
```

Most of the code or fields and labels will be familiar to you, but what about that complicated PHP code enclosed in the values?

value="<?php if (isset($_POST['fname'])) echo $_POST['fname']; ?>"></p>

This feature provides a sticky form for displaying and correcting error messages.

Sticky Forms

In the registration page, if the user makes a mistake or forgets to fill out a field, the error messages appear and the form fields are redisplayed. Users would not mind amending the incorrect bit, but they would be rather annoyed if all the correct fields also needed filling out again. A sticky form retains the entries in the fields so that only the incorrect entries need to be edited by the user.

The formatted <label> and <input> statements in the form section are usually not as complicated as our code. They normally look something like this:

```
<form action="register-page.php" method="post">

<p><label class="label" for="fname">First Name:</label>
<input id="fname" type="text" name="fname" size="30" maxlength="30"></p>
```

In our tutorial, the additional and rather complicated bit is shown in bold type as follows:

```
<form action="register-page.php" method="post">

<p><label class="label" for="fname">First Name:</label>
<input id="fname" type="text" name="fname" size="30" maxlength="30" ↵
value="<?php if (isset($_POST['fname'])) echo $_POST['fname']; ?>"></p>
```

The PHP code (in bold type) remembers the previous entries and displays (echoes) them in the reloaded form fields.

Explanation of the Code

The value is the text to be shown in the field when the form is redisplayed.

The code segment if (isset($_POST['fname'])) is saying, "If the first name has been set (entered) by the user, then…"

The echo command redisplays the content that was previously entered by the user. This content is stored in the global variable $_POST['fname']; if users enter their registration details correctly, a thank you page is displayed. We will discuss this next.

The Thank You Page

The Thank you page is show in Figure 2-11.

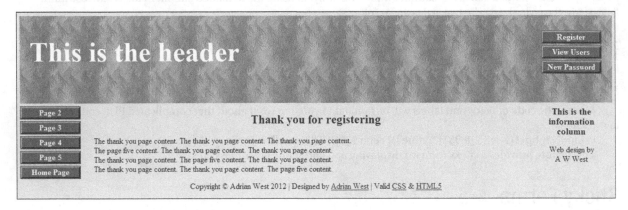

Figure 2-11. *The Thank You page*

The registration page calls up the thank you page, and this is shown in the next code snippet in bold type. You will find this in the *successful* section of the registration page's code. For convenience, I repeat it here:

```
//Start of SUCCESSFUL SECTION i.e all entries were correct
    if (empty($errors)) { // If everything's OK, register the user in the database
    require ('./mysqli_connect.php'); // Connect to the database.
    // Make the query:
$q = "INSERT INTO users (user_id, fname, lname, email, psword, registration_date) ↵
VALUES (' ', '$fn', '$ln', '$e', SHA1('$p'), NOW() )";
    $result = @mysqli_query ($dbc, $q); // Run the query.
    if ($result) { // If it ran without a problem
    header ("location: register-thanks.php");
    exit();
//End of SUCCESSFUL SECTION
```

The entire thank you page code is given in Listing 2-11.

Listing 2-11. Creating the Thank You Page (register-thanks.php)

```
<!doctype html>
<html lang=en>
<head>
<title>Registion thank you page</title>
<meta charset=utf-8>
<link rel="stylesheet" type="text/css" href="includes.css">
</head>
<body>
<div id="container">
<?php include("header.php"); ?>
<?php include("nav.php"); ?>
<?php include("info-col.php"); ?>
<div id="content"><!-- Start of the thank you page-content. -->
<h2>Thank you for registering</h2>
<p>The thank you page content. The thank you page content. The thank you page content.<br>
The thank you page.The thank you page content. The thank you page content.<br>The thank
you page content. The thank you page. The thank you page content.<br>The thank you page
content. The thank you page content. The thank you page content</p>
<!-- End of the thank you page-content. -->
</div>
</div>
<?php include("footer.php"); ?>
</body>
</html>
```

We initiated a PHP array to contain all the error messages. We will now use that array to display error messages.

Displaying Error Messages That Are Collected in an Array

If the user enters nothing in all the fields and then clicks the Register button, four errors will be created. The corresponding error messages are inserted into the errors array. These are then displayed so that the user knows what he or she has done wrong. It would be annoying if only the first error was shown and then, after clicking the Register button a second time, the second error was displayed, and so on.

Figure 2-12 shows all the errors that would be displayed if the user failed to fill out all the fields in the form.

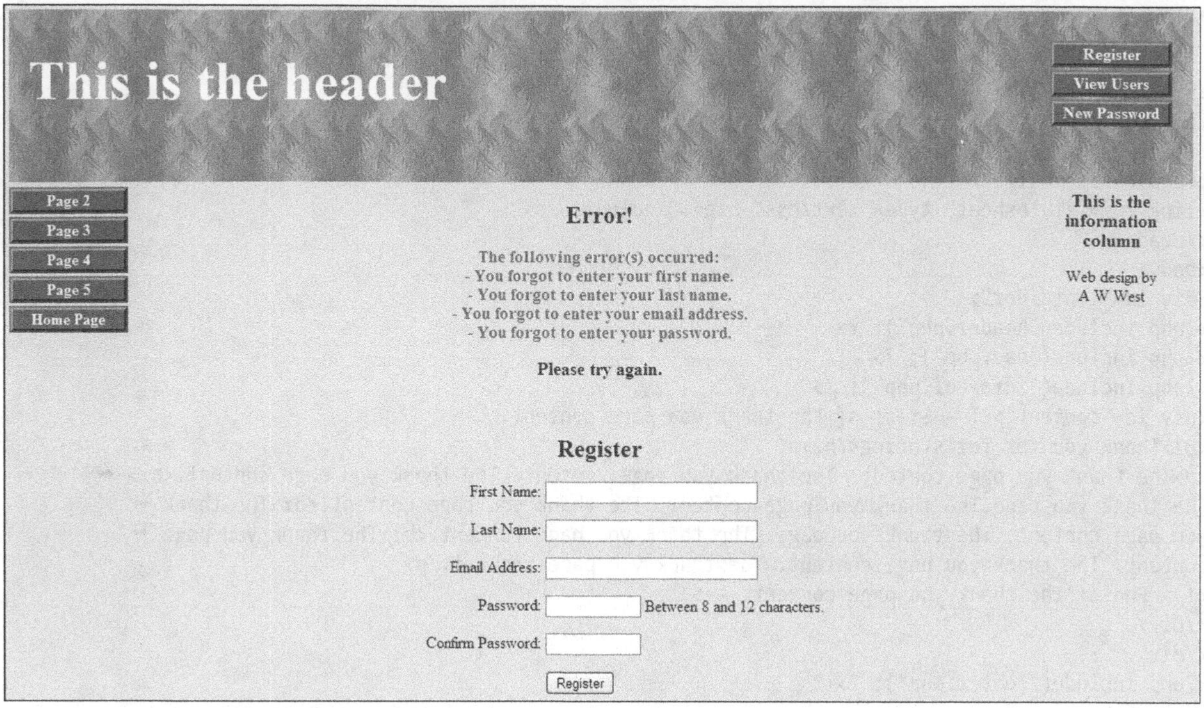

Figure 2-12. *The errors displayed if the user failed to enter any data*

The errors are displayed on the Registration page, and a sticky form is used to retain the user's entries. In the extreme case shown in Figure 2-12, the user entered nothing and then clicked the Register button.

Viewing Members' Records

When a user has registered, the web site designer can use phpMyAdmin to view the table and its entries. Access phpMyAdmin, and click the relevant database and table. Then click the Browse tab. Let's suppose a user registered last year on September 20, 2012 and she entered the following information:

First name: Rose Last name: Bush, Email: `rbush@myisp.co.uk`, and Password: redblooms

phpMyAdmin will allow you to view each record. Access phpMyAdmin, select the simpleIdb database, click the users table, and then click the Browse tab. Figure 2-13 shows Rose Bush's entries.

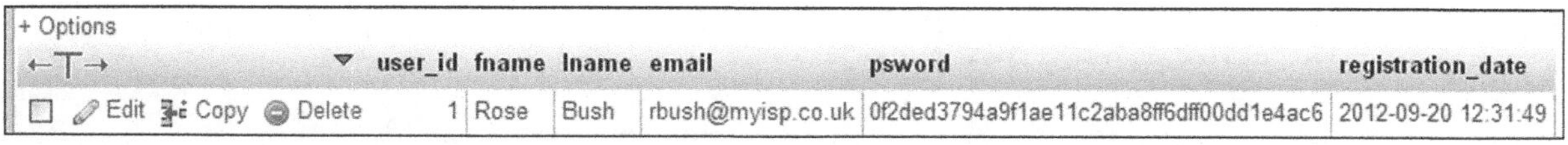

+ Options

←T→	user_id	fname	lname	email	psword	registration_date
Edit Copy Delete	1	Rose	Bush	rbush@myisp.co.uk	0f2ded3794a9f1ae11c2aba8ff6dff00dd1e4ac6	2012-09-20 12:31:49

Figure 2-13. *Viewing a record in phpMyAdmin*

Note that the password redblooms is encrypted as 0f2ded3794a9f1ae11c2aba8ff6dff00dd1e4ac6.

Often web site designers and database administrators need to view a table of database entries created by all the registered users. The next item provides the information for doing this.

The View Users Page

When the View Users button is clicked, a table of registered users is displayed as shown in Figure 2-14.

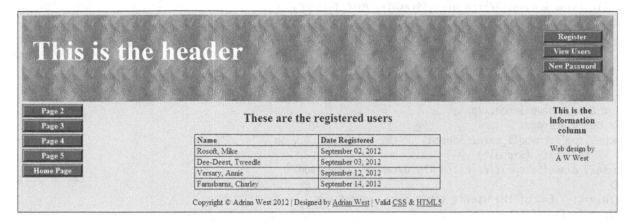

Figure 2-14. *A table of users is displayed*

The table is displayed when the user clicks the View Users button on the top-right menu. The code for displaying the table of users is given in listing 2-14.

Listing 2-14. Displaying a Table of Registered Members on the Screen (register-view-users.php)

```
<!doctype html>
<html lang=en>
<head>
<title>View users page</title>
<meta charset=utf-8>
<link rel="stylesheet" type="text/css" href="includes.css">
</head>
<body>
<div id="container">
<?php include("header.php"); ?>
<?php include("nav.php"); ?>
<?php include("info-col.php"); ?>
<div id="content"><!-- Start of the content of the table of users page. -->
<h2>These are the registered users</h2>
<p>
<?php
// This script retrieves all the records from the users table.
require('mysqli_connect.php'); // Connect to the database.
// Make the query:                                                    #1
$q = "SELECT CONCAT(lname, ', ', fname) AS name, ↵
DATE_FORMAT(registration_date, '%M %d, %Y') AS regdat FROM users
ORDER BY registration_date ASC";
$result = @mysqli_query ($dbcon, $q); // Run the query.
if ($result) { // If it ran OK, display the records.
```

49

```
// Table header.                                                              #2
echo '<table>
<tr><td><b>Name</b></td><td><b>Date Registered</b></td></tr>';
// Fetch and print all the records:                                          #3
while ($row = mysqli_fetch_array($result, MYSQLI_ASSOC)) {
echo '<tr><td>' . $row['name'] . '</td><td>' . $row['regdat'] . '</td></tr>'; }
    echo '</table>'; // Close the table so that it is ready for displaying.
    mysqli_free_result ($result); // Free up the resources.
} else { // If it did not run OK.
// Error message:
echo '<p class="error">The current users could not be retrieved. We apologize ↵
for any inconvenience.</p>';
// Debug message:
echo '<p>' . mysqli_error($dbcon) . '<br><br>Query: ' . $q . '</p>';
} // End of if ($result)
mysqli_close($dbcon); // Close the database connection.
?>
</div><!-- End of the user's table page content -->
<?php include("footer.php"); ?>
</div>
</body>
</html>
```

Explanation of the Code

You will have seen most of the code before, but here is an explanation of the new items:

```
// Make the query:                                                           #1
$q = "SELECT CONCAT(lname, ', ', fname) AS name, ↵
DATE_FORMAT(registration_date, '%M %d, %Y') AS regdat FROM users ↵
ORDER BY registration_date ASC";
$result = @mysqli_query ($dbcon, $q); // Run the query.
```

The SQL query selects and strings together (concatenates) the last name, then a comma, then the first name, and then the registration date. It sets the temporary headings for these as name and regdat. It rearranges the registration dates in the format month-day-year. It then states that the information should be extracted from the users table. Finally, it requests that each row of information be displayed in ascending date order (oldest first); the code for this is ASC for ascending. To display the records with the latest registrations first (descending order), you use DESC instead of ASC:

```
// Table header.                                                             #2
echo '<table><tr><td><b>Name</b></td><td><b>Date Registered</b>
</td></tr>';
```

This block of code displays (echoes) the first row of the table on the screen. The headings are displayed in bold type in the code and are made visible on the screen; the two headings are Name and Date Registered.

```
// Fetch and print all the records:                                         #3
while ($row = mysqli_fetch_array($result, MYSQLI_ASSOC)) {
echo '<tr>
<td>' . $row['name'] . '</td>
<td>' . $row['regdat'] . '</td>
```

```
</tr>';
    }
echo '</table>'; // Close the table.
```

This block of code loops through the rows and displays them while rows are available to display. Then, when no more rows are available, the table is closed.

Users sometimes wish to change their password. The next section demonstrates how this is done.

The Change Password Page

When the user clicks the "New Password" button on the menu at the top right of the header, the form shown in Figure 2-15 appears.

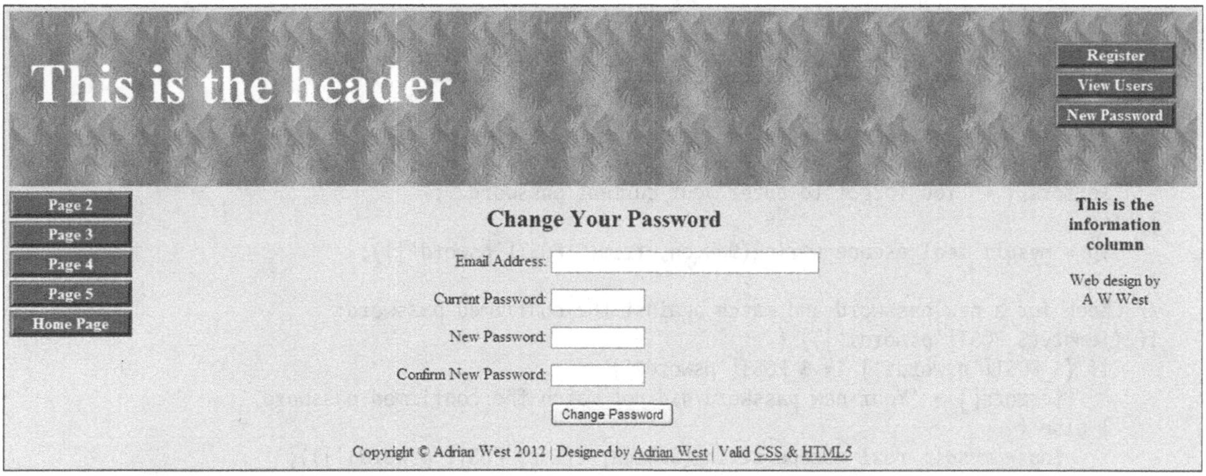

Figure 2-15. *The change password form*

The form is suitable only if the user knows her current password and e-mail address. If she has forgotten her password, a different approach is needed that will be discussed in a later chapter. However, this "new password" page is useful if the user does not like the password she originally chose. The code for the change password form is given in Listing 2-15.

Listing 2-15. Creating a Page to Allow Users to Change a Password (register-password.php)

```
<!doctype html>
<html lang=en>
<head>
<title>Change password</title>
<meta charset=utf-8>
<link rel="stylesheet" type="text/css" href="includes.css">
<style type="text/css">
p.error { color:red; font-size:105%; font-weight:bold; text-align:center; }
</style>
</head>
```

```php
<body>
<div id="container">
<?php include("header.php"); ?>
<?php include("nav.php"); ?>
<?php include("info-col.php"); ?>
<div id="content"><!-- Start of the change password page -->
<?php
// This page lets users change their password.
// Was the submit button clicked?
if ($_SERVER['REQUEST_METHOD'] == 'POST') {
    require ('mysqli_connect.php'); // Connect to the db.
    $errors = array(); // Initialize the error array.
    // Check for an email address:
    if (empty($_POST['email'])) {
        $errors[] = 'You forgot to enter your email address.';
    } else {
        $e = mysqli_real_escape_string($dbcon, trim($_POST['email']));      #1
    }
    // Check for the current password:
    if (empty($_POST['psword'])) {
        $errors[] = 'You forgot to enter your current password.';
    } else {
        $p = mysqli_real_escape_string($dbcon, trim($_POST['psword']));
    }
    // Check for a new password and match against the confirmed password:
    if (!empty($_POST['psword1'])) {
        if ($_POST['psword1'] != $_POST['psword2']) {
            $errors[] = 'Your new password did not match the confirmed password.';
        } else {
            $np = mysqli_real_escape_string($dbcon, trim($_POST['psword1']));
        }
    } else {
        $errors[] = 'You forgot to enter your new password.';
    }
    if (empty($errors)) { // If no problems occurred
    // Check that the user has entered the right email address/password combination:
    $q = "SELECT user_id FROM users WHERE (email='$e' AND psword=SHA1('$p') )";
    $result = @mysqli_query($dbcon, $q);
    $num = @mysqli_num_rows($result);
    if ($num == 1) { // Match was made.
    // Get the user_id:
    $row = mysqli_fetch_array($result, MYSQLI_NUM);
    // Make the UPDATE query:
    $q = "UPDATE users SET psword=SHA1('$np') WHERE user_id=$row[0]";
$result = @mysqli_query($dbcon, $q);
    if (mysqli_affected_rows($dbcon) == 1) { // If the query ran without a problem
    // Echo a message
    echo '<h2>Thank you!</h2>
    <h3>Your password has been updated.</h3>';
    } else { // If it encountered a problem
    // Error message
    echo '<h2>System Error</h2>
```

```php
<p class="error">Your password could not be changed due to a system error.
We apologize for any inconvenience.</p>';
	// Debugging message
	echo '<p>' . mysqli_error($dbcon) . '<br /><br />Query: ' . $q . '</p>';
	}
	mysqli_close($dbcon); // Close the database connection.
	// Include the footer and quit the script (to not show the form).
	include ('footer.php');
	exit();
	} else { // Invalid email address/password combination.
	echo '<h2>Error!</h2>
	<p class="error">The email address and password do not match those on file.</p>';
	}
	} else { // Report the errors.
	echo '<h2>Error!</h2>
	<p class="error">The following error(s) occurred:<br />';
	foreach ($errors as $msg) { // Print each error.
	echo " - $msg<br />\n";
	}
	echo '</p><p class="error">Please try again.</p><p><br /></p>';
	} // End of if (empty($errors))
	mysqli_close($dbcon); // Close the database connection.
} // End of the main Submit conditional
?>
<!--Display the form-->
<h2>Change Your Password</h2>
<form action="register-password.php" method="post">

<p><label class="label" for="email">Email Address:</label>
<input id="email" type="text" name="email" size="40" maxlength="60"
value="<?php if (isset($_POST['email'])) echo $_POST['email']; ?>" > </p>

<p><label class="label" for="psword">Current Password:</label>
<input id="psword" type="password" name="psword" size="12" maxlength="12"
value="<?php if (isset($_POST['psword'])) echo $_POST['psword']; ?>"></p>

<p><label class="label" for="psword1">New Password:</label>
<input id="psword1" type="password" name="psword1" size="12" maxlength="12"
value="<?php if (isset($_POST['psword1'])) echo $_POST['psword1']; ?>"></p>

<p><label class="label" for="psword2">Confirm New Password:</label>
<input id="psword2" type="password" name="psword2" size="12" maxlength="12"
value="<?php if (isset($_POST['psword2'])) echo $_POST['psword2']; ?>"></p>

<p><input id="submit"type="submit" name="submit" value="Change Password"></p>
</form>
<?php include ('footer.php'); ?></p>
</div><!-- End of the page-specific content. -->
</div>
</body>
</html>
```

Explanation of the Code

```
$e = mysqli_real_escape_string($dbcon, trim($_POST['email']));                    #1
```

This line of code prevents apostrophes from causing the script to stop running. The code also removes most of the characters in the users' input that would conflict with MySQL.

Take note of this pattern in line **#1**; we will be using it extensively throughout the book. The function `mysqli_real_escape_string(the connection variable, trim())` removes undesirable characters from a string (string means "some text"). This prevents some forms of database attacks by hackers. Without this function, mischief-makers could log in without a valid e-mail or password. In the example shown, the global variable `$_POST['email']` is trimmed—that is, any spaces are removed from the beginning and end of the e-mail address. Then it is located as the second argument after the connection to the database `$dbcon`. The whole lot is then cleansed of undesirable characters by the function `mysqli_real_escape_string()`.

The user would be pleased to see confirmation that the password was changed. This is demonstrated next.

Confirming a Successful Password Change

If the password change is successful, the page shown in Figure 2-16 is displayed.

Figure 2-16. *The password has been changed*

The page shown in Figure 2-16 is not a new page. It is the current "New Password" page with the form fields removed automatically. The echoed message "Thank you" replaces the form fields.

Dealing with an Apostrophe

Some characters that are input by a user can cause a page to stop working.

I recommend that you try this experiment to learn about escaping (converting) problem characters. Problem characters are characters that act as both code and text—for instance, an apostrophe is text, but to PHP it is also code because it signifies the start and finish of a piece of text. Escaping the apostrophe tells PHP that the problem character is not to be treated as code.

Try registering the following new member using the details in Table 2-1. His name contains an apostrophe that will halt the script:

Table 2-1. *Register a member who has an apostrophe in his name*

First Name	Last Name	Email	Password
Paddy	O'Brien	pobrien@myisp.co.uk	irishname

Because O'Brien contains an apostrophe, you will receive an error message and the page will halt. PHP assumes that the apostrophe is code; therefore, the page stops when it arrives at the unexpected apostrophe.

Tutorial Dealing with the Apostrophe

We were unable to register names that included an apostrophe, such as O'Brien. We will now examine this problem more closely.

The function mysqli_real_escape_string($dbcon, $variable); was used in the last example, register-password.php. If we add this function to the registration file register-page.php, it will allow users to enter names with apostrophes.

Open your htdocs folder, and save a copy of register-page.php with the new name register-page-apos.php. This is a backup in case you mess up the original page.

In the new file register-page-apos.php, find this line:

```
else { $ln = trim($_POST['lname']);
       }
```

Change the line to

```
else {$ln = mysqli_real_escape_string($dbcon, trim($_POST['lname']))  ;
}
```

IMPORTANT: The new function will work only if the language encoding is utf-8 and the database connection is opened before the function is called. The language is already set to utf-8 in the database connection file and within the meta tag (shown in bold). Next, in the file register-page-apos.php, move the database connection line `require ('mysqli_connect.php')` to the start of the PHP code. This is shown in bold in the partial listing for the register-page-apos.php file. The file is not included in the downloads because it is assumed that you will create it, a part of the code is given in the next snippet.

Listing A Snippet Showing the Amendments to the Registration Page (register-page-apos.php)

```
<!doctype html>
<html lang=en>
<head>
<title>Register page for apostrophes</title>
<meta charset=utf-8><!--important for escaping problem characters-->
<link rel="stylesheet" type="text/css" href="includes.css">
</head>
<body>
<div id="container">
<?php include("header.php"); ?>
<?php include("nav.php"); ?>
<?php include("info-col.php"); ?>
<div id="content"><!-- Registration handler content starts here -->
<p>
<?php
//The link to the database is moved here to the top of the PHP code.
require ('mysqli_connect.php'); // Connect to the db.
// This query INSERTs a record in the users table.
```

Scroll down to find the piece of code listed next, and change the line as shown in bold type:

```
// Check for a last name:
if (empty($_POST['lname'])) {
    $errors[] = 'You forgot to enter your last name.';
} else {
$ln = mysqli_real_escape_string($dbcon, trim($_POST['lname']));
}
```

Scroll down to find the piece of code listed next, and delete the line shown in bold type (or, as I have done, add two forward slashes to the front of the line to comment it out):

```
//Start of the SUCCESSFUL SECTION. i.e all the fields were filled out
    if (empty($errors)) { // If everything's OK, register the user in the database
//require ('mysqli_connect.php'); // Connect to the database.
```

Table 2-2. *The Details for Registering Paddy O'Brien*

First Name	Last Name	Email	Password
Paddy	O'Brien	pobrien@myisp.co.uk	irishname

Save the file with the new name register-page-apos.php. Fire up XAMPP, and in a browser type this into the address field: `http://localhost/simpleIdb/register-page-apos.php`. Then try registering Paddy O'Brien again using the details shown in Table 2-2. :

The registration should be accomplished successfully, and the apostrophe should be present when you view the name O'Brien using phpMyAdmin.

■ **Note** Using the two functions, mysqli_real_escape_string() and trim()is an important security step to prevent crashes and to ensure that clean data is inserted into the database table. Among the characters that are escaped by the function are the following: ', ", \, ASCII 0, \n, \r, \control+z.Since the advent of PHP 5.3, the function mysqli_real_escape_string() replaces the deprecated mysql_ escape_string() and addslashes().

The function has the format `mysqli_real_escape_string(connection variable, trim(string))`. It converts the apostrophe by escaping it. The function looks for apostrophes, and it then places a backslash in front of the apostrophe like this: O\'Brien. The backslash escapes the apostrophe—in other words, it converts the apostrophe so that PHP does not regard it as code.

You will notice that there are two items (called "arguments") within the brackets: the database connection code $dbcon is the first item, and the user's input is the second item.

■ **Note** From here forward in this book, all user input will be cleaned before being used in a database query. PHP has several ways of cleaning input, and these will be revealed and explained as we work through subsequent chapters. Since PHP version 5.2, new methods of cleaning and validating input have become available, and these will be used in Chapters 3 through 5, and a full explanation of several security measures will be given in Chapter 6.

Apostrophes Within PHP code

User input is not the only source of apostrophes, they can be introduced by the web site designer. Apostrophes can produce a PHP parsing error when they occur within a block of PHP code because they will be interpreted as code by the parser and the database. Examine this snippet for example:

```php
<?php
echo '<h2>Welcome to the Members' Page ';
if (isset($_SESSION['fname'])){
echo "{$_SESSION['fname']}";
}
echo '</h2>';
?>
```

The apostrophe after the word "Members" will result in an error message saying that there is an unexpected word Page within the line that contains the apostrophe.

To suppress the error and continue running the code, the apostrophe must be "escaped." This is achieved by means of a backslash. The backslash instructs the PHP parser "The apostrophe is not the end of a statement, therefore accept the apostrophe and display it." The backslash has been included in the next snippet:

```php
<?php
echo '<h2>Welcome to the Members\' Page ';
if (isset($_SESSION['fname'])){
echo "{$_SESSION['fname']}";
}
echo '</h2>';
?>
```

We will now add some users so that we can use a browser to display a table of registered users.

Testing the Tutorial's Pages

To see the interactive pages working, double-click the XAMPP icon on your desktop. When the control panel appears, check that Apache and MySQL are running, and then minimize the XAMPP control panel. Type http://localhost/simpleIdb/index.php into the address field of a browser, and then click the Register button so that you can enter some users.

To save you time and the effort of dreaming up fictitious persons, use the suggestions provided in Table 2-3.

Table 2-3. *Suggesions for Entering Members' Details.*

Name	Email	Password
Mike Rosoft	miker@myisp.com	willgates
Olive Branch	obranch@myisp.co.uk	anoilyone
Frank Insence	finsence@myisp.net	perfume
Annie Versary	aversary@myisp.com	birthdaygirl
Terry Fide	tfide@myisp.de	scaredstiff
Rose Bush	rbush@myisp.co.uk	redblooms

Now that you have some more data in your users table, run XAMPP and use a browser to try the menu to display the table of registered users.

___

■ **Tip** No doubt, you will encounter error messages as you create code and test it. For help, refer to the troubleshooting tips in Chapter 12.

___

Earlier in this chapter, I promised more information on the use of PHP arrays. The next section will help you understand additional aspects of this most useful feature.

More About Arrays

Arrays are used throughout this book, and if you access forums for advice on the use of PHP, you will be confronted with many arrays. Although there is no need right now to learn about the following method for assigning values to arrays, this next section will be a useful reference for the future.

Arrays can be populated with elements in several ways. If we create an array named $cereals, as follows

```php
<?php
$cereals = array();
?>
```

a few elements can be inserted as follows (note that the first array element is zero):

```php
<?php
$cereals = array();
$cereals[0] = "oats";
$cereals[1] = "barley";
$cereals[2] = "corn";
$cereals[3] = "wheat";
?>
```

To display these elements, insert the following code just before the closing tag ?>:

```php
echo ("$cereals[0] " . "$cereals[1] " . "$cereals[2] " . $cereals[3]);?>
```

The display would be
Oats barley corn wheat
The full stop between each element in the code means concatenate the elements (that is, string the elements together). Note the space after the right square bracket in the elements numbered 2 and 3. The space can also be an entity as shown in the element numbered zero. This is useful if you wish to display a character such as a bullet point between each element.

A file containing this array is included in the downloads for this chapter. To see the array elements displayed, start XAMPP and enter `http://localhost/simpleIdb/array.php` in the address bar of a browser.

___

■ **Caution** The databases created by the tutorials in this chapter are not secure. They have been deliberately stripped of most filters and cleaners so that the essential processes are uncluttered and clearly visible. An increasing number of security features will be added in later chapters.

___

Summary

In this chapter, you created your first interactive pages and tested them. You learned a little more about PHP—in particular, you should have grasped the idea of looking for and recognizing logical patterns in the code. You learned how to use two PHP functions: include() and echo(). You discovered the importance of PHP conditionals for creating interactive database pages. You also learned how to check whether the user has entered information before sending the data to the database table. In the next chapter, we will add some extra security and demonstrate how users and an administrator can log in and log out of private pages on a web site. You will also learn how to remove or replace the redundant links in the header menus.

CHAPTER 3

■ ■ ■

Login/Logout for Members and an Administrator

In Chapter 2, you created your first interactive pages using a database and a table. By now, you have probably realized that what you created was not very practical; however, you learned how to embed interactivity into a real-world page. A more practical application is to allow registered users to log in and log out of private pages. When users log in, they should be able to access extra features offered by the web site. These could be a page of special offers for members, or it could be the ability to add a comment in a blog, access the minutes of meetings, or view the dates of special events for members only.

In the previous tutorial, any user could view a table of members, but the members would not be pleased that their private details are available to everybody. We must now prevent this and allow only the administrator (a membership secretary, say) and the webmaster to view the table of members.

An administrator is a special category of user: she should be able to view the members' table and also to amend or delete records. Computer-savvy administrators can use phpMyAdmin, but many administrators will be membership secretaries with only basic computer skills. They will need a simple interface that enables them to view, alter, and delete records. This chapter will teach you how to create and implement a user-friendly interface for the administrator. Chapters 4, 5, and 6 will progressively improve this interface.

To log in to private pages on a web site, registered members and the administrator must enter information known only to them—for instance, the user's e-mail address and password or a username and a password. The database will automatically check that the login details match the user's information held in the database. If the login details are verified, the user is admitted to the private web pages.

This chapter has seven main sections that cover the following topics:

- Create the revised database and table
- Tidy the styling
- Remove or replace redundant menu buttons in the headers
- Deal with undesirable characters in the registration page
- Differentiate between two types of membership
- Create user levels to limit access to private pages
- Log in
- Create a *members' only* page
- Planning the administrator's role
- Testing the Login/Logout page

Create the Logindb Database and Table

The tutorials in this chapter are based on the templates used in Chapter 2. I will clarify the file structure by using a new name for the database and for the folder containing the PHP and HTML pages. This is necessary because I found that if students pile modification upon modification, they can get into a terrible muddle. Therefore, as a general rule, I will continue to use a separate folder and a new database name for each new chapter in this book. However, a table can have the same name (for example, *users*) as the previous tutorial. This is acceptable as long as the table is located in a different database folder.

Create a new folder and a new database as follows:

1. In the XAMPP *htdocs* folder, create a new folder called *login*.

2. Download the PHP files for Chapter 3 from the book's page at *http://www.apress.com*, and put them in the new login folder in *htdocs*. Alternatively, you can practice creating the listings by typing each file in your HTML editor as you go through the chapter. Save them in your *login* folder in the *htdocs* folder.

3. Now type **http://localhost/phpmyadmin** in the address field of your browser.

4. Click the Databases tab.

5. Create a new database called *logindb*.

6. Select the box next to *logindb*, and click *Check Privileges*.

7. Click *Add User*, and enter the following attributes:

    User name: william

    Host: localhost

    Password: catonlap

    Database name: logindb

8. Check all the global privileges, and then accept the default (zeros) for the resources.

9. Click the Go button at the bottom of the page.

10. In the *htdocs'* login folder, create the *mysqli_connect.php* file so that it connects to *logindb* as shown in the following listing:

Listing for the Snippet of Code Required for Connecting to the New Database (msqli_connect. php)

```php
<?php
// Create a connection to the logindb database and to MySQL.
// Set the encoding and the access details as constants:
DEFINE ('DB_USER', 'william');
DEFINE ('DB_PASSWORD', 'catonlap');
DEFINE ('DB_HOST', 'localhost');
DEFINE ('DB_NAME', 'logindb');
// Make the connection:
$dbcon = @mysqli_connect (DB_HOST, DB_USER, DB_PASSWORD, DB_NAME) ↵
OR die ('Could not connect to MySQL: ' . mysqli_connect_error() );
// Set the encoding...
mysqli_set_charset($dbcon, 'utf8');
```

11. In the database *logindb*, create a new table named *users* with six columns. Its layout and attributes are exactly the same as the *users* table in Chapter 2. The details are given in Table 3-1.

Table 3-1. *The attributes for the users table*

Column name	Type	Length/Value	Default	Attributes	NULL	Index	A_I
user_id	MEDIUMINT	6	None	UNSIGNED	☐	PRIMARY	☑
fname	VARCHAR	30	None		☐		☐
lname	VARCHAR	40	None		☐		☐
email	VARCHAR	50	None		☐		☐
psword	CHAR	40	None		☐		☐
registration_date	DATETIME		None		☐		☐

Next we will do a little housekeeping. We will remove the styling instructions from as many as possible of the included files and transfer the styles to the main style sheet *includes.css*

Tidy the Styling

Best practice decrees that as much as possible of the CSS styling should be incorporated in the main style sheet. Therefore, the styling has been transferred from most of the included files to the global style sheet *includes.css*.

Why is this necessary? The pages worked well without this step, so why do it? The answer is that pages will not validate successfully unless the styles are removed from the included files. Validation using the World Wide Web Consortium (W3C) validator is an important part of web development to ensure that your code conforms to the standard expected by modern browsers and web-site owners. Also, a page that validates will be more secure. Your clients will be impressed if you can demonstrate that the pages on his web site conform to the latest W3C recommendations. To demonstrate this to a client, I always add an HTML5 validation logo and code to each page. This links to the URL http://validator.w3.org. If styling instructions form part of an included file, the validator will display a red failure message and display the statement, "Element style not allowed as child of element div."

The revised style sheet is listed next. The items transferred from the included files are shown in bold type in the following code snippet for the style sheet *includes.css*:

```
/*the global style sheet includes.css*/
body { text-align:center; background-color:#D7FFEB; color:navy;
font-family: "times new roman"; font-size: 100%; color: navy; margin: auto; }
h2 { font-size:150%; color:navy; text-align:center;}
h3 { font-size:110%; color:navy; text-align:center; }
#container { position:relative; min-width:960px; max-width:1200px; margin:auto;
text-align:left; }
#header, #header-members { margin:10px auto 0 auto; min-width:960px; max-width:1200px;
height:175px; background-image: url('images/tile-pale.jpg'); background-repeat: repeat;
padding:0; color:white;
}
h1 { position:relative; top:40px; font-size:350%; color:white; margin:auto 0 auto 20px;
    width: 487px; }
#reg-navigation ul { float:right; font-size:medium; width:160px; margin:-150px 15px 0 88%; }
ul { position:absolute; top:190px; left:-10px; color:navy; width:135px;
text-align:center; margin:0; }
```

```
/* set general side button styles */
li { width:115px; list-style-type :none; margin-bottom: 3px; text-align: center; }
/* set general anchor styles */
li a { display: block; width:115px; color: white; font-weight: bold; text-decoration: none }
/* specify state styles. */
/* mouseout (default) */
li a { background: #5B78BE; border: 4px outset #aabaff; }
/* mouseover */
li a:hover { display:block; background: #0a4adf; border: 4px outset #8abaff; width:115px; }
/* onmousedown */
li a:active { background:#aecbff; border: 4px inset #aecbff; }
#midcol { width:90%; margin:auto; }
#mid-left-col { width:48%; float:left; text-align:left; }
#mid-right-col {width:48%; float:right; text-align:left; }
#content { margin-left:150px; margin-right:150px; }
table { width:500px; border:1px navy solid; border-collapse:collapse; margin:auto; }
td { border:1px navy solid; padding:1px 0 1px 4px; text-align:left; }
form { margin-left:180px; }
#footer { margin:auto; text-align:center; }
p.error { color:red; font-size:105%; font-weight:bold; }
.label { float:left; width:210px; text-align:right; clear:left; margin-right:5px; }
#submit { margin-left:215px; text-align:center; }
span.left { text-align:left; }
#loginfields input { float:left; margin-bottom:5px; }
#loginfields label { margin-bottom:5px; }
#loginfields span { float:left; }
#loginfields submit { margin:5px auto 5px auto; }
span.left { text-align:left; }
```

Later in this chapter's listings, you will see that I removed the internal styling from many included files. Now we will tidy the header menus.

Remove or Replace Redundant Menu Buttons in the Headers

As mentioned in Chapter 2, some header menu buttons have become redundant and some new buttons are needed. In this section, the header menus will be amended. We must prevent the public and ordinary members from viewing the membership table. To achieve this, we need to remove the link that displays the table of members from all the headers except the header on the administration page. We need to remove the login link on the members' page, because the member is already logged in. We must also add a logout link. The Register link is also redundant because the members and the administrator are already registered; therefore, that menu button will also be removed.

■ **Tip**   Redundant buttons are easily overlooked when you are absorbed in the coding of the database and the web-site pages. Try to cultivate the habit of checking the header on each new or revised page to ensure that there are no redundant or missing buttons.

Add a Login Button to the Home Page Header

We will now add a new button to the header menu on the home page so that members can log in. We will also remove the View Users button because we want to arrange things so that only the administrator is able to view the table of members. The revised header is shown in Figure 3-1.

Figure 3-1. *The revised header for the home page. The New Password button has been removed, and the View Users button is replaced with a Login button*

The View Users and New Password buttons have been removed, and a Login button is added. The revised header will automatically be included in the non-private pages (page-2, page-3, and so on) because the header file name is unchanged.

The new login link in the header is indicated in bold type in Listing 3-1.

Listing 3-1. Revising the Home page Header Menu (header.php)

```
<div id="header">
<h1>This is the header </h1>
<div id="reg-navigation">
    <ul>
        <li><a href="login.php">Login</a></li>
        <li><a href="register-page.php">Register</a></li>
    </ul>
</div>
</div>
```

With XAMPP running, enter **http://localhost/login/index.php** into a browser to view the home page with the new login button as shown in Figure 3-1.

Remove Redundant Buttons from the Registration and New Password Headers

A new header will be required for the registration page and the new password page because the previous headers had redundant menu buttons,

On the registration page, the user has no password and so cannot log in; therefore, the Login and New Password buttons will be removed. The Register button is redundant because the user has already accessed the registration page. We will now remove the redundant buttons from the header for the registration page and replace them with something more useful. The new header is shown in Figure 3-2.

Figure 3-2. *The new header for the Registration page and the New Password page*

The redundant buttons are replaced by two meaningful links, Erase Entries and Cancel. I chose the words "Erase Entries" rather than "Clear" or "Erase All" after testing the site with users who were fairly new computer owners. They were confused by the "Clear" and "Erase All" wording, but they immediately understood "Erase Entries." The Erase Entries button reloads the registration page and then displays empty fields. The Cancel button returns the user to the home page. Listing 3-2a gives the revised header code for the registration and new password pages.

Listing 3-2a. Replacing Redundant Buttons with Meaningful Buttons (register-header.php)

```
<div id="header">
<h1>This is the Header</h1>
<div id="reg-navigation">
    <ul>
        <li><a href="register-page.php">Erase Entries</a></li>
        <li><a href="index.php">Cancel</a></li>
    </ul>
</div>
</div>
```

The registration page for this chapter and subsequent chapters will be linked to the new header as shown in bold type in the next snippet of code shown in Listing 3-2b.

Listing 3-2b. Including the New Header in the Registration Page (register-page.php)

```
<!doctype html>
<html lang=en>
<head>
<title>Register page</title>
<meta charset=utf-8>
<link rel="stylesheet" type="text/css" href="includes.css">
</head>
<body>
<div id="container">
<?php include("register-header.php"); ?>
<?php include("nav.php"); ?>
<?php include("info-col.php"); ?>
```

The Revised Registration Page

The rest of the code is the same as the registration page in Chapter 2. The revised code is included in the downloadable files for Chapter 3.

The rest of the code for this page is unchanged. The new header will now be applied to the New Password page.

The New Header for the New Password Page

The same new header will be required for the New Password page. This was shown in Figure 3-2.

The new-password page for this chapter and subsequent chapters will be linked to the new header as shown in bold type in the next snippet of code in Listing 3-2c.

Listing 3-2c. Replacing Redundant Buttons with Meaningful Buttons (password-header.php)

```
<div id="header">
<h1>This is the Header</h1>
<div id="reg-navigation">
    <ul>
        <li><a href="register-password .php">Erase Entries</a></li>
        <li><a href="index.php">Cancel</a></li>
    </ul>
</div>
</div>
```

The Erase Entries button reloads the new-password page and displays empty fields. The Cancel button returns the user to the home page.

The included file for the header is amended in the register-password file (*register-password.php*) as given in the following code snippet:

```
<div id="container">
<?php include("password-header.php"); ?>
<?php include("nav.php"); ?>
<?php include("info-col.php"); ?>
```

The rest of the code goes here and is unchanged from Chapter 2.

A New Header Menu for the Members' Page

For the members' page, the Register button and the View Members button have been removed and a Logout button added, as shown in Figure 3-3.

Figure 3-3. *The modified header menu for the members' page*

67

Note in Figure 3-3 that when a member is logged into the members' page, the Login menu button changes to a Logout button. There are several clever ways of achieving this, but the least complicated way is to load a new header into the members' page. This is effective because sometimes the special members' page also requires a slightly changed header image or text. Note also that the redundant Register and New Password buttons have been removed from the header menu.

I named the new file *header-members.php*. The new Logout button has a link that sends the user to the page named *logout.php*. This, in turn, sends the user to the home page. Why does the link not go directly to the home page? Because the intermediate page *logout.php* contains some code for closing a session before it accesses the home page. A session is a device that will be explained in the next section. The logout link is shown in bold type in the following code snippet for the new header.

The code for the two links that remain are indicated in Listing 3-3.

Listing 3-3. *Creating the New Header for the Members' Page (header-members.php)*

```
<div id="header-members">
<h1>This is the Header</h1>
<div id="reg-navigation">
    <ul>
        <li><a href="logout.php">Logout</a></li>
        <li><a href="register-password.php">New Password</a></li>
    </ul>
</div>
</div>
```

If the web site has more than one page that is exclusively for members, you could add more buttons to the file *members-header.php* or, alternatively, you could put links in the body of the members' page.

Amend the Header for the Thank-You Page

When a user reaches the Thank-You page, she has registered and no longer requires the Register button, nor does she require any of the other buttons. The Thank-You page header only needs a button that redirects the user to the home page. The header with the Home Page button is shown in Figure 3-4.

Figure 3-4. *The revised header for the Thank-You page*

The Home Page menu button in the header redirects the user to the home page (*index.php*), as shown in Listing 3-4a.

Listing 3-4a. Creating the Code for the Revised Thank-You Header (header-thanks.php)

```
<div id="header">
<h1>This is the thank you header</h1>
<div id="reg-navigation">
    <p> </p>
    <ul>
        <li><a href="index.php">Home Page</a></li>
    </ul>
</div>
</div>
```

The Thank-You page will now be amended to include the revised header. The *includes* at the start of the Thank-You page are shown in the next snippet of code. The revised i*nclude* is shown in bold type in Listing 3-4b.

Listing 3-4b. Creating the Revised Thank-You Page (register-thanks.php)

```
<!doctype html>
<html lang=en>
<head>
<title>Registration thank you page</title>
<meta charset=utf-8>
<link rel="stylesheet" type="text/css" href="includes.css">
</head>
<body>
<div id="container">
<?php include("header-thanks.php"); ?>
<?php include("nav.php"); ?>
<?php include("info-col.php"); ?>
```

The rest of the code is unchanged from the code in Chapter 2.

The Registration Page and Undesirable Characters

In Chapter 2, you learned how the function *mysqli_real_escape_string()* converted apostrophes so that they were not regarded as PHP code; the function for achieving this also cleaned text input by removing some other undesirable characters. The same function will be used in the registration page to clean every piece of text entered by a user. However, some user entries will require further cleaning, and this is covered in Chapter 6. The function has the following format:

```
$fn = mysqli_real_escape_string($dbcon, trim($_POST['fname']));
```

We'll add that function to our registration page now. While we're at it, let's also add the updated *register-header. php* file that includes only the two buttons Erase Entries and Cancel.

Figure 3-5 shows the registration page with its new header.

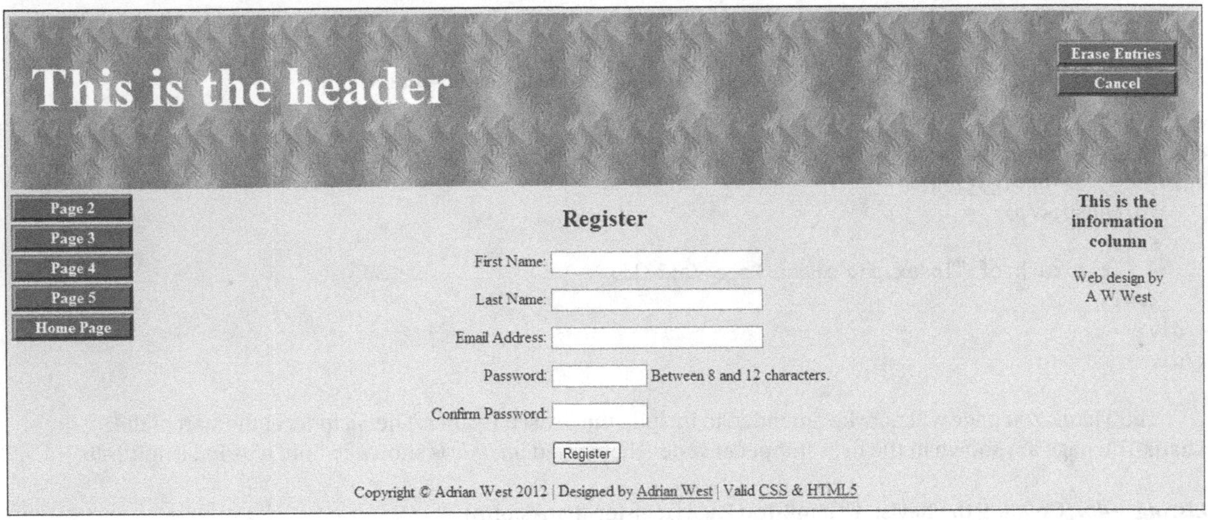

Figure 3-5. *The registration page with its new header*

Using the modified code with its new function, you will be able to enter names that include an apostrophe, such as O'Hara. The modified code for cleaning entries in *register-page.php* is shown in bold type in Listing 3-5.

Listing 3-5. Creating the Amended Registration Page (register-page.php)

```
<!doctype html>
<html lang=en>
<head>
<title>Register page</title>
<meta charset=utf-8><!--important prerequisite for escaping problem characters-->
<link rel="stylesheet" type="text/css" href="includes.css">
</head>
<body>
<div id="container">
<!--Use the revised header-->
<?php include("register-header.php"); ?>
<?php include("nav.php"); ?>
<?php include("info-col.php"); ?>
<div id="content"><!-- Registration handler content starts here -->
<p>
<?php
// The link to the database is moved to the top of the PHP code.
require ('mysqli_connect.php'); // Connect to the db.
// This query INSERTs a record in the users table.
// Has the form been submitted?
if ($_SERVER['REQUEST_METHOD'] == 'POST') {
    $errors = array(); // Initialize an error array.
    // Check for a first name:
```

```php
    if (empty($_POST['fname'])) {
        $errors[] = 'You forgot to enter your first name.';
    } else {
    $fn = mysqli_real_escape_string($dbcon, trim($_POST['fname']));

    }
    // Check for a last name
    if (empty($_POST['lname'])) {
        $errors[] = 'You forgot to enter your last name.';
    } else {
    $ln = mysqli_real_escape_string($dbcon, trim($_POST['lname']));
    }
    // Check for an email address
    if (empty($_POST['email'])) {
        $errors[] = 'You forgot to enter your email address.';
    } else {
    $e = mysqli_real_escape_string($dbcon, trim($_POST['email']));
    }
    // Check for a password and match it against the confirmed password
    if (!empty($_POST['psword1'])) {
        if ($_POST['psword1'] != $_POST['psword2']) {
        $errors[] = 'Your two passwords did not match.';
        } else {
    $p = mysqli_real_escape_string($dbcon, trim($_POST['psword1']));
        }
    } else {
        $errors[] = 'You forgot to enter your password.';
    }
    if (empty($errors)) { // If it runs
    // Register the user in the database...
// Make the query:
$q = "INSERT INTO users (user_id, fname, lname, email, psword, registration_date)
VALUES (' ', '$fn', '$ln', '$e', SHA1('$p'), NOW() )";
        $result = @mysqli_query ($dbcon, $q); // Run the query.
        if ($result) { // If it runs
        header ("location: register-thanks.php");
        exit();
        } else { // If it did not run
        // Message:
            echo '<h2>System Error</h2>
<p class="error">You could not be registered due to a system error. We apologize ⏎
for any inconvenience.</p>';
        // Debugging message:
        echo '<p>' . mysqli_error($dbcon) . '<br><br>Query: ' . $q . '</p>';
        } // End of if ($result)
        mysqli_close($dbcon); // Close the database connection.
        // Include the footer and quit the script:
        include ('footer.php');
        exit();
    } else { // Report the errors.
```

71

```
        echo '<h2>Error!</h2>
        <p class="error">The following error(s) occurred:<br>';
        foreach ($errors as $msg) { // Extract the errors from the array and echo them
              echo " - $msg<br>\n";
        }
        echo '</p><h3>Please try again.</h3><p><br></p>';
        }// End of if (empty($errors))
} // End of the main Submit conditional.
?>
<h2>Register</h2>
<form action="register-page.php" method="post">
<p><label class="label" for="fname">First Name:</label> ↵
<input id="fname" type="text" name="fname" size="30" maxlength="30" ↵
value="<?php if (isset($_POST['fname'])) echo $_POST['fname']; ?>"></p>

<p><label class="label" for="lname">Last Name:</label>
<input id="lname" type="text" name="lname" size="30" maxlength="40" ↵
value="<?php if (isset($_POST['lname'])) echo $_POST['lname']; ?>"></p>

<p><label class="label" for="email">Email Address:</label>↵
<input id="email" type="text" name="email" size="30" maxlength="60" ↵
value="<?php if (isset($_POST['email'])) echo $_POST['email']; ?>" > </p>

<p><label class="label" for="psword1">Password:</label>
<input id="psword1" type="password" name="psword1" size="12" maxlength="12"
value="<?php if (isset($_POST['psword1'])) echo $_POST['psword1']; ?>" >  ↵
Between 8 and 12 characters.</p>

<p><label class="label" for="psword2">Confirm Password:</label>
<input id="psword2" type="password" name="psword2" size="12" maxlength="12" ↵
value="<?php if (isset($_POST['psword2'])) echo $_POST['psword2']; ?>" ></p>

<p><input id="submit" type="submit" name="submit" value="Register"></p>
</form>
<?php include ('footer.php'); ?>
</p>
</div>
</div>
</body>
</html>
```

Register Some Members

At this point, you should register a few fictitious people in the database so that you will have something to play with later in the chapter. To save you time, I repeated the list of members from Chapter 2, and they are shown in Table 3-2.

Table 3-2. *Register Some Members*

Name	E-mail	Password
Patrick O'Hara	pohara@myisp.org.uk	shamrock
Mike Rosoft	miker@myisp.com	willgates
Olive Branch	obranch@myisp.co.uk	anoilyone
Frank Insence	finsence@myisp.net	perfume
Annie Versary	aversary@myisp.com	birthdaygirl
Terry Fide	tfide@myisp.de	scaredstiff
Rose Bush	rbush@myisp.co.uk	redblooms

To maintain the security of private pages, we use a device called *sessions*. A session is a server-side store of information about a user. It is deleted when a user exits a site, or it times-out after a period (typically 20 minutes) that is set by the server administrator. A session checks the credentials of users before allowing them to access a page.

Differentiating Between Two Types of Membership

The *simpleIdb* database in the previous chapter had a security problem; any non-registered user could view the table of members by simply accessing the web site. We will now ensure that the table of members can be viewed only by the developer and the membership secretary (the administrator) and not by the whole world. One solution is to instruct the membership secretary how to install and use phpMyAdmin; however, we will assume that our membership secretary is not very computer literate and does not want to learn phpMyAdmin.

Our solution will be to restrict access to the *view_table.php* page and all other administrator pages so that only the membership secretary is allowed to view them. This will be achieved by using sessions and a different *user_level* number for the administrator. The administrator will be provided with a user-friendly interface so that he can search and amend membership records.

To sum up, our rules for differentiating between types of membership will be as follows:

- Non-members will not be able to view private pages because users can't log in until they are registered.

- Registered members will be able to access members' pages because they can log in. Doing so, initiates a session that allows them to open members' pages.

- The administrator is the only person able to access administration pages. When he logs in, the act of logging in starts a session that checks his *user_level* before he can open an administrator's page. His *user_level* is different from ordinary members' user levels.

Before designing a login page, we must also create a means of differentiating between an ordinary registered member and a member who is also the administrator. The administrator will have extra privileges. In the next tutorial, you will learn how to add a new column with the title *user_level* to an existing database table. This new column will enable us to differentiate between types of membership.

Create User Levels to Limit Access to Private Pages

To limit access to the view table page, we will add a column to the users table called *user_level*. In this column, we will give the administrator a user level number *1*. That number relates to the membership secretary's login details and to no other person.

Access phpMyAdmin, and click the database *logindb*. Then click the *users* table. Click the *Structure* tab. Look below the records to find the item *Add one column*. The next steps are illustrated in Figure 3-6.

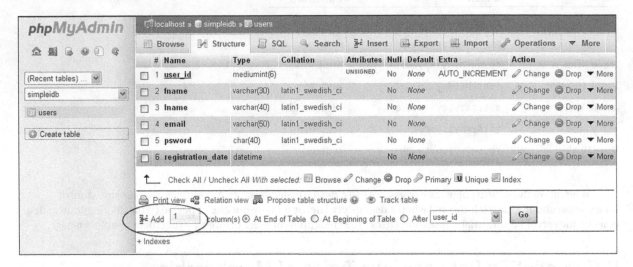

Figure 3-6. *The Add symbol (circled) can be seen at the bottom of this screen shot*

Below the list of fields, you will see where you can add another column (shown at the bottom of Figure 3-6). The details are as follows.

Find the item labeled *Add 1*, select the radio button labeled *After*, and use the drop-down menu to select *registration_date*. Alternatively, select the radio button labeled *At end of table* then click the Go button.

You will be taken to the next screen as shown in Figure 3-7.

Name	Type	Length/Values	Default	Collation	Attributes	Nu
user_level	TINYINT	1	None		UNSIGNED	

Figure 3-7. *Creating the title and attributes for the new user_level column*

Insert the new column name and its attributes as follows:

- **Name:** user_level

- **Type:** TINYINT

- **Value:** 1

- **Default:** None

- **Attributes:** UNSIGNED

When you are satisfied with the attributes, click the Save button. The new column will be created.

The next step is to launch XAMPP and access the page by entering **http://localhost/login/index.php** into the address field of a browser. When the index page appears, click the Register button on the header menu and register this user as an ordinary member:

- **First name:** James

- **Last name:** Smith

- **E-mail:** jsmith@myisp.co.uk

- **Password:** blacksmith

When using his proper e-mail address and password, James Smith can view the members' special pages but he cannot view or amend a list of members.

We will now appoint James Smith to be the membership secretary, with the right to administer the membership list. For security, he needs a second name and a pseudo e-mail address and password to access the administration section; therefore, he needs an additional registration identity. The second e-mail address is important because his office colleagues probably know his personal e-mail address. Every effort must be made to keep the administrator's login details secret. The e-mail address should be fictitious, but it must conform to the accepted format for e-mails. Now register the membership secretary a second time using his pseudonym ("Jack"), the new e-mail address, and the new password as follows:

- **First name:** Jack

- **Last name:** Smith

- **E-mail:** jsmith@outcook.com

- **Password:** dogsbody

In a real-world situation, you would not use a password that could be easily guessed. The one I used in this tutorial would not be secure, but I chose it because it is memorable and therefore helpful for exploring this tutorial.

Now use phpMyAdmin to access the database *logindb* and the *users* table. Click the Browse tab, and find the administrator Jack Smith's record, as shown in Figure 3-8. If you click the Edit link, you will be able to change his *user_level* field from *0* to *1*. Click the Go button to save the change.

Figure 3-8. *Find Jack Smith's record so that you can edit his user_level*

When James Smith logs in with his personal e-mail address and his original password, he will be taken to the members' page just like any other member. This is because when he uses his original password, his *user_level* is zero, the same as all other registered members. However, when he logs in with his different e-mail address and the administrator's password *dogsbody*, he will be taken to a page where he can administer the database because his e-mail address and the *dogsbody* password relate to *user_level* 1.

A real-world administrator would ensure that nobody could ever discover his alternative e-mail address and his new password. People contacting the administrator would use his original name and personal e-mail address.

■ **Tip** If James Smith resigns and a new administrator is appointed, the webmaster will delete Jack Smith's record. He will then give the new administrator a pseudonym and a new password. The new membership secretary would be asked to acquire an alternative e-mail address and then to register as a new member using the alternative e-mail address and a new password. The webmaster would then set the new membership secretary's *user level* to 1.

Now we will create the login page and introduce some new PHP statements.

Log In

From a user's point of view, the ability to log in or log out of a web site is pointless unless it leads to some advantage, such as a special page for members or permission to post comments in a blog. In the following sections, we will create new pages that will interact with registered users. These will be a login page, a members-only page, and an administrator's page. The same login page is used for logging into either the members' pages or the administrator's pages. You would be forgiven for thinking that the admin and members' pages are fully protected by the login process. However, imagine the following scenario.

A member has logged in to a private page and is then called away to take a telephone call. Someone could look at the member's computer and read the URL of the private page in the address field of the browser. If that person then entered the URLs on her own computer she could access the private page. Clearly, this must be prevented. This is achieved by means of the sessions described later in this chapter.

First we must create a header for the login page.

The Header for the Login Page

Figure 3-9 shows the login header with three menu buttons.

Figure 3-9. *The login page header*

The code for the login header appears in Listing 3-9.

Listing 3-9. Creating the Header for the Login Page (login-header.php)

```
<div id="header">
<h1>This is the header</h1>
<div id="reg-navigation">
    <ul>
        <li><a href="login.php">Erase Entries</a></li>
        <li><a href="register-page.php">Register</a></li>
        <li><a href="index.php">Cancel</a></li>
    </ul>
</div>
</div>
```

Now we need to look at a procedure for limiting access to the table of members. We will prevent general users and registered members from viewing the table, but we will allow the administrator to view the table and amend records.

The appearance of the login page is shown in Figure 3-10.

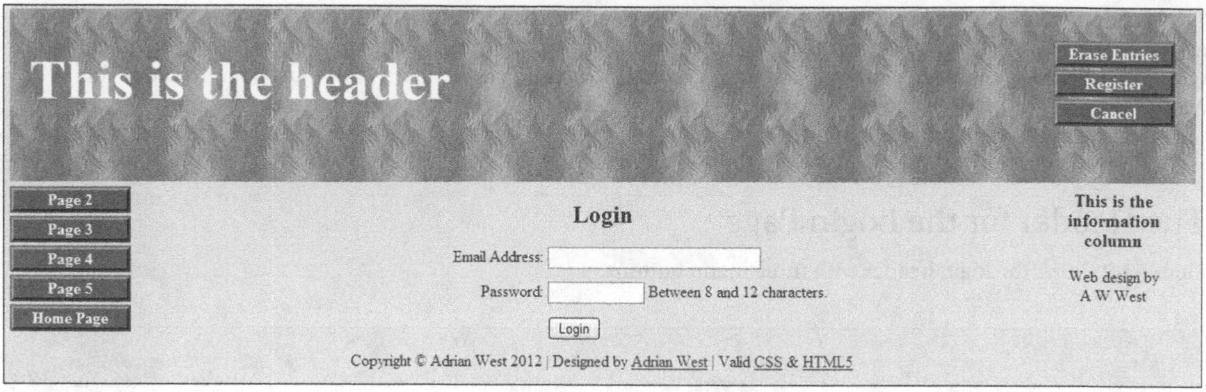

Figure 3-10. *The login page*

The form fields for the e-mail address and password could have been located in the code in the login page, but for increased security, an external included file is used. A malevolent person would then have the difficulty of assembling the components before he could interfere with the form, especially when the components are PHP files and they are located in different folders. The listing for the login page uses the *include()* function to pull the form's fields into the page from the file named *login-page.inc.php*. Note that the redundant buttons have been removed from the heading on this page.

The Login Page

Now that we have a *user_level* column, we can create the login page to include two conditionals. The conditionals will recognize the *user_level* of the administrator (*user_level 1*) and the ordinary member (*user_level 0*). When the genuine administrator logs in, he will see the administration page complete with his new menu buttons. When registered members log in, they will be redirected to the members' page. The new login page header is pulled into the page by means of the include statement in bold type in Listing 3-10a.

Listing 3-10a. Creating the Login Page (login.php)

```
<!doctype html>
<html lang=en>
<head>
<title>The Login page</title>
<meta charset=utf-8>
<link rel="stylesheet" type="text/css" href="includes.css">
</head>
<body>
<div id="container">
<?php include("login-header.php"); ?>
<?php include("nav.php"); ?>
<?php include("info-col.php"); ?>
<div id="content"><!-- Start of the login page content. -->
<?php
// This section processes submissions from the login form
// Check if the form has been submitted:
if ($_SERVER['REQUEST_METHOD'] == 'POST') {
    //connect to database
```

```
    require ('mysqli_connect.php');                                          #1
    // Validate the email address
    if (!empty($_POST['email'])) {
        $e = mysqli_real_escape_string($dbcon, $_POST['email']);
    } else {
    $e = FALSE;
        echo '<p class="error">You forgot to enter your email address.</p>';
    }
    // Validate the password
    if (!empty($_POST['psword'])) {
            $p = mysqli_real_escape_string($dbcon, $_POST['psword']);
    } else {
    $p = FALSE;
        echo '<p class="error">You forgot to enter your password.</p>';
    }
    if ($e && $p){//if no problems                                           #2
// Retrieve the user_id, first_name and user_level for that email/password combination
$q = "SELECT user_id, fname, user_level FROM users WHERE (email='$e' AND psword=SHA1('$p'))";
// Run the query and assign it to the variable $result
$result = mysqli_query ($dbcon, $q);
// Count the number of rows that match the email/password combination
if (@mysqli_num_rows($result) == 1) {//if one database row (record) matches the input:-
// Start the session, fetch the record and insert the three values in an array
session_start();                                                            #3
$_SESSION = mysqli_fetch_array ($result, MYSQLI_ASSOC);
// Ensure that the user level is an integer.
$_SESSION['user_level'] = (int) $_SESSION['user_level'];
// Use a ternary operation to set the URL                                   #4
$url = ($_SESSION['user_level'] === 1) ? 'admin-page.php' : 'members-page.php';
header('Location: ' . $url); // Make the browser load either the members' or the admin page
exit(); // Cancel the rest of the script
    mysqli_free_result($result);
    mysqli_close($dbcon);
    } else { // No match was made.
echo '<p class="error">The e-mail address and password entered do not match our records ↵
<br>Perhaps you need to register, just click the Register button on the header menu</p>';
    }
    } else { // If there was a problem.
    echo '<p class="error">Please try again.</p>';
    }
    mysqli_close($dbcon);
    } // End of SUBMIT conditional.
?>
<!-- Display the form fields-->                                             #5
<div id="loginfields">
<?php include ('login_page.inc.php'); ?>
</div><br>
<?php include ('footer.php'); ?>
</div>
</div>
</body>
</html>
```

■ **Caution**   If you type the book's listings in your text editor, do not include the line numbers (**#1, #2, #3,** and so on). These are provided to help you understand the explanation of the PHP given at the end of each listing. The downloaded files omit the line numbers. This caution applies to all the listings in the book.

Explanation of the Code

Most of the code will by now be familiar to you. Some code is explained by comments within the listing, but there are a few new PHP patterns that need explaining as follows:

```
require ('login_functions.inc.php');                              #1
```

require() is an alternative to the *include()* function. If the file in the brackets can't be located, the page will cease loading. Because the two files work together, there is no point continuing if the file in the brackets cannot be found.

```
if ($e && $p){//if no problems encountered                       #2
// Retrieve the user_id, first_name and user_level for that email/password combination:
$q = "SELECT user_id, fname, user_level FROM users WHERE (email='$e' AND psword=SHA1('$p'))";
```

If no problems are encountered (that is, if $e and $p exist), the two user entries are validated and assigned to the variable $q.

```
session_start();                                                 #3
$_SESSION = mysqli_fetch_array ($result, MYSQLI_ASSOC);
// Ensure that the user level is an integer.
$_SESSION['user_level'] = (int) $_SESSION['user_level'];
```

A session is started, and it is used to check the authorization of the person logging in. If the user_level has been saved as True or False, it needs to be converted to a whole number using *(int)*. Sessions have been introduced for the first time, and they will be explained fully at the end of this explanatory section. Meanwhile, just accept them.

```
// Use a ternary operation to set the URL                        #4
$url = ($_SESSION['user_level'] === 1) ? 'admin-page.php' : 'members-page.php';
header('Location: ' . $url); // Make the browser load either the members' or the admin page
exit(); // Cancel the rest of the script.
```

At this point, I will break the rule I set myself for this book: I am introducing a clever piece of shorthand code. However, it is not a trick invented by me; it is a common PHP device for choosing between two outcomes and is therefore particularly useful and not too difficult to understand.

The word *ternary* has nothing to do with a reserve for seabirds of the family laridae. It is a mathematical term that has been adopted by web-site script developers. It is the third operator in the series "unary, binary, ternary." In other words, *ternary* has three parts. The ternary operator is often called a *ternary conditional* because it is a very concise way of setting a conditional. The operator uses the symbols ? and :. The format we are using redirects the user to either the URL for the admin page or the URL for the members' page. The code is

```
$url = ($_SESSION['user_level'] === 1) ? 'admin-page.php' : 'members-page.php';
```

The first part of the statement on the right (enclosed in brackets) looks at the *user_level* in the session array and asks if it is identical to 1. The three equal signs mean "identical to." If it is identical to 1, the question mark turns the next two items into a conditional statement. It is saying, "If the user_level is identical to 1, then assign the *admin-page.php* to the variable named *$url*." The colon is the equivalent of "else"; therefore, if the user_level is not identical to 1, the *$url* is set to *members-page.php*. Registered members have a *user_level* of 0.

The variable *$url*, therefore, is set to a particular page and the user is redirected to that page using the familiar header statement:

```
header('Location: ' . $url); // Make the browser load either the members' or the admin page
exit(); // Quit the script.
```

The longhand equivalent of the ternary statement is

```
if ($_SESSION['user_level'] === 1) {
header('location: admin-page.php');
exit();
}else{
header('location: members-page.php');
exit();
}
<!-- Display the form fields-->
<div id="loginfields">
<?php include ('login_page.inc.php'); ?>
</div><br>
<?php include ('footer.php'); ?>
</div>
</div>
</body>
</html>
```

#5

The form fields are displayed by the included file *login_page.inc.php*. This file is described next.

The Login Form Fields

The *login_page.inc.php* file describes the form fields that will be pulled into the login page. The form is sticky—that is, the user entries are retained and redisplayed if the user makes a mistake that triggers an error message. Listing 3-10b shows the form fields.

Listing 3-7b. Displaying the Form Fields in the Login Page (login_page.inc.php)

```
<h2>Login</h2>
<form action="login.php" method="post">
<p><label class="label" for="email">Email Address:</label>
<input id="email" type="text" name="email" size="30" maxlength="60" ↵
value="<?php if (isset($_POST['email'])) echo $_POST['email']; ?>" > </p>
<br>
<p><label class="label" for="psword">Password:</label>
<input id="psword" type="password" name="psword" size="12" maxlength="12" ↵
value="<?php if (isset($_POST['psword'])) echo $_POST['psword']; ?>" > ↵
<span> Between 8 and 12 characters.</span></p>
<p> </p><p><input id="submit" type="submit" name="submit" value="Login"></p>
</form><br>
```

The form fields are formatted by the following code, which we already added to the end of the main style sheet in the earlier "Tidy the Styles" section:

```
#loginfields input { float:left; margin-bottom:5px; }
#loginfields label { margin-bottom:5px; }
#loginfields span { float:left; }
#loginfields submit { margin:5px auto 5px auto; }
span.left { text-align:left; }
```

If the user's login data does not match the data in the database table, an error message is displayed as shown in Figure 3-11.

Figure 3-11. *One of the error messages displayed when the login is unsuccessful*

The login has a sticky form so that the user's entries are retained when an error is encountered. No hint is given as to which of the two entries was incorrect; this is a security feature. For instance, if the error message stated that the e-mail address was incorrect but the password was acceptable, a hacker would be able to concentrate on trying possible e-mail addresses.

The new database *logindb* will allow registered members to log in and log out of a members' page. Non-registered users will therefore be prevented from accessing the member's page. This is not completely secure because someone could look over the member's shoulder and discover the file name of the member's page in the browser's address field. Using that name, she could then access the member's page, as previously mentioned. This security loophole will be dealt with by using sessions.

Sessions

Pages that need to be kept private will use the feature called *sessions*; therefore, sessions and their application will now be explained. Registered members should be able to log in once per visit to the web site. They should not have to log in several times to access several private pages. The login state should persist as long as that user is logged in. The time between login and logout is called a *session*. The login starts a session, and the logout closes the session. A session stores some information temporarily on the server, and additional information is stored temporarily on the user's computer in a cookie. If a session exists, extra features will be available for the logged-in user.

There is a way of using sessions without a cookie, but that is less secure. The European Union has ruled that web sites must state that they are using a cookie. The message declaring the use of a cookie can sometimes cause users to panic, but there is nothing to stop the web site adding a soothing message to the effect that the temporary cookie is quite safe to use. If users disable cookies, they won't be able to access the private pages even if they are authorized to access them. The alternative is to attach the session to the URL on each link. We will use the more secure method and employ a temporary cookie on the user's computer.

■ **Tip**   Think of a session as a sort of security pass. When a user has successfully logged in, a security pass (a session) for that person is posted in the cookie and also in the memory of the server. A security guard is stationed at the door of each private page. When the user tries to open a private page, the security guard on that page checks the security pass (the session). If the pass confirms that the person is authorized to access the page, the private page is opened. When a user logs out, the session and the cookie are destroyed. Sessions carry with them several pieces of useful information about the user that can be accessed and used in the private pages.

The process when using sessions is as follows:

1.   If a user is authorized to log in and he logs in successfully, a session is created.

2.   When a user tries to access a private page, the private page checks to see if a session for that particular user exists.

3.   If the session exists, the private page is opened.

4.   If the session does not exist, the user is directed back to the login page.

5.   By using sessions, the server can be made to differentiate between types of users, such as non-members, registered members, and administrators.

6.   Logged-in users can either move to other private pages or log out. When they log out, the session and its temporary cookie are destroyed.

A session is started as follows:

```
// Set the session data:
session_start();
```

A session is closed as follows:

```
}else{ //cancel the session
    $_SESSION = array(); // Destroy the variables.
    session_destroy(); // Destroy the session itself.
setcookie('PHPSESSID', ", time()-3600,'/', ", 0, 0);//Destroy the cookie
header("location:index.php");
exit();
```

The act of logging in creates a session that saves variables in an array named $_SESSION. When the user has logged in and tries to open a private page, the code checks that a session has been set up for that user. If it has, the private page will be opened in the user's browser.

In the following statements extracted from the code for *login.php,* the data is selected and then a session is created. Information is retained in a temporary cookie and in a temporary variable on the server for use in private pages.

```
//Select three items from a record that is defined by a combination of the user's
// e-mail and password. The three items are user_id, fname, and user_level.
$q = "SELECT user_id, fname, user_level FROM users WHERE (email='$e' AND psword=SHA1('$p'))";
//The selected data is assigned to a variable called $result
$result = mysqli_query ($dbcon, $q); //Run the query.
// If a matching record (row) is found, the number of records (rows) found will be one
if (@mysqli_num_rows($result) == 1) {//The user input matched the database record
// Start the session, fetch the record and insert the three values into the session ↵
array
session_start();
$_SESSION = mysqli_fetch_array ($result, MYSQLI_ASSOC);
```

■ **Tip** The `session_start()` function and the statements checking the session must appear before the HTML tag. Beginners are often puzzled by the `session_start()` function appearing on every private page: why does it not start a new session to replace the existing session? The answer is that if a session exists, the function does not start another session; instead, it checks the user's credentials and, if they are satisfactory, it allows the private page to load. If a session does not exist, it will start one; however, that session is not effective and a conditional statement sends the user back to the login page.

Sessions create a unique user identity. This is called a *UID* (a unique identification number). The `<?php session_start(); ?>` statement establishes a UID. It registers the user's session on the server and saves the information for use on any private pages. The following is an example of the code at the start of a private page accessible only to the administrator with a *user_level* number 1):

```
<?php
session_start();
if (!isset($_SESSION['user_level']) or ($_SESSION['user_level'] != 1))
{ header("Location: login.php");
   exit();
}
?>
<!doctype html>
```

The code can be translated as follows: "If the session does not exist, or if the user level is not equal to 1, then the user will be sent back to the login page."

Our next step is to create a members-only page protected by the login session.

A Members-only Page

Use the downloadable page *members-page.php,* or create the page by hand-coding it using Listing 3-12. The members' page created for this tutorial is shown in Figure 3-12.

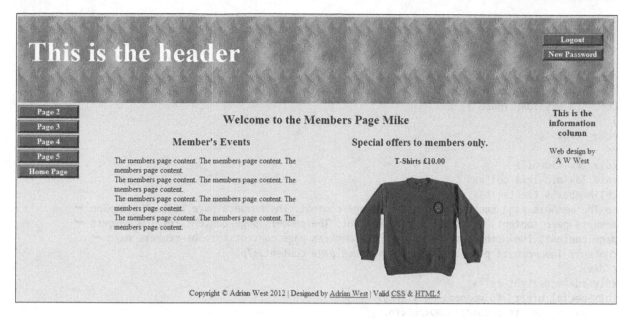

Figure 3-12. *The members-only page. Note that the member is welcomed by name*

Note the revised members' header in Figure 3-12.

Also note the session, the redirection to the login page and the included file for the new header shown in bold type in Listing 3-12.

Listing 3-12. Creating the Members Page (members-page.php)

```php
<?php                                                                    #1
session_start();
if (!isset($_SESSION['user_level']) or ($_SESSION['user_level'] != 0))
{ header("Location: login.php");
  exit();
}
?>
<!doctype html>
<html lang=en>
<head>
<title>Members page</title>
<meta charset=utf-8>
<link rel="stylesheet" type="text/css" href="includes.css">
<style type="text/css">
#mid-right-col { text-align:center; margin:auto;
}
#midcol h3 { font-size:130%; margin-top:0; margin-bottom:0;
}
</style>
</head>
<body>
<div id="container">
<?php include("header-members.php"); ?>
```

```php
<?php include("nav.php"); ?>
<?php include("info-col.php"); ?>
<div id="content"><!-- Start of the member's page content. -->
<?php
echo '<h2>Welcome to the Members Page ';
if (isset($_SESSION['fname'])){
echo "{$_SESSION['fname']}";
}
echo '</h2>';
?>
<div id="midcol">
<div id="mid-left-col">
<h3>Member's Events</h3>
<p>The members page content. The members page content. The members page content. <br>The
members page content. The members page content. The members page content.<br>The members
page content. The members page content. The members page content.<br>The members page
content. The members page content. The members page content.</p>
</div>
<div id="mid-right-col">
<h3>Special offers to members only.</h3>
    <p><b>T-Shirts &pound;10.00</b></p>
<img alt="Polo shirt" title="Polo shirt" height="207" src="images/polo.png"
width="280"><br>
<br>
</div>
</div></div><!-- End of the members page content. -->
</div>
<div id="footer">
<?php include("footer.php"); ?>
</div>
</body>
</html>
```

Explanation of the Code

```php
<?php                                                                    #1
session_start();
if (!isset($_SESSION['user_level']) or ($_SESSION['user_level'] != 0))
{ header("Location: login.php");
  exit();
}
?>
<!doctype html>
<html lang=en>
<head>
```

The snippet of PHP code must appear before the first HTML tag. As with all private pages, it begins with the session_start() function. The header redirection statement ensures that if no session was started or the user_level was not zero, the user would be redirected to the login page.

The next section demonstrates the importance of planning. Hasty decisions at this stage can cause major headaches later.

Planning the Administrator's Role

We now need to plan very carefully by considering what the membership secretary might wish to do with the web site and the database. My assumptions follow.

The membership secretary would want to do the following:

- View the members-only page using his original member's password

- View the table of members using his administrator's e-mail and password

- Change the administrator's password occasionally for extra security

To achieve these aims we need to complete the following tasks:

- Create a new header for the administration page.

- Create the administration page.

The administrator's requirements will dictate the content of the menu in the header of the administration page. Later, in Chapters 4 and 5, we will add extra features to incorporate the following requirements:

- Search for and edit members' details using his administrator's password. (Say, Miss Jones has just married and her name needs changing to Mrs. Smith.) The Search button has been added to the header, ready for this button to be functional in future chapters.

- Delete records using his administrator's password (necessary when a member has resigned or died).

- The administrator will also need to know the total number of members—someone is bound to ask him. This will be automatically displayed below the table of members.

We will now create the administrator's header and a private administrator's page.

A New Header for the Administration Page

Based on the first part of the preceding plan, the header for the administration page needs four buttons: Logout, View Members, Search, and New Password. The new header embedded in the administrator's page is shown in Figure 3-13.

Figure 3-13. *The new header is shown embedded in the administrator's page*

The header now has four buttons, and to accommodate the longer text in the heading, the <h1> style width was increased to 600 pixels in the *includes.css* style sheet. The new Logout and Search buttons are shown in bold type in Listing 3-13a.

Listing 3-13a. Creating the Administration Page Header (header-admin.php)

```
<div id="header-admin">
<h1>This is the admin header</h1>
<div id="reg-navigation">
        <ul>
            <li><a href="logout.php">Logout</a></li>
            <li><a href="register-view_users-page.php">View Members</a></li>
            <li><a href="#">Search</a></li>
            <li><a href="register-password.php">New Password</a></li>
        </ul>
    </div>
</div>
```

■ **Note**   The search button does not work because we have not yet created the Search page. We will create the Search page in Chapter 4.

In the next step, we will add the new header and session details to an administration page. The code is shown in Listing 3-13b.

The Administrator's Page

Listing 3-13b is the code for the administration page.

Listing 3-13b. Creating an Administration Page (admin-page.php)

```
<?php                                                                      #1
session_start();
if (!isset($_SESSION['user_level']) or ($_SESSION['user_level'] != 1))
{ header("Location: login.php");
exit();
}
?>
<!doctype html>
<html lang=en>
<head>
<title>Page for administrator</title>
<meta charset=utf-8>
<link rel="stylesheet" type="text/css" href="includes.css">
<style type="text/css">
p { text-align:center; }
</style>
</head>
```

```
<body>
<div id="container">
<?php include("header-admin.php"); ?>
<?php include("nav.php"); ?>
<?php include("info-col.php"); ?>
<div id="content"><!-- Start of the member's page content. -->
<?php                                                                    #2
echo '<h2>Welcome to the Admin Page ';
if (isset($_SESSION['fname'])){
echo "{$_SESSION['fname']}";
}
echo '</h2>';
?>
<div id="midcol">
<h3>You have permission to:</h3><p>&#9632;Use the View members button to see
a table of registered members.</p><p> </p>
</div>
</div>
<div id="footer">
<?php include("footer.php"); ?>
</div>
</body>
</html>
```

Explanation of the Code

```
<?php                                                                    #1
session_start();
if (!isset($_SESSION['user_level']) or ($_SESSION['user_level'] != 1))
{ header("Location: login.php");
   exit();
}
?>
```

This is the security guard (session). If the person trying to access the page has not logged in and does not have the right *user_level*—that is, his *user_level* is not *user_level* number 1—he will be unable to open the page and instead he will be redirected to the login page.

```
<?php                                                                    #2
echo '<h2>Welcome to the Admin Page ';
if (isset($_SESSION['fname'])){
echo "{$_SESSION['fname']}";
}
echo '</h2>';
?>
```

If the session detects that the person has the right credentials, the page will open and he will be welcomed by his first name as previously shown in Figure 3-13.

The Logout Page

The next page enables users to log out. The code destroys the session when it is no longer required.

This is not a page that is visible to users. It acts as an intermediary page between the login page and the home page. Listing 3-13c shows the code.

Listing 3-13c. Creating the Logout Code (logout.php)

```php
<?php
session_start();//access the current session.                               #1
// if no session variable exists then redirect the user
if (!isset($_SESSION['user_id'])) {                                         #2
header("location:index.php");
exit();
//cancel the session and redirect the user:
}else{ //cancel the session                                                 #3
    $_SESSION = array(); // Destroy the variables.
    session_destroy(); // Destroy the session
setcookie('PHPSESSID', ", time()-3600,'/', ", 0, 0);//Destroy the cookie
header("location:index.php");
exit();
}
?>
```

Explanation of the Code

```php
session_start();//access the current session.                               #1
```

The code allows the logged-in user to access the information in the memory of the session that was initiated in the login page. Line **#1** links the new page to the information stored in that session.

```php
//if no session variable then redirect the user
if (!isset($_SESSION['user_id'])) {                                         #2
header("location:index.php");
exit();
```

If the session does not exist, the user is redirected to the home page.

```php
}else{ //cancel the session                                                 #3
    $_SESSION = array(); // Destroy the variables.
    session_destroy(); // Destroy the session itself.
setcookie('PHPSESSID', ", time()-3600,'/', ", 0, 0);//Destroy the cookie
```

If the session exists, log out by destroying the session and redirecting the user to the home page. A temporary cookie was used to store the session identity (known as the SID). This cookie is also destroyed. The SID was stored in enciphered form by the item called PHPSESSID. The last line in the code block beginning with line **#3** will destroy the temporary cookie.

Testing the Login/logout Function

The web designer can access a table of members using phpMyAdmin. It is usual to allow an administrator/ membership secretary to view a table of members. The administrator would have very limited powers for security, but he should be able to edit or delete a record. This is covered in the next section.

Start XAMPP, and use a browser to test the login facility. Enter the following URL into the browser's address field:

```
http://localhost/login/login.php
```

You should now be able to load the members' page for ordinary members. You will also be able to load the administrator's page when the administrator logs in. The only button that does not yet function is *Search*. This will be dealt with in Chapter 4. Concerning the administrator's page, the table view is not very helpful yet because the administrator cannot delete or amend a record. This will be achieved in Chapter 4 by the addition of delete and edit links.

Amending and deleting individual records is easy in phpMyAdmin, but the term *Delete* is used instead of the term *DROP* that is used to delete whole tables and databases.

Amending and Deleting Individual Records

The webmaster/developer can amend and delete records as follows:

1. access phpMyAdmin by entering the following into the address field of a browser:

    ```
    http://localhost/phpmyadmin/.
    ```

2. Access the *logindb* database and then the *users* table.

3. Select the *Browse* tab, and you will see the list of registered members. This is shown in Figure 3-14.

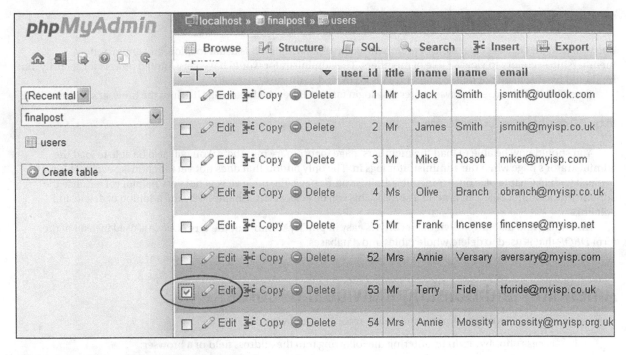

Figure 3-14. *Edit or delete an individual record*

Find the member's record to be amended or deleted and select its check box (shown ringed). When you click Edit, you will be presented with a screen that will enable you to amend any item on a record except the password. If you click Delete, you will be asked if you really mean it. You can then decline or accept.

Summary

In this chapter, you tidied the main style sheet so that, where possible, styles were no longer scattered among the included files. You amended various headers to give them more meaningful menu buttons, and you also removed redundant buttons. You discovered how to log in to private pages and how to log out of those special pages. You described a way of differentiating between different types of members by using sessions. You created a members-only page and learned how to use sessions to protect private pages. You learned how to use a session so that only the administrator could access the administrator's page.

In each tutorial, explanations were provided for the PHP and SQL code. You added a little more security by removing the ability of ordinary members to view the table of members. You prevented unauthorized persons from using a browser to enter the URLs of private pages. You learned how a developer could amend or delete individual records.

In the next chapter, you will learn how the membership secretary/administrator can search, amend, and delete records.

CHAPTER 4

■ ■ ■

Display Membership Tables for the Administrator

In this chapter, we aim to present a user-friendly set of pages for an administrator who has moderate computer skills. We are assuming the administrator is not capable of using phpMyAdmin, but that he knows enough to be able to log in, access easy-to-use displays, and use simple editing facilities. We will make the table of members interactive so that the administrator can search, edit, delete, and re-order records. Only the administrator is permitted to access these facilities for deleting and amending records. The webmaster will be restricted to using phpMyAdmin to access the records. This chapter will cover the following topics:

- The administration database
- Deleting and editing records
- Paginating the displayed records
- Searching for an individual record

■ **Caution** When we talk about tables in this book, try not to confuse tables displayed on the screen with the database tables. These types of tables are two distinct entities. For instance, Table 4-1 is a database table and is not visible to the user. Whereas, **Figure** 4-2 is a table displayed on the user's screen.

The Administration Database

The tutorials in this chapter are based on the templates used in previous chapters. We will keep things separate from previous tutorials by using new names for the database and its folder. However, a table can have the same name as earlier tutorials as long as the table lives in a different database. The table will therefore continue to be called *users*.

Create a new folder and a new database as follows:

1. In the XAMPP htdocs folder, create a new folder called *admintable*.

2. Download the PHP files from the book's page at www.apress.com, and place them in the new admintable folder.

3. Now type **http://localhost/phpmyadmin** in the address field of your browser.

4. Create a new database called *admintable*.

5. Select the check box next to *logindb*, and click *Check Privileges*.

6. Click the *Add User* button.

7. Enter a new user and password as follows:

    User: webmaster

    Password: coffeepot

    Host: localhost

8. Be sure to record the new user and password details in your notebook.

9. Scroll down, and where it says *Global privileges (Check All/Uncheck All)*, click *Check All*.

10. Scroll down to the bottom of the form, and click the *Add User* button (or the *Go* button on some versions).

To connect to the administration database, you use the following code.

Listing for creating the snippet of code for connecting to the admintable database (mysqli_connect.php)

```php
<?php
// Create a connection to the admintable database and set the encoding
DEFINE ('DB_USER', 'webmaster');
DEFINE ('DB_PASSWORD', 'coffeepot');
DEFINE ('DB_HOST', 'localhost');
DEFINE ('DB_NAME', 'admintable');
// Make the connection:
$dbcon = @mysqli_connect (DB_HOST, DB_USER, DB_PASSWORD, DB_NAME) ↵
OR die ('Could not connect to MySQL: ' . mysqli_connect_error() );
// Set the encoding...
mysqli_set_charset($dbcon, 'utf8');
```

The Users Table

In phpMyAdmin, make sure you click the new database *admintable* and then create this *users* table with seven columns. Give the columns the titles and attributes shown in Table 4-1.

Table 4-1. *The Attributes for the Users Table*

Column name	Type	Length/Values	Default	Attributes	NULL	Index	A_I
user_id	MEDIUMINT	6	None	UNSIGNED	☐	PRIMARY	☑
fname	VARCHAR	30	None		☐		☐
lname	VARCHAR	40	None		☐		☐
email	VARCHAR	50	None		☐		☐
psword	CHAR	40	None		☐		☐
registration_date	DATETIME		None		☐		☐
user_level	TINYINT	1	None	UNSIGNED	☐		☐

Use the *register-page.php* file (included in the downloadable files for Chapter 4), to register the administrator as an ordinary member using the following data:

First name: James

Last name: Smith

E-mail: jsmith@myisp.co.uk

Password: blacksmith

The registered member James Smith will be appointed as the Membership secretary using the pseudonym *Jack Smith*. We can safely assume that James Smith (alias Jack Smith) would like to view the members' page occasionally as well as viewing the administration page. He will use his membership e-mail and password to view the members' page, but he needs a different e-mail and password to access the administration section. Now register the membership secretary a second time with his pseudonym and a new password as follows:

First name: Jack

Last name: Smith

E-mail: jsmith@outcook.com,

Password: dogsbody

Important: Use phpMyAdmin to change Jack Smith's user level to 1.
Now register these members so that we have something to play with. Use the details in Table 4-2.

Table 4-2. *Suggested Details for Members*

Name	E-mail	Password
Mike Rosoft	miker@myisp.com	willgates
Olive Branch	obranch@myisp.co.uk	anoilyone
Frank Incense	fincense@myisp.net	perfume
Annie Versary	aversary@myisp.com	happyday
Terry Fide	tfide@myisp.de	scaredstiff
Rose Bush	rbush@myisp.co.uk	redblooms

You will now have a total of eight records.

■ **Note**   Now that we are using *sessions* together with the member's *user_level*, you will not be able to access any of the administration pages without first logging in as the administrator.

I amended the administrator's page from Chapter 3 so that it includes some extra facilities.

The Revised Administration Page

In Chapter 3, the admin page only had a small piece of text in the main content. It now has four items describing the extra features that will be available to the administrator. These are shown in Figure 4-1.

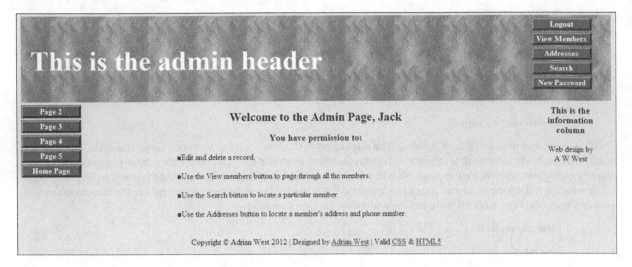

Figure 4-1. *The revised Admin Page with three extra features*

The extra items and amended features are shown in bold type in the admin page Listing 4-1.

Listing 4-1. Creating an Administrator's Page with Extra Features and a Session (admin-page.php)

```php
<?php                                                                        #1
session_start();
if (!isset($_SESSION['user_level']) or ($_SESSION['user_level'] != 1))
{
header("Location: login.php");
exit();
}
?>
<!doctype html>
<html lang=en>
<head>
<title>Admin page page</title>
<meta charset=utf-8>
<link rel="stylesheet" type="text/css" href="includes.css">
<style type="text/css">
#midcol { width:98%; }
#midcol p { margin-left:160px; }
</style>
</head>
<body>
<div id="container">
<?php include("header-admin.php"); ?>
<?php include("nav.php"); ?>
<?php include("info-col.php"); ?>
<div id="content"><!--Start of the member's page content-->
```

```php
<?php                                                                           #2
echo '<h2>Welcome to the Admin Page, ';
if (isset($_SESSION['fname'])){
echo "{$_SESSION['fname']}";
}
echo '</h2>';
?>
<div id="midcol">
    <h3>You have permission to:</h3>
<p>&#9632;Edit and delete a record.</p>                                         #3
    <p>&#9632;Use the View Members button to page through all the members.</p>
    <p>&#9632;Use the Search button to locate a particular member.</p>
    <p>&#9632;Use the Addresses button to locate a member's address and phone number. </p>
    <p> </p>
</div>
<!--End of the members page content-->
</div>
</div>
<div id="footer">
    <?php include("footer.php"); ?>
</div>
</body>
</html>
```

Explanation of the Code

```php
<?php                                                                           #1
session_start();
if (!isset($_SESSION['user_level']) or ($_SESSION['user_level'] != 1))
{
header("Location: login.php");
exit();
}
?>
```

This is the security guard in the admin page. He looks up the session details. If either (i) the session does not exist or (ii) the user level does not match the level given in the session data, he sends the user back to the login page.

```php
<?php                                                                           #2
echo '<h2>Welcome to the Admin Page, ';
if (isset($_SESSION['fname'])){
echo "{$_SESSION['fname']}";
}
echo '</h2>';
?>
```

This piece of code takes the user's first name from the session array and inserts it into the welcome message:

```html
<p>&#9632;Edit and delete a record.</p>                                         #3
<p>&#9632;Use the View Members button to page through all the members.</p>
<p>&#9632;Use the Search button to locate a particular member.</p>
<p>&#9632;Use the Addresses button to locate a member's address and phone number. </p>
```

These are the four items in the body of the page. The entity **■** provides a square bullet.

■ **Note**   If you add extra columns to a displayed table, don't forget to change its width in the main style sheet.

We display the extended table of data by means of a revised page named *view_users.php*.

Revising the View Users Page to Include Editing and Deleting

The display table needs two extra columns for links that will enable the administrator to edit and delete records. In Chapter 3, we concatenated (joined) the first and last names so that they appeared in one column. To be able to re-order records, you'll find that it's best if the first and last names are displayed in separate columns. Passwords are not included in the display because they are enciphered and would mean nothing to the administrator. The revised display for the administrator will therefore have six columns, as shown in Table 4-3. Remember that this is not the *users* database table but the table that will be displayed on the screen for the administrator; the two tables are quite different.

Table 4-3. *The Format of the New Table as It Will be Displayed for the Administrator Only*

Edit	Delete	Last Name	First Name	E-mail	Date Registered
Edit	Delete	Rosoft	Mike	miker@myisp.com	October 30, 2012

The style sheet downloadable for this chapter (*includes.css*) is almost the same as the file in Chapter 3, but the table width has been increased from 500 pixels to 700 pixels so that the table can accommodate the three extra columns.

Two of the new columns have links to enable the administrator to interact with the records. Most importantly, we intend the page to be private; therefore, it needs a security guard—in other words, a *session*.

The appearance of the interactive table is shown in Figure 4-2.

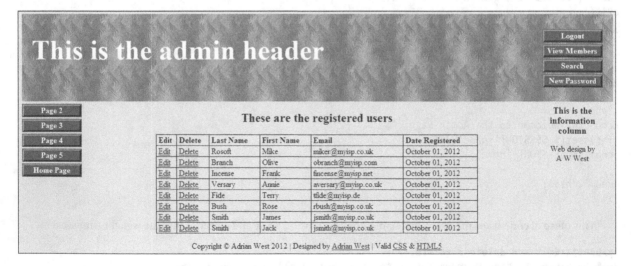

Figure 4-2. *The interactive table for an administrator*

■ **Note** You can view the table using XAMPP and a browser, but the links *edit* and *delete* will not work until we create the pages for deleting and editing a record. These pages will be described later in the chapter.

The amendments to create the new View Users page are shown in bold type in the Listing 4-2.
The administrator's page begins with session code for security:

Listing 4-2. Amending the Table View to Include Two Links (view_users-page.php)

```php
<?php                                                                    #1
session_start();
if (!isset($_SESSION['user_level']) or ($_SESSION['user_level'] != 1))
{
header("Location: login.php");
exit();
}
?>

<!doctype html>
<html lang=en>
<head>
<title>An administrator's View-members page</title>
<meta charset=utf-8>
<link rel="stylesheet" type="text/css" href="includes.css">
</head>
<body>
<div id="container">
<?php include("header-admin.php"); ?>
<?php include("nav.php"); ?>
<?php include("info-col.php"); ?>
<div id="content"><!--Start of the view_users_page content-->
<h2>These are the registered users</h2>
<p>
<?php
// This script retrieves all the records from the users table
require ('mysqli_connect.php'); // Connect to the database
// Make the query                                                        #2
$q = "SELECT lname, fname, email, DATE_FORMAT(registration_date, '%M %d, %Y') ↵
AS regdat, user_id FROM users ORDER BY registration_date ASC";
$result = @mysqli_query ($dbcon, $q); // Run the query
if ($result) { // If it ran without a problem, display the records
// Table headings                                                       #3
echo '<table>
<tr>
<td><b>Edit</b></td>
<td><b>Delete</b></td>
<td><b>Last Name</b></td>
<td><b>First Name</b></td>
<td><b>Email</b></td>
<td><b>Date Registered</b></td>
</tr>';
```

```
// Fetch and print all the records                                          #4
while ($row = mysqli_fetch_array($result, MYSQLI_ASSOC)) {
    echo '<tr>                                                              #5
    <td><a href="edit_user.php?id=' . $row['user_id'] . '">Edit</a></td>
    <td><a href="delete_user.php?id=' . $row['user_id'] . '">Delete</a></td>
    <td>' . $row['lname'] . '</td>                                          #6
    <td>' . $row['fname'] . '</td>
    <td>' . $row['email'] . '</td>
    <td>' . $row['regdat'] . '</td></tr>';
    }
    echo '</table>'; // Close the table                                     #7
    mysqli_free_result ($result); // Free up the resources
} else { // If it failed to run
// Error message
echo '<p class="error">The current users could not be retrieved. We apologize ↵
for any inconvenience.</p>';
// Debugging message
    echo '<p>' . mysqli_error($dbcon) . '<br><br />Query: ' . $q . '</p>';
} // End of if ($result)
mysqli_close($dbcon); // Close the database connection
?>
</p>
</div><!--End of page content-->
<?php include("footer.php"); ?>
</div>
</body>
</html>
```

Explanation of the Code

```
<?php                                                                       #1
session_start();
if (!isset($_SESSION['user_level']) or ($_SESSION['user_level'] != 1))
{
header("Location: login.php");
exit();
}
?>
```

This session code returns unauthorized users to the login page.

```
// Make the query:                                                          #2
$q = "SELECT lname, fname, email, DATE_FORMAT(registration_date, '%M %d, %Y') ↵
AS regdat, user_id FROM users ORDER BY registration_date ASC";
$result = @mysqli_query ($dbcon, $q); // Run the query
if ($result) { // If it ran OK, display the records
```

The code looks in the users table and selects the five items that will populate the last five columns in the displayed table. The table records are displayed in ascending order of registration date. The order can be reversed by using DESC instead of ASC.

```
// Table header                                                                  #3
echo '<table>
<tr>
<td><b>Edit</b></td>
<td><b>Delete</b></td>
<td><b>Last Name</b></td>
<td><b>First Name</b></td>
<td><b>Email</b></td>
<td><b>Date Registered</b></td>
</tr>';
```

The six headings in the title row of the table are created.

```
// Fetch and echo all the records                                               #4
while ($row = mysqli_fetch_array($result, MYSQLI_ASSOC)) {
```

The code loops through the users table's data until all the data has been displayed. This is achieved by the while() function.

```
echo '                                                                          #5
<tr>
<td><a href="edit_user.php?id=' . $row['user_id'] . '">Edit</a></td>
    <td><a href="delete_user.php?id=' . $row['user_id'] . '">Delete</a></td>
```

This code displays the first two cells in each row. Each cell contains a link to a PHP page. The links connect to the pages *edit_user.php* and *delete_user.php*. As the code loops through the data in the users table, it stores the corresponding user_id for each row. The PHP page and the user_id are combined using a device that has this pattern:

```
<a href="delete_user.php?id='the user_id for that row'">Delete</a>
```

In the preceding pattern, the user_id for the row is passed to the page that will handle the deletion. The whole line of code is a link that, when clicked, will delete the identified row. For clarification, Figure 4-3 shows a fragment of the interactive table and the two links. 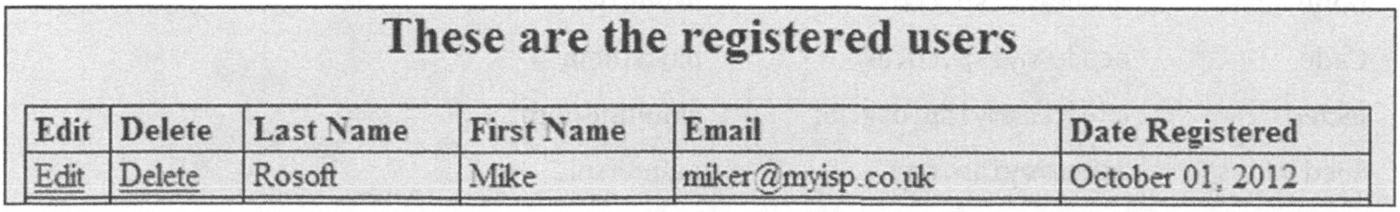

These are the registered users					
Edit	Delete	Last Name	First Name	Email	Date Registered
Edit	Delete	Rosoft	Mike	miker@myisp.co.uk	October 01, 2012

Figure 4-3. Showing one record and the two links in the first two cells

```
        <td>' . $row['lname'] . '</td>                                              #6
        <td>' . $row['fname'] . '</td>
        <td>' . $row['email'] . '</td>
        <td>' . $row['regdat'] . '</td>
    </tr>';
        }
```

In the block of code starting with line **#6**, the values for the last four cells are extracted from the arrays for each displayed record.

```
echo '</table>'; // Close the table                                                  #7
mysqli_free_result ($result); // Free up the resources
```

The table's closing tag is printed to the browser, and memory resources are freed up. The rest of the code deals with error messages and adds the footer to the displayed page.

The next section describes a method of displaying tables one page at a time.

Displaying Pages of Records (Pagination)

The table display created so far is fine for up to 30 records. A greater number of records will cause the table and the administrator to scroll down. Imagine what would happen if the database contained 1,000 records or more. Creating the ability to view the table one screen at a time would provide a solution; however, even this would be inconvenient for a large database. Later in this chapter, we will examine a slicker way of selecting and viewing one particular record in a large database; meanwhile, we will learn how to display a table so that the administrator can see one page at a time. The process is called *pagination*.

A page length of 20 rows would be a sensible choice; however, for the purposes of this tutorial, it would mean you would have to register a total of around 60 new members. That would give you at least three pages, but I am sure you would prefer to press on with the tutorial. Therefore, we will set the number of rows per displayed page to four so that you will need to register only another eight members. That will give you four pages to play with.

Table 4-4 suggests another 10 members to register.

Table 4-4. *Details for Registering Members*

First name	Last Name	E-mail address	Password
Percy	Veer	pveer@myisp.com	keepgoing
Stan	Dard	sdard@myisp.net	battleflag
Nora	Bone	nbone@myisp.com	liketerrier
Barry	Cade	bcade@myisp.co.uk	blockthem
Dee	Jected	djected@myisp.org.uk	gloomndoom
Lynn	Seed	lseed@myisp.com	paintersoi
Barry	Tone	btone@myisp.net	nicevoice
Helen	Back	hback@myisp.net	agrimsortie
Justin	Case	jcase@myisp.co.uk	cautious
Jerry	Attrik	jattrik@myisp.com	elderlyman

You will now have a total of 18 records. When you divide this by four (rows per page), you will have four and a half pages. Following this explanation, in Listing 4-4a for *admin_view_users.php*, you will see that the number of rows per page has been set by the variable *$pagerows* as follows:

```
$pagerows = 4;
```

Later, you can experiment by giving the variable a value of say 9 or 15 to see the effect.

Figure 4-4 shows the display of four records per page and the links for moving back and forward between the pages. The page also displays the total number of members.

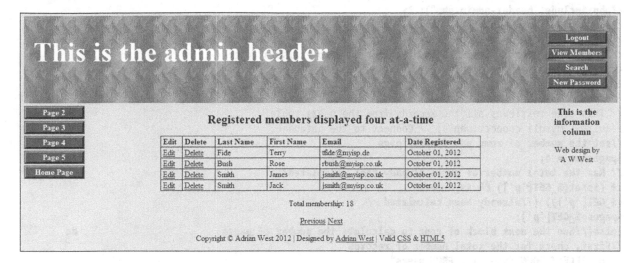

Figure 4-4. *The display now shows four records per page and indicates the total membership*

The page named *admin_view_users.php* will demonstrate pagination.

In Figure 4-4, you can see the links *Previous* and *Next* that will enable you to move from page to page. Instead of those links, we could have clickable page numbers. However, if you don't know what is on each page, a page number is not much use. The ability to browse through the pages and also having the total membership displayed will be useful to the administrator. The pagination will also enable the administrator to print each page, and this will be described in Chapter 7. For displaying one particular member's record, we will use the new Search menu button. This is described later in the chapter.

Listing 4-4a incorporates the code to enable pagination. The amendments and additions are shown in bold type.

Listing 4-4a. Creating a Table Display That Will Paginate (admin_view_users.php)

```
<?php                                                            #1
session_start();
if (!isset($_SESSION['user_level']) or ($_SESSION['user_level'] != 1))
{
header("Location: login.php");
exit();
}
?>
<!doctype html>
<html lang=en>
```

```
<head>
<title>Admin view users page for an administrator</title>
<meta charset=utf-8>
<link rel="stylesheet" type="text/css" href="includes.css">
<style type="text/css">
p { text-align:center; }                                                    #2
</style>
</head>
<body>
<div id="container">
<?php include("header-admin.php"); ?>
<?php include("nav.php"); ?>
<?php include("info-col.php"); ?>
<div id="content"><!--Start the content for the table display page-->
<h2>Registered members displayed four at a time</h2>
<p>
<?php
// This code retrieves all the records from the users table.
require ('mysqli_connect.php'); // Connect to the database.
//set the number of rows per display page
$pagerows = 4;                                                              #3
// Has the total number of pages already been calculated?
if (isset($_GET['p']) && is_numeric
($_GET['p'])) {//already been calculated
$pages=$_GET['p'];
}else{//use the next block of code to calculate the number of pages         #4
//First, check for the total number of records
$q = "SELECT COUNT(user_id) FROM users";
$result = @mysqli_query ($dbcon, $q);
$row = @mysqli_fetch_array ($result, MYSQLI_NUM);
$records = $row[0];
//Now calculate the number of pages
if ($records > $pagerows){ //if the number of records will fill more than one page
//Calculatethe number of pages and round the result up to the nearest integer
$pages = ceil ($records/$pagerows);                                         #5
}else{
$pages = 1;
}
}//page check finished
//Declare which record to start with                                        #6
if (isset($_GET['s']) && is_numeric
($_GET['s'])) {//already been calculated
$start = $_GET['s'];
}else{
$start = 0;
}
// Make the query:                                                           #7
$q = "SELECT lname, fname, email, DATE_FORMAT(registration_date, '%M %d, %Y') ↩
AS regdat, user_id FROM users ORDER BY registration_date ASC LIMIT $start, $pagerows";
```

```php
$result = @mysqli_query ($dbcon, $q); // Run the query.
$members = mysqli_num_rows($result);
if ($result) { // If it ran OK, display the records.
// Table header.
echo '<table>
<tr><td><b>Edit</b></td>
<td><b>Delete</b></td>
<td><b>Last Name</b></td>
<td><b>First Name</b></td>
<td><b>Email</b></td>
<td><b>Date Registered</b></td>
</tr>';
// Fetch and print the records:
while ($row = mysqli_fetch_array($result, MYSQLI_ASSOC)) {
echo '<tr>
<td><a href="edit_record.php?id=' . $row['user_id'] . '">Edit</a></td>
<td><a href="delete_record.php?id=' . $row['user_id'] . '">Delete</a></td>
<td>' . $row['lname'] . '</td>
<td>' . $row['fname'] . '</td>
<td>' . $row['email'] . '</td>
<td>' . $row['regdat'] . '</td>
</tr>';
}
    echo '</table>'; // Close the table
    mysqli_free_result ($result); // Free up the resources
} else { // If it failed to run
// Error message
    echo '<p class="error">The current users could not be retrieved. We apologize for ↵
any inconvenience.</p>';
    // Debug message
    echo '<p>' . mysqli_error($dbcon) . '<br><br />Query: ' . $q . '</p>';
} // End of if ($result)
//Now display the figure for the total number of records/members                  #8
$q = "SELECT COUNT(user_id) FROM users";
$result = @mysqli_query ($dbcon, $q);
$row = @mysqli_fetch_array ($result, MYSQLI_NUM);
$members = $row[0];
mysqli_close($dbcon); // Close the database connection                           #9
echo "<p>Total membership: $members</p>";
if ($pages > 1) {                                                                #10
echo '<p>';
//What number is the current page?
$current_page = ($start/$pagerows) + 1;
//If the page is not the first page then create a Previous link
if ($current_page != 1) {
echo '<a href="register-view_users.php?s=' . ($start - $pagerows) . ↵
'&p=' . $pages . '">Previous</a> ';
}
```

```
//Create a Next link                                                          #11
if ($current_page != $pages) {
echo '<a href="register-view_users.php?s=' . ($start + $pagerows) . ↵
'&p=' . $pages . '">Next</a> ';
}
echo '</p>';
}
?>
</div><!--End of content of the table display page-->
<?php include("footer.php"); ?>
</div>
</body>
</html>
```

Explanation of the Code

```
<?php                                                                          #1
session_start();
if (!isset($_SESSION['user_level']) or ($_SESSION['user_level'] != 1))
{
header("Location: login.php");
exit();
}
?>
```

The session is our security guard. He will appear in every private page used by the administrator. As in the previous tutorial, the session redirects unauthorized people to the login page.

```
p { text-align:center; }                                                       #2
```

An internal style is added to center the *Previous* and *Next* links and the *Total Membership* figure.

```
$pagerows = 4;                                                                 #3
```

Set the display to four records per page. (You would set this to about 20 in a real-world page.)

```
}else{//use the next block of code to calculate the number of pages           #4
//First, check for the total number of records
$q = "SELECT COUNT(user_id) FROM users";
$result = @mysqli_query ($dbcon, $q);
$row = @mysqli_fetch_array ($result, MYSQLI_NUM);
$records = $row[0];
//Now calculate the number of pages
if ($records > $pagerows){ //if the number of records will fill more than one page
//Calculate the number of pages and round the result up to the nearest integer
```

If the number of pages has not already been calculated by the code, the code calculates it now by counting the number of *user_ids* in the *users* table. Then it checks to see if the number of records is greater than the number of records displayed per page.

```
$pages = ceil ($records/$pagerows);                                           #5
}else{
$pages = 1;
}
}//page check finished
```

If the number of records is greater than the number of records displayed per page, round up the number of pages to a whole number. The PHP function ceil() rounds up the number of pages. In the tutorial, we have 18 records, resulting in four and a half pages (18 divided by 4). This is rounded up to five pages. The fifth page will display only two records. If the number of records is not greater than the number of rows per display, there will be only one page. The function ceil() means *set the ceiling* or *set to an integer above the actual count*; in this case, 4.5 becomes 5.

```
//Declare which record to start with                                          #6
if (isset($_GET['s']) && is_numeric
($_GET['s'])) {//already been calculated
$start = $_GET['s'];
}else{
$start = 0;
}
```

This ensures that the variable ['s'] is an integer. Then the start point for the display is set to zero.

```
// Make the query                                                             #7
$q = "SELECT lname, fname, email, DATE_FORMAT(registration_date, '%M %d, %Y') ↵
AS regdat, user_id FROM users ORDER BY registration_date ASC LIMIT $start, $pagerows";
```

The query selects the columns to be displayed and sets the number of rows to be displayed per page, starting with the record number zero. (The variable $start was set to zero.)

```
//Now display the figure for the total number of records/members             #8
$q = "SELECT COUNT(user_id) FROM users";
$result = @mysqli_query ($dbcon, $q);
$row = @mysqli_fetch_array ($result, MYSQLI_NUM);
$members = $row[0];
```

This code counts the total number of rows in the table and assigns the total to the variable $members.

```
mysqli_close($dbcon); // Close the database connection.                       #9
echo "<p>Total membership: $members</p>";
```

The database is closed, and the total number of members is displayed on the screen.

```
if ($pages > 1) {                                                            #10
echo '<p>';
//What number is the current page?
$current_page = ($start/$pagerows) + 1;
//If the page is not the first page then create a "Previous" link
if ($current_page != 1) {
echo '<a href="register-view_users.php?s=' . ($start - $pagerows) . ↵
'&p=' . $pages . '">Previous</a> ';
}
```

The link named *Previous* is created and displayed.

```
//Create a "Next" link                                                      #11
if ($current_page != $pages) {
echo '<a href="register-view_users.php?s=' . ($start + $pagerows) . ↵
'&p=' . $pages . '">Next</a> ';
}
echo '</p>';
}
?>
</div><!--End of the administration page content-->
```

The link named *Next* is created and displayed. Fire up XAMPP, and then log in as the administrator to view the pagination.

We now need to consider how to search for one particular record and then display it.

You may have noticed that the header for the *admin_view_users.php* page is changed so that the *View Members* button is a link to the *admin_view_users.php* page. Also, a new button links to the search page *search.php*. The changes are shown in bold type in Listing 4-4b.

Listing 4-4b. Creating the Revised Administration Header (header-admin.php)

```
<div id="header-admin">
<h1>This is the admin header</h1>
<div id="reg-navigation">
   <ul>
      <li><a href="logout.php">Logout</a></li>
      <li><a href="admin_view_users.php">View Members</a></li>
      <li><a href="search.php">Search</a></li>
      <li><a href="register-password.php">New Password</a></li>
   </ul>
</div>
</div>
```

Planning the Search Criteria

The administrator needs a search facility so that he does not have to scroll through scores of records to edit or delete one. The importance of forward planning cannot be over emphasized; deciding how to organize the search facility requires careful thought.

The administrator can edit and delete records. So what events would require him to use these facilities? For editing, the event would typically be members notifying the administrator of a change of e-mail address, or if a female member got married and wanted to change her last name, a new last name would need to be entered. Deletions would be required if a member resigns or dies.

Some names are very common—for instance, we may have five people named James Smith. We would need to display all five and then use their e-mail addresses to distinguish them so that we don't delete the wrong James Smith.

The next tutorial describes the creation of a page that displays the results of a search. For this, you will need to register four more members named James Smith. Table 4-5 offers some suggestions.

Table 4-5. *Some Identical Common Names*

First name	Last Name	E-mail address	Password
James	Smith	jimsmith@myisp.org.uk	chevron
James	Smith	james.smith@myisp.com	inclined
James	Smith	jimmysmith@myisp.co.uk	pedestal
James	Smith	jims@myisp.net	tungsten

When you have registered them, there will be a total of five members named James Smith and the total number of records in our database will be 22.

A Temporary Page for Displaying Specified Members

We will eventually create a search facility, but first we must create a page that will produce a table of members named James Smith. The target or end result of a search for *James Smith* will be a table, as shown in Figure 4-5.

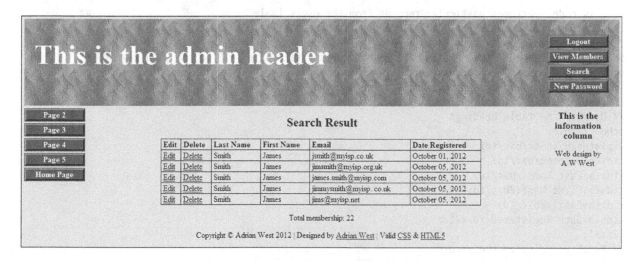

Figure 4-5. *The five James Smiths have been located and are now displayed*

To ensure that we are able to display the table shown in Figure 4-5, we need to create a page that we will call *view_found_record.php*. Because we have not created a search page, we will enter the names **James** and **Smith** directly into the page as a temporary expedient. Listing 4-5 is shown next.

Listing 4-5. Creating a Temporary Page for Displaying the Results of a Search (temp_view_found_record.php)

```php
<?php                                                                    #1
session_start();
if (!isset($_SESSION['user_level']) or ($_SESSION['user_level'] != 1))
{
header("Location: login.php");
exit();
}
?>
```

```
<!doctype html>
<html lang=en>
<head>
<title>A temporary view_found_record page</title>
<meta charset=utf-8>
<link rel="stylesheet" type="text/css" href="includes.css">
<style type="text/css">
p { text-align:center; }
</style>
</head>
<body>
<div id="container">
<?php include("header-admin.php"); ?>
<?php include("nav.php"); ?>
<?php include("info-col.php"); ?>
<div id="content"><!--Start of the page content-->
<h2>Search Result</h2>
<p>
<?php
// This code retrieves particular records from the users table               #2
require ('mysqli_connect.php'); // Connect to the database
// Make the query using hard coded names
$q = "SELECT lname, fname, email, DATE_FORMAT(registration_date, '%M %d, %Y') AS regdat, ↵
user_id FROM users WHERE lname='Smith' AND fname='James' ORDER BY registration_date ASC ";
$result = @mysqli_query ($dbcon, $q); // Run the query
if ($result) { // If it ran, display the records
// Display the table headings
echo '<table>
<tr><td><b>Edit</b></td>
<td><b>Delete</b></td>
<td><b>Last Name</b></td>
<td><b>First Name</b></td>
<td><b>Email</b></td>
<td><b>Date Registered</b></td>
</tr>';
// Fetch and display the records
while ($row = mysqli_fetch_array($result, MYSQLI_ASSOC)) {
    echo '<tr>
    <td><a href="edit_user.php?id=' . $row['user_id'] . '">Edit</a></td>
    <td><a href="delete_user.php?id=' . $row['user_id'] . '">Delete</a></td>
    <td>' . $row['lname'] . '</td>
    <td>' . $row['fname'] . '</td>
    <td>' . $row['email'] . '</td>
    <td>' . $row['regdat'] . '</td>
    </tr>';
    }
    echo '</table>'; // Close the table
    mysqli_free_result ($result); // Free up the resources
} else { // If it did not run properly
// Message
echo '<p class="error">The current users could not be retrieved. We apologize for ↵
any inconvenience.</p>';
```

```
// Debugging message
    echo '<p>' . mysqli_error($dbcon) . '<br><br>Query: ' . $q . '</p>';
} // End of if ($result). Now display the figure for total number of records/members
$q = "SELECT COUNT(user_id) FROM users";
$result = @mysqli_query ($dbcon, $q);
$row = @mysqli_fetch_array ($result, MYSQLI_NUM);
$members = $row[0];
mysqli_close($dbcon); // Close the database connection
echo "<p>Total membership: $members</p>";
?>
</div><!--End of administration page content-->
<?php include("footer.php"); ?>
</div>
</body>
</html>
```

■ **Note** This is a temporary version of the page. It is a helpful stage before producing the final version. It demonstrates an important principle and is a useful exercise for proving that a table will be displayed. The temporary version is included in the downloadable files for this chapter as *temp_view_found_record.php*.

Explanation of the Code

```
<?php                                                                    #1
session_start();
if (!isset($_SESSION['user_level']) or ($_SESSION['user_level'] != 1))
{
header("Location: login.php");
exit();
}
```

Our security guard (session) prevents unauthorized people from searching the database.

```
// This code retrieves particular records from the users table            #2
require ('mysqli_connect.php'); // Connect to the database
// Make the query using hard coded names
$q = "SELECT lname, fname, email, DATE_FORMAT(registration_date, '%M %d, %Y') AS regdat, ↵
userid FROM users WHERE lname='Smith' AND fname='James' ORDER BY registration_date ASC ";
```

This SQL query is almost the same as the one in *admin_view_users.php* except that the LIMIT on the number of rows has been removed and a new keyword, WHERE, has been introduced. Removing the limit on the number of rows ensures that all the James Smith records will be displayed no matter how many there are. The WHERE clause specifies exactly which records to display. Note that we cheated here and put some actual names in; eventually, the names will be replaced by names sent from the search page. We entered names as a temporary expedient so that we can test the page and ensure that it works as expected. This is a common technique and is known as *hard coding*. The resulting table display was shown in Figure 4-5.

■ **Note** Now that we are using sessions, you will not be able to access any of the administration pages without logging in as the administrator.

We now a have a page that will display a table of specified records. With that working correctly, the next step is to provide a search form so that the administrator can request a table showing any specified members rather than only James Smith.

The Search Form

When the administrator clicks the Search button on the header menu, he will be taken to the *search.php* page. This page has a form containing two fields where search criteria can be entered. Planning is needed to decide what the search criteria should be. A grieving widow, requesting that her husband's details be removed, may not know the e-mail address or password he used for his membership registration. The member's registration date is a poor choice for locating the member because members will inevitably forget the exact date they registered. The administrator needs to know some unique but obvious information in order to display the member's record. The obvious criteria is the member's first and last names; therefore, that is what we will use.

Figure 4-6 shows the Search form.

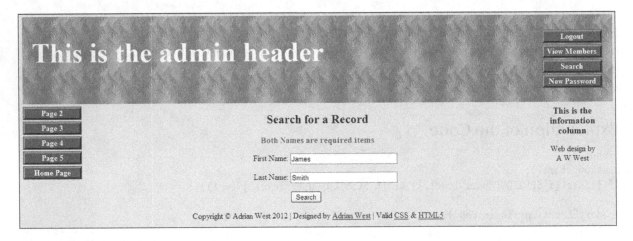

Figure 4-6. *The search form*

The search form enables the administrator to search for a particular record. If the search is successful, the *view_found_record.php* page is activated and a record (or records) will be displayed. If several people have the same first and last names, the table will display all of them.

Don't try entering a search just yet. Currently, we have set (hard coded) the *view_found_record.php* page to always show James Smith's records. This temporary page will be changed by means of the search form described in Listing 4-6. To avoid cluttering the code and to demonstrate the basic principle, the search form is extremely simple because it contains no error traps. Errors are reported in a rather primitive manner in the *view_found_record.php* page.

Listing 4-6. Creating the Search Form (search.php)

```php
<?php                                                                          #1
session_start();
if (!isset($_SESSION['user_level']) or ($_SESSION['user_level'] != 1))
{
header("Location: login.php");
exit();
}
?>
```

```
<!doctype html>
<html lang=en>
<head>
<title>Search page</title>
<meta charset=utf-8>
<link rel="stylesheet" type="text/css" href="includes.css">
<style type="text/css">
h3.red { color:red; font-size:105%; font-weight:bold; text-align:center;}
</style>
</head>
<body>
<div id="container">
<?php include("header-admin.php"); ?>
<?php include("nav.php"); ?>
<?php include("info-col.php"); ?>
<div id="content"><!--Start of search page content-->
<h2>Search for a Record</h2>
<h3 class="red">Both Names are required items</h3>
<form action="view_found_record.php" method="post">                                    #2

<p><label class="label" for="fname">First Name:</label>
<input id="fname" type="text" name="fname" size="30" maxlength="30" ⏎
value="<?php if (isset($_POST['fname'])) echo $_POST['fname']; ?>"></p>

<p><label class="label" for="lname">Last Name:</label>
<input id="lname" type="text" name="lname" size="30" maxlength="40" ⏎
value="<?php if (isset($_POST['lname'])) echo $_POST['lname']; ?>"></p>

<p><input id="submit" type="submit" name="submit" value="Search"></p>
</form>
<?php include ('footer.php'); ?>
<!--End of the search page content-->
</div>
</div>
</body>
</html>
```

Explanation of the Code

```
<?php                                                                                #1
session_start();
if (!isset($_SESSION['user_level']) or ($_SESSION['user_level'] != 1))
{
header("Location: login.php");
exit();
}
?>
```

The session is our security guard; unauthorized people will be redirected to the login page.

```
<form action="view_found_record.php" method="post">                          #2

<p><label class="label" for="fname">First Name:</label>
<input id="fname" type="text" name="fname" size="30" maxlength="30" ↵
value="<?php if (isset($_POST['fname'])) echo $_POST['fname']; ?>"></p>

<p><label class="label" for="lname">Last Name:</label>
<input id="lname" type="text" name="lname" size="30" maxlength="40"
value="<?php if (isset($_POST['lname'])) echo $_POST['lname']; ?>"></p>

<p><input id="submit" type="submit" name="submit" value="Search"></p>
</form>
```

The form posts the data to a final version of the form handler named *view_found_record.php*, which processes the search. The code supplies a *sticky form*. A sticky form is one that retains the user's entries when an error is flagged. Users can become very annoyed if they have to fill out the entire form each time they need to correct an error such as failing to fill out one field. The sticky component is the code following the value, for example:

```
value="<?php if (isset($_POST['fname'])) echo $_POST['fname']; ?>"></p>
```

We will now make the form handler *view_found_record.php* more versatile.

The Final Form Handler for Receiving Search Form Input

The code in bold type shows what has been added or modified in the first part of the code. These items enable the file to receive the first name and the last name sent from the *search.php* page. In Listing 4-6, the first and last names are assigned to variables and these variables are used to search the database so that they can be verified. The variables are then used to display the record(s).

Here's a partial listing for a snippet of code to eliminate the hard-coding and allow searches for any registered member's record:

```
<?php                                                                        #1
session_start();
if (!isset($_SESSION['user_level']) or ($_SESSION['user_level'] != 1))
{
header("Location: login.php");
exit();
}
?>
<!doctype html>
<html lang=en>
<head>
<title>View found record page</title>
<meta charset=utf-8>
<link rel="stylesheet" type="text/css" href="includes.css">
<style type="text/css">
p { text-align:center; }
</style>
</head>
<body>
```

```
<div id="container">
<?php include("header-admin.php"); ?>
<?php include("nav.php"); ?>
<?php include("info-col.php"); ?>
<div id="content"><!-- Start of the page-specific content. -->
<h2>Search Result</h2>
<?php
// This script retrieves records from the users table.
require ('mysqli_connect.php'); // Connect to the database
echo '<p>If no record is shown, this is because you had an incorrect or missing ↵
entry in the search form.<br>Click the back button on the browser and try again</p>';
$fname=$_POST['fname'];
$lname=$_POST['lname'];
$lname = mysqli_real_escape_string($dbcon, $lname);
//require ('mysqli_connect.php'); // Connect to the database.
$q = "SELECT lname, fname, email, DATE_FORMAT(registration_date, '%M %d, %Y') AS regdat,↵
user_id FROM users WHERE lname='$lname' AND fname='$fname' ORDER BY registration_date ASC ";
$result = @mysqli_query ($dbcon, $q); // Run the query
if ($result) { // If it ran successfully, display the record(s)
```

At last, you can test the search facility. Run XAMPP, and type the following into the address field of a browser:

http://localhost/admintable/login.php

Use the administrator's e-mail address and password to log in. The e-mail is *jsmith@outlook.com*, and the password is *dogsbody*. Then click the search button on the header menu. In the search form, try entering **Jack Smith** to see a single record displayed.

The result should be the record shown in Figure 4-7.

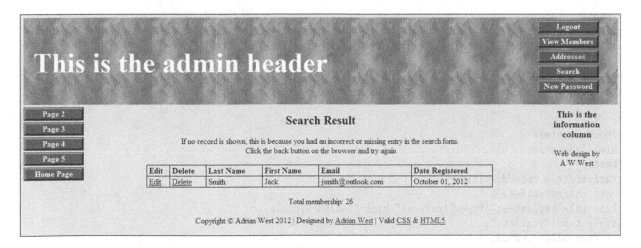

Figure 4-7. *Showing a single record selected by using the search page*

Try entering **James Smith** to see a group of records that have the same first and last names.

A sticky form is used so that when a mistake is made by the administrator, he can try again and his original entry will still be present in the search form.

Now we have reached the stage where we can demonstrate how the administrator deletes and edits the records.

Editing Records

When the administrator clicks the *Edit* link on the record displayed, he is connected to the *edit_record.php* page. The page displays the fields and the data currently held in the database table. This is illustrated in Figure 4-8.

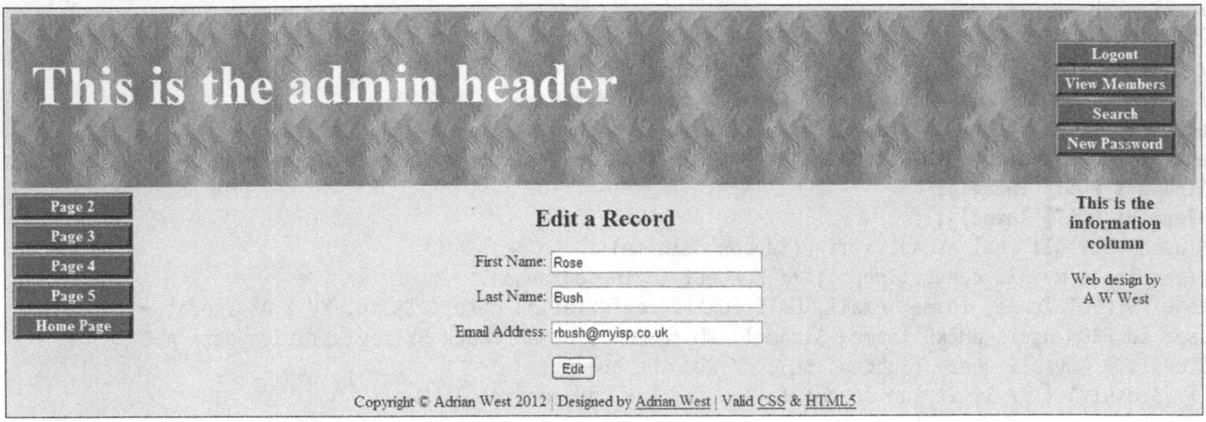

Figure 4-8. The "Edit a Record" screen showing the existing data

The administrator can amend the details and then click the Edit button to complete the editing process. The code for *edit_record.php* is shown in Listing 4-8.

Listing 4-8. Creating the Editing Interface (edit_record.php) Note that the listing starts with a session to deny access to unauthorized people:

```php
<?php
session_start();
if (!isset($_SESSION['user_level']) or ($_SESSION['user_level'] != 1))
{
header("Location: login.php");
exit();
}
?>
<!doctype html>
<html lang=en>
<head>
<title>Edit a record</title>
<meta charset=utf-8>
<link rel="stylesheet" type="text/css" href="includes.css">
<style type="text/css">
p { text-align:center; }
input.fl-left { float:left; }
#submit { float:left; }
</style>
</head>
<body>
<div id="container">
<?php include("header-admin.php"); ?>
<?php include("nav.php"); ?>
```

```php
<?php include("info-col.php"); ?>
<div id="content"><!--Start of the edit page content-->
<h2>Edit a Record</h2>
<?php
// After clicking the Edit link in the found_record.php page, the editing interface appears
// The code looks for a valid user ID, either through GET or POST                    #1
if ( (isset($_GET['id'])) && (is_numeric($_GET['id'])) ) { // From view_users.php
    $id = $_GET['id'];
} elseif ( (isset($_POST['id'])) && (is_numeric($_POST['id'])) ) { // Form submission
    $id = $_POST['id'];
} else { // If no valid ID, stop the script
    echo '<p class="error">This page has been accessed in error</p>';
    include ('footer.php');
    exit();
}
require ('mysqli_connect.php');
// Has the form been submitted?
if ($_SERVER['REQUEST_METHOD'] == 'POST') {
    $errors = array();
// Look for the first name
    if (empty($_POST['fname'])) {
        $errors[] = 'You forgot to enter the first name.';
    } else {
        $fn = mysqli_real_escape_string($dbcon, trim($_POST['fname']));
    }
    // Look for the last name
    if (empty($_POST['lname'])) {
        $errors[] = 'You forgot to enter the last name.';
    } else {
        $ln = mysqli_real_escape_string($dbcon, trim($_POST['lname']));
    }
// Look for the email address
    if (empty($_POST['email'])) {
    $errors[] = 'You forgot to enter the email address.';
    } else {
    $e = mysqli_real_escape_string($dbcon, trim($_POST['email']));
    }
if (empty($errors)) { // If everything is OK, make the update query            #2
// Check that the email is not already in the users table
$q = "UPDATE users SET fname='$fn', lname='$ln', email='$e' WHERE user_id=$id LIMIT 1";
    $result = @mysqli_query ($dbcon, $q);
    if (mysqli_affected_rows($dbcon) == 1) { // If it ran OK
// Echo a message if the edit was satisfactory
    echo '<h3>The user has been edited.</h3>';
    } else { // Echo a message if the query failed
    echo '<p class="error">The user could not be edited due to a system error. ↵
We apologize for any inconvenience.</p>'; // Error message.
    echo '<p>' . mysqli_error($dbcon) . '<br />Query: ' . $q . '</p>'; // Debugging message.
    }
    } else { // If the email address is already registered
    echo '<p class="error">The email address has already been registered.</p>';
    }
```

```
    } else { // Display the errors.
    echo '<p class="error">The following error(s) occurred:<br />';
    foreach ($errors as $msg) { // Echo each error.
    echo " - $msg<br />\n";
    }
    echo '</p><p>Please try again.</p>';

    } // End of if (empty($errors))section
} // End of the conditionals
// Select the record                                                              #3
$q = "SELECT fname, lname, email FROM users WHERE user_id=$id";
$result = @mysqli_query ($dbcon, $q);
if (mysqli_num_rows($result) == 1) { // Valid user ID, display the form.
// Get the user's information
    $row = mysqli_fetch_array ($result, MYSQLI_NUM);
// Create the form
echo '<form action="edit_record.php" method="post">

<p><label class="label" for="fname">First Name:</label>↵
<input class="fl-left" id="fname" type="text" name="fname" size="30" maxlength="30" ↵
value="' . $row[0] . '"></p>

<br><p><label class="label" for="lname">Last Name:</label>↵
<input class="fl-left" type="text" name="lname" size="30" maxlength="40" ↵
value="' . $row[1] . '"></p>

<br><p><label class="label" for="email">Email Address:</label>↵
<input class="fl-left" type="text" name="email" size="30" maxlength="50" ↵
value="' . $row[2] . '"></p>

<br><p><input id="submit" type="submit" name="submit" value="Edit"></p>
<br><input type="hidden" name="id" value="' . $id . '" />                          #4
</form>';
} else { // The record could not be validated
    echo '<p class="error">This page has been accessed in error</p>';
}
mysqli_close($dbcon);
include ('footer.php');
?>
</div>
</div>
</body>
</html>
```

Explanation of the Code

Most of the code has been explained in earlier chapters, but we will now examine some code that is new to this chapter:

```
// The code looks for a valid user ID, either through GET or POST             #1
if ( (isset($_GET['id'])) && (is_numeric($_GET['id'])) ) { // Sent from view_users.php
    $id = $_GET['id'];
} elseif ( (isset($_POST['id'])) && (is_numeric($_POST['id'])) ) {// If form submitted
```

```
    $id = $_POST['id'];
} else { // If no valid ID, stop the script
    echo '<p class="error">This page has been accessed in error.</p>';
    include ('footer.php');
    exit();
}
```

We must be sure we are editing the right record, and this is achieved by checking the id of the selected user. If the user's details were entered incorrectly or the user did not exist in the database table, an error message is shown. Note the is_numeric() function that ensures that the id is a number and therefore genuine. If the id is valid, it is assigned to the variable $id ready for the next step.

```
    if (empty($errors)) { // If everything's OK make the update query       #2
// Check that the email is not already in the users table
$q = "UPDATE users SET fname='$fn', lname='$ln', email='$e' WHERE user_id=$id LIMIT 1";
    $result = @mysqli_query ($dbcon, $q);
    if (mysqli_affected_rows($dbcon) == 1) { // If it ran OK
    // Echo a message if the edit was satisfactory
    echo '<h3>The user has been edited.</h3>';
    } else { // Echo a message if the query failed
echo '<p class="error">The user could not be edited due to a system error. ↵
We apologize for any inconvenience.</p>'; // Message
    echo '<p>' . mysqli_error($dbcon) . '<br />Query: ' . $q . '</p>';
// Debugging message
    }
```

If the error array contains no error messages, the query will run. Using the keyword UPDATE, the query updates the record in the users table for the record that has the correct user_id. Using the keyword LIMIT with the number 1 ensures that only one record is updated.

```
// Select the record                                                        #3
$q = "SELECT fname, lname, email FROM users WHERE user_id=$id";
$result = @mysqli_query ($dbcon, $q);
if (mysqli_num_rows($result) == 1) { // If valid user ID, display the form
// Get the user's information
    $row = mysqli_fetch_array ($result, MYSQLI_NUM);
// Create the form
echo '<form action="edit_record.php" method="post">

<p><label class="label" for="fname">First Name:</label>↵
<input class="fl-left" id="fname" type="text" name="fname" size="30" maxlength="30" ↵
value="' . $row[0] . '"></p>

<br><p><label class="label" for="lname">Last Name:</label>↵
<input class="fl-left" type="text" name="lname" size="30" maxlength="40" ↵
value="' . $row[1] . '"></p>

<br><p><label class="label" for="email">Email Address:</label>↵
<input class="fl-left" type="text" name="email" size="30" maxlength="50" ↵
value="' . $row[2] . '"></p>

<br><p><input id="submit" type="submit" name="submit" value="Edit"></p>
```

The form containing the selected user's data is displayed ready for editing.

```
<br><input type="hidden" name="id" value="' . $id . '" />           #4
</form>';
} else { // The record could not be validated
        echo '<p class="error">This page has been accessed in error.</p>';
}
mysqli_close($dbcon);
include ('footer.php');
?>
```

The type *hidden* (shown in bold in the preceding code) ensures that no field for the *user_id* is displayed in the form. Any item that is automatically added by the database, such as the user's id, must be hidden from the user.

Deleting Records

No special precautions were taken in the previous *Edit Record* tutorial to prevent the administrator from editing the wrong record by mistake; this was because a mistake could be easily corrected. However, if the administrator deletes the wrong record, he cannot undo the delete; therefore, he must be given another chance to check whether he is deleting the correct record. When the administrator clicks the *Delete* link on a displayed record, he is connected to the *delete_record.php* page. The *Delete a Record* screen displays the name of the person the administrator is about to delete. The administrator can then click either the Yes button or the No button, as shown in Figure 4-9.

Figure 4-9. *The screen for deleting a record*

The page displays the name of the member to be deleted and gives the administrator the chance to change his mind. Before we describe the listing for the delete page, a few more names are suggested in Table 4-6. Register them so that you can try deleting them.

Table 4-6. *Some Names You Can Register and Then Try Deleting*

First Name	Last Name	E-mail	Password
Phyllis	Tine	ptine@myisp.co.uk	vulgarian
Des	Cant	dcant@myisp.com	polyphonic
Bill	Board	bboard@myisp.net	hoarding
Eva	Nescent	enescent@myisp.de	fleeting

In the next step, we will create a page for the administrator so that he can safely delete records. (See Listing 4-9.)

Listing 4-9. Creating a Page for Deleting Records (delete_record.php)

The page is protected from unauthorized people by means of a session.

```php
<?php
session_start();
if (!isset($_SESSION['user_level']) or ($_SESSION['user_level'] != 1))
{
header("Location: login.php");
exit();
}
?>
<!doctype html>
<html lang=en>
<head>
<title>Delete a record</title>
<meta charset=utf-8>
<link rel="stylesheet" type="text/css" href="includes.css">
<style type="text/css">
p { text-align:center; }
form { text-align:center; }
input.fl-left { float:left; }
#submit-yes { float:left; margin-left:220px; }
#submit-no { float:left; margin-left:20px; }
</style>
</head>
<body>
<div id="container">
<?php include("header-admin.php"); ?>
<?php include("nav.php"); ?>
<?php include("info-col.php"); ?>
<div id="content"><!--Start of content for delete page-->
<h2>Delete a Record</h2>
<?php
// Check for a valid user ID, through GET or POST
if ( (isset($_GET['id'])) && (is_numeric($_GET['id'])) ) { //Details from view_users.php
    $id = $_GET['id'];
} elseif ( (isset($_POST['id'])) && (is_numeric($_POST['id'])) ) { // Form submission      #1
    $id = $_POST['id'];
   } else { // If no valid ID, stop the script
    echo '<p class="error">This page has been accessed in error.</p>';
    include ('footer.php');
    exit();
}
require ('mysqli_connect.php');
// Has the form been submitted?                                                              #2
if ($_SERVER['REQUEST_METHOD'] == 'POST') {
if ($_POST['sure'] == 'Yes') { // Delete the record
    // Make the query
    $q = "DELETE FROM users WHERE user_id=$id LIMIT 1";
    $result = @mysqli_query ($dbcon , $q);
```

```php
    if (mysqli_affected_rows($dbcon ) == 1) { // If there was no problem
// Display a message
        echo '<h3>The record has been deleted.</h3>';
        } else { // If the query failed to run
echo '<p class="error">The record could not be deleted.<br>Probably ↵
because it does not exist or due to a system error.</p>'; // Display error message
echo '<p>' . mysqli_error($dbcon ) . '<br />Query: ' . $q . '</p>';
// Debugging message
    }
    } else { // Confirmation that the record was not deleted
    echo '<h3>The user has NOT been deleted.</h3>';
    }
    } else { // Display the form
// Retrieve the member's data                                            #3
    $q = "SELECT CONCAT(fname, ' ', lname) FROM users WHERE user_id=$id";
    $result = @mysqli_query ($dbcon , $q);
    if (mysqli_num_rows($result) == 1) { // Valid user ID, show the form
// Get the member's data
    $row = mysqli_fetch_array ($result, MYSQLI_NUM);
// Display the name of the member being deleted
    echo "<h3>Are you sure you want to permanently delete $row[0]?</h3>";
// Display the delete page
...echo '<form action="delete_record.php" method="post">               #4
    <input id="submit-yes" type="submit" name="sure" value="Yes">
    <input id="submit-no" type="submit" name="sure" value="No">
    <input type="hidden" name="id" value="' . $id . '">
    </form>';
    } else { // Not a valid member's ID
    echo '<p class="error">This page has been accessed in error.</p>';
    echo '<p> </p>';
    }
} // End of the main conditional section
mysqli_close($dbcon );
    echo '<p> </p>';
include ('footer.php');
?>
</div>
</div>
</body>
</html>
```

Explanation of the Code

```php
elseif ( (isset($_POST['id'])) && (is_numeric($_POST['id'])) ) { // Form submission    #1
    $id = $_POST['id'];
```

If the administrator's id is available and it is numeric, assign it to the variable $id.

```php
// Has the form been submitted?                                         #2
if ($_SERVER['REQUEST_METHOD'] == 'POST') {
if ($_POST['sure'] == 'Yes') { // Delete the record
```

```
// Make the query
    $q = "DELETE FROM users WHERE user_id=$id LIMIT 1";
    $result = @mysqli_query ($dbcon , $q);
    if (mysqli_affected_rows($dbcon ) == 1) { // If there was no problem
// Echo a message
    echo '<h3>The record has been deleted.</h3>';
}
```

A check is made to see if the YES button has been clicked. If it has, the SQL code for deleting a record is run; if it is successful, a message is displayed.

```
// Display the delete page
// Retrieve the member's data                                              #3
    $q = "SELECT CONCAT(fname, ' ', lname) FROM users WHERE user_id=$id";
    $result = @mysqli_query ($dbcon , $q);
    if (mysqli_num_rows($result) == 1) { // Valid user ID, show the form
// Get the member's data
    $row = mysqli_fetch_array ($result, MYSQLI_NUM);
// Display the name of the member being deleted
    echo "<h3>Are you sure you want to permanently delete $row[0]?</h3>";
```

This code displays the "deleted" page. The member's details are retrieved and used to show a message that asks the administrator if he really wants to delete the record.

```
    echo
'<form action="delete_record.php" method="post">                           #4
    <input id="submit-yes" type="submit" name="sure" value="Yes">
    <input id="submit-no" type="submit" name="sure" value="No">
    <input type="hidden" name="id" value="' . $id . '">
    </form>';
```

The Yes and No buttons are displayed. They are positioned by means of the internal CSS style in the <head> section of the file. A reasonable space (a margin) is created between the buttons to avoid mistakenly clicking the wrong button. The result of clicking one of these buttons is to send the value Yes or No to the preceding block of code numbered **#2**.

Note   Only files that needed modifying have been described to save space. Many PHP files for this chapter have not been mentioned because they are exactly the same as the files in Chapter 3. The downloaded files for Chapter 4 can be viewed to see the code for all the files.

Summary

In this chapter, you discovered how to create a user-friendly method of allowing an administrator to amend the contents of a database. This included the ability to paginate the whole table of members. A search form was described, and this can be used for selecting specific members so that their record can be amended or deleted. Code was provided that allowed the administrator to edit and delete records. In the next chapter. we will explore a database with a few extra features. For instance, we will include the user's title and require the user's postal address and telephone number. Additional validation and security devices will also be introduced. More redundant buttons will be purged from the headers.

CHAPTER 5

■ ■ ■

Register Addresses and Phone Numbers

The tutorials in this chapter assume that web site users are applying for membership in an organization that requires a membership fee—for instance, a political party or a conservation society.

Web site databases for such organizations usually require the postal addresses and telephone numbers of their members. Some registration forms have pull-down menus that allow the user to choose a class of membership.

When a registration form has many fields, some will be required fields and some will be optional. This chapter deals with a larger registration form than the previous chapters, and two of the fields are optional. This chapter contains the following sections:

- Create a new database and a table with 17 columns

- The importance of documentation

- Create an extended registration form with a pull-down menu

- Add a PayPal debit/credit card image

- Include PayPal on the "Thank You" page

- Amend the header for the administrator's page

- Apply pagination to the View_Users table

- Searching and editing records

- Search for a member's address and phone number

The first step is to create a new database.

Create a New Database and a Table with 17 Columns

Follow these steps to create a new database and a multi-column table:

1. Open the XAMPP *htdocs* folder, and create a new folder named *postal*

2. Download the files for Chapter 5 from the book's web site at www.apress.com, and place the files in *htdocs* in the new folder called *postal*.

3. Then use a browser to access phpMyAdmin, click the *Databases* tab, and create a new database called *postaldb*.

4. Scroll down, find the newly created database, and select the box alongside it.

5. Click *Check Privileges*, click *Add User*, and add a new user and password as follows:

   User name: jenner, **Host:** Local Host, and **Password:** vaccination.
   Scroll down and click *Check All*, which is next to the *Global Privileges*.

6. At the bottom right of the window, leave *Resources limits* as the default—that is, all zeros.

7. Scroll to the bottom, and click *Add User* (or on some versions, click *Go*) to save the user's details.

8. In the left panel of phpMyAdmin, click your new database *postaldb* and then create a new table with the name *users*. Choose 17 columns and then click the *Go* button.

Create the File for Connecting to the Database

Name the following file *mysqli_connect.php*, and add it to the *postal* folder in the *htdocs* folder:

```php
<?php
// Create a connection to the postaldb database and to MySQL
// Set the encoding to utf-8
// Set the database access details as constants
DEFINE ('DB_USER', 'jenner');
DEFINE ('DB_PASSWORD', 'vaccination');
DEFINE ('DB_HOST', 'localhost');
DEFINE ('DB_NAME', 'postaldb');
// Make the connection
$dbcon = @mysqli_connect (DB_HOST, DB_USER, DB_PASSWORD, DB_NAME) ↵
OR die ('Could not connect to MySQL: ' . mysqli_connect_error() );
// Set the encoding
mysqli_set_charset($dbcon, 'utf8');
```

Now create the table with columns and attributes as described in the next section.

Create the Table

We will create a table suitable for a membership database that requires postal addresses and telephone numbers. The database table will also include extra items for the benefit of the administrator. These are class of membership and a field to indicate whether members have paid their subscription fee. The table will have columns with the titles and attributes shown in Table 5-1.

Table 5-1. *The titles and attributes for the users table*

Column name	Type	Length Values	Default	Attributes	NULL	Index	A_I
user_id	MEDIUMINT	6	None	UNSIGNED	☐	PRIMARY	☑
title	TINYTEXT	10	None		☐		☐
fname	VARCHAR	30	None		☐		☐
lname	VARCHAR	40	None		☐		☐
email	VARCHAR	50	None		☐		☐
psword	CHAR	40	None		☐		☐
uname	CHAR	15	None		☐		☐
registration_date	DATETIME		None		☐		☐
class	CHAR	20	None		☐		☐
user_level	TINYINT	2	None	UNSIGNED	☐		☐
addr1	VARCHAR	50	None		☐		☐
addr2	VARCHAR	50	None		☑		☐
city	VARCHAR	50	None		☐		☐
county	CHAR	25	None		☐		☐
pcode	CHAR	10	None		☐		☐
phone	CHAR	15	None		☑		☐
paid	ENUM	'No', 'Yes'	None		☐		☐

Note that the *addr2* (the second address) and *phone* columns have their NULL boxes selected. This is because they will be optional fields. NULL simply means that a field can be left empty by the user. Many users might not have an additional address (such as a district in a very large town). Some users are ex-directory and do not wish to disclose their telephone numbers in order to reduce the nuisance created by cold-callers.

In the USA, you would naturally change *county* to *state*. In the UK, you could omit *county* because the Royal Mail relies entirely on postal codes for sorting mail.

Using ENUM

ENUM ensures that only those values that you specify can be stored in that cell in the table. The values might be *M* and *F* (male and female) or, as in our tutorial, *No* and *Yes*. The administrator can enter a lowercase *no* or *yes* in the *paid* column and the ENUM will change the case to *No* and *Yes*. ENUM need not be limited to two values—many more can be specified . The choices must be separated by commas, and each must be surrounded by single or double quotes. If you choose NOT NULL for the *paid* column, the first value (*No*) will be the default. If you select the NULL box for an ENUM column, an empty field will also be a valid value.

The Importance of Documentation

Because the database is becoming increasingly complex, it is imperative that you continue to record everything that you do. If you don't, you will spend many unhappy hours wondering what you did and why certain changes won't work. This is especially true with a large number of pages, as in the current project. I keep careful records in a notebook, and I create a flow chart; in fact, I cannot work without a flow chart. Charts often extend over several A4 pages. I print these and paste them together.

My charts show all the pages, page titles, headers, and links between the pages. As the work progresses, I amend the flow chart by correcting faults, adding pages and adding any new features required by the client. Amending the chart as you develop a database-driven web site is vital, and you neglect this at your peril. A flow chart is particularly valuable when working in a team and when troubleshooting during development of the database. Figure 5-1 shows a small section of one of my flow charts.

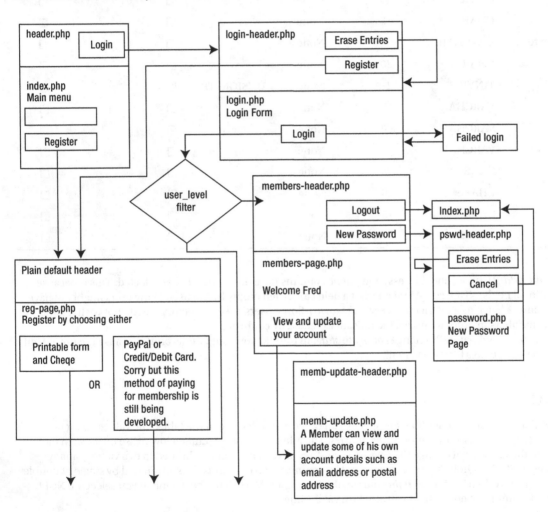

Figure 5-1. *A small section of a flow chart*

Commercial programs are available for creating flow charts, but I use the drawing toolbar and text boxes in Microsoft Word. The diamond-shaped text box denotes a switch. The switch in the flow chart shown in Figure 5-1 is a filter that detects a member's *user_level* and switches him either to the member's page or to the administrator's page. Changing the shape of a text box from a rectangle to a diamond is possible in all versions of Word. Type a question in a search engine to determine how to achieve this in your own version of Word. Visio is an expensive alternative; for an excellent free program, try Diagram Designer from the following web site:

http://meesoft.logicnet.dk/

Next, we will create a registration page based on the page used in the previous tutorials, but it will be extended to contain many extra fields. The page will also demonstrate a pull-down selection menu. The registration page will display14 of the 17 fields; the other three fields will be hidden from the user. An internal style will be used because some aspects of the form style will be required only for the form.

Extend the Registration Form, and Add a Pull-down Menu

The extended registration page is shown in Figure 5-2.

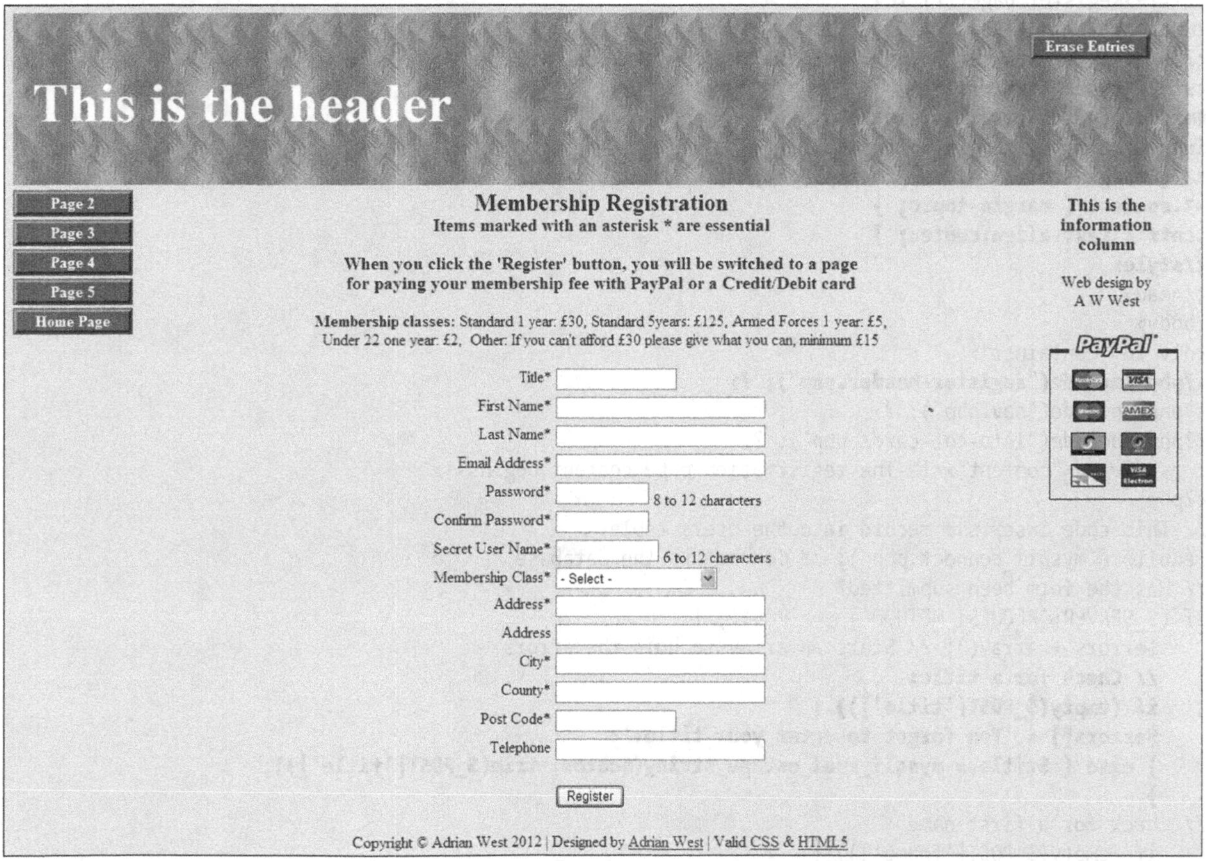

Figure 5-2. *The extended registration page*

When the fields are filled out correctly and the Register button is clicked, the user will be taken to a *Thank you* page containing a PayPal payment button and logo. The user can pay the appropriate registration fee by PayPal or by debit/credit card.

Always Announce Prices and Fee Payments Up Front

Always declare up front the full cost and the available payment methods. This is now a legal requirement in the UK. In other parts of the world, this might not be a legal requirement, but you should always declare all costs in advance. Users become very irritated if extra costs are suddenly announced at the end of a transaction. They will usually close your web site without paying. As well as stating the cost, we will add an image supplied by PayPal showing the various acceptable credit cards. However, users will not be able to pay until they submit the registration form and the *Thank You* page appears.

The registration page now contains 14 visible fields and three hidden fields. The hidden fields are *user_id*, *registration_date*, and *paid*. Hidden fields are not visible on the page that is displayed on the user's screen because they are relevant only to the administrator. The page will also contain a pull-down menu. The new fields and the new internal styling are shown in bold type in Listing 5-2.

Listing 5-2. Creating the New Registration Page with 14 Visible Fields (register-page.php)

```php
<!doctype html>
<html lang=en>
<head>
<title>Register page</title>
<meta charset=utf-8>
<link rel="stylesheet" type="text/css" href="includes.css">
<style type="text/css">                                          #1
#midcol { width:98%; margin:auto; }
input, select { margin-bottom:5px; }
h2 { margin-bottom:0; margin-top:5px};
h3.content { margin-top:0; }
.cntr { text-align:center; }
</style>
</head>
<body>
<div id="container">
<?php include("register-header.php"); ?>
<?php include("nav.php"); ?>
<?php include("info-col-cards.php"); ?>
    <div id="content"><!--The registration page content begins-->
<?php
// This code inserts a record into the users table
require ('mysqli_connect.php'); // Connect to the database
// Has the form been submitted?
if ($_SERVER['REQUEST_METHOD'] == 'POST') {
    $errors = array(); // Start an array to hold the errors
    // Check for a title:
    if (empty($_POST['title'])) {
    $errors[] = 'You forgot to enter your title.';
    } else { $title = mysqli_real_escape_string($dbcon, trim($_POST['title'])); }
    }
// Check for a first name
    if (empty($_POST['fname'])) {
        $errors[] = 'You forgot to enter your first name.';
    } else { $fn = mysqli_real_escape_string($dbcon, trim($_POST['fname'])); }
    }
// Check for a last name
    if (empty($_POST['lname'])) {
```

```
            $errors[] = 'You forgot to enter your last name.';
        } else { $ln = mysqli_real_escape_string($dbcon, trim($_POST['lname'])); 
        }
// Check for an email address
    if (empty($_POST['email'])) {
        $errors[] = 'You forgot to enter your email address.';
    } else {
        $e = mysqli_real_escape_string($dbcon, trim($_POST['email']));
    }
// Check for a password and match it against the confirmation password
    if (!empty($_POST['psword1'])) {
    if ($_POST['psword1'] != $_POST['psword2']) {
        $errors[] = 'Your two passwords did not match.';
    } else { $p = mysqli_real_escape_string($dbcon, trim($_POST['psword1']));
    }
    } else { $errors[] = 'You forgot to enter your password.';
    }
    if (empty($_POST['uname'])) {
        $errors[] = 'You forgot to enter your secret username.';
    } else {
    $uname = trim($_POST['uname']);
    }
// Check for a membership class
    if (empty($_POST['class'])) {
        $errors[] = 'You forgot to enter your membership class';
    } else { $class = trim($_POST['class']);
    }
// Check for address1
    if (empty($_POST['addr1'])) {
        $errors[] = 'You forgot to enter your address.';
    } else { $ad1 = mysqli_real_escape_string($dbcon, trim($_POST['addr1']));
    }
// Check for address2                                                        #2
    if (!empty($_POST['addr2'])) {
    $ad2 = mysqli_real_escape_string($dbcon, trim($_POST['addr2']));
}else{ $ad2 = NULL;
    }
    }
// Check for city
    if (empty($_POST['city'])) {
        $errors[] = 'You forgot to enter your City.';
    } else { $cty = mysqli_real_escape_string($dbcon, trim($_POST['city']));
    }
// Check for the county
    if (empty($_POST['county'])) {
        $errors[] = 'You forgot to enter your county.';
    } else { $cnty = mysqli_real_escape_string($dbcon, trim($_POST['county']));
    }
// Check for the post code
    if (empty($_POST['pcode'])) {
        $errors[] = 'You forgot to enter your post code.';
```

```php
    } else { $pcode = mysqli_real_escape_string($dbcon, trim($_POST['pcode']));
    }
// Check for the phone number
    if (!empty($_POST['phone'])) {
    $ph = mysqli_real_escape_string($dbcon, trim($_POST['phone']));
}else
$ph = NULL;
}
if (empty($errors)) { // If there were no errors
//Determine whether the email address has already been registered                    #3
$q = "SELECT user_id FROM users WHERE email = '$e' ";
$result=mysqli_query ($dbcon, $q) ;
if (mysqli_num_rows($result) == 0){//The mail address has not been registered ↵
already therefore register the user in the users table
// Make the query:
$q = "INSERT INTO users (user_id, title, fname, lname, email, psword, registration_date, ↵
uname, class, addr1, addr2, city, county, pcode, phone, paid) VALUES (' ', '$title', '$fn', ↵
'$ln', '$e', SHA1('$p'), NOW(), '$uname', '$class', '$ad1', '$ad2', '$cty', '$cnty', ↵
'$pcode', '$ph', '$pd' )";
$result = @mysqli_query ($dbcon, $q); // Run the query.
if ($result) { // If it ran OK
header ("location: register-thanks.php");
exit();
} else { // If it failed to run
// Error message:
    echo '<h2>System Error</h2>
    <p class="error">Registration failed because of a system error. We apologize ↵
for any inconvenience.</p>';
// Debugging message:
    echo '<p>' . mysqli_error($dbcon) . '<br><br>Query: ' . $q . '</p>';
    } // End of if ($result)
    mysqli_close($dbcon); // Close the database connection
// Include the footer and stop the script
    include ('footer.php');
    exit();
}else{//The email address is already registered                                        #4
echo     '<p class="error">The email address is not acceptable because it is already ↵
registered</p>';
}
    } else { // Report the errors
echo '<h2>Error!</h2>
    <p class="error">The following error(s) occurred:<br>';
    foreach ($errors as $msg) { // Print each error.
        echo " - $msg<br>\n";
    }
    echo '</p><h3>Please try again.</h3><p><br></p>';
    }// End of if (empty($errors))
} // End of the submit conditional
?>
<div id="midcol">
<h2>Membership Registration</h2>
<h3 class="content">Items marked with an asterisk * are essential</h3>
```

```
<p class="cntr"><b>Membership classes:</b> Standard 1 year: 30, Standard 5years: ↵
125, Armed Forces 1 year: 5,
<br>Under 21 one year: 2,  Other: If you can't afford 30 please give ↵
what you can, minimum 15</p>
<form action="register-page.php" method="post">
<label class="label" for="title">Title*</label>
<input id="title" type="text" name="title" size="15" maxlength="12" ↵
value="<?php if (isset($_POST['title'])) echo $_POST['title']; ?>">

<br><label class="label" for="fname">First Name*</label>É
<input id="fname" type="text" name="fname" size="30" maxlength="30" ↵
value="<?php if (isset($_POST['fname'])) echo $_POST['fname']; ?>">

<br><label class="label" for="lname">Last Name*</label>É
input id="lname" type="text" name="lname" size="30" maxlength="40" ↵
value="<?php if (isset($_POST['lname'])) echo $_POST['lname']; ?>">

<br><label class="label" for="email">Email Address*</label>É
<input id="email" type="text" name="email" size="30" maxlength="60" ↵
value="<?php if (isset($_POST['email'])) echo $_POST['email']; ?>" >

<br><label class="label" for="psword1">Password*</label>É
<input id="psword1" type="password" name="psword1" size="12" maxlength="12" ↵
value="<?php if (isset($_POST['psword1'])) echo $_POST['psword1']; ?>" >↵
 8 to 12 characters

<br><label class="label" for="psword2">Confirm Password*</label>É
<input id="psword2" type="password" name="psword2" size="12" maxlength="12" ↵
value="<?php if (isset($_POST['psword2'])) echo $_POST['psword2']; ?>" >
<!--The pull-down menu-->
<br><label class="label" for="class">Membership Class*</label>                      #5
<select name="class">
<option value="">- Select -</option>
<option value="30"<?php if (isset($_POST['class']) AND ($_POST['class'] == '30'))
echo ' selected="selected"'; ?>>Standard 1 year 30</option>
<option value="125"<?php if (isset($_POST['class']) AND ($_POST['class'] == '125'))
echo ' selected="selected"'; ?>>Standard 5 years 125</option>
<option value="5"<?php if (isset($_POST['class']) AND ($_POST['class'] == '5'))
echo ' selected="selected"'; ?>>Armed Forces 1 year 5</option>
<option value="2"<?php if (isset($_POST['class']) AND ($_POST['class'] == '2'))
echo ' selected="selected"'; ?>>Under 22 1 year 2**</option>
<option value="15"<?php if (isset($_POST['class']) AND ($_POST['class'] == '15'))
echo ' selected="selected"'; ?>>Minimum 1 year 15</option>
</select

<br><label class="label" for="addr1">Address*</label> ↵
<input id="addr1" type="text" name="addr1" size="30" maxlength="30" ↵
value="<?php if (isset($_POST['addr1'])) echo $_POST['addr1']; ?>">

<br><label class="label" for="addr2">Address</label>É
<input id="addr2" type="text" name="addr2" size="30" maxlength="30" ↵
value="<?php if (isset($_POST['addr2'])) echo $_POST['addr2']; ?>">
```

```
<br><label class="label" for="city">City*</label>É
<input id="city" type="text" name="city" size="30" maxlength="30" ↵
value="<?php if (isset($_POST['city'])) echo $_POST['city']; ?>">

<br><label class="label" for="county">County*</label>É
<input id="county" type="text" name="county" size="30" maxlength="30" ↵
value="<?php if (isset($_POST['county'])) echo $_POST['county']; ?>">

<br><label class="label" for="pcode">Post Code*</label>É
<input id="pcode" type="text" name="pcode" size="15" maxlength="15" ↵
value="<?php if (isset($_POST['pcode'])) echo $_POST['pcode']; ?>">

<br><label class="label" for="phone">Telephone</label>
<input id="phone" type="text" name="phone" size="30" maxlength="30" ↵
value="<?php if (isset($_POST['phone'])) echo $_POST['phone']; ?>">
<p><input id="submit" type="submit" name="submit" value="Register"></p>
</form>
</div>
</div>
</div>
<?php include ('footer.php'); ?>
<!-- End of the page content -->
</body>
</html>
```

Explanation of the Code

```
<style type="text/css">                                              #1
input, select { margin-bottom:5px; }
h2 { margin-bottom:0; }
h3.content { margin-top:0; }
.cntr { text-align:center; }
</style>
```

The internal styling differs slightly from the main style to ensure that the subheadings are centered. These styles overwrite the main style.

```
// Check for address2                                                 #2
    if (!empty($_POST['addr2'])) {
    $ad2 = mysqli_real_escape_string($dbcon, trim($_POST['addr2']));
}else{ $ad2 = NULL;
    }
```

You will not have seen this pattern before. The second address field is not a required field. On the form displayed, it has no asterisk because it can be deliberately left empty by the user. In the code, the exclamation mark in front of the word *empty* is important, The expression *!empty* means "not empty." However, if the user entered a second address, that address is assigned to the variable $ad2. If the field is empty, no error message is generated and the key word NULL has been assigned to the variable $ad2. NULL means that the field can be left empty without generating an error message. If the registration form field for *addr2* is empty, the *addr2* cell in the database table will be empty. Examine the rest of the code and see if you can find the same pattern being used for another optional field.

```
//Determine whether the email address has already been registered          #3
$q = "SELECT user_id FROM users WHERE email = '$e' ";
$result=mysqli_query ($dbcon, $q) ;
if (mysqli_num_rows($result) == 0){//The mail address has not been registered ⤶
already therefore register the user in the users table
```

The code checks whether the e-mail address is already in the database table. If it is not, the user is registered.

```
}else{//The email address is already registered                            #4
echo    '<p class="error">The email address is not acceptable because it is already ⤶
registered</p>';
}
```

This concludes the statement begun in line **#3**. If the e-mail address is already present in the database table, this else statement pauses the script and displays an error message. Duplicate e-mail addresses are not acceptable. This raises another problem: suppose a husband and wife both wish to register, and they share an e-mail address. This is best dealt with by having a membership class for a couple or even a family.

```
<br><label class="label" for="class">Membership Class*</label>              #5
<select name="class">
<option value="">- Select -</option>
<option value="30"<?php if (isset($_POST['class']) AND ($_POST['class'] == '30'))
echo ' selected="selected"'; ?>>Standard 1 year 30</option>
<option value="125"<?php if (isset($_POST['class']) AND ($_POST['class'] == '125'))
echo ' selected="selected"'; ?>>Standard 5 years 125</option>
<option value="5"<?php if (isset($_POST['class']) AND ($_POST['class'] == '5'))
echo ' selected="selected"'; ?>>Armed Forces 1 year 5</option>
<option value="2"<?php if (isset($_POST['class']) AND ($_POST['class'] == '2'))
echo ' selected="selected"'; ?>>Under 22 1 year 2**</option>
<option value="15"<?php if (isset($_POST['class']) AND ($_POST['class'] == '15'))
echo ' selected="selected"'; ?>>Minimum 1 year 15</option>
</select
```

The code uses the echo function to produce a sticky field for the pull-down menu, as shown in Figure 5-3.

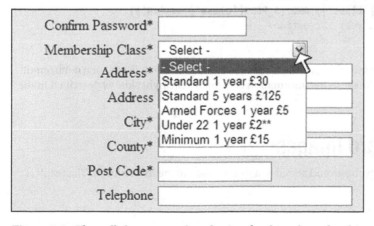

Figure 5-3. *The pull-down menu for selecting the class of membership*

If the user fails to choose one of the options, an error message is generated and inserted into the $errors array. The field containing the text - *Select* - is the same as an empty field because it has an empty variable value assigned to it. As a result, it generates an error message saying the user forgot to enter a membership class.

Sticky Fields for a Pull-down Menu

The pull-down menu in the register page detailed in Listing 5-1 had sticky field codes. A simple pull-down menu is unable to retain the entry for the class of membership. The non-sticky code is as follows:

```
<br><label class="label" for="class">Membership Class*</label>
<select name="class">
<option value="">- Select -</option>
<option value="30">Standard 1 year 30</option>
<option value="125">Standard 5 years 125</option>
<option value="5">Armed Forces 1 year 5</option>
<option value="2">Under 22 1 year 2**</option>
<option value="15">Minimum 1 year 15</option>
</select>
```

The code can be made sticky using the amendments shown in bold type in the next snippet. This snippet is not available separately in the downloadable files.

Code Snippet for a Sticky Pull-down Menu

```
<br><label class="label" for="class">Membership Class*</label>
<select name="class">
    <option value="">- Select -</option>
<option value="30"<?php if (isset($_POST['class']) AND ($_POST['class'] == '30'))
echo ' selected="selected"'; ?>>Standard 1 year 30</option>
<option value="125"<?php if (isset($_POST['class']) AND ($_POST['class'] == '125'))
echo ' selected="selected"'; ?>>Standard 5 years 125</option>
<option value="5"<?php if (isset($_POST['class']) AND ($_POST['class'] == '5'))
echo ' selected="selected"'; ?>>Armed Forces 1 year 5</option>
<option value="2"<?php if (isset($_POST['class']) AND ($_POST['class'] == '2'))
echo ' selected="selected"'; ?>>Under 22 1 year 2**</option>
<option value="15"<?php if (isset($_POST['class']) AND ($_POST['class'] == '15'))
echo ' selected="selected"'; ?>>Minimum 1 year 15</option>
</select
```

The extended registration page informs the user that membership fees can be paid using PayPal or a debit/credit card. This is achieved pictorially using a PayPal image in the information column on the right side, as described in the next section.

Add PayPal Debit/Credit Card Images

The image can be downloaded from the PayPal web site and added to a new version of the info column. The result is shown in Figure 5-4.

Figure 5-4. *The revised info column*

Listing 5-2 is the code for the new info column.

Listing 5-2. Create the Info Column with PayPal Image (info-col-cards.php)

```
<div id="info-col">
<h3>This is the information column</h3>
<p>Web design by <br>A W West</p>
<img alt="Pay by PayPal or Credit card" title="Pay by PayPal ↵
or Credit card" src="images/vertical_solution_PP.png">
</div>
```

The new *info-col-cards.php* file will be included only in the registration page and *Thank You* page. All the other pages have no need for this information; therefore, they will include the original *info-col.php*.

The Header for the Registration Page

The header for the registration page has only one menu button. The code is given in the next snippet.

The Snippet of Code for Creating the Header for the Registration Page (register-header.php)

```
<div id="header">
<h1>This is the header</h1>
<div id="reg-navigation">
```

```
    <ul>
    <li><a href="register-page.php">Erase Entries</a></li>
    </ul>
</div>
</div>
```

The "Thank You" page includes a PayPal button for paying the membership fee. This will now be described.

Include PayPal on the *Thank You* Page

A payment method will now be added to the *Thank You* page. This is shown in Figure 5-5.

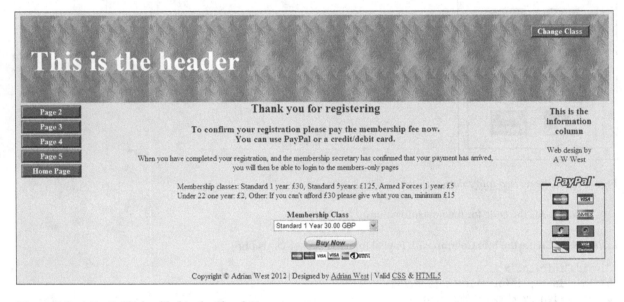

Figure 5-5. *A PayPal link added to the Thank You page*

The *Thank You* page from the previous chapter forms the basis of the new page. The user's membership application will be recorded in the database, but the *Paid* cell will contain the default value *No*. This is because the *Paid* item is an ENUM hidden from the user. The administrator is the only person allowed to enter data in that field. The administrator will change the *Paid* cell to *Yes* when he receives an e-mail from PayPal confirming the payment. The PayPal e-mail also provides the new member's postal address and e-mail address. If the administrator is satisfied that the details match the information that the user entered in the database, he will amend the member's record.

We are using PayPal in the *Thank You* page because it is the most popular payment system and it is free. A web site owner can sign up at the *paypal.com* page (or *paypal.co.uk* page), and she will be given a merchant ID and the option to generate and copy a snippet of code to embed the payment link in her page. If the owner already has a PayPal account, she can log in and then go to My Profile and My Business Info, where she can find her Merchant Account ID. That ID will enable her to access the appropriate page to generate the code to embed in her page. Listing 5-5a presents the code for the *Thank You* page.

Listing 5-5a. Creating a Combined Thank You and PayPal Payment Page (register-thanks.php)

```
<!doctype html>
<html lang=en>
<head>
<title>Registration thank-you page</title>
<meta charset=utf-8>
<link rel="stylesheet" type="text/css" href="includes.css">
<style type="text/css">
p { text-align:center; }
table, tr, td, form { margin:auto; width:180px; text-align:center; border:0; }
form input { margin:auto; }
img { border:none; }
input.fl-left { float:left; }
#submit { float:left; }
</style>
</head>
<body>
<div id="container">
<?php include("header-thanks.php"); ?>
<?php include("nav.php"); ?>
<?php include("info-col-cards.php"); ?>
    <div id="content"><!-- Start of the thank you page content. -->
<div id="midcol">
<h2>Thank you for registering</h2>
<h3>To complete your registration please pay the membership fee now. ↵
<br>You can use PayPal or a credit/debit card.</h3>
<p>When you have completed your registration and the membership secretary ↵
has confirmed that your payment has arrived,<br>you will then be able to login to the ↵
members-only pages</p>
<!--Explain the cost of membership-->
<p>Membership classes: Standard 1 year: &pound;30, Standard 5years: &pound;125, ↵
Armed Forces 1 year: &pound;5<br>
Under 22 one year: &pound;2,  Other: If you can't afford &pound;30 ↵
please give what you can, minimum &pound;15
</p>
<!--Insert the code generated by PayPal-->
<form action="https://www.paypal.com/cgi-bin/webscr" method="post">              #1
<input type="hidden" name="cmd" value="_s-xclick">
<input type="hidden" name="hosted_button_id" value="XXXXXXXXXXXXX">
<table>
<tr><td><input type="hidden" name="on0" value="Membership Class"><b>Membership ↵
Class</b></td></tr>
<tr><td>
<select name="os0">
<option value="Standard 1 Year 30">Standard 1 Year 30.00 GBP</option>
    <option value="Standard 5 Year 125">Standard 5 Year 125.00 GBP</option>
    <option value="Armed Forces 1 Year ;5">Armed Forces 1 Year 5.00 GBP</option>
    <option value="Under 22 1 Year 2">Under 22 1 Year 2.00 GBP</option>
    <option value="Other 1 Year 15 Min">Other 1 Year 15.00 GBP</option>
</select>
</td></tr>
</table>
```

```
<input type="hidden" name="currency_code" value="GBP">
<input style="margin:10px 0 0 40px" type="image" ↵
src="https://www.paypalobjects.com/en_US/GB/i/btn/btn_buynowCC_LG.gif" name="submit" ↵
alt="PayPal — The safer, easier way to pay online.">
<img alt="" src="https://www.paypalobjects.com/en_GB/i/scr/pixel.gif" width="1" height="1">
</form>
</div>
<!--End of code generated by PayPal-->
</div></div>
<!-- End of the thank-you page content. -->
<?php include("footer.php"); ?>
</body>
</html>
```

Explanation of the Code

```
<!--Insert the code generated by PayPal-->
<form action="https://www.paypal.com/cgi-bin/webscr" method="post">          #1
<input type="hidden" name="cmd" value="_s-xclick">
<input type="hidden" name="hosted_button_id" value="XXXXXXXXXXXXX">
```

This is a small portion of the code generated by PayPal. For security I have used a dummy value for the PayPal ID for this tutorial. PayPal provides a 13-character ID code.

The header now has no menu buttons because until the registrant's payment is received. The registrant can only access the home page. The home page is accessible from the main menu. The header code is given in Listing 5-5b.

Listing 5-5b. The Header for the "Thank You" Page (header-thanks.php)

```
<div id="header">
<h1>This is the header</h1>
<div id="reg-navigation">
<p> </p>
<ul>
    <li><a href="register-thanks.php">Change Class</a></li>
    </ul>
</div>
</div>
```

Before we go any further, you need to register some extra members.

Register Some Members

■ **Tip** Entering the data can be tedious. To reduce the tedium in this tutorial, the addresses and telephone numbers can be identical for each entry. A set of suitable data is suggested next.

When experimenting, I use the following data in every record. This is acceptable because no searches are made using addresses and telephone numbers:

> **Address 1**: 2 The Street
>
> **Address 2**: The Village (optional and should be omitted in some records)

City: Townsville

County or State: Devon (or CA, for example, if a USA state)

Post or Zip code: EX7 9PP (or a USA zip code)

Phone: 01234 777 888 (optional, and you should omit it in some records)

Register the following members

Table 5-2. Some members' names

Title	F name	L Name	Email address	Password	Username
Mr	James	Smith	jsmith@myisp.com	blacksmith	muscleman
Mr	Jack	Smith	jsmith@outcook.com	dogsbody	wagglytail
Mr	Mike	Rosoft	miker@myisp.com	willgates	benefactor
Ms	Olive	Branch	obranch@myisp.co.uk	anoilyone	mrspopeye
Mr	Frank	Incense	incense@myisp.net	perfume	mythking
Miss	Annie	Versary	aversary@myisp.com	happyday	celebrate
Mr	Terry	Fide	tfide@myisp.de	scaredstiff	trembling
Mrs	Rose	Bush	rbush@myisp.co.uk	redblooms	pricklystems
Mrs	Annie	Mossity	amossity@myisp.org.uk	yourenemy	acrimony
Mr	Percy	Veer	pveer@myisp.com	keepgoing	doggedly
Mr	Darrel	Doo	ddoo@myisp.co.uk	satisfied	contented
Mr	Stan	Dard	sdard@myisp.net	battleflag	battleflag
Miss	Nora	Bone	nbone@myisp.com	liketerrier	strongteeth
Mr	Barry	Cade	bcade@myisp.co.uk	blockthem	mybarrier

If you later require more data to play with, some suggestions are given in Table 5-3.

Table 5-3. Some additional suggestions for registrations

Title	F name	L Name	Email address	Password	Username
Miss	Dee	Jected	djected@myisp.org.uk	gloomndoom	pessimist
Mrs	Lynn	Seed	lseed@myisp.com	paintersoil	artistic
Mr	Barry	Tone	btone@myisp.net	nicevoice	midrange
Miss	Helen	Back	hback@myisp.net	agrimsortie	neveragain
Mr	Patrick	O'Hara	pohara@myisp.org.uk	shamrock	begorrah
Miss	Dawn	Chorus	dchorus@myisp.com	trilling	songbird
Mrs	Connie	Firs	cfirs@myisp.com	pinetrees	pinecones
Miss	Eva	Nessant	enessant@outlook.com	transient	fleeting
Mr	Al	Fresco	afresco@myisp.net	freshairfood	picnicman

■ **Important**   Jack Smith will once again act as the administrator. Enter `http://localhost/phpmyadmin` in the address field of a browser, access the users table, browse, and then change Jack Smith's user_level from 0 to 1. Also, be sure to use phpMyAdmin to change the administrator's *paid* column to *Yes*. Change some other members' *paid* columns to *Yes* and some to *No*. Remember that if you can't log in to a member's account, it is probably because his *paid* column is not set to *Yes*. This is as it should be.

A Small Amendment to the Login Page

The login page (included in the downloaded files) is almost the same as the one in the previous chapter, except that we must prevent an applicant from accessing the members-only pages before the administrator has received the membership fee. The following snippet of code shows in bold type the amendment to the query:

```
$q = "SELECT user_id, fname, user_level FROM users ↵
WHERE (email='$e' AND psword=SHA1('$p') AND paid='Yes')";
```

The error message is also modified as follows:

```
echo '<p class="error">The email address and password do not match our ↵
records.<br>Perhaps your fee has not yet arrived from PayPal.<br>If you need to ↵
register, click the Register button on the header menu</p>';
```

We must now alter the administrator's pages to match the extra columns. For instance, the membership secretary (administrator) might wish to update whether the members have paid their fees or amend an address or a telephone number. For example, Miss Eva Nessant might have just married Fred Bloggs and asked for her record to be changed to Mrs. Eva Bloggs. Her address and telephone number might also change. In Chapter 7, we will lighten the administrator's workload and allow the members to update their own records.

In this chapter, a change will be made to the administration page's header to incorporate a new button. The page content for the administrator will be similar to the previous tutorials except for some additional helpful hints for the administrator.

Amend the Administrator's Header

To avoid having a mile-wide table display, the large number of columns will be split into two separate displays: one relating to membership details, and the other relating to members' addresses and telephone numbers. A new search facility is required so that the members' addresses can be displayed in their own table. This will be launched by means of a new button on the header menu labeled *Addresses*.

This, in turn, means we need a modified header that includes the *Addresses* button, as shown in Figure 5-6. Because the header is the launch pad, we will begin by listing the new header.

Figure 5-6. *The new header containing the new Addresses button*

The new addresses button is shown in bold type in Listing 5-6.

Listing 5-6. Installing a New Addresses Button in the Header (header-admin.php)

```
<div id="header-admin">
<h1>This is the admin header</h1>
<div id="reg-navigation">
    <ul>
        <li><a href="logout.php">Logout</a></li>
        <li><a href="admin_view_users.php">View Members</a></li>
        <li><a href="search.php">Search</a></li>
        <i><a href="search_addresses.php">Addresses</a></li>
        <li><a href="register-password.php">New Password</a></li>
    </ul>
</div>
</div>
```

■ **Note** The link will not work until we have produced the *search_addresses.php* page. We will do this later in the chapter.

The table displayed by the *admin_view_users.php* file needs the two extra columns *class* and *paid*.

Apply Pagination to the *admin_view_users* Table

From the administrator's point of view, the *admin_view_users* table needs to be revised to show some of the new columns. The paginated table needs to display the columns shown in Figure 5-7.

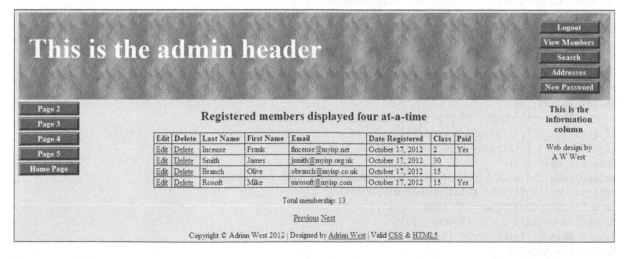

Figure 5-7. *The new table display. Note the new Class and Paid columns*

To save you the tedious task of entering a huge number of registrations, each table display has again been limited to four records. In a real-world situation, you would display about 20 to 25 rows per page. Figure 5-7 shows the table display with two extra columns.

The amendments to the code are shown in bold type in Listing 5-7. Because this is an administrator's page, we must protect it with the session details.

Listing 5-7. Creating the Paginated Table to Display Two Extra Columns (admin_view_users.php)

```php
<?php                                                                    #1
session_start();
if (!isset($_SESSION['user_level']) or ($_SESSION['user_level'] != 1))
{ header("Location: login.php");
exit();
}
?>
<!doctype html>
<html lang=en>
<head>
<title>View users page for an administrator</title>
<meta charset=utf-8>
<link rel="stylesheet" type="text/css" href="includes.css">
<style type="text/css">
p { text-align:center; }
</style>
</head>
<body>
<div id="container">
<?php include("header-admin.php"); ?>
<?php include("nav.php"); ?>
<?php include("info-col.php"); ?>
<div id="content"><!-- Start of the display page -->
<h2>Registered members are displayed four rows at-a-time</h2>
<p>
<?php
// This script retrieves all the records from the users table
require ('mysqli_connect.php'); // Connect to the database
//set the number of rows per display page
$pagerows = 4;
// Has the total number of pagess already been calculated?
if (isset($_GET['p']) && is_numeric
($_GET['p'])) {//already been calculated
$pages=$_GET['p'];
}else{//use the next block of code to calculate the number of pages
//First, check for the total number of records
$q = "SELECT COUNT(user_id) FROM users";
$result = @mysqli_query ($dbcon, $q);
$row = @mysqli_fetch_array ($result, MYSQLI_NUM);
$records = $row[0];
//Now calculate the number of pages
if ($records > $pagerows){ //if the number of records will fill more than one page
```

```
//Calculatethe number of pages and round the result up to the nearest integer
$pages = ceil ($records/$pagerows);
}else{ $pages = 1;
}
}//page check finished
//Declare which record to start with
if (isset($_GET['s']) && is_numeric
($_GET['s'])) {//already been calculated
$start = $_GET['s'];
}else{
$start = 0;
}
// Make the query                                                           #2
$q = "SELECT lname, fname, email, DATE_FORMAT(registration_date, '%M %d, %Y') ↵
É
AS regdat, class, paid, user_id FROM users ORDER BY registration_date ↵
DESC LIMIT $start, $pagerows";
$result = @mysqli_query ($dbcon, $q); // Run the query
$members = mysqli_num_rows($result);
if ($result) { // If it ran without a problem, display the records           #3
// Table header
echo '<table>
<tr><td><b>Edit</b></td>
<td><b>Delete</b></td>
<td><b>Last Name</b></td>
<td><b>First Name</b></td>
<td><b>Email</b></td>
<td><b>Date Registered</b></td>
<td><b>Class</b></td>
<td><b>Paid</b></td>
</tr>';
// Fetch and display all the records                                        #4
while ($row = mysqli_fetch_array($result, MYSQLI_ASSOC)) {
    echo '<tr>
    <td><a href="edit_record.php?id=' . $row['user_id'] . '">Edit</a></td>
    <td><a href="delete_record.php?id=' . $row['user_id'] . '">Delete</a></td>
    <td>' . $row['lname'] . '</td>
    <td>' . $row['fname'] . '</td>
    <td>' . $row['email'] . '</td>
    <td>' . $row['regdat'] . '</td>
    <td>' . $row['class'] . '</td>
    <td>' . $row['paid'] . '</td>
    </tr>';
    }
    echo '</table>'; // Close the table.
    mysqli_free_result ($result); // Free up the resources
} else { // If a problem is encountered
// Display message
echo '<p class="error">The current record could not be retrieved. ↵
We apologize for any inconvenience.</p>';
```

```php
// Debugging message
    echo '<p>' . mysqli_error($dbcon) . '<br><br>Query: ' . $q . '</p>';
} // End of if ($result).
//Now display the total number of records/members
$q = "SELECT COUNT(user_id) FROM users";
$result = @mysqli_query ($dbcon, $q);
$row = @mysqli_fetch_array ($result, MYSQLI_NUM);
$members = $row[0];
mysqli_close($dbcon); // Close the database connection
echo "<p>Total membership: $members</p>";
if ($pages > 1) {
echo '<p>';
//What number is the current page?
$current_page = ($start/$pagerows) + 1;
//If the page is not the first page then create a 'Previous' link
if ($current_page != 1) {
echo '<a href="admin_view_users.php?s=' . ($start - $pagerows) . '&p=' . $pages . '">Previous</a> ';
}
//Create a 'Next' link
if ($current_page != $pages) {
echo '<a href="admin_view_users.php?s=' . ($start + $pagerows) . '&p=' . $pages . '">↵
Next</a> ';
}
echo '</p>';
}
?>
</div><!-- End of administration page content -->
<?php include("footer.php"); ?>
</div>
</body>
</html>
```

Explanation of the Code

```php
<?php
session_start();
if (!isset($_SESSION['user_level']) or ($_SESSION['user_level'] != 1))
{
header("Location: login.php");
exit();
}
?>
```
#1

A security guard (a session) must be added to the beginning of every administration page.

```php
// Make the query
$q = "SELECT lname, fname, email, DATE_FORMAT(registration_date, '%M %d, %Y') ↵
AS regdat, class, paid, user_id FROM users ORDER BY registration_date É
DESC LIMIT $start, $pagerows";
```
#2

The two columns class and paid are added to the SELECT query. The rows are again ordered by registration date, but now they will be in descending order (DESC) because our imaginary administrator prefers to view the latest registrations at the top of the table.

```
if ($result) { // If it ran without a problem, display the records              #3
// Table header
echo '<table>
<tr><td><b>Edit</b></td>
<td><b>Delete</b></td>
<td><b>Last Name</b></td>
<td><b>First Name</b></td>
<td><b>Email</b></td>
<td><b>Date Registered</b></td>
<td><b>Class</b></td>
<td><b>Paid</b></td>
</tr>';
```

If no problem was encountered, then display the table titles including the extra two items.

```
// Fetch and display all the records                                            #4
while ($row = mysqli_fetch_array($result, MYSQLI_ASSOC)) {
    echo '<tr>
    <td><a href="edit_record.php?id=' . $row['user_id'] . '">Edit</a></td>
    <td><a href="delete_record.php?id=' . $row['user_id'] . '">Delete</a></td>
    <td>' . $row['lname'] . '</td>
    <td>' . $row['fname'] . '</td>
    <td>' . $row['email'] . '</td>
    <td>' . $row['regdat'] . '</td>
    <td>' . $row['class'] . '</td>
    <td>' . $row['paid'] . '</td>
    </tr>';
    }

    echo '</table>'; // Close the table
```

Searching and Editing Records

The search form and its code are exactly the same as those in Chapter 4; therefore, they will not be repeated here. We do, however, need to add the *Class* and *Paid* columns to the table displayed on the screen when a record is displayed using the *Search* button on the header menu.

The search result with the two new columns is shown in Figure 5-8.

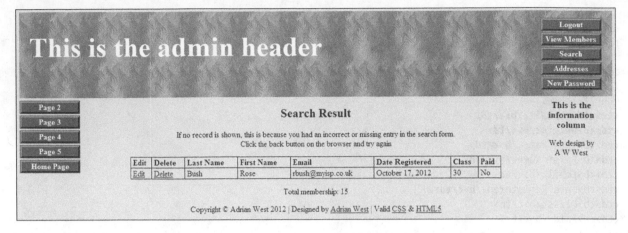

Figure 5-8. *The search result now displays a record with the two extra columns, Class and Paid*

The changes for adding the two extra columns are shown in bold type in Listing 5-8

Listing 5-8. Creating Two Extra Columns in the Table Display (view_found_record.php)

```
<?php                                                                            #1
session_start();
if (!isset($_SESSION['user_level']) or ($_SESSION['user_level'] != 1))
{
header("Location: login.php");
exit ();
}
?>
<!doctype html>
<html lang=en>
<head>
<title>View found particular record page</title>
<meta charset=utf-8>
<link rel="stylesheet" type="text/css" href="includes.css">
<style type="text/css">
p { text-align:center; }
</style>
</head>
<body>
<div id="container">
<?php include("header-admin.php"); ?>
<?php include("nav.php"); ?>
<?php include("info-col.php"); ?>
<div id="content"><!-- Start of content. -->
<h2>Search Result</h2>
<?php
// This script retrieves records from the users table
require ('mysqli_connect.php'); // Connect to the database
echo '<p>If no record is shown, this is because you had an incorrect or missing entry ⏎
in the search form.<br>Click the back button on the browser and try again</p>';
```

```php
$fname=$_POST['fname'];
$fname = mysqli_real_escape_string($dbcon, $fname);
$lname=$_POST['lname'];
$lname = mysqli_real_escape_string($dbcon, $lname);
$q = "SELECT lname, fname, email, DATE_FORMAT(registration_date, '%M %d, %Y') ↵
AS regdat, class, paid, user_id FROM users WHERE lname='$lname' AND fname='$fname ↵
ORDER BY registration_date ASC ' ";
$result = @mysqli_query ($dbcon, $q); // Run the query
if ($result) { // If it ran OK, display the record
// Table headings
echo '<table>
<tr><td><b>Edit</b></td>
<td><b>Delete</b></td>
<td><b>Last Name</b></td>
<td><b>First Name</b></td>
<td><b>Email</b></td>
<td><b>Date Registered</b></td>
<td><b>Class</b></td>
<td><b>Paid</b></td>
</tr>';
// Fetch and display the records
while ($row = mysqli_fetch_array($result, MYSQLI_ASSOC)) {
    echo '<tr>
    <td><a href="edit_record.php?id=' . $row['user_id'] . '">Edit</a></td>
    <td><a href="delete_record.php?id=' . $row['user_id'] . '">Delete</a></td>
    <td>' . $row['lname'] . '</td>
    <td>' . $row['fname'] . '</td>
    <td>' . $row['email'] . '</td>
    <td>' . $row['regdat'] . '</td>
    <td>' . $row['class'] . '</td>
    <td>' . $row['paid'] . '</td>
    </tr>';
    }
    echo '</table>'; // Close the table.
    mysqli_free_result ($result); // Free up the resources
} else { // If it did not run OK.
// Error message
echo '<p class="error">The user could not be found. We apologize ↵
for any inconvenience.</p>';
// Debugging message
    echo '<p>' . mysqli_error($dbcon) . '<br><br>Query: ' . $q . '</p>';
} // End of if ($result)
//Now display the total number of records/members
$q = "SELECT COUNT(user_id) FROM users";
$result = @mysqli_query ($dbcon, $q);
$row = @mysqli_fetch_array ($result, MYSQLI_NUM);
$members = $row[0];
mysqli_close($dbcon); // Close the database connection
echo "<p>Total membership: $members</p>";
?>
</div><!--End of view-found-record page content-->
```

```php
<?php include("footer.php"); ?>
</div>
</body>
</html>
```

Explanation of the Code

All of the code has been seen and explained before, but line **#1** is a reminder of the importance of the session for private pages.

```php
<?php                                                                    #1
session_start();
if (!isset($_SESSION['user_level']) or ($_SESSION['user_level'] != 1))
{
header("Location: login.php");
exit();
}
?>
```

The form for editing a record now needs two extra fields, and this will be described next.

Modify the Form for Editing Records

The form for editing a record will now contain two more fields, *class* and *paid*. This enables the membership secretary to view a member's chosen class of membership. He can also enter *Yes* in the paid field when the member's PayPal payment arrives. These fields are shown in Figure 5-9.

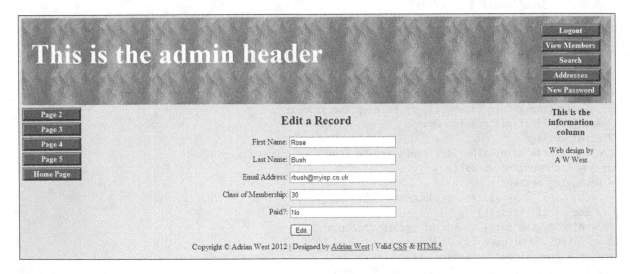

Figure 5-9. *The screen for editing a record*

All five fields can be edited by the administrator. When the Edit button is clicked, the revised data is shown, together with a message saying that the record was edited successfully. Editing an address or telephone number will be covered in Chapter 6. The code for editing a record is given in Listing 5-9

Listing 5-9. Creating an Editing Screen to Include the Two Additional Fields (edit_record.php)

```php
<?php                                                                    #1
session_start();
if (!isset($_SESSION['user_level']) or ($_SESSION['user_level'] != 1))
{
header("Location: login.php");
exit ();
}
?>
<!doctype html>
<html lang=en>
<head>
<title>Edit a record</title>
<meta charset=utf-8>
<link rel="stylesheet" type="text/css" href="includes.css">
<style type="text/css">
p { text-align:center; }
input.fl-left { float:left; }
#submit { float:left; }
</style>
</head>
<body>
<div id="container">
<?php include("header-admin.php"); ?>
<?php include("nav.php"); ?>
<?php include("info-col.php"); ?>
<div id="content"><!--Start of the edit record page-->
<h2>Edit a Record</h2>
<?php
// After clicking the Edit link in the register_found_record.php page ↵
this editing interface appears
// Look for a valid user ID, either through GET or POST
if ( (isset($_GET['id'])) && (is_numeric($_GET['id'])) ) { // From view_users.php
    $id = $_GET['id'];
} elseif ( (isset($_POST['id'])) && (is_numeric($_POST['id'])) ) { // Form submission
    $id = $_POST['id'];
} else { // No valid ID, stop the script.
    echo '<p class="error">This page has been accessed in error.</p>';
    include ('footer.php');
    exit();
}
require ('mysqli_connect.php');
// Has the form been submitted?
if ($_SERVER['REQUEST_METHOD'] == 'POST') {
    $errors = array();
    // Look for the first name
    if (empty($_POST['fname'])) {
        $errors[] = 'You forgot to enter the first name.';
    } else {
        $fn = mysqli_real_escape_string($dbcon, trim($_POST['fname']));
    }
```

151

```php
// Look for the last name
    if (empty($_POST['lname'])) {
        $errors[] = 'You forgot to enter the last name.';
    } else {
        $ln = mysqli_real_escape_string($dbcon, trim($_POST['lname']));
    }
// Look for the email address
    if (empty($_POST['email'])) {
    $errors[] = 'You forgot to enter the email address.';
    } else {
    $e = mysqli_real_escape_string($dbcon, trim($_POST['email']));
    }
// Look for the class of membership
    if (!empty($_POST['class'])) {
    $class = mysqli_real_escape_string($dbcon, trim($_POST['class']));
    }else{
    $class = NULL;
    }
// Look for the payment confirmation
    if (!empty($_POST['paid'])) {
    $paid = mysqli_real_escape_string($dbcon, trim($_POST['paid']));
    }else{
    $paid = NULL;
    }
    if (empty($errors)) { // If no problems occurred,
//determine whether the email address has already been registered for a user,
//but ignore the email address of the user being updated, he may wish to keep his
//current email address
$q = "SELECT user_id FROM users WHERE email = '$e' AND user_id != $id";
$result = @mysqli_query($dbcon, $q);
if (mysqli_num_rows($result) == 0){//The email address is not already registered or it
//belongs to the user being updated, therefore, update the users table
$q = "UPDATE users SET fname='$fn', lname='$ln', email='$e', class='$class', ↵
paid='$paid' WHERE user_id=$id LIMIT 1";
    $result = @mysqli_query ($dbcon, $q);
    if (mysqli_affected_rows($dbcon) == 1) { // If no problem was encoutered
    // Echo a message confirming that the edit was satisfactory
    echo '<h3>The user has been edited.</h3>';
    } else { // Echo a message if the query failed
        echo '<p class="error">The user was not be edited due to a system error. ↵
        We apologize for any inconvenience.</p>'; // Error message
        echo '<p>' . mysqli_error($dbcon) . '<br />Query: ' . $q . '</p>';
// Debugging message
    }
        }else{//The email address is already registered for another user
        echo '<p class="error">The email address is not acceptable because it is ↵
        already registered for another member</p>';
        }
        } else { // Display the errors
    echo '<p class="error">The following error(s) occurred:<br />';
```

```
    foreach ($errors as $msg) { // Echo each error
    echo " - $msg<br />\n";
    }
    echo '</p><p>Please try again.</p>';
    } // End of if (empty($errors))section
} // End of the conditionals
// Select the user's information
$q = "SELECT fname, lname, email, class, paid FROM users WHERE user_id=$id";
$result = @mysqli_query ($dbcon, $q);
if (mysqli_num_rows($result) == 1) { // Valid user ID, display the form.
// Get the user's information
    $row = mysqli_fetch_array ($result, MYSQLI_NUM);
// Create the form
    echo '<form action="edit_record.php" method="post">

<p><label class="label" for="fname">First Name:</label>É
<input class="fl-left" id="fname" type="text" name="fname" size="30" maxlength="30" ↵
value="' . $row[0] . '"></p>

<br><p><label class="label" for="lname">Last Name:</label>É
<input class="fl-left" type="text" name="lname" size="30" maxlength="40" ↵
value="' . $row[1] . '"></p>

<br><p><label class="label" for="email">Email Address:</label>É
<input class="fl-left" type="text" name="email" size="30" maxlength="50" ↵
value="' . $row[2] . '"></p>

<br><p><label class="label" for="class">Class of Membership:</label>É
<input class="fl-left" type="text" name="class" size="30" maxlength="50" ↵
value="' . $row[3] . '"></p>

<br><p><label class="label" for="paid">Paid?:</label>É
<input class="fl-left" type="text" name="paid" size="30" maxlength="50" ↵
value="' . $row[4] . '"></p>

<br><p><input id="submit" type="submit" name="submit" value="Edit"></p>
<br><input type="hidden" name="id" value="' . $id . '" />
</form>';
} else { // The user could not be validated
    echo '<p class="error">This page has been accessed in error.</p>';
}
mysqli_close($dbcon);
include ('footer.php');
?>
</div>
</div>
</body>
</html>
```

All the code has been seen and explained before; therefore, further explanation is unnecessary. Where anything new has been inserted, the comments within the listing give a full explanation.

Note the screen for deleting a particular record is exactly the same as in Chapter 4 and will not be repeated here to save space. However, the file *delete_record.php* is included in the downloads for Chapter 5. See this to review the code.

We need to limit the amount of information shown to the administrator. An extremely wide and confusing table would be required to display a member's full details. Therefore, a member's details will be split and displayed using two separate pages. The administrator will be able to view the addresses separately from the rest of the member's information by means of the *search-addresses.php* page. To access this page, a new *Addresses* button will be added to the menu.

Searching for Members' Addresses and Phone Numbers

When the administrator clicks the *Addresses* button, a new search page appears. This is named *search_addresses.php*. The appearance of the *search_addresses.php* page is almost identical to the previous *search.php* page except that it states that the search is for addresses, as shown in Figure 5-10.

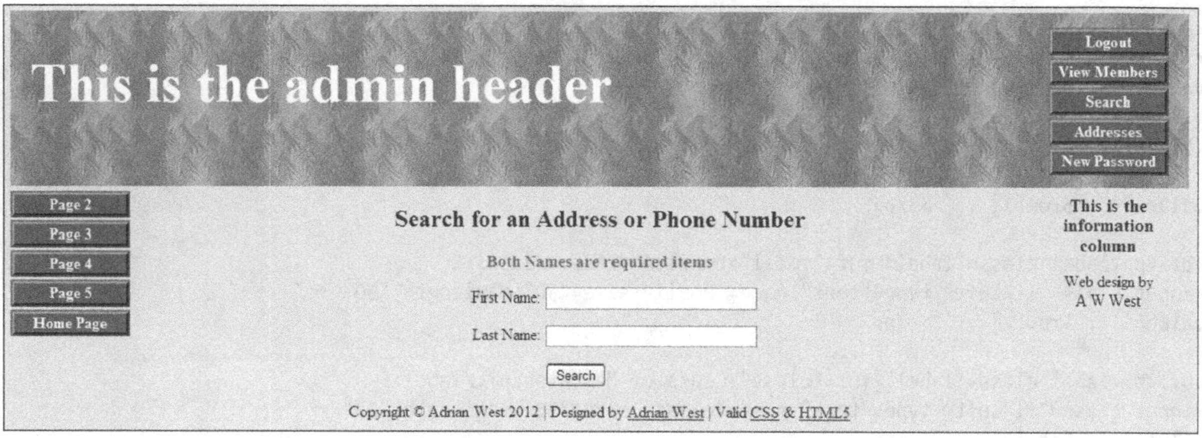

Figure 5-10. *Searching for an address or phone number*

The differences between *search.php* and *search_addresses.php* are shown in bold type in the Listing 5-10.

Listing 5-10. Creating a Screen for Searching Addresses and Phone Numbers (search_addresses.php)

```php
<?php                                                                           #1
session_start();
if (!isset($_SESSION['user_level']) or ($_SESSION['user_level'] != 1)) {
header("Location: login.php");
exit();
}
?>
<!doctype html>
<html lang=en>
<head>
<title>Search page</title>
<meta charset=utf-8>
<link rel="stylesheet" type="text/css" href="includes.css">
<style type="text/css">
h3.red { color:red; font-size:105%; font-weight:bold; text-align:center;}
</style>
```

```
</head>
<body>
<div id="container">
<?php include("header-admin.php"); ?>
<?php include("nav.php"); ?>
<?php include("info-col.php"); ?>
<div id="content"><!-- Start of search address page content -->
<h2>Search for an Address or Phone Number</h2>
<h3 class="red">Both Names are required items</h3>
<!--the form has been commented out in the downloaded file to prevent an address being accessed.
An active version of the file is provided in the downloads for Chapter 6-->
<form action="view_found_address.php" method="post">

<p><label class="label" for="fname">First Name:</label>↵
<input id="fname" type="text" name="fname" size="30" maxlength="30" ↵
value="<?php if (isset($_POST['fname'])) echo $_POST['fname']; ?>"></p>

<p><label class="label" for="lname">Last Name:</label>↵
<input id="lname" type="text" name="lname" size="30" maxlength="40" ↵
value="<?php if (isset($_POST['lname'])) echo $_POST['lname']; ?>"></p>
<p><input id="submit" type="submit" name="submit" value="Search"></p>
</form>
<?php include ('footer.php'); ?>
</div><!-- End of the search address page content -->
</div>
</body>
</html>
```

When the information is entered and the *Search* button is clicked, the *view_found_address.php* page is displayed as shown in Figure 5-11. Note that the search button will not produce a result in this chapter; a record will be retrievable in the next chapter. The screen shot of a retrieved record in Figure 5-11 was produced using the code provided in Chapter 6. Note that in Chapter 6 it will display an additional column for the member's title.

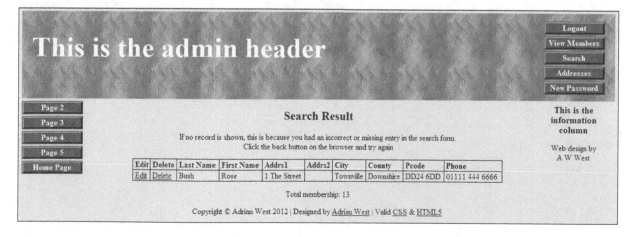

Figure 5-11. *The new table displays the address and telephone number of the selected member*

■ **Note** Only those files that needed modifying have been described to save space. Many PHP files for this chapter have not been mentioned because they are exactly the same as the files in Chapter 4. The downloaded files for Chapter 5 can be viewed to see the code for all the files.

Summary

In this chapter, we created a database containing many more fields than the ones in prior chapters. We added sessions to all the administration pages for security. We added a new *Addresses* button to the administrator's page header. We learned how to add PayPal logos and buttons to the pages. Pagination was demonstrated in a tabular display of members. The form for editing records was modified to include extra data. A page for searching addresses and phone numbers was provided.

In the next chapter, you will learn how the administrator can view and edit addresses and telephone numbers. Also in the next chapter, we will add the finishing touches to the database. The filing system will be tidied up by placing the included files in an *includes* folder. For increased security, extra user input filters will be introduced. A *title* column will be added to the table display for editing and deleting a record, and the *title* column will also be added to the table display for editing addresses and phone numbers.

CHAPTER 6

■ ■ ■

The Finishing Touches

In the previous chapter, we created the beginnings of a useful database and several interactive web-site pages. However, we were not able to edit the addresses and telephone numbers. We will now remedy this. The folder and filing system for the PHP pages will be tidied up to reduce the clutter. The previous interactive pages had a minimum of user input filtering; therefore, this chapter will introduce more security filtering and validation. The steps that are needed to finish the web site and database are described in the following sections:

- Create a copy of the database from Chapter 5 using a new name and password.
- Create a copy of the table from Chapter 5 by importing an SQL dump file.
- Tidy up the folder and filing system.
- Providing more information on security.
- Validating and sanitizing user input.
- Creating a more secure registration page.
- Searching for addresses and telephone numbers.
- Viewing and editing the retrieved addresses and phone numbers.

Create the Database

First we will create a new version of the *postaldb* database named *finalpost*:

1. Open the XAMPP *htdocs* folder, and create a new folder named *finalpost*.

2. Download the files for Chapter 6 from the book's web site at *www.apress.com*, and place the files in the new folder called *finalpost*.

3. Then use a browser to access phpMyAdmin, click the Databases tab, and create a new database called *finalpost*.

4. Scroll down and find the newly created database. Then select the check box alongside it.

5. Click *Check Privileges*, click *Add User*, and then add a new user and password as follows:

   User name: cabbage

   Password: in4aPin4aL

   Host: local host

   Scroll down; next to *Global Privileges*, click *Check All*.

6.   Accept the default for the *Resource limits*.

7.   Scroll to the bottom, and click *Add User* (or *Go* in some versions) to save the user's details.

Create the File for Connecting to the Database

Create a new connection file named *mysqli_connect.php*. (If you don't need to practice creating the file from scratch, it is already included in the downloaded files for Chapter 6.)

The Database Connection File (mysqli_connect.php)

```php
<?php
// Create a connection to the postaldb database
// Set the database access details as constants and set the encoding to utf-8
DEFINE ('DB_USER', 'cabbage');
DEFINE ('DB_PASSWORD', 'in4aPin4aL');
DEFINE ('DB_HOST', 'localhost');
DEFINE ('DB_NAME', 'finalpost');
// Make the connection
$dbcon = @mysqli_connect (DB_HOST, DB_USER, DB_PASSWORD, DB_NAME) OR die ↵
('Could not connect to MySQL: ' . mysqli_connect_error() );
// Set the encoding
mysqli_set_charset($dbcon, 'utf8');
```

■ **Tip** When composing a password for use in the real-world, you should make it as complex as possible. Ensure that it is not related in any way to the name of the database. A complex password can be easily remembered by means of a mnemonic. The mnemonic can then be written down and placed under lock and key. The mnemonic chosen for the password (in4aPin4aL) in this tutorial is the old British saying, "In for a penny, in for a pound." One of the meanings of this maxim is, "If we start this, we must make sure we finish it; there must be no drawing back." In the password itself, the uppercase *P* stands for *Penny*, and the uppercase *L* is the archaic symbol for a British Pound (100 pennies).

Create the Table by Importing an SQL Dump File

We now need to create a table named *users* with 17 columns.

I think I can hear you groaning, "Oh, no! Not another table!" Don't worry, I am about to show you a shortcut using the Import/Export facility in phpMyAdmin.

I already compiled the table for you and exported it into a file called *users.sql*. You will find this among the downloaded files that you installed in the folder *finalpost*.

To import the *.sql file*: in the home page of phpMyAdmin, click the database *finalpost* and then create a table called *users* with 17 columns, but STOP at that point. Don't insert any attributes.

When the message appears confirming that your table was created, you can click the *Import* tab.

Click the *Browse* button (shown circled) on the *Import* screen in Figure 6-1.

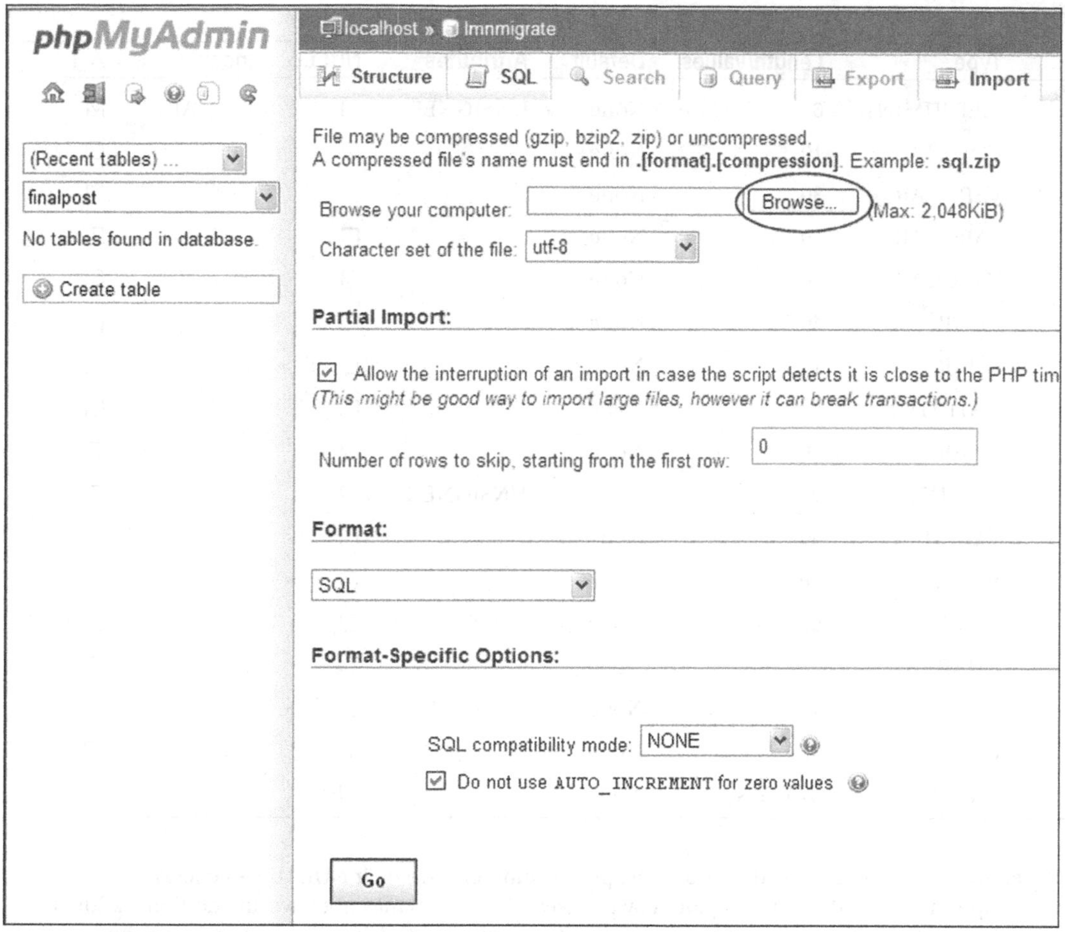

Figure 6-1. *The Import screen in phpMyAdmin*

The browse button allows you to navigate to the file *users.sql*. Open the *users.sql* file, and then click *Go* and the file will be imported. If you now open the *users* table in phpMyAdmin, you will be able to view the table and its data.

If you wish to Create the Table Manually

If you need the practice, you can create the table from scratch as follows.

Use phpMyAdmin to create the membership table named *users*. Name the table *users*, and create 17 columns. Give the columns the titles and attributes shown in Table 6-1.

Table 6-1. *The Titles and Attributes for the users Table*

Column name	Type	Length/Values	Default	Attributes	NULL	Index	A_I
user_id	MEDIUMINT	6	None	UNSIGNED	☐	PRIMARY	☑
title	TINYTEXT	10	None		☐		☐
fname	VARCHAR	30	None		☐		☐
lname	VARCHAR	40	None		☐		☐
email	VARCHAR	50	None		☐		☐
psword	CHAR	40	None		☐		☐
uname	CHAR	15	None		☐		☐
registration_date	DATETIME		None		☐		☐
class	CHAR	20	None		☐		☐
user_level	TINYINT	2	None	UNSIGNED	☐		☐
addr1	VARCHAR	50	None		☐		☐
addr2	VARCHAR	50	None		☑		☐
city	VARCHAR	50	None		☐		☐
county	CHAR	25	None		☐		☐
pcode	CHAR	10	None		☐		☐
phone	CHAR	15	None		☑		☐
paid	ENUM	'No', 'Yes'	None		☐		☐

Note that the columns for the second address and the phone number have their NULL boxes checked. This is because they will be optional fields that can be ignored by the user. Many users may not have an additional address, such as the district of a very large town. Some users are ex-directory and do not wish to disclose their telephone numbers in order to reduce the cold-call nuisance.

In the UK, the *county* column can be omitted because the Royal Mail relies entirely on the Post Code for mail delivery. In the USA, *county* would be replaced by *state* and abbreviations would be acceptable, such as *CA* for *California*. To cover both territories, the column title might be *county_state*.

Registering Some Members Manually

If you decide to enter the members manually, create the empty table, run XAMPP, and then use a browser to enter this URL:

```
http://localhost/finalpost/safer-register-page.php
```

The file *safer-register-page.php* is a more secure version of the *register-page.php* file from Chapter 5. The file is included in the downloadable files for Chapter 6. The security enhancements for the safer file are described later in this chapter. First, register these two members: Mr James Smith and the administrator Mr Jack Smith, as you did in Chapter 5. The procedure is repeated here.

Register the following user as a member:

Title: Mr

First name: James

Last name: Smith

E-mail: jsmith@myisp.co.uk

Password: blacksmith

Username: muscleman

James Smith has been appointed as the membership secretary. We can safely assume that James Smith would like to view the members page occasionally as well as viewing the administration page. He will use his membership password to view the members page. He needs a different password and e-mail address to access the administration section; therefore, he needs a new registration identity as follows:

Title: Mr

First name: Jack

Last name: Smith

E-mail: jsmith@outcook.com

Password: dogsbody

Username: wagglytail

In a real-world situation, an administrator would need a much more complex password and a less obvious pseudonym, but this is not important for this tutorial.

Use phpMyAdmin to change the administrator's *user_level* to 1.

Register several more members so that you have something to play with. Table 6-2 suggests some users' details.

Table 6-2. *Suggested Details for Registering Members Manually*

Title	Fname	Lname	E-mail address	Password	User Name
Mr	Mike	Rosoft	miker@myisp.com	willgates	benefactor
Ms	Olive	Branch	obranch@myisp.co.uk	anoilyone	mrspopeye
Mr	Frank	Incense	incense@myisp.net	perfume	mythking
Miss	Annie	Versary	aversary@myisp.com	happyday	celebrate
Mr	Terry	Fide	tfide@myisp.de	scaredstiff	trembling
Mrs	Rose	Bush	rbush@myisp.co.uk	redblooms	pricklystems
Mrs	Annie	Mossity	amossity@myisp.org.uk	yourenemy	acrimony
Mr	Percy	Veer	pveer@myisp.com	keepgoing	doggedly
Mr	Darrel	Doo	ddoo@myisp.co.uk	satisfied	contented
Mr	Stan	Dard	sdard@myisp.net	battleflag	warbanner
Miss	Nora	Bone	nbone@myisp.com	liketerrier	strongteeth
Mr	Barry	Cade	bcade@myisp.co.uk	blockthem	mybarrier
Miss	Dee	Jected	djected@myisp.org.uk	gloomndoom	pessimist
Mrs	Lynn	Seed	lseed@myisp.com	paintersoil	artistic
Mr	Barry	Tone	btone@myisp.net	nicevoice	midrange

■ **Tip** For your convenience, I repeat the tip given in the previous chapter as follows: Entering the data can be tedious using the manual method. To reduce the tedium in this tutorial, you can enter identical addresses and telephone numbers for each user. A set of suitable data is suggested next.

When experimenting, I use the following data in every record. This is acceptable because no searches will be made in this tutorial using addresses and telephone numbers. Instead, searches are made using the members' first and last names.

Address 1	2 The Street
Address 2	The Village (This is optional and should be omitted when registering some of the members' addresses.)
City	Townsville
County or State	Devon
Post or Zip code	EX7 9PP (or CA if a USA state)
Phone	01234 777 888 (This is optional and should be omitted when registering some of the members' telephone numbers.)

Now we need to do some more housekeeping because the ever-increasing number of PHP and HTML files needs to be organized into folders.

Tidy the Folders and Filing System

The number of files in the postal folder in the previous chapter increased as each chapter added more features. The clutter can be confusing. To tidy the new *finalpost* folder, we need to place all the included files in their own folder. I already did this in the downloadable files for this chapter. Note the new *includes* folder and the fact that, in the main files, all the PHP includes now have the prefix *includes/*, as shown in the following snippet:

```php
<?php include("includes/header-admin.php"); ?>
<?php include("includes/nav.php"); ?>
<?php include("includes/info-col.php"); ?>
```

The info column for the registration page *safer-register-page.php* contains a credit/debit card logo, which is provided by PayPal. The code for this is in the included file *info-col-cards.php* and is as follows:

```php
<?php include("includes/info-col-cards.php"); ?>
```

The Style Sheet

If you examine the downloaded *includes* files (contained in the *includes* folder) you will see that their internal styles have been removed. This ensures that the web site pages will validate. The styles for the included files have been placed in the main style sheet as follows:

The New Main Style Sheet (includes.css)

```
body {text-align:center; background-color:#D7FFEB; color:navy; font-family: ↵
"times new roman"; font-size: 100%; color: navy; margin: auto; }
h2 { font-size:150%; color:navy; text-align:center; }
h3 { font-size:110%; color:navy; text-align:center; }
#container {position:relative; min-width:960px; max-width:1200px; margin:auto; ↵
text-align:left; }
#header, #header-members, #header-admin { margin:10px auto 0 auto; min-width:960px; ↵
max-width:1200px; height:175px; background-image: url('images/tile-pale.jpg'); ↵
background-repeat: repeat; padding:0; color:white; }
h1 {position:relative; top:40px; font-size:350%; color:white; margin:auto 0 auto 20px; ↵
width: 600px; }
ul { position:absolute; top:180px; left:-40px; color:navy; width:135px; text-align:center; ↵
margin:0; }
#nav ul { position:absolute; top:190px; left:-10px; color:navy; width:135px; ↵
text-align:center; margin:0; }
#info-col { position:absolute; top:190px; right:10px; color:navy; width:135px; ↵
text-align:center; margin:5px 5px 0 0; }
/* set general side button styles */
li { width:115px; list-style-type :none; margin-bottom: 3px; text-align: center; }
/* set general anchor styles */
li a { display: block; width:115px; color: white; font-weight: bold; text-decoration: none }
/* specify state styles. */
/* mouseout (default) */
li a { background: #5B78BE; border: 4px outset #aabaff; }
/* mouseover */
li a:hover { display:block; background: #0a4adf; border: 4px outset #8abaff; width:115px; }
/* onmousedown */
li a:active { background:#aecbff; border: 4px inset #aecbff; }
#reg-navigation ul { float:right; font-size:medium; width:160px; margin:-150px 15px 0 88%; }
#midcol {width:90%; margin:auto; }
#mid-left-col { width:48%; float:left; text-align:left; }
#mid-right-col {width:48%; float:right; text-align:left; }
#content { margin-left:150px; margin-right:150px; }
table { width:800px; border:1px navy solid; border-collapse:collapse; margin:auto; }
td { border:1px navy solid; padding:1px 0 1px 4px; text-align:left; }
form { margin-left:180px; }
#footer { margin:auto; text-align:center; }
p.error { color:red; font-size:105%; font-weight:bold; text-align:center; }
.label { float:left; width:210px; text-align:right; clear:left; margin-right:5px; }
#submit { margin-left:215px; text-align:center; }
span.left { text-align:left; }
```

■ **Tip**   If you have more than one style sheet in a web site, it is good practice to create a folder for them named *styles*. The links for the styles would then have the following format:
<link rel="stylesheet" type="text/css" href="styles/somestylesheet.css">.

Ensuring the security of a database will be discussed next. Security is the most important aspect of the development process and perhaps the most tedious. Inappropriate input from a user can insert faulty data into a database table. More seriously, it can cause a leakage of private information or allow nefarious people to trash a table. Unacceptable input can be the work of criminals, or it could simply be users' mistakes. Therefore, all user input must be filtered to ensure that it is fit for your database and for the server.

Degrees of Security

A database can be insecure or partially secure; it can never be 100% secure. However, this statement must be qualified because the risk depends on several other factors besides the built-in security of the database. Criminals will not bother targeting small concerns; they will go for big firms that host many users' details, especially if money is handled and credit-card details are included in the data. Postal addresses, e-mail addresses, and users' preferences can be harvested from an insecure database and sold for substantial amounts of money.

Databases for small firms, clubs, or societies must have at least a minimum layer of security built in.

The Minimum Layer of Security

The database must have a unique name (up to 16 characters long), a password (as complex as possible), a host name (usually *localhost*), a designated user, and a set of permissions.

Multiple users are permissible and their permissions should differ, but the number of users must be severely restricted for maximum security. Additional users should not have permissions such as GRANT, SHUTDOWN, or DROP.

MySQL encrypts the password before storing it on the server. The webmaster should choose a password that is difficult to deduce. Never use a word that can be found in a dictionary or a word that is an anagram of the webmaster's name. You could take a popular saying such as "Raining again, good weather for ducks" and create a password something like RaGw4dux.

Always assume that everything a user enters will be a danger to the database. Also, the data should be as accurate as possible. For instance, e-mail addresses with incorrect formats are of no use to the user or to the owner of the database.

Trim all string entries, and run them through the function `mysqli_real_escape_string()` as follows:

```
$q = mysqli_real_escape_string($dbcon, trim($_POST['first_name']));
```

`mysql_real_escape_string()` calls MySQL's library function `mysql_real_escape_string`, which prefixes backslashes to the following characters: \x00, \n, \r, \, ', " and \x1a.

Validate e-mail addresses, phone numbers, and all numerical items, but clean everything else. The two techniques *validation* and *sanitization* will be explained later in this chapter.

Filter all user input so that HTML tags and scripts cannot be inserted into a database. Scripts can infiltrate the database using HTML tags, such as *<script>*, in conjunction with JavaScript.

Where possible, store the file that accesses the database in a folder located one level above the root folder. (The root folder is *htdocs* or *www*.) Contact your remote host to see if this is possible. The connection code we have been using is

```
require ('mysqli_connect.php');
```

When using a file in a folder one level above the root level, the connection code is

```
require ('../mysqli_connect.php');
```

The downloadable PHP files for this tutorial will retain the code *require (mysqli_connect.php')*; because the database will be located on your computer and not on a remote host.

You could rename the connection file so that a hacker would dismiss it as not what he is searching for. If the web site is selling original paintings, you might change the name of the connection file to *canvas.php*. The new name fits the theme of the web site but is not conspicuous. However, if you chose the name *monalisa.php*, a hacker would be suspicious because there is no way that you would have the Mona Lisa for sale. The hacker would guess you are hiding something important.

Always insert and retrieve passwords using SH1 or SH2 encoding like this SH1($password).

Where possible, prevent browsers from displaying error messages that reveal the structure of the database. These messages can help a hacker find his way around your database.

Always use sessions to restrict access to vulnerable pages, such as an administration page and members' special pages.

You can safely accept payments through a web site by using PayPal, Stripe, or a similar secure payment system. But NEVER store members' bank/debit/credit card details.

An Increased Layer of Security

If your clients wish to use an internal payment system rather than using PayPal, they will need a very expensive security budget. For sites where national security is at risk, or when users' financial details are stored, the site will require specialist staff or an expensive agency to supervise and continually monitor the web site.

A secure server is the main requirement for such vulnerable databases. The client would have to pay a substantial annual fee for a server using Secure Sockets Layer (SSL).

Validation and Sanitization

Here, we will demonstrate the difference between validation and sanitization.

- **Validating:** The validator checks the format of the users' input. If the format is incorrect, the form page halts and an error message asks the user to correct the input. Validation ensures that e-mail addresses and phone numbers have the correct characters. This prevents incorrect data from being entered into a database table. It also protects against the injection of dangerous code.

- **Sanitizing:** This can be achieved by two methods: (i) using standard PHP cleaners or (ii) using the new *filter_var()* function with the *SANITIZE* attribute. Sanitizing removes undesirable characters automatically before the data is sent to the database table. When you are using the new *SANITIZE* attribute, no error message is displayed. Users are not alerted to the fact that they have made a mistake or that their input contains dangerous characters or scripts. If an error message would be useful, the web designer must add his or her own error message. Sanitization can remove HTML tags and JavaScript commands that could harm a database.

■ **Caution** The *filter_var()* with *sanitization* should not be used to clean e-mail addresses. Sanitizing does not check that e-mails are in the correct format. An e-mail address must have the correct format; otherwise, it is useless. Therefore, *VALIDATE* is the appropriate attribute for filtering e-mail addresses.

Validation and sanitization can be applied by means of the function *filter_var()*.

The filter_var() Function

The function filter_var() is included with PHP version 5.2 and later. Its purpose is to simplify the validation and sanitization of user input. The function is used in conjunction with either the *FILTER_VALIDATE* or *FILTER_SANITIZE* attribute. For more detailed information on this function, see http://php.net/manual/en/function.filter-var.php.

Validation

In Chapter 5, the registration page had no built-in validation or sanitization. A user could enter data that would either damage the web page or interfere with the database. The user could enter items that were in the wrong format. As an example of a wrong format, a user could make a mistake when entering an e-mail address. The incorrect address could contain spaces or unacceptable characters as follows:

rbush 'myisp.co m

That faulty e-mail address contains no @ symbol, and it has two spaces and an apostrophe. These are unacceptable e-mail characters. The VALIDATION attribute will recognize the problems and provide an error message asking the user to correct the e-mail address.

In Chapter 5, in the file *register-page.php*, the code for the e-mail was as follows:

```
// Check that an email address has been entered
if (empty($_POST['email'])) {
    $errors[] = 'You forgot to enter your email address.';
} else {
$e = mysqli_real_escape_string($dbcon, (trim($_POST['email'])));
}
```

The code merely cleaned the input and checked that the field contained some characters. However, the e-mail address format might be complete nonsense, and that nonsense would have been entered into the database table. In the past, I would have used regex (Regex is an abbreviation of *Regular Expressions*). to validate the format of the e-mail address, but with the advent of PHP 5.2 and later versions, the *filter_var()* function became available and this was a great improvement. Validation by means of regex is rather complicated and prone to typing errors, as you will see from the following example shown in bold type:

```
$email = "name@usersisp.com";
if (preg_match('/^[^0-9][a-zA-Z0-9_]+([.][a-zA-Z0-9_]+)*[@][a-zA-Z0-9_]+([.]↵
[a-zA-Z0-9_]+)*[.][a-zA-Z]{2,4}$/',$email)) {
echo "Your email is in the acceptable format";
} else {
echo "Your email address does not have an acceptable format";
}
```

Validating by means of the *filter_var()* function is a great improvement, as you will see in line **#4** in the next snippet of code for validating an e-mail address. This is used in the registration form *safer_register_page.php*.

```
// Set the email alias as FALSE and check for an email address
$e = FALSE;                                                                    #1
// Check that an email address has been entered                               #2
if (empty($_POST['email'])) {
$errors[] = 'You forgot to enter your email address.';
}
//remove spaces from beginning and end of the email address and validate it   #3
if (filter_var((trim($_POST['email'])), FILTER_VALIDATE_EMAIL)) {             #4
//A valid email address is then registered
$e = mysqli_real_escape_string($dbcon, (trim($_POST['email'])));
}else{                                                                         #5
$errors[] = 'Your email address is invalid or you forgot to enter your ↵
email address.';
}
```

Explanation of the Code

```
// Set the email alias as FALSE and check for an email address
$e = FALSE;                                                                    #1
```

Assigning the keyword FALSE to the e-mail constant $e may seem an odd thing to do. However, it is a useful trick because it reduces the amount of code required in the conditionals that follows that statement.

```
// Check that an email address has been entered                               #2
if (empty($_POST['email'])) {
$errors[] = 'You forgot to enter your email address.';
```

This first conditional is the same as the one in Chapter 5.

```
}else{                                                                         #3
//remove any spaces from beginning and end of the email address and validate it
```

Any unwanted spaces at the beginning or end of the e-mail address will be removed by means of the PHP trim() function. This filter is then embedded in the next statements:

```
if (filter_var((trim($_POST['email'])), FILTER_VALIDATE_EMAIL)) {             #4
$e = mysqli_real_escape_string($dbcon, (trim($_POST['email'])));
```

The PHP function filter_var() is introduced into the code here. The pattern for using it is as follows:

```
If (filter_var(a variable, the type of filter)) {
```

If the function determines that the e-mail address has the correct format, the e-mail address is assigned to the variable $e. The variable $e is no longer FALSE. In other words, the e-mail address is accepted and entered into the database table.

```
}else{                                                                         #5
$errors[] = 'Your email is not in the correct format.';
}
```

When an e-mail address is in an incorrect format, the variable $e is unchanged. In the else clause, the variable $e remains FALSE because it was set to FALSE in line #1. An error message is then inserted into the *errors* array.

■ **Tip** A negative form of a function is available by simply placing an exclamation mark in front of the function as follows: if (!filter_var(variable, FILTER_VALIDATE_EMAIL)) { This means, "if the email does not have the correct format. . .".

Some text input might not have a valid format because it does not conform to a set pattern—for instance, a text area for comments or a person's title. In the UK, we have titles that are a holdover from medieval feudalism, quaint things like Baroness, Lord, Lady, or Sir. Some retired military members will use their armed forces titles like Major or Colonel. Text that does not conform to a set pattern can be cleaned by means of either a *regex* function or possibly with *filter_var()* and the *SANITIZE* attribute.

Sanitization

The *filter_var()* function used with the *SANITIZE* attribute will not be used in this book because it is tricky to implement and this book presents a simplified approach to database design. Also, many PHP gurus seem to discourage its use. This is not a problem because another solution is available that does not use SANITIZE. Instead, it uses two other PHP functions: strip_tags() and mb_strlen(). The first function removes HTML tags, and the second checks the length of the string input by the user. If the string length is less than one (i.e., it is zero), the user has failed to enter a string. The following snippet of code illustrates the use of these two functions to sanitize a string:

```
// Trim the user's input
$name = trim($_POST['fname']);
// Strip HTML tags and apply escaping
$stripped = mysqli_real_escape_string($dbcon, strip_tags($name));
// Get string lengths
$strlen = mb_strlen($stripped, 'utf8');
// Check stripped string
if( $strlen < 1 ) {
    $errors[] = 'You forgot to enter your first name.';
}
```

This code will produce an error message if the field has not been filled in. If a user injects some HTML or JavaScript into a field, the function strip_tags() not only strips out tags such as <p> but it removes the characters between the opening and closing HTML tags. That does not matter because anyone entering HTML tags or JavaScript is usually attacking the database.

Text Areas and Sanitization

Obviously, a text area (a field accepting many lines of text) cannot conform to a format for validation. Sanitization by means of regex must be used for a text area. This is covered in Chapter 10.

Validating Telephone Numbers

At the time of this writing, PHP does not have a built-in validation attribute for telephone numbers. Telephone numbers do not conform to a common format. Users will enter any combination of numbers, spaces, hyphens, and brackets. Also there are international differences. To complicate matters, some users will write the numbers in groups as follows:

0111 222 333 or (0111) 222 333 or 0111-222-333

We must therefore resort to a regex method of validation. Phone numbers have national differences. To help you cope with this, many regex expressions are available. This book offers a simplified approach. The neatest solution is to strip out every character that is not a number. Brackets, letters, spaces, and hyphens can be removed by using a regex function. This function is used in the revised registration page that is described next.

A More Secure Registration Page

To make the registration page more secure, several techniques were employed. The revised registration page has exactly the same appearance as the registration page in the Chapter 5, as shown in Figure 6-2.

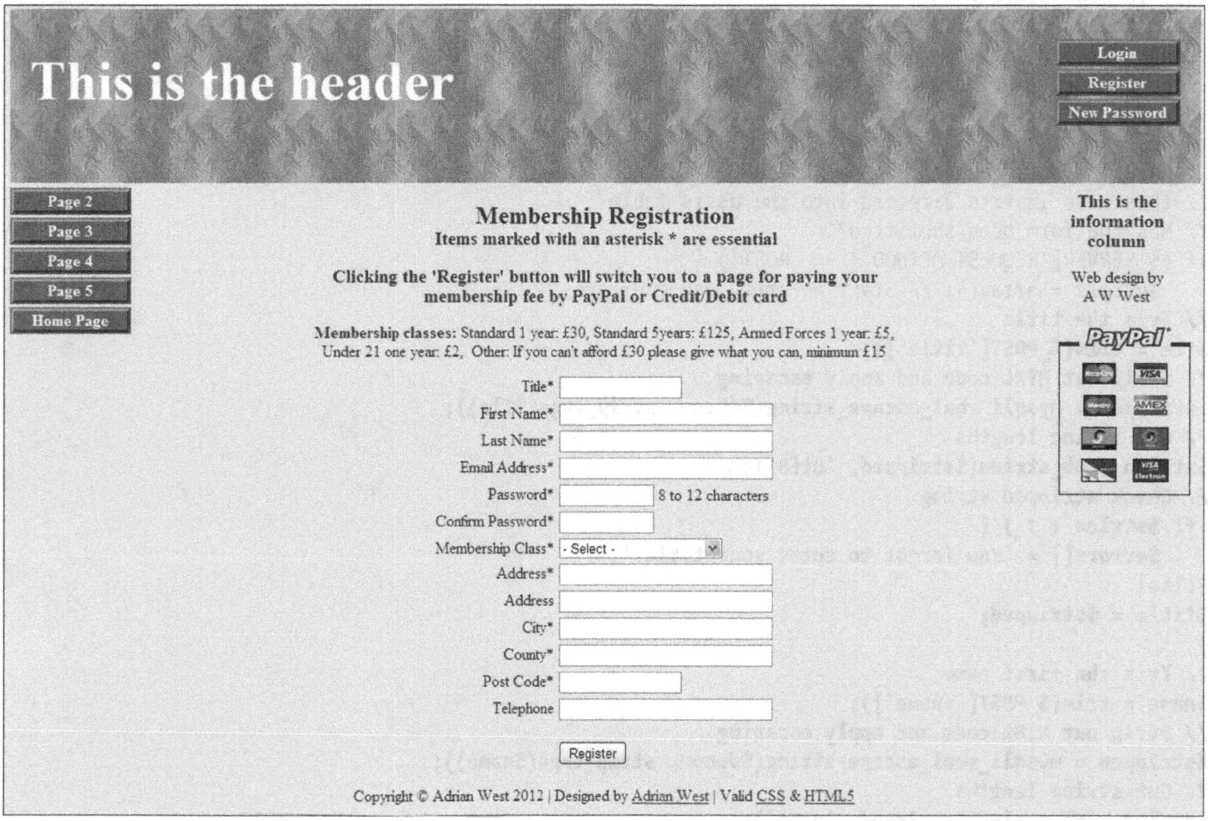

Figure 6-2. *The registration page*

Additional security and cleaning has been included, and this will be explained at the end of Listing 6-2. The modified items are shown in bold type.

Listing 6-2. Creating a More Secure Registration Page (safer-register-page.php).

//The form contains an internal style sheet because the styling of the form elements is unique to this page.

```
<!doctype html>
<html lang=en>
<head>
<title>Safer register pagepage</title>
<meta charset=utf-8>
<link rel="stylesheet" type="text/css" href="includes.css">
<style type="text/css">
#midcol { width:98%; margin:auto; }
input, select { margin-bottom:5px; }
h2 { margin-bottom:0; margin-top:5px; }
h3.content { margin-top:0; }
.cntr { text-align:center; }
</style>
</head>
<body>
<div id="container">
<?php include("includes/register-header.php"); ?>
<?php include("includes/nav.php"); ?>
<?php include("includes/info-col-cards.php");?>
<div id="content"><!--Start of the registration page content-->
<?php
require ('mysqli_connect.php'); // Connect to the database
// This code inserts a record into the users table
// Has the form been submitted?
if ($_SERVER['REQUEST_METHOD'] == 'POST') {
    $errors = array(); // Start an array named errors
// Trim the title                                                        #1
$tle = trim($_POST['title']);
// Strip out HTML code and apply escaping
$stripped = mysqli_real_escape_string($dbcon, strip_tags($tle));
// Get string lengths
$strlen = mb_strlen($stripped, 'utf8');
// Check stripped string
if( $strlen < 1 ) {
    $errors[] = 'You forgot to enter your title.';
}else{
$title = $stripped;
}
// Trim the first name
$name = trim($_POST['fname']);
// Strip out HTML code and apply escaping
$stripped = mysqli_real_escape_string($dbcon, strip_tags($name));
// Get string lengths
$strlen = mb_strlen($stripped, 'utf8');
// Check stripped string
if( $strlen < 1 ) {
$errors[] = 'You forgot to enter your first name.';
}else{
```

```php
$fn = $stripped;
}
// Trim the last name
$lnme = trim($_POST['lname']);
// Strip HTML and apply escaping
$stripped = mysqli_real_escape_string($dbcon, strip_tags($lnme));
// Get string lengths
$strlen = mb_strlen($stripped, 'utf8');
// Check stripped string
if( $strlen < 1 ) {
$errors[] = 'You forgot to enter your last name.';
}else{
$ln = $stripped;
}
//Set the email variable to FALSE                                             #2
$e = FALSE;
// Check that an email address has been entered
if (empty($_POST['email'])) {
$errors[] = 'You forgot to enter your email address.';
}
//remove spaces from beginning and end of the email address and validate it
if (filter_var((trim($_POST['email'])), FILTER_VALIDATE_EMAIL)) {
//A valid email address is then registered
$e = mysqli_real_escape_string($dbcon, (trim($_POST['email'])));
}else{
$errors[] = 'Your email is not in the correct format.';
}
// Check that a password has been entered, if so, does it match the confirmed password
if (empty($_POST['psword1'])){                                                #3
$errors[] ='Please enter a valid password';
}
if(!preg_match('/^\w{8,12}$/', $_POST['psword1'])) {                          #4
$errors[] = 'Invalid password, use 8 to 12 characters and no spaces.';
} else{
$psword1 = $_POST['psword1'];
}                                                                             #4
if($_POST['psword1'] == $_POST['psword2']) {                                  #5
$p = mysqli_real_escape_string($dbcon, trim($psword1));
}else{
$errors[] = 'Your two password do not match.';
}
// Trim the username
$unme = trim($_POST['uname']);
// Strip HTML and apply escaping
$stripped = mysqli_real_escape_string($dbcon, strip_tags($unme));
// Get string lengths
$strlen = mb_strlen($stripped, 'utf8');
// Check stripped string
if( $strlen < 1 ) {
    $errors[] = 'You forgot to enter your secret username.';
}else{
$uname = $stripped;
}
```

171

```php
// Check for a membership class
if (empty($_POST['class'])) {
$errors[] = 'You forgot to choose your membership class.';
} else {
$class = trim($_POST['class']);
}
// Trim the first address
$add1 = trim($_POST['addr1']);
// Strip HTML and apply escaping
$stripped = mysqli_real_escape_string($dbcon, strip_tags($add1));
// Get string lengths
$strlen = mb_strlen($stripped, 'utf8');
// Check stripped string
if( $strlen < 1 ) {
$errors[] = 'You forgot to enter your address.';
}else{
$ad1 = $stripped;
}
// Trim the second address
$ad2 = trim($_POST['addr2']);
// Strip HTML and apply escaping
$stripped = mysqli_real_escape_string($dbcon, strip_tags($ad2));
// Get string lengths
$strlen = mb_strlen($stripped, 'utf8');
// Check stripped string
if( $strlen < 1 ) {
$ad2=NULL;
}else{
$ad2 = $stripped;
}
// Trim the city
$ct = trim($_POST['city']);
// Strip HTML and apply escaping
$stripped = mysqli_real_escape_string($dbcon, strip_tags($ct));
// Get string lengths
$strlen = mb_strlen($stripped, 'utf8');
// Check stripped string
if( $strlen < 1 ) {
$errors[] = 'You forgot to enter your city.';
}else{
$cty = $stripped;
}
// Trim the county
$conty = trim($_POST['county']);
// Strip HTML and apply escaping
$stripped = mysqli_real_escape_string($dbcon, strip_tags($conty));
// Get string lengths
$strlen = mb_strlen($stripped, 'utf8');
// Check stripped string
if( $strlen < 1 ) {
$errors[] = 'You forgot to enter your county.';
}else{
```

#6

```
$cnty = $stripped;
}
// Trim the post code
$pcod = trim($_POST['pcode']);
// Strip HTML and apply escaping
$stripped = mysqli_real_escape_string($dbcon, strip_tags($pcod));
// Get string lengths
$strlen = mb_strlen($stripped, 'utf8');
// Check stripped string
if( $strlen < 1 ) {
$errors[] = 'You forgot to enter your county.';
}else{
$pcode = $stripped;
}
// Has a phone number been entered?                                         #7
if (empty($_POST['phone'])){
$ph=($_POST['phone']);
}
elseif (!empty($_POST['phone'])) {
//  Strip out everything that is not a number
$phone = preg_replace('/\D+/', '', ($_POST['phone']));
$ph=$phone;
}
if (empty($errors)) { // If no problems occurred
//Determine whether the email address has already been registered for a user
$q = "SELECT user_id FROM users WHERE email = '$e' ";
$result=mysqli_query ($dbcon, $q) ;
if (mysqli_num_rows($result) == 0){//The mail address was not already registered ↵
therefore register the user in the users table
// Make the query:
$q = "INSERT INTO users (user_id, title, fname, lname, email, psword, registration_date,↵
 uname, class, addr1, addr2, city, county, pcode, phone, paid) VALUES (' ', '$title', ↵
'$fn', '$ln', '$e', SHA1('$p'), NOW(), '$uname','$class', '$ad1', '$ad2', '$cty', ↵
'$cnty', '$pcode', '$ph', '$pd ' )";
    $result = @mysqli_query ($dbcon, $q); // Run the query
    if ($result) { // If the query ran OK
    header ("location: register-thanks.php");
    exit();
    } else { // If the query did not run OK
    // Errosr message
    echo '<h2>System Error</h2>
<p class="error">You could not be registered due to a system error. We apologize for ↵
the inconvenience.</p>';
// Debugging message
echo '<p>' . mysqli_error($dbcon) . '<br><br>Query: ' . $q . '</p>';
} // End of if ($result)
mysqli_close($dbcon); // Close the database connection
// Include the footer and stop the script
include ('includes/footer.php');
exit();
```

```
            } else {//The email address is already registered
                echo '<p class="error">The email address is not acceptable because it is already registered</p>';
        }
    }else{ // Display the errors
echo '<h2>Error!</h2>';
<p class="error">The following error(s) occurred:<br>';
foreach ($errors as $msg) { // Echo each error
echo " - $msg<br>\n";
}
echo '</p><h3>Please try again.</h3><p><br></p>';
}// End of if (empty($errors))
} // End of the main Submit conditional
?>
<div id="midcol">
<h2>Membership Registration</h2>
<h3 class="content">Items marked with an asterisk * are essential</h3>
<h3 class="content">When you click the 'Register' button, you will be switched to ↵
a page<br>for paying your membership fee with PayPal or a Credit/Debit
card</h3>
<p class="cntr"><b>Membership classes:</b> Standard 1 year: &pound;30, Standard 5years:↵
&pound;125, Armed Forces 1 year: &pound;5,<br>Under 21 one year: &pound;2,  ↵
Other: If you can't afford &pound;30 please give what you can, minimum &pound;15 </p>
<form action="safer-register-page.php" method="post">
<label class="label" for="title">Title*</label>
<input id="title" type="text" name="title" size="15" maxlength="12" ↵
value="<?php if (isset($_POST['title'])) echo $_POST['title']; ?>">
<br><label class="label" for="fname">First Name*</label>
<input id="fname" type="text" name="fname" size="30" maxlength="30" ↵
value="<?php if (isset($_POST['fname'])) echo $_POST['fname']; ?>">
<br><label class="label" for="lname">Last Name*</label>
<input id="lname" type="text" name="lname" size="30" maxlength="40" ↵
value="<?php if (isset($_POST['lname'])) echo $_POST['lname']; ?>">
<br><label class="label" for="email">Email Address*</label>↵
<input id="email" type="text" name="email" size="30" maxlength="60" ↵
value="<?php if (isset($_POST['email'])) echo $_POST['email']; ?>" >
<br><label class="label" for="psword1">Password*</label>↵
<input id="psword1" type="password" name="psword1" size="12" maxlength="12" ↵
value="<?php if (isset($_POST['psword1'])) echo $_POST['psword1']; ?>" >↵
 8 to 12 characters
<br><label class="label" for="psword2">Confirm Password*</label><input id="psword2" ↵
type="password" name="psword2" size="12" maxlength="12" ↵
value="<?php if (isset($_POST['psword2'])) echo $_POST['psword2']; ?>" >
<br><label class="label" for="uname">Secret User Name*</label><input id="uname" ↵
type="text" name="uname" size="12" maxlength="12" ↵
value="<?php if (isset($_POST['uname'])) echo $_POST['uname']; ?>"> 8 to 12 characters
<br><label class="label" for="class">Membership Class*</label>
<select name="class">
<option value="">- Select -</option>
<option value="30"<?php if (isset($_POST['class']) AND ($_POST['class'] == '30'))
echo ' selected="selected"'; ?>>Standard 1 year &pound;30</option>
<option value="125"<?php if (isset($_POST['class']) AND ($_POST['class'] == '125'))
echo ' selected="selected"'; ?>>Standard 5 years &pound;125</option>
```

```
<option value="5"<?php if (isset($_POST['class']) AND ($_POST['class'] == '5'))
echo ' selected="selected"'; ?>>Armed Forces 1 year &pound;5</option>
<option value="2"<?php if (isset($_POST['class']) AND ($_POST['class'] == '2'))
echo ' selected="selected"'; ?>>Under 22 1 year &pound;2**</option>
<option value="15"<?php if (isset($_POST['class']) AND ($_POST['class'] == '15'))
echo ' selected="selected"'; ?>>Minimum 1 year &pound;15</option>
</select
<br><label class="label" for="addr1">Address*</label><input id="addr1" ↵
type="text" name="addr1" size="30" maxlength="30" ↵
value="<?php if (isset($_POST['addr1']))
echo $_POST['addr1']; ?>">
<br><label class="label" for="addr2">Address</label><input id="addr2" ↵
type="text" name="addr2" size="30" maxlength="30" ↵
value="<?php if (isset($_POST['addr2']))
echo $_POST['addr2']; ?>">
<br><label class="label" for="city">City*</label><input id="city" ↵
type="text" name="city" size="30" maxlength="30" ↵
value="<?php if (isset($_POST['city']))
echo $_POST['city']; ?>">
<br><label class="label" for="county">County*</label><input id="county" ↵
type="text" name="county" size="30" maxlength="30" ↵
value="<?php if (isset($_POST['county']))
echo $_POST['county']; ?>">
<br><label class="label" for="pcode">Post Code*</label><input id="pcode" ↵
type="text" name="pcode" size="15" maxlength="15" ↵
value="<?php if (isset($_POST['pcode']))
echo $_POST['pcode']; ?>">
<br><label class="label" for="phone">Telephone</label><input id="phone" ↵
type="text" name="phone" size="30" maxlength="30" ↵
value="<?php if (isset($_POST['phone']))
echo $_POST['phone']; ?>">
    <p><input id="submit" type="submit" name="submit" value="Register"></p>
</form>
</div></div></div>
<?php include ('includes/footer.php'); ?>
<!--End of the registratation page content-->
</body>
</html>
```

Explanation of the Code

```
// Trim the title                                                          #1
$tle = trim($_POST['title']);
// Strip HTML and apply escaping
$stripped = mysqli_real_escape_string($dbcon, strip_tags($tle));
// Get string lengths
$strlen = mb_strlen($stripped, 'utf8');
```

```
// Check stripped string
if( $strlen < 1 ) {
$errors[] = 'You forgot to enter your title.';
}else{
$title = $stripped;
}
```

The title is trimmed to remove any spaces from the beginning and end. Any HTML tags are then removed using the function strip_tags(). The stripped input is then run through the mysqli_real_escape_string() function for extra security. Next the input is checked for its length with the function mb_strlen(). If the string length is zero (less than one character), an error message is inserted in the $errors array. Note that I changed the variable's name ($_POST['title')] at each step of the security checks; this is a convention I adopt to remind me that a change has occurred. The variable finally reverts to the name $title ready for entry into the database table.

This security-check pattern is repeated several times in the rest of the code. See if you can recognize it.

```
$e = FALSE;                                                          #2
// Has an email address has been entered?
if (empty($_POST['email'])) {
$errors[] = 'You forgot to enter your email address.';
}
//remove spaces from the beginning and end of the email address and validate it
if (filter_var((trim($_POST['email'])), FILTER_VALIDATE_EMAIL)) {
//A valid email address is then registered
$e = mysqli_real_escape_string($dbcon, (trim($_POST['email'])));
}else{
$errors[] = 'Your email is not in the correct format.';
}
```

Setting the variable as *FALSE* at the start of a set of statements is a common PHP pattern. This can reduce the amount of subsequent code required. The *filter_var()* function checks the e-mail address for validity. If it conforms to the correct pattern, the address is assigned to the variable *$e* ready to be entered into the user's record.

```
// Check that a password has been entered, if so, does it match the confirmed password
if (empty($_POST['psword1'])){                                      #3
$errors[] ='Please enter a valid password';
}
```

The code in line **#3** checks whether the user has entered a password.

```
if(!preg_match('/^\w{8,12}$/', $_POST['psword1'])) {               #4
$errors[] = 'Invalid password, use 8 to 12 characters and no spaces.';
} else{
$psword1 = $_POST['psword1'];
}
```

Note the exclamation mark in front of *preg_match*. This means "If the password has NOT been entered, put an error message into the *$errors* array." The Regex function *preg_match()* checks the first password for unacceptable characters. The regex pattern uses the symbol \w to accept the characters 0–9, a–z and A–Z, but no spaces. It also ensures that it contains between 8 and 12 characters. For more information on *preg_match*, see:

http://php.net/manual/en/function.preg-match.php.

```
if($_POST['psword1'] == $_POST['psword2']) {                              #5
$p = mysqli_real_escape_string($dbcon, trim($psword1));
}else{
$errors[] = 'Your two password do not match.';
}
```

If the first password is in an acceptable format, a check is made to ensure that the first password matches the confirmation password. If the checks is satisfactory, the password is assigned to the variable $p ready to be entered into the user's record. If the passwords do not match, an error message is placed in the $errors array.

```
// Trim the second address
$ad2 = trim($_POST['addr2']);                                            #6
// Strip HTML and apply escaping
$stripped = mysqli_real_escape_string($dbcon, strip_tags($ad2));
// Get string lengths
$strlen = mb_strlen($stripped, 'utf8');
// Check stripped string
if( $strlen < 1 ) {
$ad2=NULL;
}else{
$ad2 = $stripped;
}
```

The pattern is similar to most of the other entries except that, should the form field be empty, no error message is displayed because the field is optional. The column for this field was set to NULL when the table was created; therefore, an empty field is acceptable.

```
// Has a phone number been entered?                                      #7
if (empty($_POST['phone'])){
$ph=($_POST['phone']);
}
elseif (!empty($_POST['phone'])) {
//Remove all characters except numbers
$phone = preg_replace('/\D+/', '', ($_POST['phone']));
$ph=$phone;
}
```

Phone number entries may contain numbers, spaces, brackets, and hyphens. Only the numbers are valid; therefore, all characters except numbers are stripped out by the function *preg_replace()*. The code in the brackets allows numbers, but it replaces all other characters with nothing. For instance, if the user enters (01297) 877-111, the number is changed to 01297877111, which is an acceptable phone number for entry into the database table. If the user accidentally typed a letter within the phone number, the letter would be removed. This will also strip out '+' characters from international numbers, which may be undesirable. You might be able to find a regex function that will cope with this problem.

For more information on preg_replace, see *http://www.php.net/manual/en/function.preg-replace.php.*

■ **Note**   In the downloadable files, the links in the headers that have a *Register* menu button, now connect to the safer registration page.

Run XAMPP, and enter `http://localhost/finalpost/safer-register-page.php` in the address field of a browser. Then register some members, but make deliberate errors to see the results.

In the previous chapter, we created and listed a screen for searching addresses and phone numbers. We will now make use of that screen so that we can edit addresses and phone numbers.

Search for an Address and Telephone Number

The screen for searching an address/phone number was shown and listed in the last chapter. Figure 6-3 is shown again as a reminder.

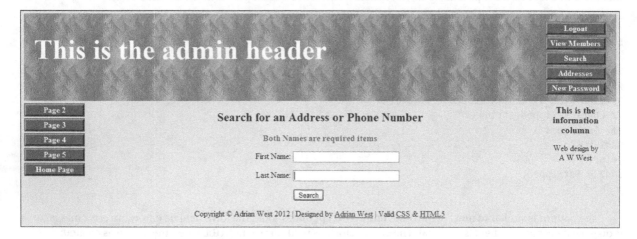

Figure 6-3. *Searching for an address or phone number*

The code will not be repeated in this chapter because it was listed in Chapter 5. However, if you wish to review the code, it can be seen in the downloaded files for Chapter 6. Just to remind you, the code begins with a session to ensure that only the administrator can view and amend the member's record. In this case, we have assumed that the administrator's session is sufficient protection. Only the administrator can search for users' records.

Listing 6-3. Creating the Search Address Page (search_address.php)

```php
<?php
session_start();
if (!isset($_SESSION['user_level']) or ($_SESSION['user_level'] != 1))
{
header("Location: login.php");
exit();
}
?>
<!doctype html>
<html lang=en>
<head>
```

The *<form>* section of the file has been amended in the downloadable file so that it connects to the file *view_found_address.php* as follows:

```
<form action="view_found_address.php" method="post">
```

We will now examine the screen for the retrieved addresses and phone numbers.

Note that the *Delete* column is absent from the table displayed in Figure 6-4 because the act of deleting is rather final; it must be done using the *delete_record.php* page, where the administrator is given a second chance to decide whether to delete the record.

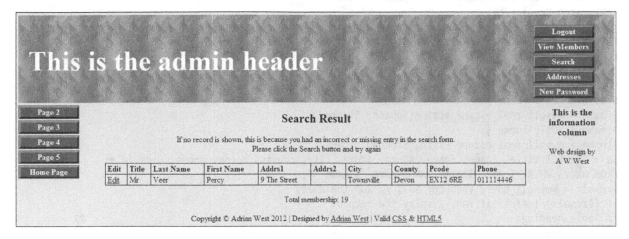

Figure 6-4. *The new table displays the address and telephone number of the selected member*

Viewing the Retrieved Address and Phone Number

The screen shot shown in Figure 6-4 appeared at the end of Chapter 5, where I promised that the listing would be given in this chapter.

The code that displays the two new columns is shown in bold type in Listing 6-4.

Listing 6-4. Displaying a Table with Address and Phone Number (view_found_address.php)

```php
<?php
session_start();
if (!isset($_SESSION['user_level']) or ($_SESSION['user_level'] != 1)) {
header("Location: login.php");
exit();
}
?>
<!doctype html>
<html lang=en>
<head>
<title>View found address page</title>
<meta charset=utf-8>
<link rel="stylesheet" type="text/css" href="includes.css">
<style type="text/css">
```

```
p { text-align:center; }                                                        #1
table, tr { width:850px; }
</style>
</head>
<body>
<div id="container">
<?php include("includes/header-admin.php"); ?>
<?php include("includes/nav.php"); ?>
<?php include("includes/info-col.php"); ?>
<div id="content"><!--Start of the page content-->
<h2>Search Result</h2>
<?php
// This script fetches selected records from the users table
require ('mysqli_connect.php'); // Connect to the database
echo '<p>If no record is shown, this is because of an incorrect or missing entry in ↵
the search form.<br>Click the Search button and try again</p>';
$fname=$_POST['fname'];
$fname = mysqli_real_escape_string($dbcon, $fname
$lname=$_POST['lname'];
$lname = mysqli_real_escape_string($dbcon, $lname);
$q = "SELECT title, lname, fname, addr1, addr2, city, county, pcode, phone, user_id ↵
FROM users WHERE lname='$lname' AND fname='$fname' ";
$result = @mysqli_query ($dbcon, $q); // Run the query
if ($result) { // If it ran, display the records
// Table headings                                                               #2
echo '<table>
<tr><td><b>Edit</b></td>
<td><b>Title</b></td>
<td><b>Last Name</b></td>
<td><b>First Name</b></td>
<td><b>Addrs1</b></td>
<td><b>Addrs2</b></td>
<td><b>City</b></td>
<td><b>County</b></td>
<td><b>Pcode</b></td>
<td><b>Phone</b></td>
</tr>';
// Fetch and display the records                                                #3
while ($row = mysqli_fetch_array($result, MYSQLI_ASSOC)) {
    echo '<tr>
    <td><a href="edit_address.php?id=' . $row['user_id'] . '">Edit</a></td>
<td>' . $row['title'] . '</td>
<td>' . $row['lname'] . '</td>
<td>' . $row['fname'] . '</td>
<td>' . $row['addr1'] . '</td>
<td>' . $row['addr2'] . '</td>
<td>' . $row['city'] . '</td>
<td>' . $row['county'] . '</td>
<td>' . $row['pcode'] . '</td>
<td>' . $row['phone'] . '</td>
    </tr>';
    }
```

```
    echo '</table>'; // Close the table
    mysqli_free_result ($result); // Free up the resources
} else { // If it failed to run
// Display message
echo '<p class="error">The current users could not be retrieved. We apologize for ↵
any inconvenience.</p>';
// Debugging message
    echo '<p>' . mysqli_error($dbcon) . '<br><br>Query: ' . $q . '</p>';
} // End of the if ($result)
//Now display a figure for the total number of records/members
$q = "SELECT COUNT(user_id) FROM users";
$result = @mysqli_query ($dbcon, $q);
$row = @mysqli_fetch_array ($result, MYSQLI_NUM);
$members = $row[0];
mysqli_close($dbcon); //Close the database connection
echo "<p>Total membership: $members</p>";
?>
</div><!-- End of found address page -->
<?php include("includes/footer.php"); ?>
</div>
</body>
</html>
```

Explanation of the Code

```
table, tr { width:850px; }
```
#1

This internal style increases the table width to accommodate the extra columns for the address and telephone number. This overrides the table style in the main style sheet.

```
// Table headings
echo '<table>
<tr><td><b>Edit</b></td>
<td><b>Title</b></td>
<td><b>First Name</b></td>
<td><b>Last Name</b></td>
<td><b>Addrs1</b></td>
<td><b>Addrs2</b></td>
<td><b>City</b></td>
<td><b>County</b></td>
<td><b>Pcode</b></td>
<td><b>Phone</b></td>
</tr>';
```
#2

The column headings now include the member's address and telephone number.

```
// Fetch and display the records
while ($row = mysqli_fetch_array($result, MYSQLI_ASSOC)) {
    echo '<tr>
    <td><a href="edit_address.php?id=' . $row['user_id'] . '">Edit</a></td>
    <td>' . $row['title'] . '</td>
```
#3

```
<td>' . $row['lname'] . '</td>
<td>' . $row['fname'] . '</td>
<td>' . $row['addr1'] . '</td>
<td>' . $row['addr2'] . '</td>
<td>' . $row['city'] . '</td>
<td>' . $row['county'] . '</td>
<td>' . $row['pcode'] . '</td>
<td>' . $row['phone'] . '</td>
    </tr>';
    }
    echo '</table>'; // Close the table
```

The table is displayed and populated with the member's address and telephone number. Note the link for editing the address/phone table is now *edit_address.php*. We will be creating this file now.

Edit Addresses and Telephone Numbers

When the record is found and the *Edit* link is clicked, the screen shown in Figure 6-5 appears. This allows the administrator to edit any field in the display. Note that the administrator cannot delete a record from the address/phone search because this must be done using the record displayed by the *delete.php* page. Deleting a record from the *delete.php* page automatically removes the address and phone details because they are part of the record.

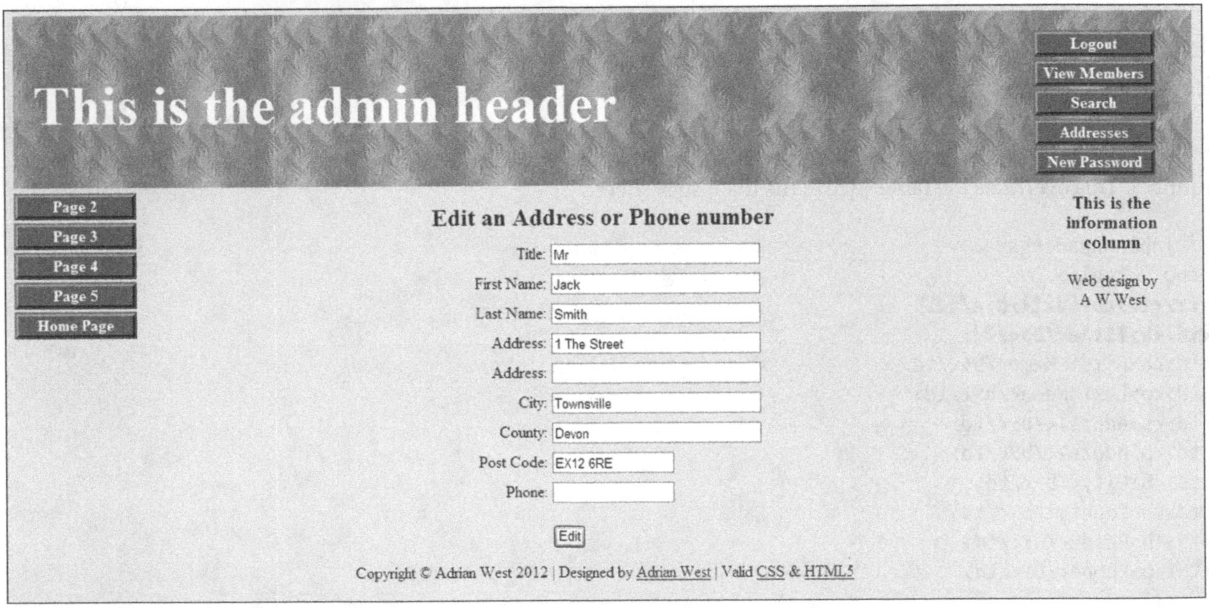

Figure 6-5. *The screen for editing fields in the address/phone display*

In this screen, all the fields can be edited. The second address and the phone fields are optional—that is, they can remain empty if necessary. The code for the screen is given in Listing 6-5.

Listing 6-5. Creating a Screen for Editing the Address and Phone Number (edit_address.php)

```php
<?php
session_start();                                                              #1
if (!isset($_SESSION['user_level']) or ($_SESSION['user_level'] != 1))
{
header("Location: login.php");
exit();
}
?>
<!doctype html>
<html lang=en>
<head>
<title>Edit an address or phone number</title>
<meta charset=utf-8>
<link rel="stylesheet" type="text/css" href="includes.css">
<style type="text/css">
p { text-align:center; }
input.fl-left { float:left; }
#submit { float:left; }
</style>
</head>
<body>
<div id="container">
<?php include("includes/header-admin.php"); ?>
<?php include("includes/nav.php"); ?>
<?php include("includes/info-col-cards.php"); ?>
<div id="content"><!--Start of the page-for editing addresses and phone numbers-->
<h2>Edit an Address or Phone number</h2>
<?php
// Click the Edit link in view_found_address.php page and this editing interface appears
// Look for a valid user ID, either through GET or POST
if ( (isset($_GET['id'])) && (is_numeric($_GET['id'])) ) { // From view_users.php
    $id = $_GET['id'];
} elseif ( (isset($_POST['id'])) && (is_numeric($_POST['id'])) ) { // Form submission
    $id = $_POST['id'];
} else { // If no valid ID, quit the script
    echo '<p class="error">This page has been accessed in error.</p>';
    include ('includes/footer.php');
    exit();
}
require ('mysqli_connect.php');
// Has the form been submitted?
if ($_SERVER['REQUEST_METHOD'] == 'POST') {
    $errors = array();
// Look for the title
    if (empty($_POST['title'])) {
        $errors[] = 'You forgot to enter the title.';
    } else {
        $title = mysqli_real_escape_string($dbcon, trim($_POST['title']));
    }
```

```php
// Look for the first name
if (empty($_POST['fname'])) {
    $errors[] = 'You forgot to enter the first name.';
} else {
    $fn = mysqli_real_escape_string($dbcon, trim($_POST['fname']));
}
// Look for the last name
if (empty($_POST['lname'])) {
    $errors[] = 'You forgot to enter the last name.';
} else {
    $ln = mysqli_real_escape_string($dbcon, trim($_POST['lname']));
}
// Look for the 1st address
if (empty($_POST['addr1'])) {
$errors[] = 'You forgot to enter the first address.';
} else {
$addr1 = mysqli_real_escape_string($dbcon, trim($_POST['addr1']));
}
// Look for the address 2
if (!empty($_POST['addr2'])) {
$addr2 = mysqli_real_escape_string($dbcon, trim($_POST['addr2']));
}else{
$addr2 = NULL;
}
// Look for the city
if (empty($_POST['city'])) {
$errors[] = 'You forgot to change the city.';
} else {
$city = mysqli_real_escape_string($dbcon, trim($_POST['city']));
}
// Look for the county
if (empty($_POST['county'])) {
$errors[] = 'You forgot to change the county.';
} else {
$county = mysqli_real_escape_string($dbcon, trim($_POST['county']));
}
// Look for the post code
if (empty($_POST['pcode'])) {
$errors[] = 'You forgot to enter the post code.';
} else {
$pcode = mysqli_real_escape_string($dbcon, trim($_POST['pcode']));
}
// Look for the phone number
if (!empty($_POST['phone'])) {
$phone = mysqli_real_escape_string($dbcon, trim($_POST['phone']));
    }else{
    $phone = NULL;}
 if (empty($errors)) { // If the entries are OK
// Make the query
    $q = "SELECT user_id FROM users WHERE lname='$ln' AND user_id != $id";
    $result = @mysqli_query($dbcon, $q);
```

```
            if (mysqli_num_rows($result) == 0) {
// Make the update query
$q = "UPDATE users SET title='$title', fname='$fn', lname='$ln', addr1='$addr1', ↵
addr2='$addr2', city='$city', county='$county', pcode='$pcode', phone='$phone' ↵
WHERE user_id=$id LIMIT 1";
            $result = @mysqli_query ($dbcon, $q);
            if (mysqli_affected_rows($dbcon) == 1) { // If it ran OK.
// Echo a message if the edit was satisfactory:
                echo '<h3>The user has been edited.</h3>';
            } else { // Echo an error message if the query failed.
            echo '<p class="error">The user was not edited due to a system error. ↵
We apologize for the inconvenience.</p>'; // Error message
echo '<p>' . mysqli_error($dbcon) . '<br />Query: ' . $q . '</p>'; // Debugging message.
            }
            } else { // Display the errors
            echo '<p class="error">The following error(s) occurred:<br>';
            foreach ($errors as $msg) { // Echo each error.
            echo " - $msg<br />\n";
            }
            echo '</p><p>Please try again.</p>';
        } // End of if (empty($errors))section.
} // End of the conditionals
// Select the user's information
$q = "SELECT title, fname, lname, addr1, addr2, city, county, pcode, phone FROM users ↵
WHERE user_id=$id";
$result = @mysqli_query ($dbcon, $q);
if (mysqli_num_rows($result) == 1) { // Valid user ID, display the form.
// Get the user's information:
    $row = mysqli_fetch_array ($result, MYSQLI_NUM);
// Create the form
echo '<form action="edit_address.php" method="post">
<p><label class="label" for="title">Title:</label><input class="fl-left" id="title" ↵
type="text" name="title" size="30" maxlength="30" value="' . $row[0] . '"></p>
<p><label class="label" for="fname">First Name:</label><input class="fl-left" id="fname" ↵
type="text" name="fname" size="30" maxlength="30" value="' . $row[1] . '"></p>
<p><label class="label" for="lname">Last Name:</label><input class="fl-left" id="lname" ↵
type="text" name="lname" size="30" maxlength="40" value="' . $row[2] . '"></p>
<p><label class="label" for="addr1">Address:</label><input class="fl-left" id="addr1" ↵
type="text" name="addr1" size="30" maxlength="50" value="' . $row[3] . '"></p>
<p><label class="label" for="addr2">Address:</label><input class="fl-left" ↵
id="addr2"type="text" name="addr2" size="30" maxlength="50" value="' . $row[4] . '"></p>
<p><label class="label" for="city">City:</label><input class="fl-left" id="city" ↵
type="text" name="city" size="30" maxlength="30" value="' . $row[5] . '"></p>
<p><label class="label" for="county">County:</label><input class="fl-left" ↵
id="county"type="text" name="county" size="30" maxlength="30" value="' . $row[6] . '"></p>
<p><label class="label" for="pcode">Post Code:</label><input class="fl-left" ↵
id="pcode"type="text" name="pcode" size="15" maxlength="15" value="' . $row[7] . '"></p>
<p><label class="label" for="phone">Phone:</label><input class="fl-left" id="phone" ↵
type="text" name="phone" size="15" maxlength="15" value="' . $row[8] . '"></p>
<br><br><p><input id="submit" type="submit" name="submit" value="Edit"></p><br>
<input type="hidden" name="id" value="' . $id . '">
</form>';
```

```
} else { // The user could not be validated
    echo '<p class="error">The page was accessed in error.</p>';
}
mysqli_close($dbcon);
include ('includes/footer.php');
?>
</div>
</div>
</body>
</html>
```

Explanation of the Code

The majority of the code you will have seen before. The administrator is not allowed to view users' passwords or secret user names. This explained snippet of code is a reminder of the importance of using sessions to protect a private page.

```
<?php                                                                    #1
session_start();
if (!isset($_SESSION['user_level']) or ($_SESSION['user_level'] != 1))
{
header("Location: login.php");
exit();
}
?>
```

If an unauthorized person tries to access this file, the session redirects him to the login page.

■ **Note** The listings for all the other files are not included in this chapter because most of them are exactly the same as those in Chapter 5. To view the code, see the downloadable files for Chapter 6.

Summary

In this chapter, we created a copy of the database from Chapter 5 using a new name and password. We then created the table. The process for importing an SQL file was described, and the chapter provided a quick method for creating tables. The traditional method of manually creating a table was given in case you need more practice.

Next we tidied the filing system by putting all the included files into a folder named *includes*. We discussed security, briefly mentioned *sanitization*, and investigated the term *validation*. We then created a new safer registration page. We learned how to create pages for searching and editing addresses and telephone numbers.

In the next chapter, you will learn how to make those inevitable last-minute changes and also how to migrate a database to a remote host. Advice will be given on how to back up tables.

■ ■ ■

CHAPTER 7

Migrating to a Host and Backing Up Your Web Site Database

You might think that the database-driven web site created in Chapter 6 is finished and ready for migrating to the host. However, in a real-world situation the client has had time to think about the site and will ask for some last-minute changes. A web designer/developer cannot anticipate everything that a client might expect to achieve with a database driven web site. Also, last-minute changes might be necessary when new laws require the database to exclude certain information or to include additional information.

This chapter contains the following sections:

- Making last-minute changes

  - Include members' titles in the paginated display

  - Allow members to update their own details

  - Provide for safe e-mailing

  - Create a secure feedback form

- Migrating the database to a remote host

- Backing up your database

Making Last-Minute Changes

In our example, we assume that the client asked for some last-minute changes as follows:

- In the database in Chapter 6, the membership secretary noticed that, although the title column was present in the administrator's individual record display, the title was absent from the paginated table display. We will correct this omission.

- To reduce the workload of the membership secretary, he asked us to allow registered members to update their own details. For instance, telephone numbers and e-mail addresses can change. If a woman is recorded as "Miss," her title and last name might need changing when she gets married. We will therefore allow members to update their titles, last names, addresses, telephone numbers and e-mail addresses.

- The client asked for a live but secure e-mail address to be displayed on the web site. This will allow users to contact the organization and the webmaster.

- The client asked for an inquiry form so that users can ask for more information about the organization before registering as members.

We will begin by creating a new database and table.

Create a New Database

The last-minute changes were requested for the database that we created in the last chapter, but to avoid confusion we will implement the changes in a new version of the database called *lmnmigrate*, short for *Last Minute* and *Migrate*. (The first letter of the name is a lowercase *L*, not an uppercase *I*.) In the *htdocs* folder within the *xampp* folder, create a new folder called *lmnmigrate*.

Download the files for Chapter 7 from the book's page at www.apress.com, and load them into the new lmnmigrate folder:

1. Use a browser to access phpMyAdmin, click the *Databases* tab, and create a new database called *lmnmigrate*.

2. Scroll down and find the newly created database, and select the box next to it.

3. Click *Check Privileges* and then click *Add User*. Add a new user and password as follows:

   User name: trevithick
   Host: select Local,
   Password: locomotive

4. Scroll down to the item named *Global Privileges*, and click *Check All*.

Scroll to the bottom, and click *Add User* (or *Go* in some versions)to save the database user's details.

Details of the Downloaded File for Connecting to the Database

The file *mysqli_connect.php* is already created for you in the download files for this chapter.

```php
<?php
// Connect to the lmnmigrate database and set the encoding to utf-8
DEFINE ('DB_USER', 'trevithick');
DEFINE ('DB_PASSWORD', 'locomotive');
DEFINE ('DB_HOST', 'localhost');
DEFINE ('DB_NAME', 'lmnmigrate');
// Make the connection
$dbcon = @mysqli_connect (DB_HOST, DB_USER, DB_PASSWORD, DB_NAME) OR die ↵
('Could not connect to MySQL: ' . mysqli_connect_error() );
// Set the encoding
mysqli_set_charset($dbcon, 'utf8');
```

We now need to create a table named *users* with 17 columns.

I already compiled the table for you and exported it into a file called *users.sql*. You will find this among the downloaded files you just installed in the folder lmnmigrate.

In phpMyAdmin, open the database lmnmigrate.

In the home page of phpMyAdmin, click the database lmnmigrate. Then use the *import* tab to import the file *users.sql* you downloaded and installed in htdocs.

To locate the *users.sql* file in the *Import* interface, click the *Browse* button shown circled in Figure 7-1.

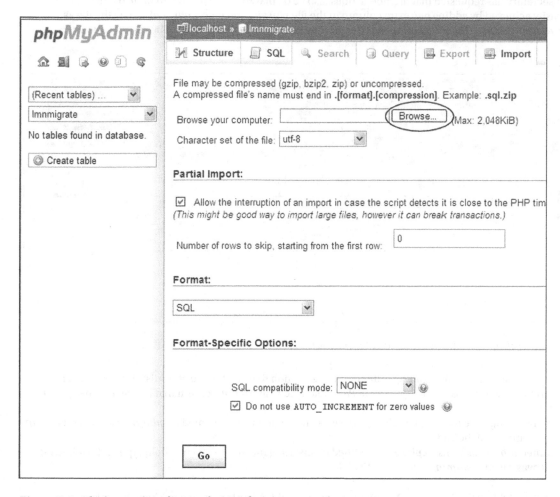

Figure 7-1. *The Import interface in phpMyAdmin*

The Browse button will allow you to navigate to the downloaded file *users.sql*. Open the file and then click the *Go* button. The file will be imported. If you now open the *users* table in phpMyAdmin, you will be able to view the table and its data by clicking, in turn, the *Structure* tab and the *Browse* tab.

■ **Note** The PHP files in this chapter make no attempt to accommodate styling for Internet Explorer 8; for this a conditional style sheet would be required. The files work in all the most popular browsers, but make sure your copy of Mozilla FireFox is the latest version; otherwise, you will not be able to access the administration pages with FireFox. In fact, FireFox is rather picky, and unlike the other browsers, it will detect the tiniest error in the PHP code and throw the user back to the login page.

Displaying the Members' Titles in the Paginated Table

In Chapter 6, the members' titles were included in some screen displays but not in the paginated table display. The membership secretary has requested that members' titles also be displayed in the paginated table display.

This is easily achieved by adding one extra column in the file *php view-members.php* and saving the file as *admin_view_users_title.php*. The *Title* column is added in front of the *Last name* column. The result is shown in Figure 7-2.

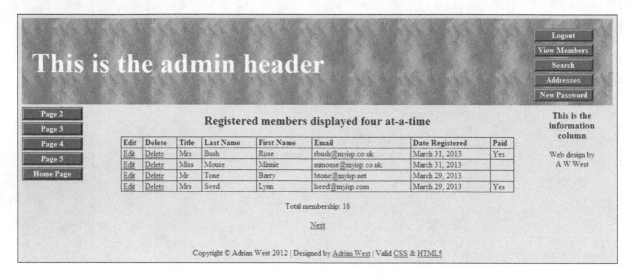

***Figure 7-2.** The members' titles are now visible in the paginated table*

The records are displayed in descending order of the registration date so that the administrator can quickly view the latest registrations. This helps him to update the *Paid* field when PayPal notifies him that a registrant has paid the membership fee.

To achieve the change, the file *view-members.php* has been amended and renamed as *admin_view_users_title.php*. Listing 7-1 gives a snippet of the code.

The file named *admin_view_users.php* was modified by inserting the items shown in bold type in the following snippet. The file was saved as *admin_view_users_title.php*.

Partial Listing 7-1. Adding the Title to the Members' Paginated Table View (admin_view_users_title.php)

```
// Make the query
$q = "SELECT title, lname, fname, email, DATE_FORMAT(registration_date, '%M %d, %Y') ↵
AS regdat, class, paid, user_id FROM users ORDER BY registration_date DESC ↵
LIMIT $start, $pagerows";
$result = @mysqli_query ($dbcon, $q); // Run the query
$members = mysqli_num_rows($result);
if ($result) { // If the query ran OK, display the records
// Table headings
echo '<table>
<tr><td><b>Edit</b></td>
<td><b>Delete</b></td>
<td><b>Title</b></td>
```

```
<td><b>Last Name</b></td>
<td><b>First Name</b></td>
<td><b>Email</b></td>
<td><b>Date Registered</b></td>
<td><b>Class</b></td>
<td><b>Paid</b></td>
</tr>';
// Fetch and display all the records
while ($row = mysqli_fetch_array($result, MYSQLI_ASSOC)) {
    echo '<tr>
    <td><a href="edit_record.php?id=' . $row['user_id'] . '">Edit</a></td>
    <td><a href="delete_record.php?id=' . $row['user_id'] . '">Delete</a></td>
    <td>' . $row['title'] . '</td>
    <td>' . $row['lname'] . '</td>
    <td>' . $row['fname'] . '</td>
    <td>' . $row['email'] . '</td>
    <td>' . $row['regdat'] . '</td>
    <td>' . $row['class'] . '</td>
    <td>' . $row['paid'] . '</td>
    </tr>';
    }
    echo '</table>'; // Close the table
    mysqli_free_result ($result); // Free up the resources
    } else { // If the query did not run OK
// Error message
```

No changes were needed to the rest of the file.

For you to be able to access the amended file, the menu button link in the file *header_admin.php* has been changed from *admin_view_users.php* to *admin_view_users_title.php*.

■ **Caution**   Remember to log in as administrator to view the table of members.
The login details are **e-mail:** jsmith@outcook.com and **password:** dogsbody.

The membership secretary has asked for a change so that members can update their own records to a limited extent. This is a common feature in database-driven web sites. For instance, in PayPal, members can update their profile (their own account details). A provision was already made for members to change their password; therefore, this feature will not be included again in the members' update interface that follows.

Allow Members to Update Their Own Records

When members have logged in, they can be permitted to update their own accounts. They have no access to any other member's account; this is controlled by means of a session and a LIMIT that allows only one record to be displayed by the member. The member's amendments are validated and sanitized. If members want to change a password, they must use the *New Password* button on the header menu. The items that can be amended are limited for security reasons, and they are as follows: title, first name, last name, e-mail address, postal address, and telephone number.

■ **Tip** The membership secretary might ask the member to send an e-mail notifying the secretary that an amendment has been made. If so, this must be stipulated clearly on the edit page. The member should be asked to use the *Contact Us* button on the menu. This will open the feedback form described later in this chapter.

The first step consists of changing the header for the "members' only" page so that registered members can view and amend their records. The header shown in Figure 7-3 is modified to allow this.

Figure 7-3. *The new "Your Account" button in the header for the members' page*

The code for the revised header is shown in Listing 7-2. This is in the *includes* folder in the download code.

Listing 7-2. Creating the New Header for the Members' Page (header_members_account.php)

```
<div id="header-members">
<h1>This is the header</h1>
<div id="reg-navigation">
    <ul>
        <li><a href="logout.php">Logout</a></li>
        <li><a href="edit_your_account.php">Your Account</a></li>
        <li><a href="register-password.php">New Password</a></li>
    </ul>
    </div>
</div>
```

When the *Your Account* button is clicked, a new page is displayed as shown in Figure 7-4.

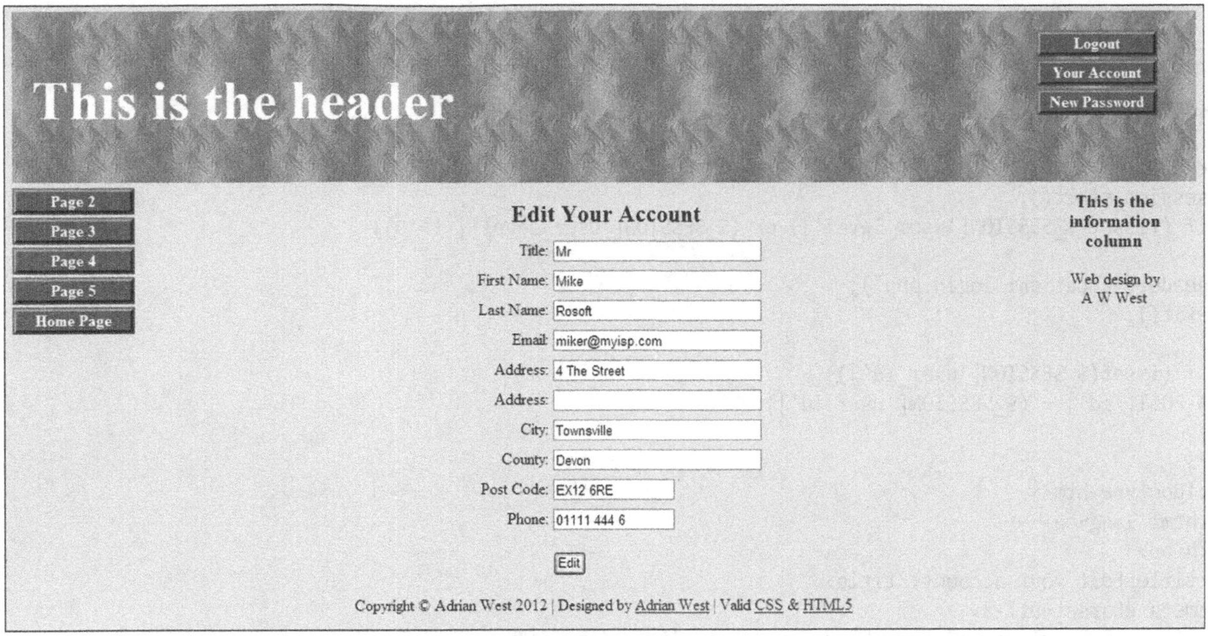

Figure 7-4. *This screen shot shows the data that a registered member is allowed to update*

The importance of logging out is stressed on the members' page and on the update screens. When fields are edited and the Edit button is clicked, the confirmation message appears as shown in Figure 7-4a.

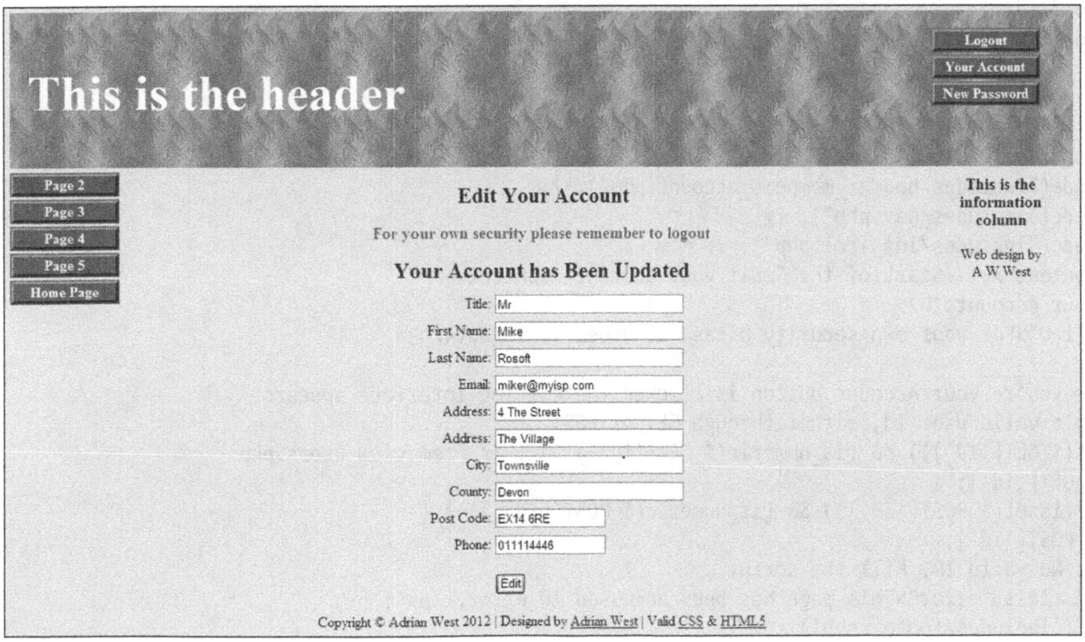

Figure 7-4a. *The update is confirmed*

The code for the screens shown in Figures 7-4 and 7-4a is given in Listing 7-3 as follows:

Listing 7-3. Creating an Interface for Members to Edit Their Accounts (edit_your_account.php)

The member must log in to access this page; therefore, it begins with session statements.

```php
<?php
session_start();                                                    #1
if (!isset($_SESSION['user_level']) or ($_SESSION['user_level'] != 0))
{
header("Location: login.php");
exit();
}
if (isset($_SESSION['user_id'])){
$_POST['id'] = ($_SESSION['user_id']);
}
?>
<!doctype html>
<html lang=en>
<head>
<title>Edit your account</title>
<meta charset=utf-8>
<link rel="stylesheet" type="text/css" href="includes.css">
<style type="text/css">
p { text-align:center; }
label {margin-bottom:5px; margin-top:5px; }
input.fl-left { float:left; margin-bottom:5px; margin-top:5px; padding-bottom:0; }
/*#submit { margin-left:-660px; margin-top:260px; margin-bottom:10px; }*/
#submit { position:absolute; top:595px; left:330px; }
.red { color:red; }
footer { position:absolute; top:600px; left:370px;;}
</style>
</head>
<body>
<div id="container">
<?php include("includes/header_members_account.php"); ?>
<?php include("includes/nav.php"); ?>
<?php include("includes/info-col.php"); ?>
<div id="content"><!--Start of the "edit your account" content-->
<h2>Edit Your Account</h2>
<h3 class="red">For your own security please remember to logout</h3>
<?php
// When the you're your-Account button is clicked the editing interface appears
// Look for a valid user id, either through GET or POST
if ( (isset($_GET['id'])) && (is_numeric($_GET['id'])) ) { // From view_users.php
   $id = $_GET['id'];
} elseif ( (isset($_POST['id'])) && (is_numeric($_POST['id'])) ) {
   $id = $_POST['id'];
} else { // No valid ID, kill the script
   echo '<p class="error">This page has been accessed in error.</p>';
   include ('includes/footer.php');
   exit();
}
```

194

```php
require ('mysqli_connect.php');
// Has the form been submitted?
if ($_SERVER['REQUEST_METHOD'] == 'POST') {
    $errors = array();
// Trim the title                                                           #2
$tle = trim($_POST['title']);
// Strip HTML and apply escaping
$stripped = mysqli_real_escape_string($dbcon, strip_tags($tle));
// Get string lengths
$strLen = mb_strlen($stripped, 'utf8');
// Check stripped string
if( $strlen < 1 ) {
    $errors[] = 'You forgot to enter your title.';
}else{
$title = $stripped;
}
// Trim the first name
$name = trim($_POST['fname']);
// Strip HTML and apply escaping
$stripped = mysqli_real_escape_string($dbcon, strip_tags($name));
// Get string lengths
$strlen = mb_strlen($stripped, 'utf8');
// Check stripped string
if( $strLen < 1 ) {
    $errors[] = 'You forgot to enter your first name.';
}else{
$fn = $stripped;
}
// Trim the last name
$lnme = trim($_POST['lname']);
// Strip HTML and apply escaping
$stripped = mysqli_real_escape_string($dbcon, strip_tags($lnme));
// Get string lengths
$strlen = mb_strlen($stripped, 'utf8');
// Check stripped string
if( $strlen < 1 ) {
$errors[] = 'You forgot to enter your last name.';
}else{
$ln = $stripped;
}
//Set the email variable to FALSE                                           #3
$e = FALSE;
// Check that an email address has been entered
if (empty($_POST['email'])) {
$errors[] = 'You forgot to enter your email address.';
}
//remove spaces from beginning and end of the email address and validate it
if (filter_var((trim($_POST['email'])), FILTER_VALIDATE_EMAIL)) {
//A valid email address is then registered
$e = mysqli_real_escape_string($dbcon, (trim($_POST['email'])));
}else{
```

```php
$errors[] = 'Your email is not in the correct format.';
}
// Trim the first address
$add1 = trim($_POST['addr1']);
// Strip HTML and apply escaping
$stripped = mysqli_real_escape_string($dbcon, strip_tags($add1));
// Get string lengths
$strlen = mb_strlen($stripped, 'utf8');
// Check stripped string
if( $strlen < 1 ) {
    $errors[] = 'You forgot to enter your address.';
}else{
    $addr1 = $stripped;
}
// Trim the second address
$addr2 = trim($_POST['addr2']);
// Strip HTML and apply escaping
$stripped = mysqli_real_escape_string($dbcon, strip_tags($addr2));
// Get string lengths
$strlen = mb_strlen($stripped, 'utf8');
// Check stripped string
if( $strLen < 1 ) {
    $ad2=NULL;
}else{
$addr2 = $stripped;
}
// Trim the city
$ct = trim($_POST['city']);
// Strip HTML and apply escaping
$stripped = mysqli_real_escape_string($dbcon, strip_tags($ct));
// Get string lengths
$strlen = mb_strlen($stripped, 'utf8');
// Check stripped string
if( $strlen < 1 ) {
    $errors[] = 'You forgot to enter your city.';
}else{
$city = $stripped;
}
// Trim the county
$conty = trim($_POST['county']);
// Strip HTML and apply escaping
$stripped = mysqli_real_escape_string($dbcon, strip_tags($conty));
// Get string lengths
$strlen = mb_strlen($stripped, 'utf8');
// Check stripped string
if( $strlen < 1 ) {
    $errors[] = 'You forgot to enter your county.';
}else{
$county = $stripped;
}
```

```
// Trim the post code
$pcod = trim($_POST['pcode']);
// Strip HTML and apply escaping
$stripped = mysqli_real_escape_string($dbcon, strip_tags($pcod));
// Get string lengths
$strlen = mb_strlen($stripped, 'utf8');
// Check stripped string
if( $strlen < 1 ) {
    $errors[] = 'You forgot to enter your county.';
}else{
$pcode = $stripped;
}
// Has a phone number been entered?                                              #4
if (empty($_POST['phone'])){
$ph=($_POST['phone']);
}
elseif (!empty($_POST['phone'])) {
//Remove spaces, hyphens, letters and brackets
$phone = preg_replace('/\D+/', '', ($_POST['phone']));
$ph=$phone;
}
if (empty($errors)) { // If everything's OK
//  make the query
    $q = "SELECT user_id FROM users WHERE lname='$ln' AND user_id != $id";
    $result = @mysqli_query($dbcon, $q);
    if (mysqli_num_rows($result) == 0) {
// Make the update query                                                         #5
$q = "UPDATE users SET title='$title', fname='$fn', lname='$ln', email='$e', ↵
addr1='$addr1', addr2='$addr2', city='$city', county='$county', pcode='$pcode', ↵
phone='$phone' WHERE user_id=$id LIMIT 1";
    $result = @mysqli_query ($dbcon, $q);
    if (mysqli_affected_rows($dbcon) == 1) { // If the query was successful
    // Echo a message if the edit was satisfactory
    echo '<h3>Your Account has Been Updated.</h3>';
    } else { // Echo a message if the query failed
echo '<p class="error">The user could not be edited due to a system error. ↵
We apologize for any inconvenience.</p>'; // Message
echo '<p>' . mysqli_error($dbcon) . '<br />Query: ' . $q . '</p>'; // Debugging message
    }
    }
    } else { // Display the errors
    echo '<p class="error">The following error(s) occurred:<br>';
    foreach ($errors as $msg) { // Echo each error
     echo " - $msg<br/>\n";
    }
    echo '</p><p>Please try again.</p>';
    } // End of the if (empty($errors))section
    } // End of the conditionals
```

```
// Select the member's information                                              #6
$q = "SELECT title, fname, lname, email, addr1, addr2, city, county, pcode, phone ↵
FROM users WHERE user_id=$id";
$result = @mysqli_query ($dbcon, $q);
if (mysqli_num_rows($result) == 1) { // If the user id is valid, display the form
// Get the member's information
    $row = mysqli_fetch_array ($result, MYSQLI_NUM);
// Create the form                                                              #7
echo '<form action="edit_your_account.php" method="post">
<p><label class="label" for="title">Title:</label>
<input class="fl-left" id="title" type="text" name="title" size="30" maxlength="30" ↵
value="' . $row[0] . '"></p>
<p><label class="label" for="fname">First Name:</label>
<input class="fl-left" id="fname" type="text" name="fname" size="30" maxlength="30" ↵
value="' . $row[1] . '"></p>
<p><label class="label" for="lname">Last Name:</label>
<input class="fl-left" id="lname" type="text" name="lname" size="30" maxlength="40" ↵
value="' . $row[2] . '"></p>
<p><label class="label" for="email">Email:</label>
<input class="fl-left" id="email" type="text" name="email" size="30" maxlength="50" ↵
value="' . $row[3] . '"></p>
<p><label class="label" for="addr1">Address:</label>
<input class="fl-left" id="addr1" type="text" name="addr1" size="30" maxlength="50" ↵
value="' . $row[4] . '"></p>
<p><label class="label" for="addr2">Address:</label>
<input class="fl-left" id="addr2"type="text" name="addr2" size="30" maxlength="50" ↵
value="' . $row[5] . '"></p>
<p><label class="label" for="city">City:</label>
<input class="fl-left" id="city" type="text" name="city" size="30" maxlength="30"↵
value="' . $row[6] . '"></p>
<p><label class="label" for="county">County:</label>
<input class="fl-left" id="county"type="text" name="county" size="30" maxlength="30" ↵
value="' . $row[7] . '"></p>
<p><label class="label" for="pcode">Post Code:</label>
<input class="fl-left" id="pcode"type="text" name="pcode" size="15" maxlength="15" ↵
value="' . $row[8] . '"></p>
<p><label class="label" for="phone">Phone:</label>
<input class="fl-left" id="phone" type="text" name="phone" size="15" maxlength="15" ↵
value="' . $row[9] . '"></p>
<br><br><p><input id="submit" type="submit" name="submit" value="Edit"></p><br>
<input type="hidden" name="id" value="' . $id . '">
</form>';
} else { // The user could not be validated
...echo '<p class="error">This page has been accessed in error.</p>';
}
mysqli_close($dbcon);
include ('includes/footer.php');
?>
</div>
</div>
</body>
</html>
```

Explanation of the code

```
session_start();                                                                #1
if (!isset($_SESSION['user_level']) or ($_SESSION['user_level'] != 0))
{
header("Location: login.php");
exit();
}
if (isset($_SESSION['user_id'])){
$_POST['id'] = ($_SESSION['user_id']);
}
```

To ensure that no ordinary registered member can view and edit the member's account, a session is started that contains the logged-in member's details.

```
// Trim the title                                                               #2
$tle = trim($_POST['title']);
// Strip HTML and apply escaping
$stripped = mysqli_real_escape_string($dbcon, strip_tags($tle));
// Get string lengths
$strLen = mb_strlen($stripped, 'utf8');
// Check stripped string
if( $strLen < 1 ) {
$errors[] = 'You forgot to enter your title.';
}else{
$title = $stripped;
}
```

We saw this code before in the safer registration page in Chapter 6. It prevents HTML tags and JavaScript from being inserted into the database table. This sanitizing format is applied many times in this listing. This test applies only if the user has altered the title in an unacceptable manner, or the user has cleared the field and then forgotten to enter a new title.

```
//Set the email variable to FALSE                                              #3
$e = FALSE;
// Check that an email address has been entered
if (empty($_POST['email'])) {
$errors[] = 'You forgot to enter your email address.';
}
//remove spaces from beginning and end of the email address and validate it
if (filter_var((trim($_POST['email'])), FILTER_VALIDATE_EMAIL)) {
//A valid email address is then registered
$e = mysqli_real_escape_string($dbcon, (trim($_POST['email'])));
}else{
$errors[] = 'Your email is not in the correct format.';
}
```

This method of validating an email address was demonstrated in Chapter 6 and is repeated here.

```
// Has a phone number been entered?                                            #4
if (empty($_POST['phone'])){
$ph=($_POST['phone']);
}
```

```
elseif (!empty($_POST['phone'])) {
//Remove spaces, hyphens, letters and brackets
$phone = preg_replace('/\D+/', '', ($_POST['phone']));
$ph=$phone;
}
```

This method of sanitizing and formatting a phone number was explained in Chapter 6 and is repeated here.

```
// Make the update query:                                              #5
$q = "UPDATE users SET title='$title', fname='$fn', lname='$ln', email='$e', ↵
addr1='$addr1', addr2='$addr2', city='$city', county='$county', pcode='$pcode', ↵
phone='$phone' WHERE user_id=$id LIMIT 1";
```

There are 10 fields in the form; therefore, there must be 10 items in the update query.

```
// Select the member's information                                     #6
$q = "SELECT title, fname, lname, email, addr1, addr2, city, county, pcode, phone ↵
FROM users WHERE user_id=$id";
$result = @mysqli_query ($dbcon, $q);
if (mysqli_num_rows($result) == 1) { // If the user id is valid, display the form
// Get the member's information
   $row = mysqli_fetch_array ($result, MYSQLI_NUM);
```

The 10 column names in the member's selected information must exactly match the 10 names in the code block beginning at line **#4**.

```
// Create the form                                                     #7
echo '<form action="edit_your_account.php" method="post">
<p><label class="label" for="title">Title:</label>
<input class="fl-left" id="title" type="text" name="title" size="30" maxlength="30" ↵
value="' . $row[0] . '"></p>
<p><label class="label" for="fname">First Name:</label>
<input class="fl-left" id="fname" type="text" name="fname" size="30" maxlength="30" ↵
value="' . $row[1] . '"></p>
<p><label class="label" for="lname">Last Name:</label>
<input class="fl-left" id="lname" type="text" name="lname" size="30" maxlength="40" ↵
value="' . $row[2] . '"></p>
```

This shows part of the sticky form for editing the member's account.

■ **Caution** Carefully check the array items shown bold in the block of code beginning with reference line **#7** in the preceding code. They must be in numerical order. In this table display, they are numbered from 0 to 9 because there are 10 fields. When inserting an extra field or deleting a field, it is only too easy to forget to renumber the array items in square brackets. This would result in either the same data appearing in two adjacent fields or inappropriate data appearing in some fields.

That concludes the tutorial on the database *lmnmigrate*. Some useful additions to a database-driven web site (or any web site) will now be described.

To enable users to contact the web site's owner, the client has asked for a live e-mail address to be included in one of the web site pages. This could be a magnet for spammers. The webmaster should encode the live e-mail address so that spam spiders cannot harvest it.

Safe E-mailing

This useful item is for information only. A live but secure e-mail link is not included in any page of this chapter's example web site. An influx of spam will cause distress to the site owner, and this breach of privacy can sow seeds of doubt about the security of the rest of the web site, especially the security of the database. This also damages the reputation of the web designer. This section describes a method for preventing spam.

Escrambler is a free, anti-spam device. It was originally produced as a plain, clickable e-mail link, and it was later enhanced by the addition of an image of the e-mail address by InnerPeace.org. Their web page is at `http://innerpeace.org/escrambler.shtml`. The web site will quickly generate the code for you, or you can adapt the JavaScript snippet that follows.

The JavaScript code allows for two conditions:

- The full e-mail address appears on the screen in the form of an image that is clickable but invisible to spam spiders.

- If no image is available, a link having the words *E-mail Me* appears on the web page.

Clicking either the image or the words *E-mail Me* causes the user's default e-mail program to open with the e-mail address already filled in. Users might need to be told that the e-mail might go into their Outbox and, therefore, the user must send it by clicking the *Send/Receive* button.

I usually create the image of the e-mail address in MS Paint, and then I import it into my image-manipulation program, crop it, and export it as a transparent *.gif* or *.png* file.

Insert the following JavaScript snippet into the *<body>* section where you want the e-mail address to appear. The JavaScript code also places a picture of the e-mail address on the page so that the user can click it or make note of it for future use. For your own e-mail scrambler, just change the items in bold type in the following example, which hides the address fredbloggs@aol.com:

```
<p>
<script type="text/javascript">
<!--
function escramble(){
var a,b,c,d,e,f,g,h,i
a='<a href=\"mai'
b='fredbloggs'
c='\">'
a+='lto:'
b+='@'
b+='aol.com'
e='</a>'
f=''
g='<img src=\"'
h='images/bloggs-email.jpg'
i='\" alt="Email Me" border="0">'
if(f) d=f
else if(h) d=g+h+i
else d=b
```

```
document.write(a+b+c+d+e)
}
escramble()
//-->
</script></p>
```

The JavaScript breaks down the traditional email address into little bits and then reassembles it. Spam spiders have great difficulty reading JavaScript and images; even if they could read JavaScript, the email address is so fragmented that spam spiders would not make sense of it.

■ **Caution**   The variable *f* is followed by two single quotes, not a double quote. The line *g='<img src=\"'* ends in a double quote followed by a single quote.

A Minor Problem

Your client might decide not to put her e-mail address on the web site. She might prefer to use a feedback form because it is a more secure approach. However, there is nothing to prevent someone from ignoring the form and contacting her directly by guessing her e-mail address. This very rarely happens, and the sender is not necessarily a mass spammer. This is known as *link exchange spam,* so tell your client not to be alarmed. I have personally received only a handful of these e-mails in a decade. This is a minor problem and can be ignored.

So how does the sender know your client's e-mail address? He knows because he found her web site. Why does he try to contact her? He wants to establish a reciprocal link from her web site to his web site. Because the secure feedback form (described in the next section) is designed to prevent the sender from entering URLs, he must use a normal e-mail; therefore, he makes an intelligent guess.

He tries *info@clientswebsite.co.uk* or *sales@clientswebsite.co.uk,* and so on. Link exchange spam can be the result of viewing the web site's e-mail address posted in *Whois,* a directory of web-site owners. If your client has a *catchall* e-mail address, the person could also type something like *postmaster@clientswebsite.co.uk* and it might reach your client. His e-mail would then include his URL. He normally won't include a dodgy URL because he could be traced through his e-mail. By requesting and establishing a reciprocal link, he is hoping to improve his search engine ranking by having as many external links as possible that link to his site. Your client should not click a link in the e-mail to look at the person's web site(s); if she did take the risk, she would usually find that his content is in no way related to her own web site, so she should not agree to a reciprocal link. Also, she will most likely find that his link page has between 50 and 150 links on it. If she agrees to a reciprocal link, search engines will assume she is using a link farm and, as a consequence, they might penalize her web site.

If your client is receiving this type of e-mail, she can avoid it by using a different e-mail address in the feedback form handler. She could use her home address, *clientsemailaddress@herisp.co.uk.* No one will be able to guess her home e-mail address by looking at her web site, but the downside is that her business replies won't be distinguished from her personal e-mails.

A Secure Feedback Form

A Contact Us form is not strictly related to databases; however, it is an interactive element and provides an excellent application of PHP code.

E-mails and feedback forms are the most popular contact methods for allowing users to communicate easily with web-site owners. Unfortunately, both contact methods can be abused. E-mail addresses are harvested and sold to spammers. Both actions cause distress and an influx of spam to the site owner, and they don't enhance the reputation of the web designer. Hackers can hijack a form and use it to send frequent nonsense messages to the web-site owner.

These usually contain malware that can be activated via a link in the text area. This section describes some options to prevent these risks.

When designing feedback forms, we need to consider the following three points:

- Because layout tables are deprecated, CSS must be used to align the input fields neatly.

- Blind and severely visually-impaired users can use screen readers to read and reply to forms. Accessibility rules must be observed

- Filters must be built into the form handler to prevent the form from being hijacked for nefarious purposes.

Bogus Replies

Concerning the third point, when I first began to design web sites, I added feedback forms to many of my clients' web sites and all of them were plagued by people using robots to send bogus replies to the site owners. The replies contained gobbledygook and dodgy URLs. These e-mails were often sent once or twice a week. The site owners were naturally disappointed and puzzled because they thought they had received an order. Fortunately, they did not click a link on these bogus replies, but they contacted me immediately for a solution. What do bogus replies look like?

A typical bogus reply is shown next. For your security, I altered the URLs and the e-mail address. The replies contain gobbledygook as well as live URL links that lead to dodgy web sites. A web-site owner unfamiliar with the weird behavior of hackers might be tempted to click a link, which could lead to all sorts of mayhem. Note the large number of live URLs:

```
Content-type: text/html;charset="iso-8859-1"
From: ezrxsk@xyzvjox.com
X-Antivirus: AVG for Email 8.0.100 [270.4.1/1510]
From: Damon Rosario
Telephone No: 24315931045
Mobile phone: 25803805787
Address of sender: pkPb80 <a href=\"http://lpwqwncrqwel.com/\">lpwqwncrqwel</a>,
superobligation hobbledehoyish foreread minaway wips taenioid chancellorism unsocket
3Sy6Rl <a href=\"http://qmuxlytwkukt.com/\">qmuclytwkuxt</a>,
[url=http://iqdqouydsqzn.com/]iqdqouydsqzn[/url],
[link=http://lvcukrrfrlpj.com/]lvkuckrfrlsj[/link], http://uiaopyzucuiyba.com/
<a href=http://www.axtemplate.com/ >Axtemplate.com</a>
http://www.moley.co.jp/
```

The robot is designed to send URLs; therefore, the way to kill the replies—and also cause the robot to have hysterics and crash—is to put a URL filter in the form handler.

What Does a Genuine Reply Look Like?

The following is a genuine e-mail received from a secure form and its handler:

```
This message was sent from:
http://www.my-website.co.uk/feedbackform.html
------------------------------------------------------------
Name of sender: Andrew Eastman
Email of sender: aeastman@myisp.co.uk
Telephone No: 01111 222333
XP?: No
Vista?: No
```

Windows7?: No
Windows 8: Yes
Laptop?: Yes
Desktop?; No
------------------------ MESSAGE ----------------------------
How can I change back to Windows 7?

The Feedback Form

Figure 7-5 shows a typical feedback form.

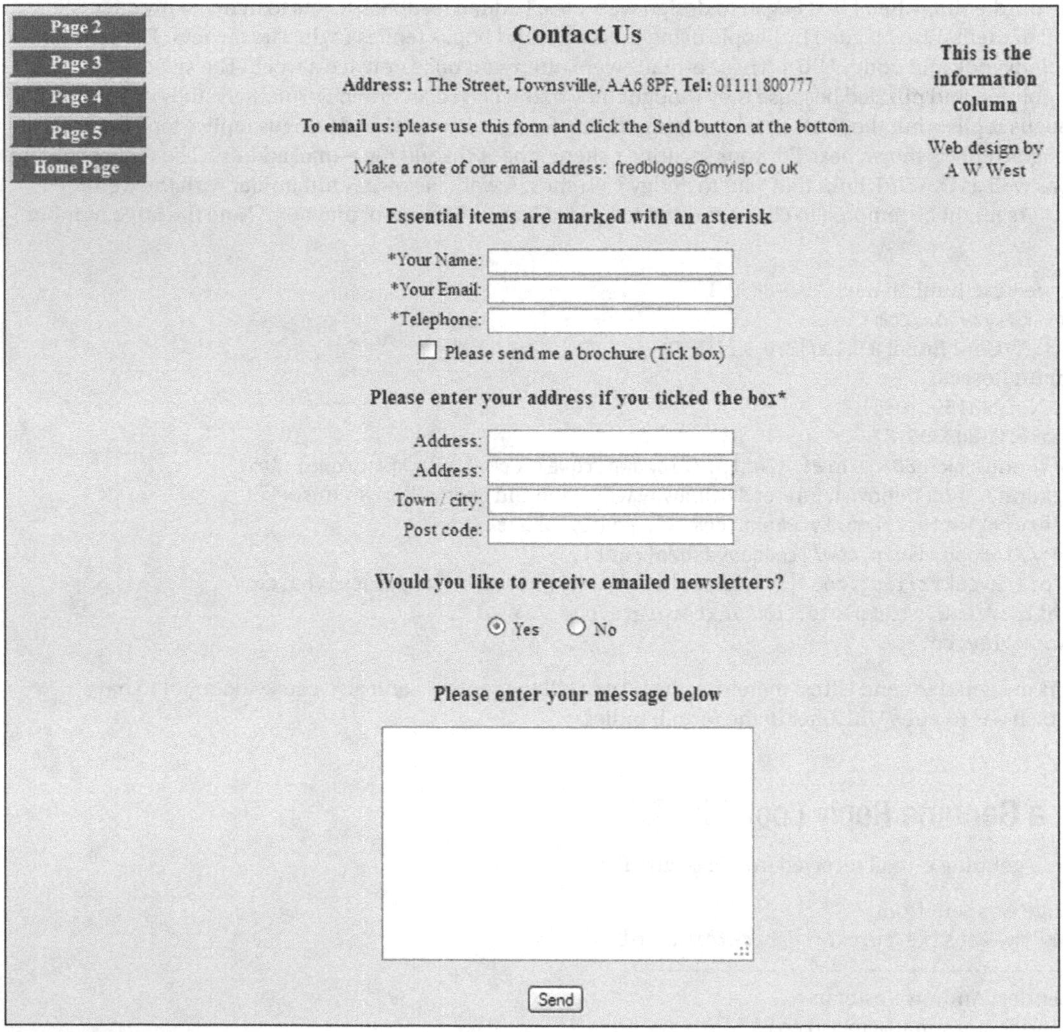

Figure 7-5. *The feedback form. In this screenshot, the header and footer are cropped away to save space*

The code for the feedback page concentrates on preventing URLs from being entered because these are the main concern with forms filled in by robots.

The formatting of a form can be rather time consuming, and you will need a conditional style sheet for Internet Explorer 8. The Listing 7-4a that follows contains an additional link to a style sheet for the feedback form and also a link to a conditional style sheet for Internet Explorer 8. Conditional style sheets must always be listed after the other style sheets. The code [if lt IE 9] means "if less than Internet Explorer 9." Note the space between IE and 9.

Listing 7-4a. Creating the "Contact Us" Form (feedback-form.php)

```
<!doctype html>
<html lang=en>
<head>
<title>The feedback form</title>
<meta charset=utf-8>
<link rel="stylesheet" type="text/css" href="includes.css">
<link rel="stylesheet" type="text/css" href="feedback_form.css">
<!--[if lt IE 9]>
<link rel="stylesheet" type="text/css" href="feedback-ie8.css">
<![endif]-->
</head>
<body>
<div id='container'>
<div id='content'><!--Start of feedback form content.-->
<div id="form">
<form action="feedback_handler.php" method="post" ><h2>Contact Us</h2>
<div class="cntr">
<strong>Address:</strong> 1 The Street, Townsville, AA6 8PF, <b>Tel:</b> 01111 800777</div>
<p class="cntr"><strong>To email us:</strong> please use this form and click the Send button at the
bottom.</p>
<p class="cntr"><span class="small">Make a note of our email address:</span>
<img alt="Email Address" title="Email Address" src="images/fredbloggs.gif"></p>
<h3 >Essential items are marked with an asterisk</h3>
<!--START OF TEXT FIELDS-->
<label for="username" class="label"><span class="red">*</span>Your Name: </label>
<input id="username" name="username" size="30">
<label for="useremail" class="label"><span class="red">*</span>Your Email:</label>
<input id="useremail" name="useremail" size="30">
<label for="phone" class="label"><span class="red">*</span>Telephone:</label>
<input id="phone" name="phone" size="30">
<div class="chk1">
<input id="chkbox1" name="brochure" value="Yes" type="checkbox">
<label for ="chkbox1> Please send me a brochure (Tick box)</label>
</div>
<h3>Please enter your address if you ticked the box<span class="star">*</span></h3>
<div>
<label for="addrs1" class="label">    Address: </label>
<input id="addrs1" name="addrs1" size="30">
<label for="addrs2" class="label">    Address: </label>
<input id="addrs2" name="addrs2" size="30">
<label for="city" class="label"> Town/city: </label>
<input id="city" name="city" size="30">
<label for="postcode" class="label"> Post code:</label>
```

```
<input id="postcode" name="postcode" size="30"></div>
<h3>Would you like to receive emailed newsletters?</h3>
<div id="rad">
<input checked="checked" id="radio1" name="letter" type="radio" value="yes">
<label for="radio1">Yes</label>    
<input id="radio2" name="letter" value="no" type="radio">
<label for="radio2">No  </label>
</div><br><br>
    <h3><span class="red">*</span>Please enter your message below</h3>
<textarea id="comment" name="comment" rows="12" cols="40"></textarea><br>
<!--THE SUBMIT BUTTON GOES HERE-->
<input id="sb" value="Send" title="Send" alt="Send" type="submit"><br>
</form>
</div><!--End of the feedback form content.-->
<div id="footer">
<?php include('includes/footer.php'); ?>
</div></div></div><br>
</body>
</html>
```

Bogus feedback from the feedback form can be stopped by means of a PHP handler file. If a URL has been entered into any text field, the form handler causes an error message to appear when the submit button is clicked. This stops bogus replies completely. Hackers do not hijack a form to send advertisements for Viagra; they are hoping the site owner will click the URL link and fire up the sender's dodgy web site(s). The web sites usually contain malware such as a Trojan horse that would take control of the site owner's computer. The PHP code for the handler is shown in Listing 7-4b.

Listing 7-4b. Creating the Feedback Form Handler (feedback_handler.php)

Note that dummy e-mail addresses and URLs have been used. Replace them with your client's details.

```
<?php
/* Feedback form handler*/
// set to the email address of the recipient
$mailto = "clientsemailaddress@clients-isp.com" ;                              #1
//$mailto = "webmaster@someisp.com" ;
$subject = "Message from my website" ;
// list the pages to be displayed
$formurl = "http://www.clients-isp.com/feedback_form.html" ;
$errorurl = "http://www.clients-isp.com/error.html" ;
$thankyouurl = "http://www.clients-isp.com/thankyou.html" ;
$emailerrurl = "http://www.clients-isp.com/emailerr.html" ;
$errorcommenturl = "http://www.clients-isp.com/commenterror.html" ;
$uself = 0;
// Set the information received from the form as short variables           #2
$headersep = (!isset( $uself ) || ($uself == 0)) ? "\r\n" : "\n" ;
$username = $_POST['username'] ;
$useremail = $_POST['useremail'] ;
$phone = $_POST['phone'];
$brochure = $_POST['brochure'];
$addrs1 = $_POST['addrs1'];
$addrs2=$_POST['addrs2'];
```

```php
$city=$_POST['city'];
$postcode = $_POST['postcode'] ;
$letter=$_POST['letter'];
$comment = $_POST['comment'] ;
$http_referrer = getenv( "HTTP_REFERER" );
//Check that all four essential fields are filled out
if (empty($username) || empty($useremail) || empty($phone)|| empty($comment)) {
header( "Location: $errorurl" );
exit ; }
//check that no URLs have been inserted in the username text field
if (strpos ($username, '://')||strpos($username, 'www') !==false){
header( "Location: $errorsuggesturl" );
exit ; }

if (preg_match( "[\r\n]", $username ) || preg_match( "[\r\n]", $useremail )) {
header( "Location: $errorurl" );
exit ; }
#remove any spaces from beginning and end of email address
$useremail = trim($useremail);
#Check for permitted email address patterns
$_name = "/^[-!#$%&\'*+\\.\/0-9=?A-Z^_`{|}~]+";
$_host = "([-0-9A-Z]+\.)+";
$_tlds = "([0-9A-Z]){2,4}$/i";
if(!preg_match($_name."@".$_host.$_tlds,$useremail)) {
header( "Location: $emailerrurl" );
exit ; }
// Has a phone number been entered?
if (!empty($_POST['phone'])) {
//Remove spaces, hyphens, letters and brackets.
$phone = preg_replace('/\D+/', '', ($_POST['phone']));
}
//Has the brochure box been checked?
if(!$brochure) {$brochure = "No";}
//check that no URLs have been inserted in the addrs1 text field
if (strpos ($addrs1, '://')||strpos($addrs1, 'www') !==false){
header( "Location: $errorsuggesturl" );
exit ; }
//Check whether URLs have been inserted in the addrs2 text field
if (strpos ($addrs2, '://')||strpos($addrs2, 'www') !==false){
header( "Location: $errorsuggesturl" );
exit ; }
//Check whether URLs have been inserted in the city text field
if (strpos ($city, '://')||strpos($city, 'www') !==false){
header( "Location: $errorsuggesturl" );
exit ; }
//Check whether URLs have been inserted in the pcode text field
if (strpos ($pcode, '://')||strpos($pcode, 'www') !==false){
header( "Location: $errorsuggesturl" );
exit ; }
//Check whether URLs have been inserted in the comment text area
if (strpos ($comment, '://')||strpos($comment, 'www') !==false){
```

#3

#4

#5

207

```
header( "Location: $errorcommenturl" );
exit ; }
if($letter !=null) {$letter = $letter;}
$messageproper =                                                              #6
"This message was sent from:\n" .
"$http_referrer\n" .
"------------------------------------------------------------\n" .
"Name of sender: $username\n" .
"Email of sender: $useremail\n" .
"Telephone: $phone\n" .
"brochure?: $brochure\n" .
"Address: $addrs1\n" .
"Address: $addrs2\n" .
"City: $city\n" .
"Postcode: $postcode\n" .
"Newsletter:$letter\n" .
"----------------------- MESSAGE ------------------------\n\n" .
$comment .
"\n\n-----------------------------------------------------\n" ;
mail($mailto, $subject, $messageproper, "From: \"$username\" <$useremail>" );
header( "Location: $thankyouurl" );
exit ;
?>
```

■ **Caution** Because the XAMPP package may not contain an e-mail client such as *Mercury*, to test the form and its handler, the form and its associated files MUST be uploaded and tested on a remote host.

Explanation of the Code

Note that URLs cannot be inserted into the check box or the radio button fields. URLs cannot be inserted into the phone field because it only allows numbers.

```
$mailto = "clientsemailaddress@clients-isp.com" ;                             #1
//$mailto = "webmaster@someisp.com" ;
$subject = "Message from my website" ;
// list the pages to be displayed
$formurl = "http://www.clients-isp.com/feedback_form.html" ;
$errorurl = "http://www.clients-isp.com/error.html" ;
$thankyouurl = "http://www.clients-isp.com/thankyou.html" ;
$emailerrurl = "http://www.clients-isp.com/emailerr.html" ;
$errorphoneurl = "http://www.clients-isp.com/phonerror.html" ;
$errorcommentturl = "http://www.clients-isp.com/commenterror.html" ;
```

The dummy email addresses and URLs will need to be replaced by real-world addresses and URLs. To test the feedback form, the webmaster will comment-out the client's email address and remove the comment symbols from his own email address. When he is satisfied that the form works, he will reverse this process so that the client receives the feedback. In the last five lines, five files are assigned to short form variables. The last four lines refer to pages containing error messages.

```
// Set the information received from the form as short variables          #2
$headersep = (!isset( $uself ) || ($uself == 0)) ? "\r\n" : "\n" ;
$username = $_POST['username'] ;
$useremail = $_POST['useremail'] ;
$phone = $_POST['phone'];
$brochure = $_POST['brochure'];
$addrs1 = $_POST['addrs1'];
$addrs2=$_POST['addrs2'];
$city=$_POST['city'];
$postcode = $_POST['postcode'] ;
$letter=$_POST['letter'];
$comment = $_POST['comment'] ;
```

The long variables are assigned to short variables to make the form easier to read and debug.

```
//check that no URLs have been inserted in the username text field        #3
if (strpos ($username, '://')||strpos($username, 'www') !==false){
header( "Location: $errorsuggesturl" );
exit ; }
```

The PHP function *strpos()* checks whether the URL symbols // and *www* are present within the string input by the user. The function actually finds the position of the first occurrence of a string within a string. If URL symbols are present, a page containing an error message is displayed. The function is used to check most of the fields in the form.

```
#remove any spaces from beginning and end of email address               #4
$useremail = trim($useremail);
#Check for permitted email address patterns
$_name = "/^[-!#$%&\'*+\\.\/0-9=?A-Z^_`{|}~]+";
$_host = "([-0-9A-Z]+\.)+";
$_tlds = "([0-9A-Z]){2,4}$/i";
if(!preg_match($_name."@".$_host.$_tlds,$useremail)) {
header( "Location: $emailerrurl" );
exit ; }
```

This code uses a regular expression to validate the e-mail address, if the e-mail address does not validate, a page containing an error message is displayed.

```
//Has the brochure box been checked?                                      #5
if(!$brochure) {$brochure = "No";}
```

If the brochure check box has not been selected, the word *No* is assigned to the variable $brochure; otherwise, the word *Yes* will be assigned by default.

```
$messageproper =                                                          #6
"This message was sent from:\n" .
"$http_referrer\n" .
"------------------------------------------------------------\n" .
"Name of sender: $username\n" .
"Email of sender: $useremail\n" .
"Telephone: $phone\n" .
"brochure?: $brochure\n" .
```

```
"Address: $addrs1\n" .
"Address: $addrs2\n" .
"City: $city\n" .
"Postcode: $postcode\n" .
"Newsletter:$letter\n" .
"----------------------- MESSAGE ------------------------\n\n" .
$comment .
"\n\n-------------------------------------------------------------\n" ;
mail($mailto, $subject, $messageproper, "From: \"$username\" <$useremail>" );
header( "Location: $thankyouurl" );
```

This block of code constructs the e-mail using the variables provided in the feedback form by the user. Note the full stops after each item; these are very important. The code \n inserts a line break (or Enter) between each item. The last two lines send the e-mail using the PHP function mail().

The Style Sheets for the Feedback Form

Two style sheets are provided, one is a *conditional* to ensure that the fields format properly with Internet Explorer 8.

Listing 7-4c. Creating the Style Sheet for the Feedback Form (feedback_form.css)

```
body {margin:0; padding:0; }
form {position:relative; margin-left:90px; margin-bottom:0; width:590px; }
.cntr { text-align:center; }
#rad { width:140px; position:absolute; left:210px; }
.chk1 { margin-left:150px; }
textarea { margin-left:120px; }
label, input { margin-bottom:3px; }
#sb { width:50px; margin-left:250px; margin-top:10px;}
img { vertical-align: top; }
h3 { width:590px; text-align:center; }
.red { color:red; }
```

Listing 7-4d. Creating the Conditional Style Sheet for Use With IE8 (feedback-ie8.css)

```
body {margin:0; padding:0; }
form {position:relative; margin-left:90px; margin-bottom:0; width:590px; }
.cntr { text-align:center; }
#rad { width:140px; position:absolute; left:210px; }
.chk1 { margin-left:150px; }
textarea { position:absolute; left:15px; margin-bottom:45px;}
label, input { margin-bottom:3px; }
#sb { position:absolute; top:770px; width:50px; margin-left:250px; margin-top:50px; }
img { vertical-align: top; }
h3 { width:590px; text-align:center; }
.red { color:red; }
#footer {margin-top:190px; }
```

The *Thank You* Page and the Error Messages

The *thank you* page confirms that the e-mail was sent successfully. It would be a pity to lose the visitor, so add a *Return to Home Page* button. The *thank you* page is shown in Figure 7-6, and the code is Listing 7-5a. The page has a *Go Back* button with the text *Return to Home Page*, but you can replace this button with your main navigation menu. The styling for the button is incorporated in the style sheet feedback.css.

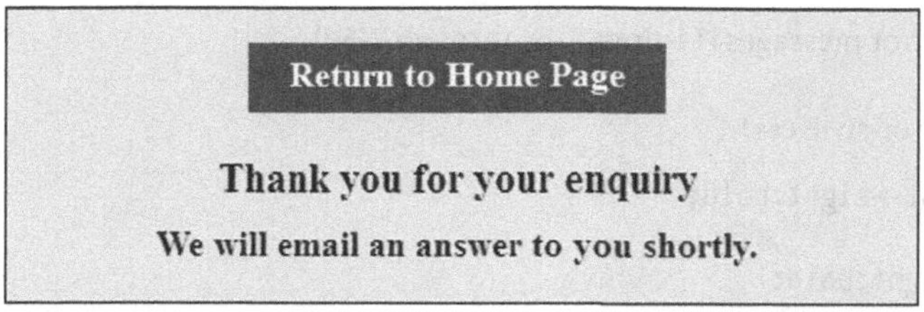

Figure 7-6. *The "thank you" page message*

Listing 7-5a. Creating the "Thank You" Page (thankyou.html)

```
<!doctype html>
<html lang=en>
<head>
<title>Thank you for your enquiry</title>
<meta charset=utf-8>
<link rel="stylesheet" type="text/css" href="feedback.css">
</head>
<body>
<p> </p>
<div id="back-button"><a title="Return to the Home page" href="index.php">Return to ↵
Home Page</a>
</div>
<div><br>
<h2>Thank you for your enquiry</h2>
<h3>We will email an answer to you shortly.</h3>
</div>
</body>
</html>
```

If the e-mail message was not sent successfully, an explanatory error message will appear.

Why use error pages instead of echoing a piece of text to the screen? I found that many of my clients prefer the distinct message, and the help that a page provides, rather than the usual small error messages in red that can be overlooked or that are so often too brief. If you prefer to echo messages to the page, create an $error() array to hold the messages as we did in the registration page.

Listing 7-5b. The Style Sheet for the "Thank You" Page (feedback.css)

```
/*FEEDBACK.CSS*/
/*reset browsers for cross-client consistency*/
body,h2,h3,p {margin:0; padding:0 }
body {text-align:center; background-color:#D7FFEB; color:black; ↵
font-family: "times new roman"; max-width:100%; min-width:960px;
```

```
font-size: medium; color: #000000; margin: auto; width:95%;}
#back-button { margin:20px auto 0 auto; text-align:center; width:200px; height:25px; ↵
padding:5px; background-color:brown; color:white; font-size:110%; font-weight:bold; }
#back-button a { text-decoration:none; color:white; }
#back-button a:hover { color:red; }
h2 { margin-top:15px; margin-bottom:10px; font-size:130%; font-weight:bold;}
h3 { font-size:110%; font-weight:bold; text-align:center;}
```

The style sheet in Listing 7-5c is used for all three error messages (Listings 7-5c through 7-5e).

Listing 7-5c. The Style Sheet for the Error Messages (error-style.css)

```
body { text-align:center; font-size: large; font-weight:bold;
}
span.red {color:red; font-size:xlarge; font-weight:bold;
}
```

Listing 7-5d provides the code for the error message for empty fields.

Listing 7-5d. Creating the Page for Empty Field Errors (error.html)

```html
<!doctype html>
<html lang=en>
<head>
<title>Error message. Missing essentials</title>
<meta charset=utf-8>
<link rel="stylesheet" type="text/css" href="error-style.css">
</head>
<body>
<p> </p>
<p> </p>
<p>One or more of the essential items in the form has not been filled in.</p>
<p>Essential items have a red asterisk like this <span>*</span></p>
<p>Please return to the form<br> and then fill in the missing items</p>
<form method="post" action=" ">
<input type="button" value="Return to form" onclick="history.go(-1)">
</form>
</body>
</html>
```

Listing 7-5e shows the code for the e-mail error message.

Listing 7-5e. Error Message for an Invalid E-mail Address (emailerr.html)

```html
<!doctype html>
<html lang=en>
<head>
<title>Email error message</title>
<meta charset=utf-8>
<link rel="stylesheet" type="text/css" href="error-style.css">
</head>
```

```
<body>
<p> </p>
<p>Your email address has an incorrect format.</p>
<p>Please return to the form<br>and then correct your email address.</p>
<form method="post" action=" ">
<input type="button" value="Return to form" onclick="history.go(-1)">
</form>
</body>
</html>
```

Listing 7-5f provides the code for the message forbidding the entry of URLs.

Listing 7-5f. Error Message for Unacceptable Comment Content (commenterror.html)

```
<!doctype html>
<html lang=en>
<head>
<title>Error message. Do not enter URLs</title>
<meta charset=utf-8>
<link rel="stylesheet" type="text/css" href="error-style.css">
</head>
<body>
Sorry, but website addresses are not allowed<br><br>
<p>Please click the Back button on your internet browser<br>and then remove any ↩
website addresses from the form.</p>
</body>
</html>
```

■ **Note**　You will need to add one more button to the main menu (includes/nav.php). Label the button "Contact Us", and link it to the file *feedback_form.php*.

Migrating the Database and Tables to a Remote Host

Having created a database and table(s) using XAMPP, how can we transfer them to a hosting company? The process for migrating a database from XAMPP (or any other WAMP) to a remote host worries beginners more than any other aspect of database development. This is because MySQL manuals and Internet tutorials rarely provide proper explanations for the procedure; in fact, the many manuals I possess (or have borrowed) either omit or hardly mention this important topic.

For this tutorial, I chose to use the *admintable* database from Chapter 4 simply because it is shorter than the databases in Chapters 5 and 6 and will take up less space in this chapter.

■ **Caution**　You will need to determine which operating system is used in your chosen hosting package. Linux and Windows require a slightly different migration procedure.

A Puzzling Error Message

I experienced an occasional problem when trying to transfer a database to another computer. I use phpMyAdmin to create a new empty database in the destination computer, and then I try to import the SQL dump for the table(s). An error message sometimes appears saying that the table already exists. This is weird because there is definitely not a table in that empty database. The solution is to access the XAMPP folder on the first computer and drill down to the MySQL folder and then the Data folder. I then save a copy of the *somefilename.frm* file on a pen drive (memory stick). I copy that file into the same Data folder on the destination computer and the problem is solved. Being rather paranoid about backups, I regularly save copies of the **.frm* files as well as the SQL dumps.

Creating and Exporting the SQL File

The first stage for migrating a database consists of creating an SQL file (the dump file). You will be able to export two types of dumps: (i) for the table(s) only or (ii) f or the database and table(s). We will be using the table(s) only file because dumps of whole databases can be fraught with snags when you import them. They can also be huge and therefore unacceptable to many hosts. Use phpMyAdmin to export a file. The exported SQL file for the table(s) is a simple text file of the type *filename.sql,* although other file types can be chosen for the exported file. The content of the file and the process will be explained next.

To Create a Dump File of a Table or Tables

Open a browser, and in the address bar, type **http://localhost/phpmyadmin/**.

In the left panel of phpMyAdmin, click the database containing the *admintable* tables to be exported. Then click the Export tab as shown in Figure 7-7.

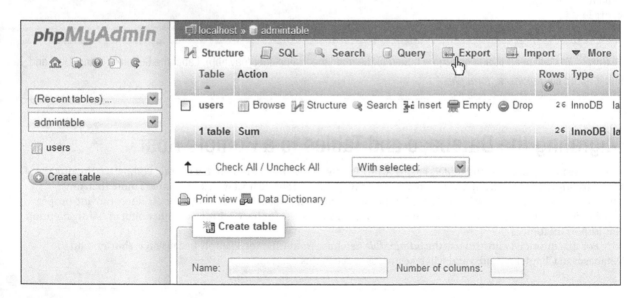

Figure 7-7. *The screen for dumping the database table*

When the Export tab is selected, the next screen appears as shown in Figure 7-8.

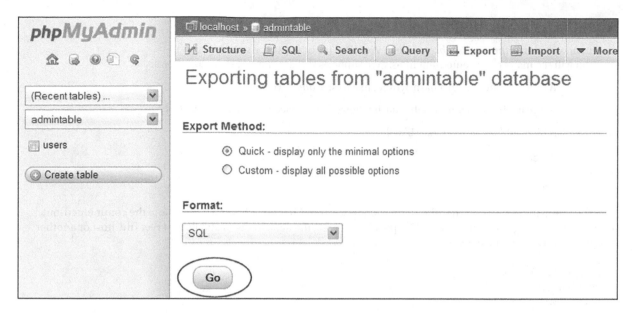

Figure 7-8. *Export the SQL file*

Select the *Quick* option, and ensure that the format is SQL. Then click the *Go* button shown circled. Depending on your browser and settings, you will be asked whether to open or save the file as shown in Figure 7-9.

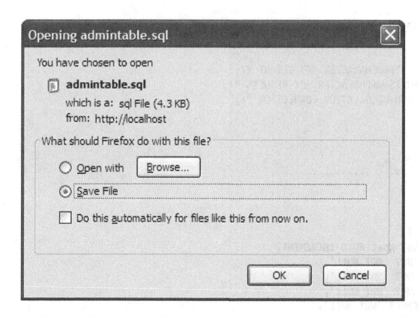

Figure 7-9. *Choose to save the SQL file*

Choose to save the file, and click OK. You will be taken to a screen where you can decide where to save it. Save the file in a folder where you can access it for uploading it to the host later with your FTP client. The default is the *Downloads* folder.

What Does an SQL Dump Look Like?

We will now examine the *admintable.sql* file in WordPad (or better still, use Notepad++).

You will see many commented-out lines. SQL supports three comment styles as follows:

- A line beginning with a hash symbol like this: *#some text*

- A line beginning with a double dash followed by a space like this: *-- some text*

- A block of text between tags like this:

```
/*some text
some text
some text*/
```

The dump for the table in the admintable database (from Chapter 4) is shown next. Note the commented-out code. The remaining code, shown in bold type, will re-create the table in the destination server (the host or another computer with XAMPP installed).

```
-- phpMyAdmin SQL Dump
-- version 3.5.2
-- http://www.phpmyadmin.net
--
-- Host: localhost
-- Generation Time: Dec 27, 2012 at 06:51 PM
-- Server version: 5.5.25a
-- PHP Version: 5.4.4

SET SQL_MODE="NO_AUTO_VALUE_ON_ZERO";
SET time_zone = "+00:00";

/*!40101 SET @OLD_CHARACTER_SET_CLIENT=@@CHARACTER_SET_CLIENT */;
/*!40101 SET @OLD_CHARACTER_SET_RESULTS=@@CHARACTER_SET_RESULTS */;
/*!40101 SET @OLD_COLLATION_CONNECTION=@@COLLATION_CONNECTION */;
/*!40101 SET NAMES utf8 */;
--
-- Database: `logindb`
--

-- --------------------------------------------------------
--
-- Table structure for table `users`
--
CREATE TABLE IF NOT EXISTS `users` (
  `user_id` mediumint(6) unsigned NOT NULL AUTO_INCREMENT,
  `fname` varchar(30) NOT NULL DEFAULT 'NOT NULL',
  `lname` varchar(40) NOT NULL DEFAULT 'NOT NULL',
  `email` varchar(50) NOT NULL DEFAULT 'NOT NULL',
  `psword` varchar(40) NOT NULL DEFAULT 'NOT NULL',
  `registration_date` datetime NOT NULL,
  `user_level` tinyint(1) unsigned NOT NULL,
  PRIMARY KEY (`user_id`),
  UNIQUE KEY `fname` (`fname`)
```

```
) ENGINE=InnoDB  DEFAULT CHARSET=latin1 AUTO_INCREMENT=21 ;
--
-- Dumping data for table `users`
--
INSERT INTO 'users' ('user_id', 'fname', 'lname', 'email', 'psword', ↵
   'registration_date', 'user_level') VALUES
(1, 'Rose', 'Bush', 'rbush@myisp.co.uk', '0f2ded3794a9f1ae11c2aba8ff6dff00dd1e4ac6', ↵
   '2012-09-20 12:31:49', 0),
(3, 'Mike', 'Rosoft', 'miker@myisp.co.uk', '315806a3a2ae3ae81d1294746df09ac6ceaa587c', ↵
   '2012-09-29 20:08:29', 0),
(4, 'Olive', 'Branch', 'obranch@myisp.com', '0d05e04b8b1cf237dcdaab55468c54733c7fdeb1', ↵
   '2012-09-29 20:09:15', 0),
(5, 'Frank', 'Incense', 'fincense@myisp.net', '71ea58aa789b63d377fa73c441348da5840bd0dc', ↵
   '2012-09-29 20:11:34', 0),
(6, 'Annie', 'Versary', 'aversary@myisp.co.uk', '2f635f6d20e3fde0c53075a84b68fb07dcec9b03', ↵
   '2012-09-29 20:14:09', 0),
(7, 'Terry', 'Fide', 'tfide@myisp.de', '55deee02330052a7bb715168f9405b33ef752662', ↵
   '2012-09-29 20:15:41', 0),
(11, 'James', 'Smith', 'jsmith@myisp.co.uk', '34ae707a963ad8a1fb248f8c1f50a4d3d5dd2e64', ↵
   '2012-09-29 20:28:53', 0),
(16, 'Jack', 'Smith', 'jsmith@outlook.com', 'bda7aeb2f7a4cf6f6f26b7c9e96e009913b2594b', ↵
   '2012-10-14 19:17:32', 1),
(18, 'Helen', 'Back', 'hback@myisp.net', 'f16879eb900436b07ee6f31a46da0819ffba6a94', ↵
   '2012-12-07 19:09:13', 0),
(19, 'Patrick', 'O''Hara', 'pohara@myisp.org.uk', '3d8385096ef3b5712bdee38e4e385cf626d5de9c', ↵
   '2012-12-09 16:12:07', 0),
(20, 'Lynn', 'Seed', 'lseed@myisp.com', 'a2614195adf5952916965acba1b4111058453ba4', ↵
   '2012-12-09 16:18:14', 0);

/*!40101 SET CHARACTER_SET_CLIENT=@OLD_CHARACTER_SET_CLIENT */;
/*!40101 SET CHARACTER_SET_RESULTS=@OLD_CHARACTER_SET_RESULTS */;
/*!40101 SET COLLATION_CONNECTION=@OLD_COLLATION_CONNECTION */;
```

The next steps are to do the following:

- Examine the destination server (the host), and prepare it to receive the SQL file and the contents of the *htdocs* folder.

- Upload the SQL file and web-site files to the host.

- Import the SQL file using phpMyAdmin in the host.

Investigate the Remote Host's Server

We will assume that you have reserved a space for the web site and registered the domain name with your remote host. Also, you should have determined whether your chosen hosting package uses Linux or Windows.

A remote host must have PHP and MySQL installed. If you are not sure whether PHP and MySQL are installed at the host, type the following in a text editor and save it as *phpinfo.php*:

```
<?php
phpinfo();
?>
```

Use your FTP client to upload the file to the host and open it in a browser. You will see a table like the one in Figure 7-10. Scroll down the table, and you should see details of the MySQL and MySQLi installation on the host's server.

PHP Version 5.3.9	php
System	Windows NT ADRIAN-3CBBE1C0 5.1 build 2600 (Windows XP Home Edition Service Pack 3) i586
Build Date	Jan 10 2012 16:15:55
Compiler	MSVC9 (Visual C++ 2008)
Architecture	x86
Configure Command	cscript /nologo configure.js "--enable-snapshot-build" "--disable-isapi" "--enable-debug-pack" "--disable-isapi" "--without-mssql" "--without-pdo-mssql" "--without-pi3web" "--with-pdo-oci=D:\php-sdk\oracle\instantclient10\sdk,shared" "--with-oci8=D:\php-sdk\oracle\instantclient10\sdk,shared" "--with-oci8-11g=D:\php-sdk\oracle\instantclient11\sdk,shared" "--enable-object-out-dir=../obj/" "--enable-com-dotnet" "--with-mcrypt=static" "--disable-static-analyze"
Server API	Apache 2.0 Handler
Virtual Directory Support	enabled
Configuration File (php.ini) Path	C:\WINDOWS
Loaded Configuration File	C:\Program Files\EasyPHP-5.3.9\apache\php.ini
Scan this dir for additional .ini files	(none)
Additional .ini files parsed	(none)
PHP API	20090626
PHP Extension	20090626
Zend Extension	220090626
Zend Extension Build	API220090626,TS,VC9
PHP Extension Build	API20090626,TS,VC9
Debug Build	no

Figure 7-10. *The result of opening phpinfo.php in a server*

■ **Caution**   Some basic hosting packages do not accept databases. In this case, you will have to upgrade to a more expensive package. Check the product range on your intended host before proceeding further.

Using the GUIs on a Remote Host's Server

Access the control panel of the host, and ensure that it allows you to upload a database. Scroll down the control panel until you see the section shown in Figure 7-11.

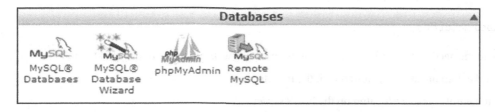

Figure 7-11. *The database section of the control panel*

If a database section is not shown in the control panel, it means that the hosting packet needs to be upgraded. Assuming that the host will accept databases, follow these steps:

- Click the phpMyAdmin icon, and create an empty database. In this example, we will pretend to create the *admintable* database.

When creating the *admintable* database, the resulting database will either have the name *admintable* or the host will add a prefix to the database name. Most hosts add a prefix, and it is nearly always the web-site owner's username for accessing the control panel. Let's assume that the owner's username is *mywebsite*; the host will create the database name as *mywebsite_admintable*. In this example, we will assume that the database name has the prefix *myusername*.

- Now you must immediately protect the newly created database by giving it a user and a password. Do this by using phpMyAdmin as described in Chapter 1. (Some hosts will automatically provide the user name—if that's the case, use that one.)

  Create a user with the following details:

  User: webmaster (or a name provided by the host)
  Password: coffeepot
  Host: localhost

The password in a real-world database must be much more complex than *coffeepot*. Make a careful note of the database name, password, and user.

Connecting to the Database on the Remote Host

Now that we know the name of the empty database (in this example, it is *myusername_admintable*), we can amend the connection file to suit the remote host. Do not create this in XAMPP's htdocs folder on your computer. If you do, you will no longer be able to run the *admintable* database on your computer's server. Use a text editor such as notepad++ to create the file and store the new *mysqli_connect.php* file anywhere except in the htdocs folder. The amended file is not included in the downloadable files because it would be unique for your database. The amendment might be as shown in bold type in the next snippet of code.

The Snippet of Code for Connecting to the New Database (msqli_connect.inc.php).

```php
<?php
// Create a connection to the admintable database and set the encoding
// The user name might be provided by the host. If not, use the name from your XAMPP version
DEFINE ('DB_USER', 'webmaster');
DEFINE ('DB_PASSWORD', 'coffeepot');
DEFINE ('DB_HOST', 'localhost');
DEFINE ('DB_NAME', 'myusername_admintable');
// Make the connection
$dbcon = @mysqli_connect (DB_HOST, DB_USER, DB_PASSWORD, DB_NAME) OR die ↩
 ('Could not connect to MySQL: ' . mysqli_connect_error() );
```

```
// Set the encoding
mysqli_set_charset($dbcon, 'utf8');
```

You now have all the items necessary for migrating the database-driven web site to the remote host as follows:

- An account and a domain name registered with the remote host.

- A newly created empty database located on the host's server.

- The SQL dump files for the tables.

- The folder containing the *includes*, and the folder containing the *images*.

- The modified *mysqli_connect.php* file.

The main PHP and HTML files need an amendment before they can be uploaded, and this amendment is described in the next section.

Securely Upload the *mysqli_connect.php* File

For maximum security, the database connection file should be located outside the root folder. The file is then not directly accessible via the web site. We will also give it a name that would confuse a hacker who is searching for the file. Figure 7-12 shows an FTP window for viewing the folder structure on a remote host.

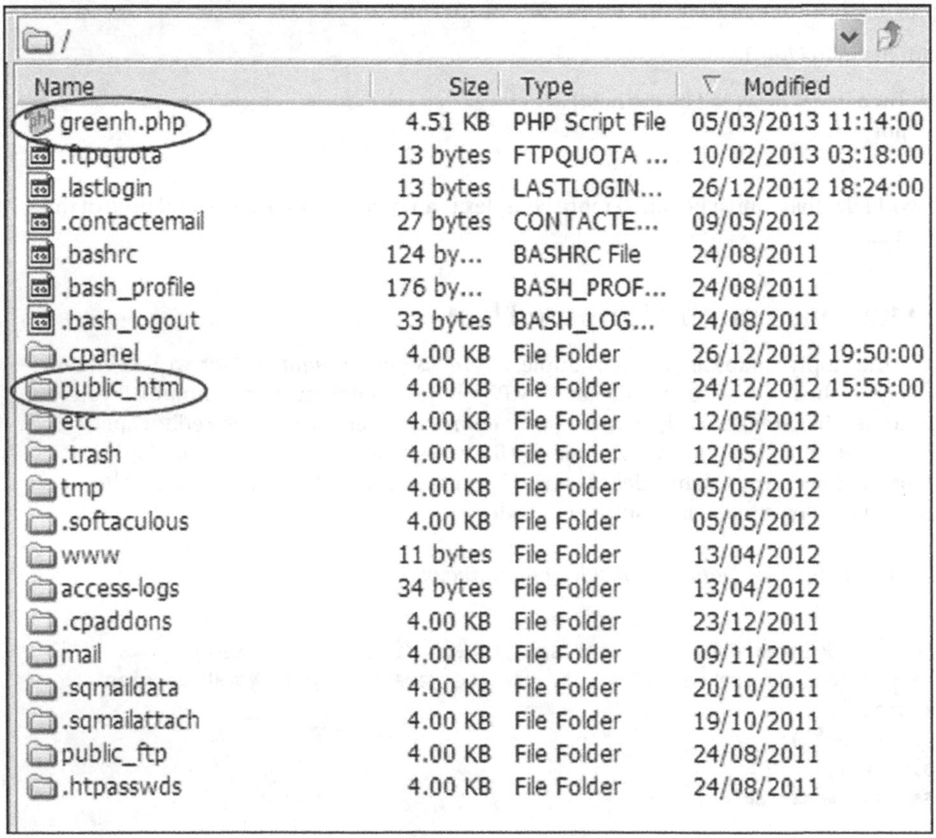

Name	Size	Type	▽ Modified
greenh.php	4.51 KB	PHP Script File	05/03/2013 11:14:00
.ftpquota	13 bytes	FTPQUOTA ...	10/02/2013 03:18:00
.lastlogin	13 bytes	LASTLOGIN...	26/12/2012 18:24:00
.contactemail	27 bytes	CONTACTE...	09/05/2012
.bashrc	124 by...	BASHRC File	24/08/2011
.bash_profile	176 by...	BASH_PROF...	24/08/2011
.bash_logout	33 bytes	BASH_LOG...	24/08/2011
.cpanel	4.00 KB	File Folder	26/12/2012 19:50:00
public_html	4.00 KB	File Folder	24/12/2012 15:55:00
etc	4.00 KB	File Folder	12/05/2012
.trash	4.00 KB	File Folder	12/05/2012
tmp	4.00 KB	File Folder	05/05/2012
.softaculous	4.00 KB	File Folder	05/05/2012
www	11 bytes	File Folder	13/04/2012
access-logs	34 bytes	File Folder	13/04/2012
.cpaddons	4.00 KB	File Folder	23/12/2011
mail	4.00 KB	File Folder	09/11/2011
.sqmaildata	4.00 KB	File Folder	20/10/2011
.sqmailattach	4.00 KB	File Folder	19/10/2011
public_ftp	4.00 KB	File Folder	24/08/2011
.htpasswds	4.00 KB	File Folder	24/08/2011

Figure 7-12. *The remote host's files and folders shown in an FTP program's window*

In Figure 7-12, the database connection file (circled) has been renamed as *greenh.php* and uploaded outside the *public_html* root folder (circled).

Having uploaded the connection file outside the root folder on the host, none of your interactive pages will be able to find it. To solve this, use your code editor to open every file that contains a *mysqli_connect.php* link and run a *Find-and-Replace-All* to amend its location as follows.

Find *mysqli_connect.php* and replace it with *../greenh.php*. The symbols *../* tell the pages that the file is located one level above the current folder. For connecting to the database on your own computer/server, you have always used *require ('mysqli_connect.php');*

Now that the connection file is safely hidden from hackers and the interactive pages have been modified to match, you can upload the HTML and PHP pages to the remote host.

Uploading the Interactive Pages to the Host

The final steps are as follows:

- Most hosts will be using Linux. In this case, there will not be an *htdocs* folder in the *public_html* folder. Therefore, you need to use your FTP client to upload the HTML and PHP pages from your admintable's *htdocs* folder into the *public_html* folder in the host's server. Because you already uploaded an amended and renamed *mysqli_connect.php* file, take great care not to upload the unmodified version into the *public_html* folder.

- If your host uses Windows, use your FTP client to upload the content of your admintable's *htdocs* folder into the host's *htdocs* folder.

- Use your FTP client to upload the SQL files for the tables into the *public_html* folder.

- Log in to the control panel at the host, and open phpMyAdmin.

- In the left panel, click the name of the newly created empty database, and then click the *Import* tab.

- You will be asked to name the SQL file to be imported. Browse to the *public_html* folder, and find each uploaded SQL file. Open them one at a time, and then click *Go*.

- At some earlier date, you might have uploaded a file named *index.html*. Your new *index.php* file must replace the html file; otherwise, *index.html* will load instead of your *index.php file*. Rename the *index.html* file at the host as *old-index.html*, or delete it.

■ **Note**   Beginners are often puzzled by the lack of an *htdocs* folder on the host server because MySQL and Apache normally look for files in the *htdocs* folder. To explain the mystery, if the host is using Linux, then the host will have configured Apache and MySQL so that it looks in the *public_html* folder.

View your uploaded interactive web site online by typing your web site's URL into the address field of a browser. You should see your home page, and from there you can test the database features. Be aware that you might have to wait a little while because some hosts might take time to update their server.

As with any computer work, backups are an essential precaution against hardware or software failure. Also, you might want to roll back to an earlier version when experimenting with files.

Back Up Your Database

While you are learning to create and use databases, four steps are essential:

1. Continue writing in your notebook.

2. Be sure to update your flow chart.

3. Use the Export tab in phpMyAdmin to back up your tables.

4. Back up your *htdocs* folder.

Recording important steps and details such as usernames and password has saved me a lot of grief. During my learning period, when I created many experimental databases and variations of those databases, I could not possibly remember the details of each one. Also, I recorded details of the stage that I had reached and what I intended to do next. This was especially important if I had to stop for two or three days to update some of my clients web sites. Clients never seem to request updates singly; they come in bunches, with four or five clients clamoring for updates at the same time.

I also recorded useful web-site URLs. If I came across a helpful tip in a manual, I made a note of the page number. This saved me from having to trawl though the manual to find the item again. I recorded the URLs, usernames, and password for the many forums that I contacted for help. A ring-back notebook is ideal because you can insert dividers to help you find where you wrote that vital bit of information.

For backups, I recommend using phpMyAdmin to export SQL dumps for the tables from each database. Then copy them to a CD or USB pen drive so that you can create a copy in another computer.

Make a copy of the *htdocs* folder on a CD or pen drive so that it can be copied to another computer. Having suffered the occasional hard disk or OS failure, I also make a complete copy of each database-driven web site on one or two other computers. The other computers each have XAMPP and an FTP program installed. Extra work is entailed in keeping each web site up to date, but if a computer dies, I can continue working on another computer. Peace of mind is a wonderful thing.

Summary

In this chapter, we added some last-minute improvements suggested by the client and the membership secretary. These included adding a title column to the paginated table display, allowing registered members to update their own details, and adding a live e-mail address to be displayed on the web site. The client also asked for an inquiry form for the web site. All these additions to the web site were described and listed. The chapter then gave a full description of the procedures for migrating a database to a host and backing up database tables.

In the next chapter, we will learn how to create a product catalog for a real estate agent.

■ ■ ■

CHAPTER 8

Creating a Product Catalog

You have learned the basics of PHP and MySQL, so now we will create a full database-driven web site, using a product catalog as an example. Most e-commerce web sites incorporate a catalog to display products and services. Some web sites use catalogs to display items that cannot be purchased over the Internet, such as tourist attractions or houses. The tutorial in this chapter uses a real estate agency offering various types of houses in a limited region. Real estate is an excellent example of a web site that has a catalog but buying the product over the Internet is impractical. Sensible buyers will view a property and its location before even considering the purchase.

Because so many people are involved in the purchase and sale of a house, their actions must all be carefully coordinated. The parties involved are the seller, the buyer, the real estate agent, separate lawyers for the buyer and seller, the buyer's and seller's banks or mortgage companies, and the buyer's surveyor. In addition, there will probably be a chain of events involved—for example, the sellers cannot proceed with the transaction until they have found and agreed to buy another house. Similarly, buyers cannot proceed until they have a firm offer on their current house. Therefore, a catalog for a real estate web site is purely a catalog and does not include provisions for financial transactions or personal details.

The sections in this chapter are as follows:

- Prepare the database and administration plan.

- Create a new database and table for a real estate agent.

- Create a home page where users can search for a suitable house.

- Create a page so that the administrator can view the entire stock of houses or search for and view a specific house.

- Create pages to give the full specification of each property. To save space, only one page will be provided for this tutorial.

- Create a page so that the administrator can add new houses.

- Create an inquiry form for users interested in viewing a house.

Prepare the Database and Administration Plan

After discussing the requirements with the real estate agent's owner, the follow priorities were agreed upon:

- The most important page is the search page. This must enable users to quickly find what they are looking for.

- The top priorities when searching for a house are the following:

  - Location

  - Price

- Number of bedrooms

- Type of house

Therefore, the search page would contain fields for those four items.

- The approximate location of a house will be disclosed, but the street name and house number must not be disclosed. This prevents users from bypassing the real estate agent and going directly to the house owner. It also means that, because no personal details will be recorded in the database, it might not be subject to the territory's data protection laws.

- The term "Vacant Possession" will not be used. A house that is empty is a magnet for miscreants.

- The real estate agent's photographer will provide each house's thumbnail image as a .jpg, .gif, or .png file 150 pixels wide with a maximum height of, say, 120 pixels. The photographer also will provide enlarged versions of the photographs for the full specification pages; these will be standardized at, say, 350 pixels wide.

■ **Caution** A catalog always contains images, but the real estate's administrator might not be capable of handling them. Also, the administrator might not be capable of placing new images or full specification pages inside the appropriate folder at the remote host using an FTP client. An administrator with no knowledge of HTML, PHP, and CSS would not be capable of producing the pages containing the full specifications of the properties. The solution I adopted is to ask the webmaster to be the administrator. If the webmaster is a member of the real estate agent's staff, he would be the ideal administrator.

First we need to create the new database.

Create a New Database

In the *htdocs* folder within the *xammp* folder, create a new folder called *estate*.

Download the files for Chapter 8 from the book's page at www.apress.com, and load them into the new folder *estate*. To create a new database, follow these steps:

1. Use a browser to access phpMyAdmin. Type http://localhost/phpmyadmin/ into the address field of the browser. In phpMyAdmin, click the *Databases* tab and create a new database called *estatedb*.

2. In the right pane, scroll down to find the newly created database and select the box alongside it.

3. Click *Check Privileges*. Then click *Add User*, and add a new user and password as follows:

    User name: smeeton
    Password: Lighthouse

4. Scroll down to the item named *Global Privileges*, and click *Check All*. Scroll to the bottom, and click *Add User* (or *Go* in some versions)to save the user's details.

Create the File for Connecting to the Database

Name the file *mysqli_connect.php*. If you are using the download files, this file is already created for you and can be found in the folder named *estate*.

```php
<?php
// Create a connection to the estatedb database and set the encoding to utf-8
DEFINE ('DB_USER', 'smeeton');
DEFINE ('DB_PASSWORD', 'Lighthouse');
DEFINE ('DB_HOST', 'localhost');
DEFINE ('DB_NAME', 'estatedb');
// Make the connection
$dbcon = @mysqli_connect (DB_HOST, DB_USER, DB_PASSWORD, DB_NAME) OR die
('Could not connect to MySQL: ' . mysqli_connect_error() );
// Set the encoding
mysqli_set_charset($dbcon, 'utf8');
?>
```

We will assume two types of user: (i) persons viewing the web site, and (ii) the webmaster, who will maintain and update the catalog table and also use FTP to upload the images and full specification pages to the host.

I already compiled the catalog table for you and exported it into a populated file called *houses.sql*. You will find this among the downloaded files you just installed in the folder *estate*. You can import it using phpMyAdmin or compile the table manually as follows:

- In phpMyAdmin, open the database *estatedb*.

- In the home page of phpMyAdmin, click the database *estatedb*, and then create a table called *houses* with nine columns as follows:

Table 8-1. *The attributes for the houses database table*

Columnname	Type	Length/Value	Default	Attributes	NULL	Index	A_I
ref_num	MEDIUMINT	6	None	UNSIGNED	☐	PRIMARY	☑
loctn	TINYTEXT	60	None		☐		☐
price	DECIMAL	9,2	None		☐		☐
type	TINYTEXT	50	None		☐		☐
mini_descr	VARCHAR	100	None		☐		☐
b_rooms	TINYINT	2	None		☐		☐
thumb	VARCHAR	45	None		☐		☐
full_spec	VARCHAR	60	None		☐		☐
status	TINYTEXT	30	None		☐		☐

The house reference number will be used by viewers when they inquire about a property. The column type MEDIUMINT (when unsigned) allows integers from 0 to 65,535.

TINYTEXT allows up to 255 characters.

DECIMAL allows prices up to the limit set by the first figure shown in the table. The second figure indicates the number of decimal places. The size 9,2 means that when entering nine figures, such as 123456789, the recorded result will be 1234567.89.

The thumbnail thumb holds the URL of an image—for example, *images/house_01.jpg*. I allowed 45 characters in the thumbnail image column because the file names for thumbnails are often long—for instance, *images/bungalow_South_Devon_150px.png*.

The *full_spec* column will contain the URL link for each house's HTML page, which contains a full description and an enlarged image of the property.

The *status* column indicates whether the house is available, under offer, withdrawn from the market, or sold.

Security

As previously described, an unskilled administrator would not be able to cope with the preparation of images and might not be capable of using an FTP program to place new images or full-specification pages inside the appropriate folder at the remote host. An administrator with no knowledge of HTML, PHP, and CSS would not be capable of producing the pages containing the full specifications of the properties. Because these tasks must be performed by the webmaster, the webmaster will be the administrator. This approach eliminates a real security risk and reduces the number of special pages for administering the site. For instance, pages for editing and deleting houses would have been a security risk; instead, the webmaster can use phpMyAdmin. He is the approved user for the *houses* database, and no other person can access phpMyAdmin.

Based on his decisions, the required pages will be as follows:

- The home page that doubles as a search page for the user *(index.php)*.

- The search results page for displaying the houses selected by the user's search criteria.

- Full-specification pages, one for each house. The user accesses these by clicking a link on the page for displaying the selected category of house.

- The *Contact Us* page for user inquiries.

- An administration page so that the webmaster can conveniently view the whole stock of houses.

- An administration page so that the webmaster can search for and view a specific house.

- An administration page so that the webmaster can add new houses. Only the webmaster knows the URL for this page, and it is not accessible from the web site.

None of the preceding pages allow the list of houses to be edited or deleted, the administrator uses phpMyAdmin to edit and delete houses. We now need to create a home page for the real estate web site.

Creating a Home Page with Search Capability

The home page is shown in Figure 8-1.

Figure 8-1. *The home page for a real estate web site*

In this tutorial, the background of the home page (and all the other pages) is a vertical gradient and the main content panel is transparent so that the gradient is visible within the panel. A gradient can be created using CSS3, but this will not work with Internet Explorer 8 (IE8). Because that browser will be around for a few years yet, I chose to use a 3-pixel-wide gradient that is repeated horizontally across the page. All the previous chapters used HTML5, but for the sake of simplicity I did not use semantic tags in those chapters, (semantic tags will not work with IE8). In this chapter, I will use semantic HTML5 tags with a JavaScript workaround for IE8. When IE8 is eventually replaced by newer versions, the JavaScript workaround can be dispensed with.

■ **Tip** If you would like to learn more about enhancing the appearance, accessibility, and usefulness of a web site, try my book *Practical HTML5 Projects* (Apress, 2012).

The home page has four pull-down menus to eliminate user-input errors and ensure that only acceptable data is entered into the database table. To save space, the database in this tutorial is simplified by restricting the choices in these pull-down menus. British prices and terminology are used in the menus. In the USA, you use some different terminology—for instance, the term *semi-detached* might be replaced by *side-by-side-duplex*. In the UK, a *bungalow* is a single-story building, whereas a *house* has two or more stories.

Although I limited the drop-down choices severely to save both space and code, a real-world house catalog would adopt the same principle but use a more extensive choice of location, price, and type of house.

In the body of the home page, the code for the main menu (*menu.inc*) is given in the following snippet:

```
<ul>
    <li><a href="about.php" title="About Us">About Us</a></li>
    <li><a href="faqs.php" title="Frequently Asked Questions">FAQs</a></li>
    <li><a href="contact.php" title="Contact Us">Contact Us</a></li>
    <li><a href="index.php" title="Return to Home Page">Home Page</a></li>
</ul>
```

In the downloadable menu file, the About Us and FAQs links are dead because no target pages have been made available for those two links in this tutorial.

We will now examine the header for the home page and the majority of the web pages.

The Header for the Majority of the Pages

The general header in this tutorial is not a separate included file; it is part of the HTML of the pages. The following extract from the HTML in the home page (*index.php*) shows in bold type how it fits between the container *div* and the content *div*. The background, border, and positioning of the text and rosette are set by the *transparent.css* style sheet.

```
<div id="container">
<header>
<h1>Devon Real Estate</h1>
<h2>Try our award-winning service</h2>
<img id="rosette" alt="Rosette" title="Rosette" height="127"
src="images/rosette-128.png" width="128">
</header>
<div id="content">
```

The main style sheet formats the header and provides the background image.

■ **Note**   In the two previous chapters, we used sticky pull-down lists but the pages did not validate. In the code shown in Listing 8-1a, a sticky form is not used for the pull-down lists. However, with most modern browsers, the user's entries will remain in the fields if the browser's back button is clicked, thus creating the equivalent of a sticky form.

The Home Page Code

We must now examine the home page, which also doubles as a search page.

Listing 8-1a. Creating the Home Page (index.php)

I used an internal style in addition to the main style sheet because some features are unique to the home page.

```
<!doctype html>
<html lang=en>
<head>
<title>Real estate home page.</title>
<meta charset=utf-8>
```

```
<link rel="stylesheet" type="text/css" href="transparent.css">
<!--[if lte IE 8]>
<link rel="stylesheet" type="text/css" href="ie8.css">
<![endif]-->
<style type="text/css">
#leftcol h3 { margin-bottom:-10px; }
#midcol h3 { margin-top:-10px; }
.black { color:black; }
form { margin-left:15px; font-weight:bold; color:black; }
select { margin-bottom:5px; }
h3 { font-size:130%; }
</style>
<!--Add conditional JavaScript for IE8-->
<!--[if lte IE 8]>
<script src="html5.js">
</script>
<![endif]-->
</head>
<body>
<div id="container">
<header>
<h1>Devon Real Estate</h1>
<h2>Try our award-winning service</h2>
<img id="rosette" alt="Rosette" title="Rosette" height="127"
src="images/rosette-128.png" width="128">
</header>
<div id="content">
<div id="leftcol">
<h3>Search for your dream house</h3><br><span class="black"><strong>IMPORTANT: You must ↵
select an item in<br>ALL the fields, otherwise the search will fail.</strong></span><br>
<form action="found_houses.php" method="post">
Location<br>
<select name="loctn">
    <option value="">- Select -</option>
    <option value="South_Devon">South Devon</option>
    <option value="Mid_Devon">Mid Devon</option>
    <option value="North_Devon">North Devon</option>
    </select><br>
Maximum Price<br>
    <select name="price">
    <option value="">- Select -</option>
    <option value="200000">&pound;200,000</option>
    <option value="300000">&pound;300,000</option>
    <option value="400000">&pound;400,000</option>
    </select><br>
Type<br>
    <select name="type">
    <option value="">- Select -</option>
    <option value="Det-bung">Detached Bungalow</option>
    <option value="Semi-det-bung">Semi-detached Bungalow</option>
    <option value="Det-house">Detached House</option>
```

```
    <option value="Semi-det-house">Semi-detached House</option>
    </select><br>
Number of Bedrooms<br>
<select name="b_rooms">
    <option value="">- Select -</option>
    <option value="2">2</option>
    <option value="3">3</option>
    <option value="4">4</option>
</select>
<p><input id="submit" type="submit" name="submit" value="Search"></p>
</form></div>
<div id="rightcol">
<nav>
<?php include('includes/menu.inc'); ?>
</nav>
</div><!--end of side menu column-->
<div id="midcol">
<h3>All houses are situated in the beautiful green<br>rolling countryside of Devon, ↩
England, UK</h3>
<img alt="SW England" height="238" src="images/devon-map-crop.jpg" width="345">
</div>
<br class="clear">
</div><!--End of page content-->
<footer>footer goes here
</footer>
</div>
</body>
</html>
```

The main style sheet is shown next in Listing 8-1b.

Listing 8-1b. Creating the Main Style Sheet for the Web Site Pages (transparent.css)

```
/*equalize all the margins, paddings and borders built into various browsers*/
div body #header #content { margin:0; padding:0; border:0; }
body { background:#FFF url(images/green-grad-800.jpg) repeat-x;}
/*add the display attribute for the semantic tags*/
header, footer, section, article, nav { display:block; }
header {width:920px; height:180px; padding:0; border:10px white solid; ↩
position:relative; background: url(images/header3.jpg); background-repeat:no-repeat; ↩
margin:10px auto; }
#header-button ul { position:absolute; top:30px; right:-80px; font-size:medium; width:160px; }
h1 { font-size:300%; color :white; position: relative; left:90px; top: 25px; width:480px; }
h2 { position:relative; left:425px; }
#rosette { position:relative; left:750px; top:-75px; }
#container { width:984px; margin:auto; }
#content { background-color:transparent; border-left:10px white solid; ↩
border-right:10px white solid; border-bottom:10px white solid; width: 904px; ↩
margin-top:-10px; margin-left:auto; margin-right:auto; padding:8px; font-size:medium; }
h2 { font-size:x-large; color:white; margin:0 0 10px 0; }
h3 { font-size:large; color:white; margin:0 0 6px 0; }
```

```
#leftcol { float:left; width: 310px; vertical-align:top; }
#rightcol { width: 135px; float:right; height: 252px; margin-right:10px; }
#midcol { margin-left:15px; margin-right:145px; margin-top:10px; vertical-align:top; }
/* set side menu block position and width*/
nav, #header-button { margin:10px 30px 0 10px; width:135px; float:right; }
/*Set list style within the menu block only. This removes bullets*/
nav li, #header-button li { list-style-type:none; }
/* set general side button styles */
nav li, #header-button li {  margin-bottom: 3px; text-align: center; width:130px; }
/* Set general anchor styles */
nav li a, #header-button li a {  display: block; color: white; font-weight: bold; ↵
text-decoration: none; }
/* Specify mouse state styles */
/* mouseout (default) */
nav li a, #header-button li a {  background:#559a55; color: white; ↵
border: 5px outset #559a55; padding-bottom:3px; }
/* mouseover */
nav li a:hover, #header-button li a:hover { background: red; color:white; ↵
border: 5px outset red; }
/*mouse active*/
nav li a:active { background:maroon;  border: 5px inset maroon; }
#header-button { position:absolute; top:-35px; left:710px; }
#midcol img { margin-left:10px;  }
footer { clear:both; color:black; text-align:center; margin:auto; }
#loginfields { display:block; margin-left:50px; }
#ftr { margin:auto; text-align:center; }
br.clear { clear:both;  }
#midcol img { margin-left:10px; }
footer { clear:both; color:black; margin:auto; text-align:center; }
table tr td { background-color:#FFFFFF; text-align:center; border: 1px black solid; ↵
border-collapse:collapse;}
```

The Conditional Style Sheet for Internet Explorer 8

A conditional style sheet is necessary to display the page correctly in IE8. The code for the conditional style sheet is given in Listing 8-1c.

Listing 8-1c. Creating the Conditional Style Sheet for the IE8 Web Site Pages (ie8.css)

```
/*add display attributes for the semantic tags*/
header, footer, section, article, nav { display:block; }
header {width:920px; height:160px; padding:0; border:10px white solid;
background: url(images/header3.jpg); background-repeat:no-repeat; margin:10px auto; }
h1 { font-size:300%; color :white; position: relative; left:90px; top: 60px; width:480px; }
h2 { position:relative; left:425px; top:50px; }
#rosette { position:relative; left:750px; top:-25px; }
/* set menu block position and width*/
nav { margin:20px 30px 0 -30px; width:135px; float:right; }
#header-button { position:absolute; top:-25px; left:710px; }
```

Displaying the Catalog

After the user enters the search criteria into the home page fields (*index.php* as shown in Figure 8-1), clicking the *Search* button will reveal the selected houses as shown in Figure 8-2.

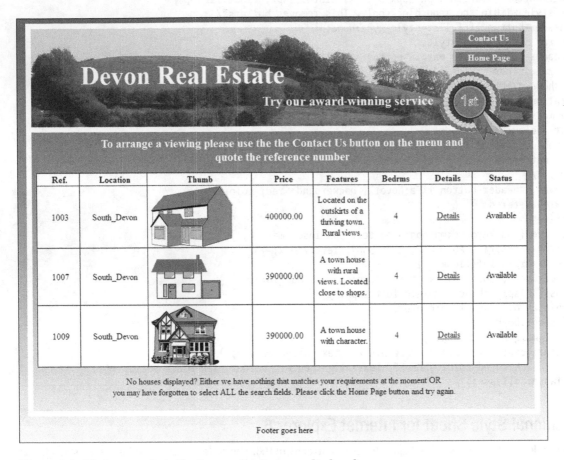

Figure 8-2. *The houses selected by the search criteria are displayed*

The search criteria resulting in the display shown in Figure 8-2 were as follows:
Location: South Devon
Max Price: £400,000
Type: Detached house
Bedrooms: 4

■ **Caution** To save space and avoid having to compile dozens of PHP pages for this book, all the *Details* links in the downloadable files are deliberately disabled except for the first one shown in Figure 8-2. When a *Details* link is clicked, the user will be directed to a page showing an enlarged image and a full specification of the house. The *Details* page is described and shown later in this chapter. (See Figure 8-10.)

The code for displaying the found houses is given in Listing 8-2.

Listing 8-2. Creating the Results Page (found_houses.php)

The main menu is removed so that the table can span the width of the page. To enable the user to return to the home page, a *Home Page* button has been added to the header.

```
<!doctype html>
<html lang=en>
<head>
<title>The found_houses page</title>
<meta charset=utf-8>
<link rel="stylesheet" type="text/css" href="transparent.css">
<!--Add conditional JavaScript for IE8-->                             #1
<!--[if lte IE 8]><script src="html5.js">
</script>
<![endif]-->
<!--[if lte IE 8]>
<link rel="stylesheet" type="text/css" href="ie8_admin.css">
<![endif]-->
<style type="text/css">
p{ text-align:center; }
table, td, th { width:900px; border-collapse:collapse; border:1px black solid; ↵
 background:white;}
td, th { padding-left:5px; padding-right:0; text-align:center; }
#content h3 { text-align:center; font-size:130%; font-weight:bold; }
img { display:block; }                                                 #2
#header-button { margin-top:-5px; }
</style>
</head>
<body>
<div id="container">
<header>
<?php include("includes/header_found_houses.inc"); ?>
<img id="rosette" alt="Rosette" title="Rosette" height="127"
src="images/rosette-128.png" width="128">
</header>
<div id="content"><!--Start of table display content-->
<h3>To arrange a viewing please use the the Contact Us button on the menu and<br> ↵
quote the reference number</h3>
<p>
<?php
$loctn=$_POST['loctn'];                                                #3
$price=$_POST['price'];
$type=$_POST['type'];
$b_rooms=$_POST['b_rooms'];
// This code retrieves all the records from the houses table
require ('mysqli_connect.php'); // Connect to the database
// Make the query
$q = "SELECT ref_num, loctn, thumb, price, mini_descr, type, b_rooms, full_spec, ↵   #4
status FROM houses WHERE loctn='$loctn' AND (price <= '$price') AND ↵
(price >= ('$price'-100000)) AND type='$type' AND b_rooms='$b_rooms' ORDER BY ↵
```

233

```php
ref_num ASC ";
$result = @mysqli_query ($dbcon, $q); // Run the query
if ($result) { // If the query ran OK, display the records
// Table header
echo '<table>
<tr>
<th><b>Ref.</b></th>
<th><b>Location</b></td>
<th><b>Thumb</b></th>
<th><b>Price</b></th>
<th><b>Features</b></th>
<th><b>Bedrms</b></th>
<th><b>Details</b></th>
<th><b>Status</b></th>
</tr>';
// Fetch and print the records
while ($row = mysqli_fetch_array($result, MYSQLI_ASSOC)) {
    echo '<tr>
    <td>' . $row['ref_num'] . '</td>
    <td>' . $row['loctn'] . '</td>
    <td>  <img src='.$row['thumb'] . '></td>
    <td>' . $row['price'] . '</td>
    <td>' . $row['mini_descr'] . '</td>
    <td>' . $row['b_rooms'] . '</td>
    <td>' . $row['full_spec'] . '</td>
    <td>' . $row['status'] . '</td>
    </tr>';
    }
    echo '</table>'; // Close the table
    mysqli_free_result ($result); // Free up the resources
} else { // If it did not run OK
// Message
echo '<p class="error">The record could not be retrieved. We apologize for any ↵
inconvenience.</p>';
// Debugging error message
    echo '<p>' . mysqli_error($dbcon) . '<br><br>Query: ' . $q . '</p>';
} // End of if ($result). Now display the total number of records/houses
$q = "SELECT COUNT(ref_num) FROM houses";
$result = @mysqli_query ($dbcon, $q);
$row = @mysqli_fetch_array ($result, MYSQLI_NUM);
$houses = $row[0];
mysqli_close($dbcon); // Close the database connection
?>
<p>No houses displayed? Either we have nothing that matches your requirements at the ↵
moment OR<br>you may have forgotten to select ALL the search fields. Please click ↵
the Home Page button and try again.</p>
</div><!--End of table display content-->
<?php include("includes/footer.inc"); ?>
</div>
</body>
</html>
```

Explanation of the Code

```
<link rel="stylesheet" type="text/css" href="transparent.css">
<!--Add conditional JavaScript for IE8-->
<!--[if lte IE 8]><script src="html5.js">
</script>
<![endif]-->
<!--[if lte IE 8]>
```
#1

The JavaScript enables Internet Explorer 8 to see HTML5 semantic tags. The JavaScript file is assumed to be in the same folder as the web-site pages. This block of conditional code must be the last item within the <head> </head> section. The free JavaScript file was devised by Remy Sharp, and it is included in the downloadable files for this chapter. The file will work only if the <body></body> tags are included in the HTML page, even though HTML will function without the <body> tags.

```
img { display:block; }
```
#2

This little trick removes the unsightly white space beneath an image that is located in a table cell.

```
$loctn=$_POST['loctn'];
$price=$_POST['price'];
$type=$_POST['type'];
$b_rooms=$_POST['b_rooms'];
```
#3

The entries provided by the pull-down menus are assigned to variables.

```
// This script retrieves all the records from the houses table
require ('mysqli_connect.php'); // Connect to the database
// Make the query
$q = "SELECT ref_num, loctn, thumb, price, mini_descr, type, b_rooms, ↵
full_spec, status FROM houses WHERE loctn='$loctn' AND (price <= '$price') ↵
AND (price >= ('$price'-100000)) AND type='$type' AND b_rooms='$b_rooms' ↵
ORDER BY ref_num ASC ";
```
#4

By now, you understand most of this query, but the price needs some explanation. The statement is as follows:

```
(price <= '$price') AND (price >= ('$price'-100000)
```

If the price was simply <= '$price', a search using a maximum price £400,000 would display every house valued at £400,000 or less. People looking for a house with maximum price of £400,000 would not be interested in houses at say £280,00 or £120,000. Therefore, the statement

```
AND (price >= ('$price'-100000)
```

is used to give a minimum price that is £100,000 below the searcher's maximum. The display is ordered by ascending reference numbers; however, you could change this to order it by price in descending order.

The Header for the Page of Search Results

The header is shown in Figure 8-3.

Figure 8-3. *One of the two buttons is a ContactUs button so that the user can request an appointment to view the house*

The code for the header is given in Listing 8-3.

Listing 8-3. Creating the Search Result Header (header_found_houses.inc)

```
<div id="header-button">
   <ul>
     <li><a href="contact.php">Contact Us</a></li>
     <li><a href="index.php">Home Page</a></li>
   </ul>
</div>
<h1>Devon Real Estate</h1>
<h2>Try our award-winning service</h2>
```

Adding houses in phpMyAdmin can be rather tedious, so we will allow the user to add houses by means of a web page known only to the webmaster. The page is not accessible via the web site.

Creating the Admin/Add a House Page

The administrator's page is shown in Figure 8-4a.

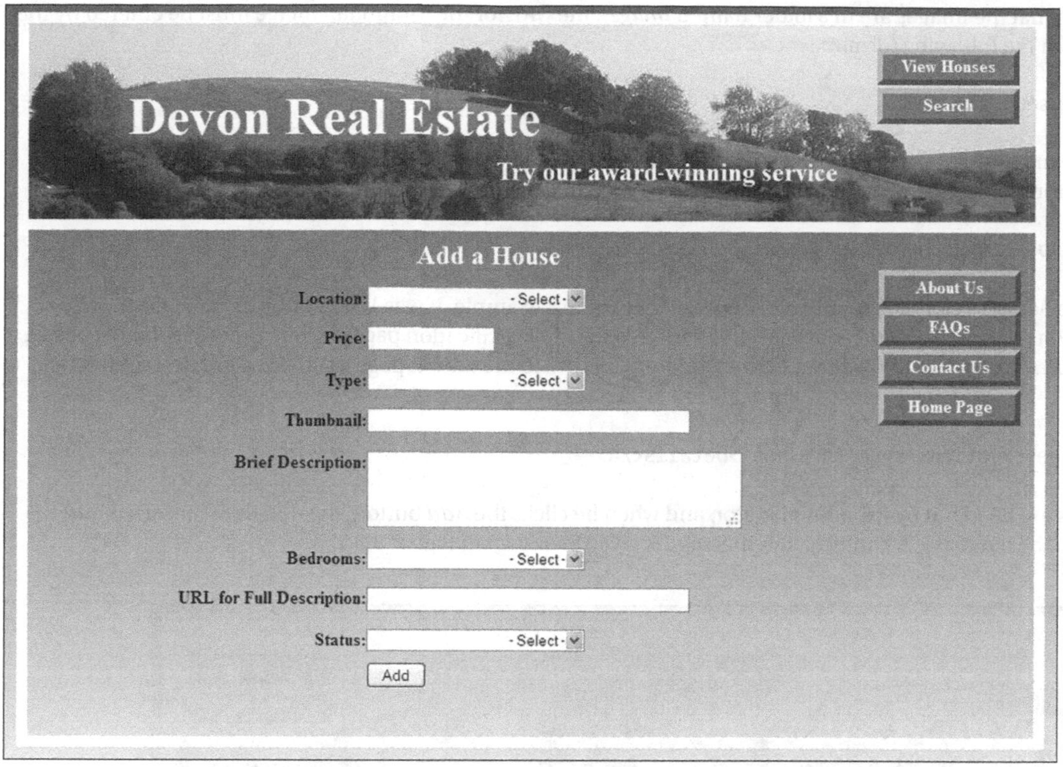

Figure 8-4a. *The admin and add-a-house page*

Figure 8-4a shows the administrator's page *(admin_page.php)* that also acts as a page for adding new houses to the *houses* table in the database.

Let's examine the elements on the administrator's page. The page contains four pull-down menus, three of them are replicas of the pull downs in the *index php* page; these are location, type, and the number of bedrooms. The status menu is the fourth pull-down menu and is used to inform the user whether the house is available, under offer, or already sold. The price field is not a pull-down because house values are rarely set at precisely £400,000 or £300,000, or £200,000.

Concerning the status, you might wonder why we would enter *Sold*. Why not delete the house from the database if it is sold? Real estate agents do this for two reasons:

1. Prospective buyers might have used the site at some earlier date and were attracted by a particular house. Later, when they see that the house is sold, they would have no need to contact the agent to see if it still on the market.

2. If prospective vendors see several sold houses listed on the web site, they will be confident that the agent is actively selling houses.

The administrator will use phpMyAdmin to delete sold houses after a suitable time interval.

Assuming that the images are in a folder named *images*, the URL for the thumbnail image must be entered by the administrator in the following format:

```
images/house06.gif
```

The price must be entered (without currency symbols) in this format: 300000
The URL for the full-specification pages must be entered in the following format:

```
<a href='spec_1003.php'>Details</a>
```

I used the house's reference number for convenience (in this example, it was 1003), but you can choose any full-specification page name to suit yourself. I prefer to keep the full-specification pages within a special folder. (I used a folder named *descriptions* in this tutorial.) I then entered the URL in the admin page's URL for a full description field as follows:

```
<a href='descriptions/spec_1003.php'>Details</a>
```

The fields are filled out by the administrator, and when he clicks the *Add* button, the details are inserted into the *houses* table in the database. A confirmation message is given as shown in Figure 8-4b.

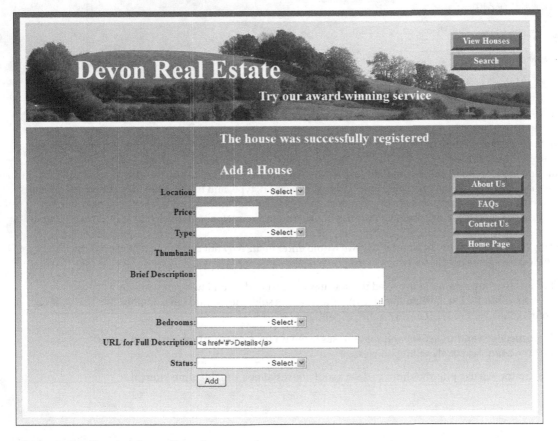

Figure 8-4b. *Showing the confirmation message*

■ **Note** No filtering or error messages are included in the listings in order to simplify the code and to make the general principles stand out clearly. The pull-down menus remove most of the risks. In a real-world situation, the administrator's page might be protected by either a login system using sessions or a password. Because the page is not accessible via the web site, it is reasonably secure anyway. It could even be located outside the *htdocs* folder. Only the administrator would be allowed to know the URL for his page. In addition, the web site's database holds no personal or financial details; therefore, it is most unlikely to tempt hackers. Having said that, an unscrupulous rival real estate office might be tempted to interfere with the site.

The code for the administrator's page is given in Listing 8-4.

Listing 8-4. Creating the Administator's Page (admin_page.php)

```
<!doctype html>
<html lang=en>
<head>
<title>Admin page</title>
<meta charset=utf-8>
<link rel="stylesheet" type="text/css" href="transparent.css">
<link rel="stylesheet" type="text/css" href="admin_form.css">
<style type="text/css">
p.error { color:red; font-size:105%; font-weight:bold; text-align:center;}
</style>
</head>
<body>
<div id="container">
<header>
<?php include('includes/header_admin.inc'); ?>
</header>
    <div id="content"><!--Start of admin page content-->
<?php
// This code is a query that INSERTs a house into the houses table
// Check that the form has been submitted
if ($_SERVER['REQUEST_METHOD'] == 'POST') {
    $errors = array(); // Initialize an error array
// Check for location
    if (empty($_POST['loctn'])) {
      $errors[] = 'You forgot to select the location';
      } else {
          $loctn = trim($_POST['loctn']);
      }
// Has a price been entered?
if (empty($_POST['price'])){
$errors[] ='You forgot to enter the price.' ;
}
elseif (!empty($_POST['price'])) {
//Remove unwanted characters
//Use regex to ensure that the remaining characters are digits
$price = preg_replace('/\D+/', '', ($_POST['price']));
}
```

```php
// Check for a type
   if (empty($_POST['type'])) {
   $errors[] = 'You forgot to select the type of house.';
   } else {
   $type = trim($_POST['type']);
   }
// Check for brief description
   if (empty($_POST['mini_descr'])) {
   $errors[] = 'You forgot to enter the brief description';
   } else {
$mini_descr = strip_tags(($_POST['mini_descr']));
   }
// Check for number of bedrooms
   if (empty($_POST['b_rooms'])) {
   $errors[] = 'You forgot to select the number of bedrooms';
   } else {
   $b_rooms = ($_POST['b_rooms']);
   }
// Check if a thumbnail url has been entered
   if (empty($_POST['thumb'])) {
   $errors[] = 'You forgot to enter the thumbnail url';
   } else {
   $thumb = ($_POST['thumb']);
   }
// Check for the status of the house
   if (empty($_POST['status'])) {
   $errors[] = 'You forgot to select the status of the house';
   } else {
   $status = ($_POST['status']);
   }
if (empty($errors)) { // If the query ran OK
// Register the house in the database
   require ('mysqli_connect.php'); // Connect to the database
// Make the query
$q = "INSERT INTO houses (ref_num, loctn, price, type, mini_descr, b_rooms, thumb, ↵
status) VALUES (' ', '$loctn', '$price', '$type', '$mini_descr', '$b_rooms', '$thumb', ↵
'$status' )";
   $result = @mysqli_query ($dbcon, $q); // Make the query
   if ($result) { // If the query ran OK
   echo '<h2>The house was successfully registered</h2><br>';
   } else { // If it did not run OK
   // Error message
   echo '<h2>System Error</h2>
<p class="error">The house could not be added due to a system error. We apologize ↵
for any inconvenience.</p>';
   // Debugging message
   echo '<p>' . mysqli_error($dbcon) . '<br><br>Query: ' . $q . '</p>';
   } // End of if ($result)
   mysqli_close($dbcon); // Close the database connection
   } else { // Report the errors
   echo '<h2>Error!</h2>
```

```
    <p class="error">The following error(s) occurred:<br>';
    foreach ($errors as $msg) { // display each error
    echo " - $msg<br>\n";
    }
    echo '</p><h3>Please try again.</h3><p><br></p>';
    }// End of if (empty($errors))
} // End of the main Submit conditionals
?>
<div id="rightcol">
<nav>
<?php include('includes/menu.inc'); ?>
</nav>
</div>
<h2>Add a House</h2>
<form  action="admin_page.php" method="post">
<p><label class="label"><b>Location:</b></label>
<select name="loctn" >
    <option value="">- Select -</option>
    <option value="South_Devon">South Devon</option>
    <option value="Mid_Devon">Mid Devon</option>
    <option value="North_Devon">North Devon</option>
</select><br>
<p><label class="label" for="price"><b>Price:</b></label><input id="price" ↵
type="text" name="price" size="9" maxlength="9" ↵
value="<?php if (isset($_POST['pricee'])) echo $_POST['price']; ?>">
</p>

<p><label class="label"><b>Type:</b></label>
<select name="type" >
    <option value="">- Select -</option>
    <option value="Det-bung">Detached Bungalow</option>
    <option value="Sem-det-bung">Semi-detached Bungalow</option>
    <option value="Det-house">Detached House</option>
    <option value="Semi-det-house">Semi-detached House</option>
</select><br> .

<p><label class="label" for="thumb"><b>Thumbnail:</b></label><input id="thumb" ↵
type="text" name="thumb" size="45" maxlength="45" value="<?php if (isset($_POST['thumb'])) ↵
echo $_POST['thumb']; ?>"></p>
<p><label class="label"><b>Brief Description:</b></label><textarea name="mini_descr" ↵
rows="3" cols="40"></textarea></p>

<p><label class="label"><b>Bedrooms:</b></label>
<select name="b_rooms" >
    <option value="">- Select -</option>
    <option value="2">2</option>
    <option value="3">3</option>
    <option value="4">4</option>
    <option value="5">5</option>
    </select><br>

<p><label class="label"><b>URL for Full Description:</b></label><input id="full_spec" ↵
type="text" name="full_spec" size="60" maxlength="60" ↵
value="<?php if (isset($_POST['full_spec'])) echo $_POST['full_spec']; ?>">
```

```
<p><label class="label"><b>Status:</b></label>
<select name="status" >
    <option value="">- Select -</option>
    <option value="Available">Available</option>
    <option value="Under offer">Under offer</option>
    <option value="Withdrawn">Withdrawn</option>
    <option value="Sold">Sold</option>
    </select></p>
    <div id="submit">
    <p><input id="submit" type="submit" name="submit" value="Add"></p>
    </div>
</form><!--End of the admin page content-->
<div><br class="clear">
</div>
</div>
<div></div></div>
</body>
</html>
```

■ **Note** We can be sure that the webmaster/administrator will not be using Internet Explorer 8; therefore, no conditionals for IE8 are included in any of the administrator's pages.

You will have noticed that the header for the administrator's page differs from the general header. We will examine this next.

The Header for the Administrator's Page

The rosette is removed to allow room for more menu buttons in case the administrator needs extra facilities in the future. The buttons now allow the administrator to view the entire stock of houses or to search for one particular house.

The admin page header is shown in Figure 8-5.

Figure 8-5. *The heading for the administrator's page*

The code for the administrator's heading is given in Listing 8-5.

Listing 8-5. Creating the Header for the Administrator's Page (header_admin.inc)

The header menu needs no other buttons because the main menu is available on the admin page.

```
<div id="header-button">
    <ul>
    <li><a href="admin_view_houses.php">View Houses</a></li>
    <li><a href="admin_search.php">Search</a></li>
    </ul>
</div>
<h1>Devon Real Estate</h1>
<h2>Try our award-winning service</h2>
```

Three of the admin pages need two extra buttons because the wide table display fills the content area, leaving no room for the main menu.

The Header with Two Extra Buttons

The two extra buttons are shown in Figure 8-6.

Figure 8-6. *Showing the two extra menu buttons*

The code for the administrator's header is given in Listing 8-6.

Listing 8-6. Creating the Header with Two Extra Menu Buttons (header_admin_found.inc)

```
<div id="header-button">
    <ul>
        <li><a href="admin_view_houses.php">View Houses</a></li>
        <li><a href="admin_search.php">Search</a></li>
        <li><a href="admin_page.php">Add a House</a></li>
        <li><a href="index.php">Home Page</a></li>
    </ul>
</div>
<h1>Devon Real Estate</h1>
<h2>Try our award-winning service</h2>
```

The administrator can view the entire stock using a paginated display. This is discussed next.

Administrator's View of the Entire Stock of Houses for Sale

Figure 8-7 shows the first page of the full-stock view.

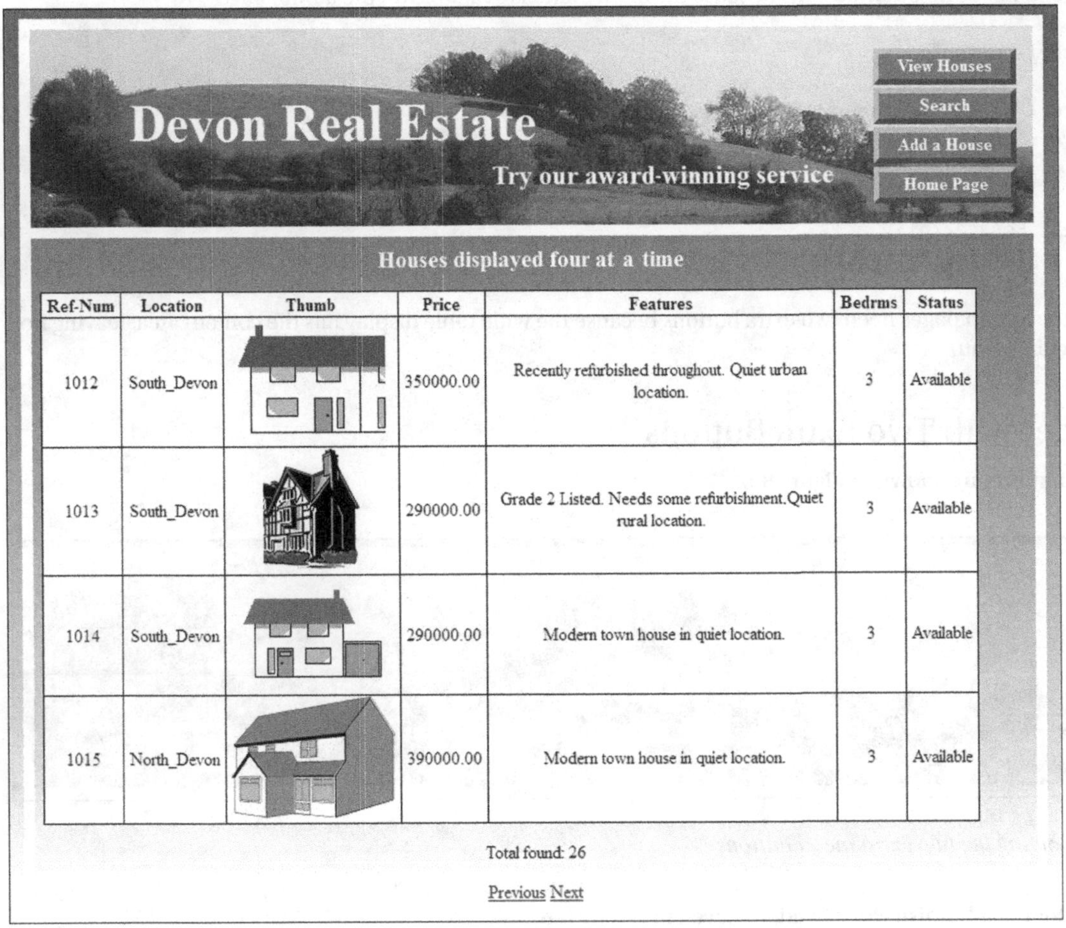

Figure 8-7. *One of the pages in a full stock display*

The code for displaying the stock of houses is given in Listing 8-7a.

Listing 8-7a. Creating a Paginated Table of the Entire Stock of Houses (admin_view_houses.php)

The code for the full-stock display uses a table and pagination very similar to those described in previous chapters. Therefore, no explanation of the code will be given.

```
<!doctype html>
<html lang=en>
<head>
<title>Admin view houses page</title>
<meta charset=utf-8>
<link rel="stylesheet" type="text/css" href="transparent.css">
```

```
<style type="text/css">
p{ text-align:center; }
table { width:860px; border-collapse:collapse; }
td { padding-left:5px; padding-right:5px; }
#content h3 { text-align:center; font-size:130%; font-weight:bold; }
</style>
</head>
<body>
<div id="container">
<header>
<?php include("includes/header_admin_found.inc"); ?>
</header>
<div id="content"><!--Start of table display page-->
<h3>Houses displayed four at-a-time</h3>
<p>
<?php
// This code fetches all the records from the houses table
require ('mysqli_connect.php'); // Connect to the database
//set the number of rows displayed per page
$pagerows = 4;
// Has the total number of pages already been calculated?
if (isset($_GET['p']) && is_numeric
($_GET['p'])) { //already been calculated
$pages=$_GET['p'];
}else{ //use the next block of code to calculate the number of pages
//First, check for the total number of records
$q = "SELECT COUNT(ref_num) FROM houses";
$result = @mysqli_query ($dbcon, $q);
$row = @mysqli_fetch_array ($result, MYSQLI_NUM);
$records = $row[0];
//Now calculate the number of pages
if ($records > $pagerows){ //if the number of records will fill more than one page
//Calculate the number of pages and round the result up to the nearest integer
$pages = ceil ($records/$pagerows);
}else{
$pages = 1;
}
}//page check finished. Declare which record to start with
if (isset($_GET['s']) && is_numeric
($_GET['s'])) { //already been calculated
$start = $_GET['s'];
}else{
$start = 0;
}
// Make the query
$q = "SELECT ref_num, loctn, thumb, price, mini_descr, b_rooms, status FROM houses ↵
ORDER BY ref_num ASC LIMIT $start, $pagerows";
$result = @mysqli_query ($dbcon, $q); // Run the query
if ($result) { // If the query ran OK, display the records
// Table header
echo '<table>
```

```
<tr>
<td><b>Ref-Num</b></td>
<td><b>Location</b></td>
<td><b>Thumb</b></td>
<td><b>Price</b></td>
<td><b>Features</b></td>
<td><b>Bedrms</b></td>
<td><b>Status</b></td>
</tr>';
// Fetch and print all the records
while ($row = mysqli_fetch_array($result, MYSQLI_ASSOC)) {
    echo '<tr>
    <td>' . $row['ref_num'] . '</td>
    <td>' . $row['loctn'] . '</td>
    <td>  <img src='.$row['thumb'] . '></td>
    <td>' . $row['price'] . '</td>
    <td>' . $row['mini_descr'] . '</td>
    <td>' . $row['b_rooms'] . '</td>
    <td>' . $row['status'] . '</td>
    </tr>';
    }
    echo '</table>'; // Close the table
    mysqli_free_result ($result); // Free up the resources
} else { // If it did not run OK
// Error message
echo '<p class="error">The record could not be retrieved. We apologize ↵
for any inconvenience.</p>';
// Debugging message
    echo '<p>' . mysqli_error($dbcon) . '<br><br>Query: ' . $q . '</p>';
} // End of if ($result). Now display the total number of records/houses
$q = "SELECT COUNT(ref_num) FROM houses";
$result = @mysqli_query ($dbcon, $q);
$row = @mysqli_fetch_array ($result, MYSQLI_NUM);
$houses = $row[0];
mysqli_close($dbcon); // Close the database connection
echo "<p>Total found: $houses</p>";
if ($pages > 1) {
echo '<p>';
//What number is the current page?
$current_page = ($start/$pagerows) + 1;
//If the page is not the first page, then create a Previous link
if ($current_page != 1) {
echo '<a href="admin_view_houses.php?s=' . ($start - $pagerows) . '&p=' . $pages .
'">Previous</a> ';
}
//Create a Next link
if ($current_page != $pages) {
echo '<a href="admin_view_houses.php?s=' . ($start + $pagerows) . '&p=' . $pages . '">Next</a> ';
}
echo '</p>';
}
?>
```

```
</div><!--End of table display-->
</div>
</body>
</html>
```

The administrator can also search for individual records by using the house reference number as described in the next section.

The Administrator's Search Page

Figure 8-8 shows the administrator's search page.

Figure 8-8. *The administrator can search for a specific house*

The code for the administrator's search page is given in Listing 8-8a.

Listing 8-8a. The Administrator's Search Page (admin_search.php)

```
<!doctype html>
<html lang=en>
<head>
<title>Administrator's search page</title>
<meta charset=utf-8>
<link rel="stylesheet" type="text/css" href="transparent.css">
<link rel="stylesheet" type="text/css" href="admin_search.css">
</head>
<body>
<div id="container">
<header>
<?php include('includes/header_admin_found.inc'); ?>
</header>
```

```
<div id="content"><!--Start of search page content-->
<h2 class="center" >Search for a Record</h2>
<h3>Enter the Reference Number</h3>
<form action="view_found_record.php" method="post">
<p><label for="ref_num"><b>Reference Number:</b></label><input id="ref_num" ↵
type="text" name="ref_num" size="6" maxlength="6" ↵
value="<?php if (isset($_POST['ref_num'])) echo $_POST['refnum']; ?>"></p>
<p><input id="submit" type="submit" name="submit" value="Search"></p>
</form>
<!--End of the admin search page-->
</div>
</div>
</body>
</html>
```

The code for styling the administrator's search page is given in Listing 8-8b.

Listing 8-8b. The Style for the Search Page (admin_search.css)

```
h2.center { width:280px; margin-left:-70px; }
h3 { text-align:center; }
label { margin-left:150px; width:250px; float:left; text-align:right; }
#submit { margin-left:398px; }
```

When the Search button is clicked, the record relating to the house reference number is displayed.

The Result of a Search

Figure 8-9 shows that any specified house can be displayed by the administrator.

Figure 8-9. *The record is selected and displayed*

The code for displaying a specific record is given in Listing 8-9.

Listing 8-9. Creating the Display of Specific Record (view_found_record.php)

Note that the page contains no way of editing or deleting a house. The page exists purely so that the webmaster can check that the details are correct for a newly added house. The webmaster is the administrator, and he is the only person allowed to edit or delete a house; for these tasks, he uses phpMyAdmin.

```
<!doctype html>
<html lang=en>
<head>
<title>View found record</title>
<meta charset=utf-8>
<link rel="stylesheet" type="text/css" href="transparent.css">
<link rel="stylesheet" type="text/css" href="admin_form.css">
<!--Add conditional Javascript-->
<!--[if lte IE 8]><script src="html5.js">
</script>
<![endif]-->
<!--[if lte IE 8]>
<link rel="stylesheet" type="text/css" href="ie8_admin.css">
<![endif]-->
<style type="text/css">
p.error { color:red; font-size:105%; font-weight:bold; text-align:center;}
table { width:900px; border-collapse:collapse; }
</style>
</head>
<body>
<div id="container">
<header>
<?php include('includes/header_admin_found.inc'); ?>
</header>
<div id="content"><!--Start of the view found record content -->
<h2>Search Result</h2>
<?php
// This code fetches a record from the houses table
require ('mysqli_connect.php'); // Connect to the db
$ref_num=$_POST['ref_num'];
$q = "SELECT ref_num, loctn, thumb, price, type, mini_descr, b_rooms, status ↵
      FROM houses WHERE ref_num='$ref_num' ";
$result = @mysqli_query ($dbcon, $q); // Make the query.
if ($result) { // If the query ran OK, display the record
// Table header
   echo '<table>
   <tr>
     <td><b>Ref_Num</b></td>
     <td><b>Image</b></td>
     <td><b>Price</b></td>
     <td><b>Features</b></td>
     <td><b>Bedrms</b></td>
     <td><b>Status</b></td>
   </tr>';
```

```
// Fetch and display the record
while ($row = mysqli_fetch_array($result, MYSQLI_ASSOC)) {
    echo '<tr>
        <td>' . $row['ref_num'] . '</td>
        <td>  <img src='.$row['thumb'] . '></td>
        <td>' . $row['price'] . '</td>
        <td>' . $row['mini_descr'] . '</td>
        <td>' . $row['b_rooms'] . '</td>
        <td>' . $row['status'] . '</td>
    </tr>';
    }
    echo '</table>'; // Close the table
    mysqli_free_result ($result); // Free up the resources
    } else { // If the query failed to run
// Error message:
    echo '<p class="error">The current houses could not be retrieved. We apologize for any
inconvenience.</p>';
// Debugging message:
    echo '<p>' . mysqli_error($dbcon) . '<br><br>Query: ' . $q . '</p>';
    } // End of if ($result).
?>
</div><!--End of the "view found record" content-->
</div>
</body>
</html>
```

When users search for a suitable house, they are shown a selection that matches their search criteria. The displayed table includes a column named Details. If they click the Details link, they will be shown a full description of a house and an enlarged picture of the house.

■ **Caution**   Using the downloaded files, only one of the *Details* links is a live link. To see it in action, start at the home page and search for a detached house in South Devon with 4 bedrooms and a maximum price of £400,000. When you see the displayed table of houses, click the *Details* link in the row for the house reference number 1003.

Displaying the Full Description of a House

Figure 8-10 shows an example of a page that displays the full specification of a house.

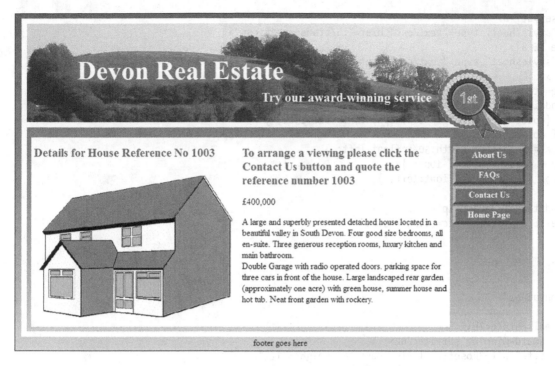

Figure 8-10. *Showing the full specification of house reference number 1003*

A real-world full description would contain much more information, such as room dimensions and the details of the heating system.

■ **Note**   Each house will need its own full description page. I have shown and listed just one of those pages.

When the administrator added the house reference 1003 to the *houses* table, the Details link for house reference 1003 was entered in the *full_spec* column of the houses table as

```
<a href='descriptions/spec_1003.php'>Details</a>.
```

The code for displaying the full description of the house reference 1003 is given in Listing 8-10.

Listing 8-10. Creating a Full Description Page (spec1003.php)

This code assumes that the description pages are stored in the folder named *descriptions*. An internal style is included for elements that are unique to full-description pages. A piece of JavaScript is included so that IE8 can read the HTML5 semantic tags. This listing is the template for all full-description pages; the items that change with each house are shown in bold type.

```
<!doctype html>
<html lang=en>
<head>
<title>Spec 1003</title>
```

251

```
<meta charset=utf-8>
<link rel="stylesheet" type="text/css" href="../transparent.css">
<!--[if lte IE 8]>
<link rel="stylesheet" type="text/css" href="../ie8.css">
<![endif]-->
<style type="text/css">
#midcol {padding:5px; margin-left:0; margin-right:140px; background:white; color:green; }
#midcol h3 {color:green; margin-top:10px; font-size:130%; }
#midcol p { color:black; }
#leftcol {margin-left:0; width:50%; float:left; }
#leftcol h3 { margin-bottom:-10px; }
mid-right-col { width:40%; float:left; }
</style>
<!--Add conditional Javascript-->
<!--[if lte IE 8]><script src="../html5.js">
</script>
<![endif]-->
</head>
<body>
<div id="container">
<header>
<h1>Devon Real Estate</h1>
<h2>Try our award-winning service</h2>
<img id="rosette" alt="Rosette" title="Rosette" height="127"
src="../images/rosette-128.png" width="128">
</header>
<div id="content">
<div id="rightcol">
<nav>
<?php include('spec_menu.inc'); ?>                                        #1
</nav>
</div><!--end of side menu column-->
<div id="midcol">
<div id="leftcol">
    <h3><strong>Details for House Reference No 1003</strong></h3><br><br>
<img alt="house reference 1003 " height="255" src="../images/house10.gif" width="350"><br>
</div>
<div id="mid-right-col">
</div>
<h3>To arrange a viewing please click the Contact Us button and quote the ↵
reference number 1003</h3>
<p>&pound;400,000</p>
<p>A large and superbly presented detached house located in a beautiful valley in ↵
South Devon. Four good size bedrooms, all en-suite. Three generous reception rooms, luxury ↵
kitchen and main bathroom.<br>Double Garage with radio operated doors. Parking space for ↵
three cars in front of the house. Large landscaped rear garden (approximately one acre) ↵
with green house, summer house and hot tub. Neat front garden with rockery.</p>
<br class="clear">
</div></div><!--content closed-->
</div>
```

```
<footer>footer goes here
</footer>
</body>
</html>
```

Explanation of the Code

The code is quite straightforward, but note that the URLs for the included items are all prefixed with two dots and a forward slash (../). This is because the *includes*, JavaScript, style sheets, and images are all located one level above the descriptions folder.

However, the item on line **#1** is not straightforward and needs some explanation as follows:

```
<?php include('spec_menu.inc'); ?>                                                    #1
```

A copy of the main menu (*menu.inc*) was placed in the *descriptions* folder and renamed *spec_menu.inc*. This is because the path to the four files in the main menu is complex. By locating the modified menu file in the *descriptions* folder, the paths are simplified. The code for *spec_menu.inc* is as follows:

```
<ul>
    <li><a href="#" title="About Us">About Us</a></li>
    <li><a href="#" title="Frequently Asked Questions">FAQs</a></li>
    <li><a href="../contact.php" title="Contact Us">Contact Us</a></li>
    <li><a href="../index.php" title="Return to Home Page">Home Page</a></li>
</ul>
```

The first and second items are dead links because the downloadable files do not include the *About us* and *FAQs* files. If they were included the path would be *../about.php*, which is preceded by two dots and a forward slash because the file *about.php* would be located one level above the file that calls it. The same applies to the path for the FAQs file.

If extra buttons are added to the main menu, the webmaster must remember to also add them to the *spec_menu.inc* file.

When users wish to visit and inspect a house, they are asked to click the *Contact Us* button. This button loads the *Contact Us* form, which will be described next.

The *Contact Us* Page

Figure 8-11 shows an example of a suitable *Contact Us* page. This is a cut-down version of the *Contact Us* page from Chapter 7.

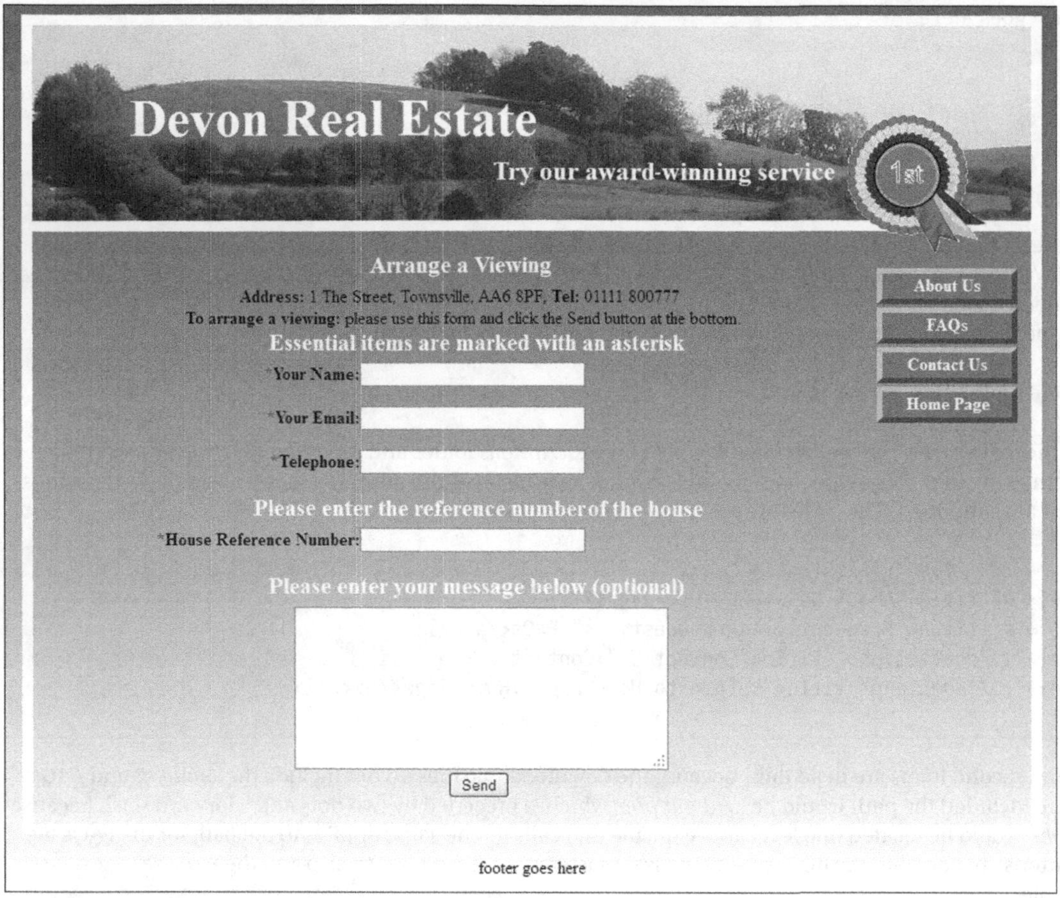

Figure 8-11. *The Contact Us page*

The code that displays the form is given in Listing 8-11a.

Listing 8-11a. Creating the "Contact Us" Page (contact.php)

An internal style is used to format the fields because their layout is unique to this page.

```
<!doctype html>
<html lang=en>
<head>
<title>Contact page - Devon Real Estate</title>
<meta charset=utf-8>
<link rel="stylesheet" type="text/css" href="transparent.css">
<!--[if lte IE 8]>
<link rel="stylesheet" type="text/css" href="ie8.css">
<![endif]-->
<style type="text/css">
span.red { color:red; }
```

```
div.cntr { text-align:center; }
form { margin-left:15px; font-weight:bold; color:black; }
#midcol h3 { font-size:130%; text-align:center;}
form { margin-left:30px; }
form h3 { text-align:center; }
label { width:250px; float:left; text-align:right; }
input { float:left; }
textarea { margin-left:190px; }
#sb { margin-left:330px; }
</style>
<!--Add conditional JavaScript for IE8-->
<!--[if lte IE 8]>
<script src="html5.js">
</script>
<![endif]-->
</head>
<body>
<div id="container">
<header>
<h1>Devon Real Estate</h1>
<h2>Try our award-winning service</h2>
<img id="rosette" alt="Rosette" title="Rosette" height="127"
src="images/rosette-128.png" width="128">
</header>
<div id="content">
<div id="rightcol">
<nav>
<?php include('includes/menu.inc'); ?>
</nav>
</div><!--End of side menu column-->
<div id="midcol">
<h3>Arrange a Viewing</h3>
<div class="cntr">
<strong>Address:</strong> 1 The Street, Townsville, AA6 8PF, <b>Tel:</b> 01111 800777
<br> <strong>To arrange a viewing:</strong> please use this form and click the ↵
Send button at the bottom.
</div>
<div id="form">
<form action="contact_handler.php" method="post" >
<h3 >Essential items are marked with an asterisk</h3>
<!--Start of text fields-->
<label for="username"><span class="red">*</span>Your Name: </label>
<input id="username" name="username" size="30"><br>
<br><label for="useremail" ><span class="red">*</span>Your Email:</label>
<input id="useremail" name="useremail" size="30"><br>
<br><label for="phone" ><span class="red">*</span>Telephone:</label>
<input id="phone" name="phone" size="30"><br><br>
<h3>Please enter the reference number of the house</h3>
<label for="ref_num" ><span class="red">*</span>House Reference Number: </label>
<input id="ref_num" name="ref_num" size="30"><br><br>
<h3>Please enter your message below (optional)</h3>
```

```
<textarea id="comment" name="comment" rows="8" cols="40"></textarea>
<br>
<!--The submit button goes here-->
<input id="sb" value="Send" title="Send" alt="Send" type="submit"><br>
</form>
</div>
</div>
<br class="clear">
</div> <!--End of the feedback form content-->
<footer>
Footer goes here
</footer>
</div>
</body>
</html>
```

We will now examine the contact form handler in Listing 8-11b.

Listing 8-11b. Creating the Contact Form Handler (contact_handler.php)

```php
<?php
/* Contact form handler*/
// set to the email address to the recipient, eg
//$mailto = "webmaster@myisp.com" ;
$mailto = "info@devonrealestate.co.uk" ;
$subject = "Message from the Devon Real Estate contact form" ;
// list the pages to be displayed
$formurl = "http://www.devonrealestate.co.uk/contact.php" ;
$errorurl = "http://www.devonrealestate.co.uk/error.html" ;
$thankyouurl = "http://www.devonrealestate.co.uk/thankyou.html" ;
$emailerrurl = "http://www.devonrealestate.co.uk/emailerr.html" ;
$errorcommenturl =  "http://www.devonrealestate.co.uk/commenterror.html" ;
$uself = 0;
// Set the information received from the form as short variables
$headersep = (!isset( $uself ) || ($uself == 0)) ? "\r\n" : "\n" ;
$username = $_POST['username'] ;
$useremail = $_POST['useremail'] ;
$phone = $_POST['phone'];
$ref_num = $_POST['ref_num'];
$comment = $_POST['comment'] ;
$http_referrer = getenv( "HTTP_REFERER" );
$errors = array(); // Initialize an error array
//Check that all four essential fields are filled out
if (empty($username) || empty($useremail) || empty($phone)|| empty($comment)) {
header( "Location: $errorurl" );
   exit ; }
//check that no URLs have been inserted in the username text field
if (strpos ($username, '://')||strpos($username, 'www') !==false){
header( "Location: $errorsuggesturl" );
exit ; }
```

```php
if (preg_match( "[\r\n]", $username ) || preg_match( "[\r\n]", $useremail )) {
header( "Location: $errorurl" );
exit ; }
#remove any spaces from beginning and end of email address
$useremail = trim($useremail);
#Check for permitted email address patterns
$_name = "/^[-!#$%&\'*+\\.\/0-9=?A-Z^_`{|}~]+";
$_host = "([-0-9A-Z]+\.)+";
$_tlds = "([0-9A-Z]){2,4}$/i";
if(!preg_match($_name."@".$_host.$_tlds,$useremail)) {
header( "Location: $emailerrurl" );
exit ; }
if (!empty($_POST['phone'])) {
//Remove spaces, hyphens, letters and brackets
$phone = preg_replace('/\D+/', '', ($_POST['phone']));
}
if (!empty($_POST['ref_num'])) {
//Remove spaces, hyphens, letters and brackets
$ref_num = preg_replace('/\D+/', '', ($_POST['ref_num']));
}
//check that no URLs have been inserted in the comment text area
if (strpos ($comment, '://')||strpos($comment, 'www') !==false){
header( "Location: $errorcommenturl" );
exit ; }
$messageproper =
"This message was sent from:\n" .
"$http_referrer\n" .
"------------------------------------------------------------\n" .
"Name of sender: $username\n" .
"Email of sender: $useremail\n" .
"Telephone: $phone\n" .
"Reference Num: $ref_num\n" .
"----------------------- MESSAGE -----------------------\n\n" .
$comment .
"\n\n------------------------------------------------------------\n" ;
mail($mailto, $subject, $messageproper, "From: \"$username\" <$useremail>" );
header( "Location: $thankyouurl" );
exit ;
?>
```

When the message is sent, a Thank You page appears. The code for this is given in Listing 8-12a.

Listing 8-12a. The "Thank You" Page (thankyou.html)

```html
<!doctype html>
<html lang=en>
<head>
<title>Thank you for your enquiry</title>
<meta charset=utf-8>
<link rel="stylesheet" type="text/css" href="feedback.css">
</head>
```

```
<body>
<p> </p>
<div id="back-button"><a title="Return to the Home page" href="index.php">↵
Return to Home Page</a>
</div>
<div><br>
<h2>Thank you for your enquiry</h2>
<h3>We will email an answer to you shortly.</h3>
</div>
</body>
</html>
```

Listing 8-12b. The Styling for the "Thank You" Page (feedback.css)

```
/*FEEDBACK.CSS*/
/*reset browsers for cross-client consistency*/
body,h2,h3,p {margin:0; padding:0 }
body {text-align:center; background-color:#D7FFEB; color:black; ↵
font-family: "times new roman"; max-width:100%; min-width:960px;
font-size: medium; color: #000000; margin: auto; width:95%;}
#back-button { margin:20px auto 0 auto; text-align:center; width:200px; height:25px; ↵
padding:5px; background-color:brown; color:white; font-size:110%; font-weight:bold; }
#back-button a { text-decoration:none; color:white; }
#back-button a:hover { color:red; }
h2 { margin-top:15px; margin-bottom:10px; font-size:130%; font-weight:bold;}
h3 { font-size:110%; font-weight:bold; text-align:center;}
```

■ **Note**   The three error-message pages are included in the downloadable files, and they are the same as those in Chapter 7.

Summary

In this chapter, you learned how to plan a database for a real estate catalog. We created a home page in which users could search for a suitable house. We provided the administrator with a page so that he could add new houses. We produced a page that allowed the administrator to view the entire stock of houses, or to search for and view a specific house. We then learned how to create a page to show users the full specification of a particular property. We created an inquiry form for users who wished to inspect a house.

In the next chapter, you will learn how to extract data from multiple tables by joining them, how to create a form to allow payments by check, and an economical method for printing online forms.

CHAPTER 9

■ ■ ■

Adding Multiple Tables and Other Enhancements

Web sites with databases can benefit from the three practical enhancements described in this chapter. For instance, (i) multiple tables can give more specific search results and are essential for the administration of forums and e-commerce sites, (ii) membership fees can be paid by check as well as by using PayPal and credit/debit cards, (iii) check payments can be accompanied by printable application forms. These three enhancements will be used in subsequent chapters. The sections in this chapter are as follows:

- Introduction to multiple tables

- Payment by check

- Printing online forms

Introduction to Multiple Tables

Previous chapters used databases with one table. These databases are called *flat file* databases. Sometimes databases use several tables that can be related to each other. These databases are called *relational* databases. Data from each table can be joined (combined) to form virtual tables that can be displayed in a browser. In this tutorial, we will concentrate entirely on the process of joining tables. For simplicity and clarity, the web site for this tutorial will be stripped of several features, such as logging in, registration, and administration. The buttons for these functions will appear on the headers, but they will be dead links.

You may wonder why we need more than one table. Why not put all the data in one table? We could use one huge table, but it would lead to no end of trouble. A great deal of information would be entered many times, causing the database to be very inefficient, and the administration would be time consuming and extremely tedious.

As an example, suppose we had an e-commerce web site selling telephones and intercoms. We could have a set of records as shown in Table 9-1.

Table 9-1. *A table with many duplicate entries*

Order_id	Customer name	Address	Product	Stock
1006	Charlie Smith	3 Park Road Townsville TV77 99JP	Phone 123	1
1007	Charlie Smith	3 Park Road Townsville TV77 99JP	Intercom 456	4
1008	Robert Bruce	4 Linden Street Urbania UT88 66XY	Intercom 456	5
1009	Nellie Dean	7 Elm Avenue Milltown MT 78 88WZ	Phone 456	6
1010	Robert Bruce	4 Linden Street Urbania UT88 66XY	Phone 678	1
1011	Nellie Dean	7 Elm Avenue Milltown MT78 88WZ	Intercom 396	3
1012	Charlie Smith	3 Park Road Townsville TV77 99JP	Phone dock A2	4

This single table containing the latest orders has many problems.

Charlie Smith has ordered three items, and his address is repeated three times. If he changed his address, we would need to amend three rows in the table. Charlie's name and address should be kept in a separate table; then we need to change his address only once. The stock level will change so that we would have to scroll through the records to determine the lowest stock level for a particular item. The stock level and the product description should be kept in another table so that only that table would need updating. The user and the administrator would then see an accurate figure for the stock level when the product is displayed.

Normalization

The process of eliminating redundancies and other maintenance problems is called *normalization*. Table 9-1 contains items that illustrate very bad practices. The first name and last name should be in separate columns, The address should be split into separate columns for street, town, and ZIP code or postal code. This process is known by the rather clumsy name of *atomicity* because, like atoms, the data is separated into minimal components. It is then *atomic* or *indivisible*.

Normalization is achieved by applying rigorous *atomicity* and splitting the data into several tables, instead of using just one table, so that each table has a very specific and singular purpose. Also, the information in each table must have closely related data, such as first name, last name, and e-mail address; if the customer changes his or her e-mail address, you have to amend only one record. Normalization allows a database to be easily extended so that it can hold more types of information. For instance, a table could be added to hold the colors of the phones, or you could have a table for dispatch dates.

Normalization can be difficult to understand at first, but you will be automatically normalizing your tables if you apply atomicity and then group closely related data into separate tables. By breaking data down to the lowest level, you allow for future growth and better data control, and you leave yourself more options in the future to modify and manipulate the data. Being able to have a one-to-many relationship on multiple tables ensures less data redundancy.

We will now create a database with two tables.

Create the Database and Tables

For the first part of this tutorial, we must create a database to contain two small tables. In *htdocs*, create a new folder and name it *birds*. In phpMyAdmin, create a database called *birdsdb* and then set up a user and a password as follows:

Database name: birdsdb

User: faraday

Password: dynamo1831

Host: localhost

Download the files from the book's page at apress.com, and load them into your *birds* folder.

View the Connection File

The file *mysqli_connect.php* has the following code:

```php
<?php
// This creates a connection to the birdsdb database; it also sets the encoding to utf-8
DEFINE ('DB_USER', 'faraday');
DEFINE ('DB_PASSWORD', 'dynamo1831');
DEFINE ('DB_HOST', 'localhost');
DEFINE ('DB_NAME', 'birdsdb');
// Make the connection
$dbcon = @mysqli_connect (DB_HOST, DB_USER, DB_PASSWORD, DB_NAME) ↵
OR die ('Could not connect to MySQL: ' . mysqli_connect_error() );
// Set the encoding
mysqli_set_charset($dbcon, 'utf8');
?>
```

Use phpMyAdmin to import the *birds.sql* file, or create a table manually named *birds* with four columns and the attributes given in Table 9-2.

Table 9-2. *The* birds *table*

Columnname	Type	Length/value	Default	Attributes	NULL	Index	A_I
bird_id	MEDIUMINT	4	None	UNSIGNED	☐	PRIMARY	☑
bird_name	TINYTEXT	60	None		☐		☐
rarity	TINYTEXT	60	None		☐		☐
best_time	TINYTEXT	60	None		☐		☐

The *birds* table contains a column named *bird_id*. This column is configured as the PRIMARY key.

Using phpMyAdmin, import the file *location.sql*, or create the table manually with four columns as shown in Table 9-3 and name it *location*.

Table 9-3. *The attributes for the* location *table*

Column name	Type	Length/value	Default	Attributes	NULL	Index	A_I
location_id	MEDIUMINT	4	None	UNSIGNED	☐	PRIMARY	☑
location	TINYTEXT	60	None		☐		☐
location_type	TINYTEXT	60	None		☐		☐
bird_id	MEDIUMINT	4	None	UNSIGNED	☐		☐

Foreign Keys

The *location* table contains the *location_id*, *location*, and *location_type*. In addition, it contains a column named *bird_id* that duplicates the *bird_id* column that is the PRIMARY key in the *birds* table. The *birds_id* column in the *location* table is called a *foreign key* because this is a key from a different table (the *birds* table). This foreign key enables us to join the two tables by means of a SELECT and INNER JOIN statement; the various JOIN methods will be explained later. By this means, we can select certain data from both tables and display the result in a browser as a single table.

IMPORTANT: Foreign keys link to PRIMARY keys in another table, and they must be the same type and length as the PRIMARY key. Also, foreign keys must all be indexed. Indexing these keys ensures fast queries. In our tutorial, all the PRIMARY keys and their linked foreign keys are of the type MEDIUMINT and their length is 4. PRIMARY keys are automatically indexed, but foreign keys must be indexed by the web-site developer. This can be done in phpMyAdmin, as you will see shortly. If you try to set a foreign key that links to a PRIMARY key with a different length or value, you will see an error message stating that the reference to the PRIMARY key could not be created.

■ **Caution**   Do not enter data in the tables. We will do this later when the tables have been prepared for joining.

Meanwhile, we must begin with some preparation.

Preparing the Tables for Joining

So that we can join the tables, we must establish a link between the *bird_id* in the first table and the *bird_id* in the second table. But first, we need to set the storage method.

MySQL uses two methods for storing tables; they are called INNODB, the default for MySQL, and MyISAM. Note that MySQL supports foreign keys only when INNODB storage is used; therefore, we must check that both tables are using the INNODB storage engine. You can quickly check the storage method for all tables by looking on the database *Structure* tab. In the *Type* column, it will list the storage type. Alternatively, in phpMyAdmin, select the box next to the *birds* table and click the *Operations* tab. Then go to the *Table options* section If the storage engine is not listed as INNODB, change it to INNODB. Repeat this for the second table. The *Operations* dialog screen is shown in Figure 9-1.

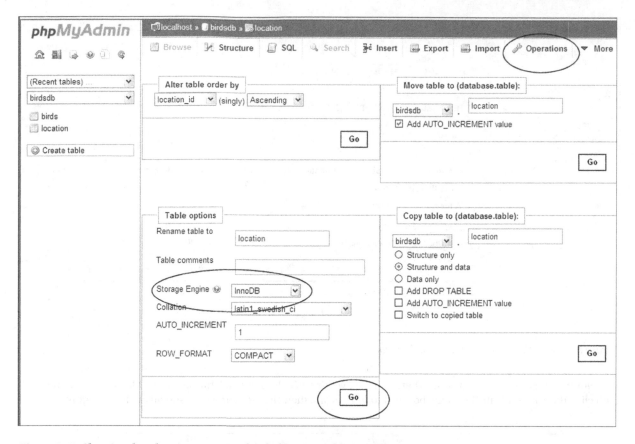

Figure 9-1. *Showing that the storage engine for the* location *table is INNODB*

■ **Note** It is possible to extract and display data from multiple tables even if they do not all use the INNODB storage engine. However, for simplicity, we will not be using MyISAM storage on any of the tables in this tutorial.

Now the indexes need to be set. The index is already prepared in the first table because the column named *bird_id* is a PRIMARY key, which is an index by default. The foreign key named *bird_id* in the *location* table needs to be indexed. In phpMyAdmin, select the *location* table and then the *Structure* tab, and select the box next to the *bird_id* column. Then click the word *Index* shown circled at the bottom right of Figure 9-2. phpMyAdmin shows a message to confirm that the index has been created, and you can also click the "+ indexes" pull-down item in the *Structure* tab to see the indexes.

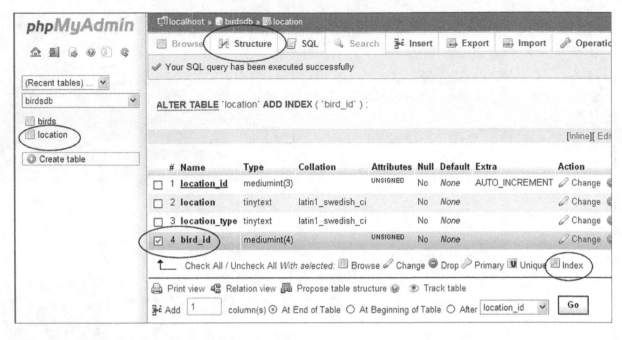

Figure 9-2. *Creating an index for the* bird_id *column*

Now we must create a relationship between the two *bird_id* columns. Click the *location* table in the left panel and then click the *Structure* tab. Select the box next to *bird_id* and then click *Relation view* shown circled in Figure 9-3.

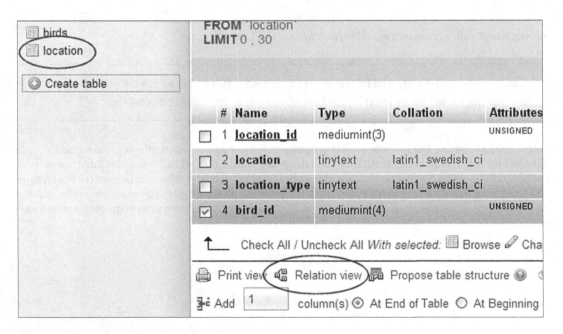

Figure 9-3. *Click* Relation view *for the location table*

A new dialog will appear, as shown in the next screen shot Figure 9-4.

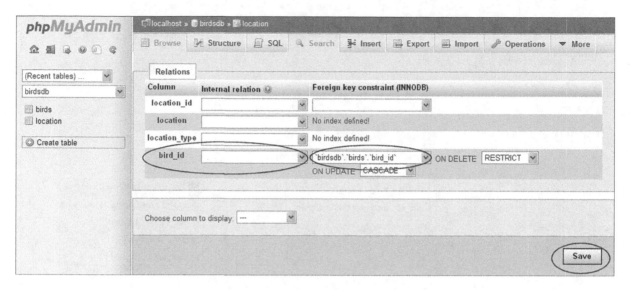

Figure 9-4. *Selecting the key in the* birds *table that matches the foreign key in the location table. In later versions of phpMyAdmin, you will see an additional field between the FOREIGN KEY and the ON DELETE field*

Using the phpMyAdmin interface shown in Figure 9-4, we will select the constraints for the birds table by using the following steps:

1. With the details of the *location* table on the screen, use the pull-down menu in the column headed *Foreign key constraint* to select the matching PRIMARY key in the *birds* table. The field next to *bird_id* in the column under the heading *Internal relation* should remain empty. If you click the circled question mark next to the heading *Internal relation,* a tool tip will explain why.

2. In the field named *On delete*, select RESTRICT. In the field named ON UPDATE, select CASCADE. The terms RESTRICT and NO ACTION are synonymous, and they ensure that when you're attempting to delete data (say, a user's record) in one table, the data (matching record) in the linked table is not affected adversely. This is prevented because a warning message is displayed. CASCADE ensures that when a table is updated the linked tables are also updated; this a great help for maintaining database tables.

3. Click *Save*. The foreign key *bird_id* in the *location* table is then related to the PRIMARY key *bird_id* in the *birds* table.

When you click *Save*, the code is displayed above the main pane. You will see the ON DELETE and CASCADE settings. You can use phpMyAdmin to view the link between the two tables. In the home page of phpMyAdmin, click the database *birdsdb* and then use the *MORE* pull-down menu to select *Designer*. You will see a diagrammatic view of the two tables illustrating the link between the PRIMARY key and the foreign key, as shown in Figure 9-5. Drag the tables around to give a neat diagram clearly displaying the tables and their link. While you are using the *Designer* view, explore it to see several useful control features.

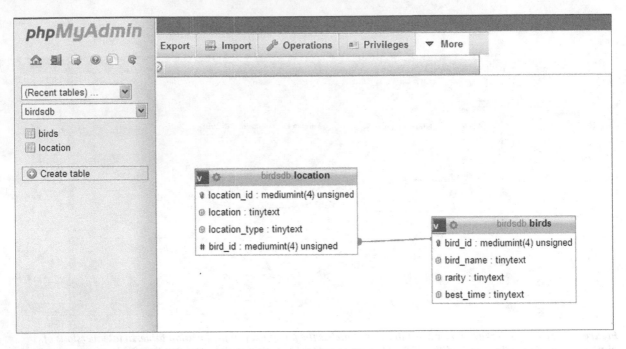

Figure 9-5. *The Designer view showing the link between the two tables*

Add Some Data

Import the file *birds.sql*, which is already populated, but if you wish to create the table manually, use the *Insert* tab in phpMyAdmin to insert the data shown in Table 9-4 into the *birds* table.

Table 9-4. *The* birds *table*

bird_id	bird_name	rarity	best_time
1	Goldeneye	Common	Winter
2	Wryneck	Rare	Summer
3	Avocet	Common	Winter
4	Moorhen	Common	Any time

If you wish to populate the *location* table manually, use phpMyAdmin and click the location table in the left panel. Then, using the *Insert* tab in phpMyAdmin, insert the data shown in Table 9-5. Note that because we linked the two *bird_id* columns, you will see a pull-down menu containing the *bird_id* numbers for entering the foreign key *bird_id* in the *location* table.

Table 9-5. *The* location *table*

location_id	location	location_type	bird_id
1	Southpark	Ponds	4
2	Westlands	Estuary	3
3	Lakeland	Lakes	1
4	Moorfield	Moorland	2
5	Heathville	Heath	2

The following criteria were used to enter data for the foreign key *bird_id* in the fourth column.

We assumed that some birds can be seen only in certain reserves. For instance, goldeneyes are found in the lake at the Lakeland reserve; therefore, we entered the goldeneye's id (1) in the Lakeland row. Wrynecks are found only in the Moorfield and Heathville bird reserves; therefore, we entered the wryneck's id (2) in the rows containing those two locations. The avocet is an estuary bird; therefore, its id (3) was entered in the row for the Westlands reserve, which is an estuary. Moorhens prefer ponds; therefore, the moorhen's id (4) was entered in the row for the Southpark reserve because that reserve has several ponds.

Now that we have learned about keys (indexes), we can discuss how to use them to join tables.

Joins

We will digress here to discuss the theory of JOINS. Refer to Tables 9-6 and 9-7 as I explain three ways of joining tables by using a SELECT query.

Table 9-6. *The* users *table*

user_id	user	phone
1	Mrs Bush	01222 123456
2	Mr Rosoft	01333 123456
3	Mr Druff	01444 123456
4	Mr Druff	01555 123456

Table 9-7. *The* town *table*

town_id	user_id	town
1	1	Exeter
2	3	Axminster
3	3	Plymouth
4	4	Taunton
5	5	Seaton

Note how I placed the tables. I will refer to them as the LEFT table and the RIGHT table. This reflects the order of the tables in the SELECT query that we will use to join the two tables. The first table in a JOIN query we think of as the LEFT table, and the second table in a JOIN query we regard as the RIGHT table.

The IDs (indexes) are the keys to understanding joins. Look through each table, and take particular note of the IDs. Some deliberate (but unlikely) registration errors have been introduced so that the various joins can be demonstrated. The errors are (i) Mr Duff has registered twice because his work means he has addresses in two towns, and a secure database would not normally allow a person to register twice, (ii) the second *user_id* in the table on the right has been entered as 3 instead of 2, (iii) the details for *user_id* 5 are missing from the table on the left. We will now examine various types of join using Tables 9-6 and 9-7.

INNER Joins

INNER joins are the most frequently used joins for the public display of tables. This is because OUTER joins can display columns containing NULL entries that are helpful for maintaining a database, but they are not good for public display.

If you use a SELECT query to create an INNER JOIN, you will select all the records where the *user_id* matches in both tables. Where *user_ids* in the table on the right do not match, the records are not selected. The SELECT query would be as follows:

```
SELECT user, phone, town FROM users INNER JOIN USING (user_id);
```

The resulting table display using an INNER join is shown in Table 9-8.

Table 9-8. *The result of an INNER join*

user	phone	town
Mrs Bush	01222 123456	Exeter
Mr Druff	01444 123456	Plymouth
Mr Druff	01555 123456	Taunton

Mr Rosoft doesn't appear because the ID in the *users* table has no matching ID in the *town* table. The fifth entry in the *town* table doesn't show up because there is no equivalent entry in the *users* table (which is the one we performed the Join query on).

The INNER join query can have the following alternative format:

```
SELECT user, phone, town FROM users JOIN town ON users.user_id = town.user_id;
```

Outer Joins

In OUTER joins, the word OUTER is normally not used; instead, they are referred to as LEFT joins and RIGHT joins. However, the word OUTER may be optionally added after the words LEFT or RIGHT. The words LEFT and RIGHT refer to the database tables shown in Tables 9-6 and 9-7, they are on the left and the right of the book's page, respectively. As previously stated, they are also the first and second tables, respectively, in the SELECT query.

LEFT JOIN

With a LEFT outer join, you will SELECT the same matching data as before (Table 9-8), but you will also select items from the table on the left of this page (the first table in the SELECT query) so that every name and phone number is listed. However, you will see NULL in the columns where no matching ID is found.

The OUTER LEFT join would have the following format:

```
SELECT user, phone, town FROM users LEFT JOIN town ON users.user_id = town.user_id;
```

The result is as shown in Table 9-9.

Table 9-9. *The result of the LEFT outer join*

user	phone	town
Mrs Bush	01222 123456	Exeter
Mr Rosoft	01333 123456	NULL
Mr Druff	01444 123456	Plymouth
Mr Druff	01555 123456	Taunton

The LEFT JOIN lists every user and phone number because these are in the LEFT table (the first table in the SELECT query). But in the case of Mr Rosoft, you will see NULL in the town column because his ID (number 2) is not present in the RIGHT table (the second table in the SELECT query).

RIGHT JOIN

With a RIGHT OUTER JOIN, you select all the records that match (as in Table 9-8), but you will also select a record for each unmatched record in the table on the RIGHT. This means that all the towns are selected, but NULL will be seen in the user and phone columns where no match is found in the LEFT table. The SELECT query is as follows:

```
SELECT user, phone, town FROM users RIGHT JOIN town ON ↵
users.user_id = town.user_id;
```

The data selected is as shown in Table 9-10.

Table 9-10. *The result of a RIGHT OUTER JOIN*

user	phone	town
Mrs Bush	01222 123456	Exeter
NULL	NULL	Axminster
Mr Druff	01444 123456	Plymouth
Mr Druff	01555 123456	Taunton
NULL	NULL	Seaton

All three columns have entries for Mrs. Bush and Mr. Druff because their IDs are present in both tables (as shown in Table 9-8). All the towns are listed because we used a RIGHT JOIN and all the towns are present in the RIGHT table (the second table in the SELECT query). However, because the people living in Axminster and Seaton have no corresponding ID in the LEFT table (*users*), their *user* and *phone* columns contain NULL.

Joined tables are virtual tables; they cannot be stored in the *data* folder within the MySQL folder. However, they can be displayed using a browser. That is the end of the JOINS theory section. We will now return to the *birds* database and apply the theory. As a reminder, we will view the two *birdsdb* database tables (Table 9-4 and Table 9-5) once more.

We will use an INNER JOIN to extract and display information from both tables. An INNER join is the most frequently employed method for joining tables, because it never shows NULL fields in a public display.

The INNER JOIN will combine only the records (rows) that have a common item ID in both tables. We want the location to appear in the first column of the table display, so the syntax for INNER joining the two tables birds (tableA) and locations (tableB) is as follows:

```
$q = "SELECT location.location, birds.bird_name, birds.rarity, birds.best_time ↵
FROM location INNER JOIN birds ON location.bird_id=birds.bird_id";
```

After the SELECT keyword, add the column names in the order that you want them to be displayed on the screen. Separate the column names using commas. After the FROM key word, JOIN the two tables using the ON keyword (which is the equivalent of WHERE). The statement after the ON key word means "where tableB.FOREIGN key equals the tableA.PRIMARY key". Note that the dot between the table names and the keys (the IDs) is very important.

The query result is shown in Table 9-11.

Table 9-11. *The result of the INNER JOIN query*

location	bird_name	rarity	Best_time
Lakeland	Goldeneye	Common	Winter
Moorfield	Wryneck	Rare	Summer
Heathville	Wryneck	Rare	Summer
Westlands	Avocet	Common	Winter
Southpark	Moorhen	Common	Any time

To demonstrate that the word "INNER" can be omitted in a plain SELECT statement, you could use the following query:

```
$q = "SELECT location, bird_name, rarity, best_time FROM location JOIN birds ↵
ON location.bird_id=birds.bird_id";
```

We will briefly examine a LEFT OUTER JOIN for completeness.

What Happens If You Use a LEFT Outer Join

OUTER joins are inclusive. If we add the robin to our list of birds with a *bird_id* of 5, the robin will be included in the OUTER LEFT joined table, but the robin's location will contain a NULL entry as shown next in Table 9-12. Tables containing NULL entries are not for public viewing but can be helpful for a web site administrator.

Table 9-12. *An outer join using LEFT JOIN*

bird_name	rarity	Best_time	location
Goldeneye	Common	Winter	Lakeland
Wryneck	Rare	Summer	Moorfield
Wryneck	Rare	Summer	Heathville
Avocet	Common	Winter	Westlands
Moorhen	Common	Any time	Southpark
Robin	Common	Any time	NULL

The query statement for the preceding OUTER LEFT JOIN is as follows:

```
$q = "SELECT birds.bird, birds.rarity, bird,best_time, location.location ↵
FROM birds LEFT JOIN location USING (bird_id) ";
```

The previous sections demonstrated the creation of *virtual* joined tables We will now create an environment for displaying those *virtual* joined tables. This will be achieved by using menu buttons in the home page.

The Home Page for the Multiple Tables Tutorial

To save space and to simplify the tutorial, you do not need to log in or administer the web site because no members' table is provided in the downloadable files or listings. In addition to these omissions, no provision is made for an Internet Explorer 8 conditional style sheet.

The home page menu buttons are on the left as shown in Figure 9-6. When the buttons are clicked, they will display two separate tables and two joined tables, Later in the chapter we will add a third table so that the fifth button will display three joined tables. The code for the home page is given in Listing 9-6a.

Figure 9-6. *The Devon Bird Reserves home page*

Listing 9-6a. Creating the home page for demonstrating joined tables (index.php)

```
<!doctype html>
<html lang=en>
<head>
<title>Home Page</title>
<meta charset=utf-8>
<link rel="stylesheet" type="text/css" href="birds.css">
</head>
<body>
<div id="container">
<?php include("includes/header.php"); ?>
```

```php
<?php include("includes/nav.php"); ?>
<?php include("includes/info-col.php"); ?>
<div id="content"><!--Start of the home page content-->
<div id="midcol">
<h2>Help Save Our Devon Birds From Extinction</h2>
<div id="mid-left-col">
<p class="dark">The Devon Bird Reserves were established in an effort to combat the
massive decline in the bird population due to intensive farming.<br>The reserves are
pesticide-free havens for birds and other wildlife. They provide an ideal habitat where
birds are able to nest and safely search for food. </p>
    <p class="dark">The reserves have comfortable bird hides where you may observe the
wildlife without disturbing it. Each hide has an information panel and also a chalkboard
 where you can inform others about your sightings.</p>
 </p>
</div>
<div id="mid-right-col">
<h3>Become a member and support our cause</h3>
<p class="dark">The annual membership subscription permits free entry or reduced entrance
fees to the reserves. Members receive a free quarterly magazine and news
updates. You will also be able to log in and view the members' special events.</p>
    <p class="dark">To join, please click the Register button.  </p>
</div><!--End of the home page content--></div>
</div></div><br class="clear">
<div id="footer">
<footer>
<?php include("includes/footer.php"); ?>
</footer></div>
</body>
</html>
```

The elements on the home page are positioned using the CSS code given in Listing 9-6b.

Listing 9-6b. The main style sheet for the pages (birds.css)

```css
body {text-align:center; background-color:#CCFF99; color:green;
font-family:"times new roman"; font-size: 100%; margin: auto; }
h2 { font-size:150%; margin-bottom:0; color:#003300; text-align:center; }
h3 { font-size:110%; color:#003300; text-align:center; }
#container {position:relative; min-width:960px; max-width:1200px; margin:auto;
text-align:left; }
#header, #header-members, #header-admin { position:relative; margin:10px auto 0 auto;
min-width:960px; max-width:1200px; height:183px;
background-image: url('images/header3.jpg'); background-repeat: no-repeat; padding:0;
color:white;}
h1 {position:relative; top:50px; font-size:350%; color:white; margin:auto 0 auto 20px;
width: 700px; }
ul { position:absolute; top:180px; right:-40px; color:navy; width:135px;
text-align:center; margin:0; }
#nav ul { position:absolute; top:190px; left:-40px; color:navy; width:135px;
text-align:center; margin:0; }
#info-col { position:absolute; top:190px; right:10px; color:navy; width:135px;
text-align:center; margin:5px 5px 0 0; }
```

```
#reg-navigation ul { position:absolute; top:30px; right:-20px; font-size:medium; width:160px; }
#midcol { margin-left:150px; margin-right:150px; }
#mid-left-col{      float:left; width:46%; text-align:left; }
#mid-right-col{ float:right; width:46%; text-align:left; }
p.dark {font-size:120%; color:#003300; }
#mid-right-col h3 { text-align:left; font-size:130%; color:#003300; margin-bottom:0; }
#footer { text-align:center; }
.clear { clear:both; }
/* set general side button styles */
li { width:115px; list-style-type :none; margin-bottom: 3px; text-align: center; }
/* set general anchor styles */
li a { display: block; width:115px; color: white; font-weight: bold; text-decoration: none; }
/* specify state styles. */
/* mouseout (default) */
li a { background: #559a55; border: 4px outset #559a55; }
/* mouseover */
li a:hover { display:block; background: red;  color:white; border: 5px outset red; ↵
width:115px; }
/* onmousedown */
li a:active { background:maroon;  border: 5px inset maroon; }
```

■ Note   As previously mentioned, joined tables are virtual tables. They cannot be seen until they are displayed in a browser. The pages in this tutorial are designed specifically to demonstrate the results of joining tables. The table displays are selected by clicking buttons on the menu. A real-world web site would not have buttons labeled *Join 2 Tables* and *Join 3 Tables*. (We will be adding a third table later.) These labels are for your convenience only.

We will now examine the menu for viewing the various tables.

The Main Menu for the Home Page

Buttons on the main menu will be used to select the various tables. The buttons are shown in Figure 9-7.

Figure 9-7. *The menu for demonstrating the tables*

The menu code is given in Listing 9-7 and the file can be found in the *includes* folder in the downloaded files.

Listing 9-7. Creating the Menu for Selecting Various Tables (includes/nav.php)

```
<div id="nav"><!--The side menu column contains the vertical menu-->
<ul>
<li><a href="#" title="Page two">About Us</a></li>
<li><a href="birds.php" title="The Birds">The Birds</a></li>
<li><a href="reserves.php" title="The Reserves">The Reserves</a></li>
<li><a href="join-2.php" title="Two tables joined">Join 2 Tables</a></li>
<li><a href="join-3.php" title="Three tables joined">Join 3 Tables</a></li>
<li><a href="index.php" title="Return to Home Page">Home Page</a></li>
</ul>
</div><!--end of side column and menu -->
```

The Header for the Home Page

The header for the home page contains two menu buttons as shown in Figure 9-8.

Figure 9-8. *The home page header*

The code for the header is shown in Listing 9-8

Listing 9-8. Creating the Header Menu Buttons (includes/header.php)

```
<div id="header">
<h1>The Devon Bird Reserves</h1>
<div id="reg-navigation">
    <ul>
        <li><a href="#">Login</a></li>
        <li><a href="member_reg.php">Register</a></li>
    </ul>
</div>
</div>
```

■ **Caution** To save space, a member's table is not included in the database for this tutorial. Therefore, you will not be able to register members. However, you will be able to click the Register button to view the registration page. Note that the *Login* link is dead because without a database table for members, it is not possible to log in.

Displaying a Table of Birds

We will now display a single un-joined table using the data from the *birds* table. The table will display as shown in Figure 9-9.

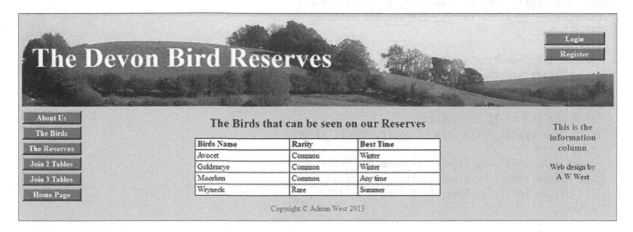

Figure 9-9. *Displaying the table of birds*

The code for displaying the table of birds is given in Listing 9-9.

Listing 9-9. Creating the Page for Displaying a Table of Birds (birds.php)

An internal style is used because the table is unique to this page.

```
<!doctype html>
<html lang=en>
<head>
<title>View birds page</title>
<meta charset=utf-8>
<link rel="stylesheet" type="text/css" href="birds.css">
<style type="text/css">                                                    #1
table { width:500px; background:white; color:black; border:1px black solid; ↵
border-collapse:collapse; margin:auto; }
td { border:1px black solid; padding:1px 0 1px 4px; text-align:left; }
</style>
</head>
<body>
<div id="container">
<?php include("includes/header.php"); ?>
<?php include("includes/nav.php"); ?>
<?php include("includes/info-col.php"); ?>
<div id="content"><!--Start of the view birds page content-->
<div id="midcol">
<h2>The Birds that can be seen on our Reserves</h2>
<p>
<?php
```

```php
// This script retrieves the records from the birds table
require ('mysqli_connect.php'); // Connect to the database
// Make the query
$q = "SELECT bird_name, rarity, best_time FROM birds ORDER BY bird_name ASC";
$result = @mysqli_query ($dbcon, $q); // Run the query
if ($result) { // If it ran OK, display the records
// Table header
echo '<table>
<td align="left"><b>Bird's Name</b></td>
<td align="left"><b>Rarity</b></td>
<td align="left"><b>Best Time</b></td>
</tr>';
// Fetch and print all the records
while ($row = mysqli_fetch_array($result, MYSQLI_ASSOC)) {
    echo '<tr>
    <td align="left">' . $row['bird_name'] . '</td>
    <td align="left">' . $row['rarity'] . '</td>
    <td align="left">' . $row['best_time'] . '</td>
    </tr>';
    }
    echo '</table>'; // Close the table
    mysqli_free_result ($result); // Free up the resources
} else { // If it did not run OK
// Message
        echo '<p class="error">The current birds could not be retrieved. We apologize ↵
        for any inconvenience.</p>';
// Debugging message
    echo '<p>' . mysqli_error($dbcon) . '<br><br />Query: ' . $q . '</p>';
} // End of if ($result)
mysqli_close($dbcon); // Close the database connection
?></p>
</div>
</div><!--End of the view birds page content-->
<?php include("includes/footer.php"); ?>
</div>
</body>
</html>
```

The page can be viewed by clicking the *Birds* menu button on the home page.

Explanation of the Code

You will have seen all this code in earlier chapters, but the use of an internal style needs explaining as follows:

```css
<style type="text/css">                                                    #1
table { width:500px; background:white; color:black; border:1px black solid; ↵
border-collapse:collapse; margin:auto; }
td { border:1px black solid; padding:1px 0 1px 4px; text-align:left; }
</style>
```

I always find it convenient to use an internal style for displaying tables. This is partly because most tables are unique to the page and partly because a neat layout is easier to control using an internal style.

We will now examine the *locations* table, which is the second single unjoined table for this tutorial. It can be viewed by clicking the menu button labeled *The Reserves*.

Displaying a Table of Locations

The displayed table of locations is shown in Figure 9-10.

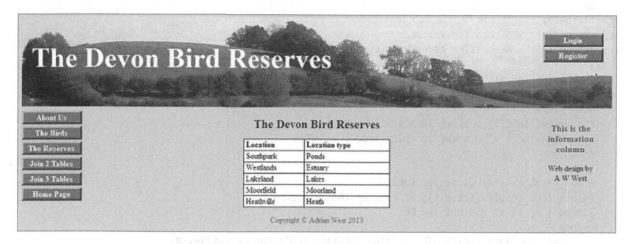

Figure 9-10. *The table display for the locations*

The code for displaying the locations table is given in Listing 9-10.

Listing 9-10. Creating the Page for Displaying the Locations (location.php)

```
<!doctype html>
<html lang=en>
<head>
<title>View the location page</title>
<meta charset=utf-8>
<link rel="stylesheet" type="text/css" href="includes.css">
<style type="text/css">
table { width:500px; background:white; color:black; border:1px black solid; ↵
border-collapse:collapse; margin:auto; }
td { border:1px black solid; padding:1px 0 1px 4px; text-align:left; }
</style>
</head>
<body>
<div id="container">
<?php include("includes/header.php"); ?>
<?php include("includes/nav.php"); ?>
<?php include("includes/info-col.php"); ?>
<div id="content"><!-- Start of the view location page content -->
<div id="midcol">
```

```
<h2>The Devon Bird Reserves</h2>
<p>
<?php
// This script retrieves all the records from the location table
require ('mysqli_connect.php'); // Connect to the database
// Make the query:
$q = "SELECT location, location_type FROM location ORDER BY location_id ASC";
$result = @mysqli_query ($dbcon, $q); // Run the query
if ($result) { // If it ran OK, display the records
// Table header
echo '<table>
<td align="left"><b>Location</b></td>
<td align="left"><b>Location type</b></td>
</tr>';
// Fetch and print all the records
while ($row = mysqli_fetch_array($result, MYSQLI_ASSOC)) {
    echo '<tr>
    <td align="left">' . $row['location'] . '</td>
    <td align="left">' . $row['location_type'] . '</td>
    </tr>';
    }
    echo '</table>'; // Close the table
    mysqli_free_result ($result); // Free up the resources
    } else { // If it did not run OK
// Message
        echo '<p class="error">The current location could not be retrieved. ↵
        We apologize for any inconvenience.</p>';
// Debugging message
    echo '<p>' . mysqli_error($dbcon) . '<br><br />Query: ' . $q . '</p>';
} // End of if ($result)
        mysqli_close($dbcon); // Close the database connection
?>
</p>
</div></div><!-- End of the view location page content. -->
<?php include("includes/footer.php"); ?>
</div>
</body>
</html>
```

We will now show the display for two joined tables.

Displaying Data from the Joined Tables

When the two tables are joined, some data from each will be displayed as shown in Figure 9-11.

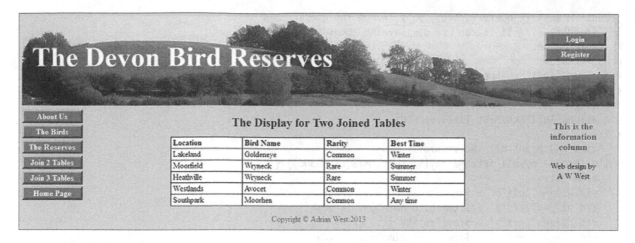

Figure 9-11. *Displaying two joined tables*

The code for displaying selected data from the two joined tables is given in Listing 9-11.

Listing 9-11. Creating the Page for Displaying Selected Data from Two Joined Tables (join-2.php)

```
<!doctype html>
<html lang=en>
<head>
<title>The display for a pair of joined tables</title>
<meta charset=utf-8>
<link rel="stylesheet" type="text/css" href="birds.css">
<style type="text/css">
table { width:600px; background:white; color:black; border:1px black solid; ↵
border-collapse:collapse; margin:auto; }
td { border:1px black solid; padding:1px 0 1px 4px; text-align:left; }
</style>
</head>
<body>
<div id="container">
<?php include("includes/header.php"); ?>
<?php include("includes/nav.php"); ?>
<?php include("includes/info-col.php"); ?>
<div id="content"><!--Start of the view birds page content using two joined tables-->
<div id="midcol">
<h2>The Display for Two Joined Tables</h2>
<p>
<?php
// This script retrieves all the records from the birds table joined with the location table
require ('mysqli_connect.php'); // Connect to the database
// Make the query
$q = "SELECT location.location, birds.bird_name, birds.rarity, birds.best_time ↵
FROM location INNER JOIN birds ON location.bird_id=birds.bird_id" ;
```

279

```
$result = @mysqli_query ($dbcon, $q); // Run the query
if ($result) { // If it ran OK, display the records
// Table header
echo '<table>
<td align="left"><b>Location</b></td>
<td align="left"><b>Bird Name</b></td>
<td align="left"><b>Rarity</b></td>
<td align="left"><b>Best Time</b></td>
</tr>';
// Fetch and print all the records
while ($row = mysqli_fetch_array($result, MYSQLI_ASSOC)) {
    echo '<tr>
    <td align="left">' . $row['location'] . '</td>
    <td align="left">' . $row['bird_name'] . '</td>
    <td align="left">' . $row['rarity'] . '</td>
    <td align="left">' . $row['best_time'] . '</td>
    </tr>';
    }
    echo '</table>'; // Close the table
    mysqli_free_result ($result); // Free up the resources
    } else { // If it did not run OK
// Message
echo '<p class="error">The current birds could not be retrieved. We apologize for ⏎
any inconvenience.</p>';
// Debugging message
    echo '<p>' . mysqli_error($dbcon) . '<br><br />Query: ' . $q . '</p>';
} // End of if ($result)
mysqli_close($dbcon); // Close the database connection
?></p>
</div></div><!--End of the view birds page content using two joined tables-->
<?php include("includes/footer.php"); ?>
</div>
</body>
</html>
```

Note that the order of the items following the ON word can be reversed and you will get the same result. For example,

```
ON location.bird_id=birds.bird_id)" ;
```

can be written as follows:

```
ON birds.bird_id=location.bird_id";
```

You can view the two joined tables by clicking the menu button labeled *Join 2 Tables*. You will be able to see that the table contains data from both tables, as shown in Figure 9-11.

We will often have to join more that two tables, and to demonstrate this we will create or import a third table.

Joining More Than Two Tables

Use phpMyAdmin to import the table file *rsv_info.sql*, or create it manually using the information in Table 9-13. The table has five columns, and it contains useful information about the reserves.

Table 9-13. *The structure and attributes for the* rsv_info *table*

Column name	Type	Length/Value	Default	Attributes	NULL	Index	A_I
resv_id	MEDIUMINT	4	None	UNSIGNED	☐	PRIMARY	☑
bird_hides	ENUM	'yes','no'	None		☐		☐
entr_memb	TINYTEXT	60	None		☐		☐
entr_n_memb	TINYTEXT	60	None		☐		☐
location_id	MEDIUMINT	4	None	UNSIGNED	☐	INDEX	☐

Note that we are inserting the index for *location_id* directly into this table. We could have added the indexes in this way in earlier tables, but it can be advantageous to learn alternative methods.

Using the Insert tab in phpMyAdmin, enter the data shown in Table 9-14.

Table 9-14. *The data for the* rsv_info *table (*entr *refers to the entrance fee)*

rsv_id	bird_hides	entr_memb	entr_n_memb	location_id
1	yes	free	£1	1
2	yes	£1	£2	2
3	yes	free	£1	3
4	no	free	free	4
5	no	free	free	5

After creating the table, click the *More* tab in phphMyAdmin and select *Designer*. You will see the first two tables with their connecting link, but the third table will not be linked, as shown in Figure 9-12.

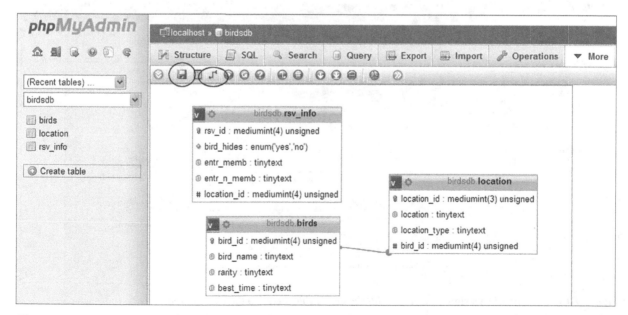

Figure 9-12. *Designer view showing that the third table is not yet linked to the second table*

Keep the designer view on the screen while you explore this alternative method of linking the tables. In the Designer view in phpMyAdmin, drag the tables around by their title bars so that they are arranged in a convenient pattern. (See Figure 9-14 for an example.) Dragging the tables around is strictly to make it easier for you to view them and does not effect their functionality.

Above the tables, you will see a row of icons. Two are shown circled in Figure 9-12. Hover over the right ringed icon and you will see a "Create relation" tool tip. Click that icon and then click the referenced key *location_id*, which is the first item in the location table on the right. This is the PRIMARY key that we want our new table to link with. A tool tip will appear asking you to click the foreign key. Then click the foreign key in the *rsv_info* table, which in this case is the last item in the *rsv_info* table. A dialog box will appear at the bottom right of the window. This is shown in Figure 9-13.

Figure 9-13. *The dialog box*

The dialog requests more information about the foreign key. At the item named *On delete*, select RESTRICT. At the item named *On update*, select CASCADE and click OK. You will see the new relational link appear, as shown in Figure 9-14. To save the *Designer* diagram, click the floppy disk icon on the toolbar.

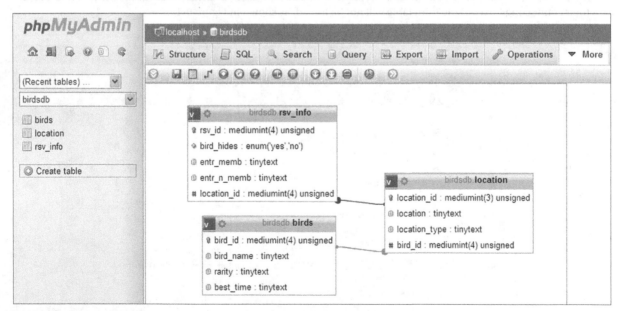

Figure 9-14. *Showing the* Designer *diagram with the third table linked to the second table*

Next we will explore the code for displaying the three linked tables.

Create a Page to Display the Three Joined Tables

Now that the relationships have been set, we can learn how to select and display data from the three tables. The principle is quite logical: first join two tables to produce a virtual table, and then join that to the third table. The syntax for a query for joining and selecting data from three tables is as follows:

```
$q= "SELECT some column, some other column, another column
FROM table1
INNER JOIN table2 USING (the key that links table1 and table2)
INNER JOIN table 3 USING (the key that links table2 and table3) ";
```

Select some data from our three joined tables:

```
$q = "SELECT bird_name, best_time, location, bird_hides, entr_memb, entr_n_memb ↵
FROM birds
INNER JOIN location USING (bird_id)
INNER JOIN rsv_info USING (location_id) ";
```

The resulting display is shown in Figure 9-15.

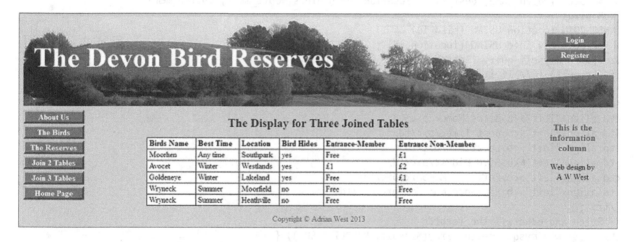

Figure 9-15. *Three tables joined and displayed in a browser*

The table can be viewed by clicking the menu button labeled *Join 3 Tables*.
The code for the page showing three joined tables is given in Listing 9-15.

Listing 9-15. Creating the Page for Displaying Three Joined Tables (join-3.php).

Once again an internal style is used.

```
<!doctype html>
<html lang=en>
<head>
<title>Display three joined tables</title>
<meta charset=utf-8>
<link rel="stylesheet" type="text/css" href="birds.css">
```

```php
<style type="text/css">
table { width:700px; background:white; border:1px black solid; border-collapse:collapse; ↵
margin:auto; }
td { border:1px black solid; padding:1px 0 1px 4px; text-align:left; color:black; }
</style>
</head>
<body>
<div id="container">
<?php include("includes/header.php"); ?>
<?php include("includes/nav.php"); ?>
<?php include("includes/info-col.php"); ?>
<div id="content"><!-- Start of content of the display three tables page -->
<div id="midcol">
<h2>The Display for Three Joined Tables</h2>
<p>
<?php
// This code fetches data from the three tables
require ('mysqli_connect.php'); // Connect to the database
// Make the query                                                          #1
$q = "SELECT bird_name, best_time, location, bird_hides, entr_memb, entr_n_memb
FROM birds
INNER JOIN location USING (bird_id)
INNER JOIN rsv_info USING (location_id)";
$result = @mysqli_query ($dbcon, $q); // Run the query
if ($result) { // If it ran OK, display the records
// Table header                                                            #2
echo '<table>
<td align="left"><b>Birds Name</b></td>
<td align="left"><b>Best Time</b></td>
<td align="left"><b>Location</b></td>
<td align="left"><b>Bird Hides</b></td>
<td align="left"><b>Entrance-Member</b></td>
<td align="left"><b>Entrance Non-Member</b></td>
</tr>';
// Fetch and echo all the records
while ($row = mysqli_fetch_array($result, MYSQLI_ASSOC)) {
    echo '<tr>
    <td align="left">' . $row['bird_name'] . '</td>
    <td align="left">' . $row['best_time'] . '</td>
    <td align="left">' . $row['location'] . '</td>
    <td align="left">' . $row['bird_hides'] . '</td>
    <td align="left">' . $row['entr_memb'] . '</td>
    <td align="left">' . $row['entr_n_memb'] . '</td>
    </tr>';
    }
    echo '</table>'; // Close the table                                    #3
    mysqli_free_result ($result); // Free up the resources
} else { // If it did not run OK
// Error message
        echo '<p class="error">The current data could not be retrieved. We apologize ↵
        for any inconvenience.</p>';
```

```
// Debugging message
    echo '<p>' . mysqli_error($dbcon) . '<br><br />Query: ' . $q . '</p>';
        } // End of if ($result)
        mysqli_close($dbcon); // Close the database connection
        ?>
        </p>
</div></div><!-- End of the view three tables content -->
<?php include("includes/footer.php"); ?>
</div>
</body>
</html>
```

Explanation of the Code

```
// Make the query                                                    #1
$q = "SELECT bird_name, best_time, location, bird_hides, entr_memb, entr_n_memb
FROM birds
INNER JOIN location USING (bird_id)
INNER JOIN rsv_info USING (location_id)";
$result = @mysqli_query ($dbcon, $q); // Run the query
if ($result) { // If it ran OK, display the records
```

The code is very similar to the code for two tables except for the lines beginning with line **#1**.

We selected some data (but not all) from the three joined tables. Six items were selected from three tables using the SELECT query. Then we used that data in the code in lines **#2** through **#3** to display the table in a browser.

We will now learn how to add an alternative method of paying for goods or membership fees using a check instead of PayPal or debit/credit cards.

Payments by Check

A surprising number of uses prefer to pay by check because either they do not have a PayPal account or they prefer not to disclose their debit/credit card details over the Internet. Check payments usually need to be accompanied by a printed form containing the payer's name, address, e-mail address, and telephone number.

This tutorial uses a simplified printable form for an organization that requires online registration for the users' full details, together with a choice of payment methods. This is ideal for web sites that require membership registrations.

Let's assume that Devon Bird Reserves requires an online registration form, as shown in Figure 9-16.

Figure 9-16. *The registration page*

You can view the registration page by clicking the *Register* button on the home page header, but as previously mentioned, you will not be able to register members because a members' table is not included in the database for this tutorial. The registration page is essentially the same as the page used in Chapter 7. The majority of the code from Chapter 7 is embedded into the birds template and saved as *member_reg.php*. When users register successfully, the *Register* button redirects them to a *thank you* page that contains the alternative methods of paying the membership fee. The redirection instruction differs from the one in Chapter 7, and the code is given in Listing 9-16.

Listing 9-16. The Snippets of Code for Redirecting the User (extracted from member_reg.php)

Once again, an internal style for formattimg the form fields has been used, in addition to the main style sheet; this is because the style is unique to this page.

```
<!doctype html>
<html lang=en>
<head>
<title>The members' reg page</title>
<meta charset=utf-8>
```

```
<link rel="stylesheet" type="text/css" href="birds.css">
        <style type="text/css">
        #container { min-width:960px; max-width:1100px; }
        #midcol { margin-left:150px; margin-right:150px; color:#003300; }
        label {font-weight:bold; width:330px; float:left; text-align:right }
        input, select { margin-bottom:5px; }
        #submit { margin-left:330px; }
        h2 { margin-bottom:0; margin-top:5px; color:#003300;}
        h3.content { margin-top:0; color:#003300;}
        .cntr { text-align:center; }
        </style>
</head>
```

Between these two blocks of code, the code is the same as the registration page in Chapter 7.

```
if (empty($errors)) {                       // If it runs OK
// Register the user in the database using an INSERT query
$q = "INSERT INTO users (user_id, title, fname, lname, email, psword, registration_date, ↵
uname, class, addr1, addr2, city, county, pcode, phone, paid) ↵
VALUES (' ', '$title', '$fn', '$ln', '$e', SHA1('$p'), NOW(), '$uname','$class', ↵
'$ad1', '$ad2', '$cty', '$cnty', '$pcode', '$ph', ' ' )";
    $result = @mysqli_query ($dbcon, $q); // Run the query
    if ($result) {                          // If it ran OK
    header ("location: choose_pay.php");
    exit();
```

The code shown in bold type is the redirection instruction so that the user can choose from three methods of payment: check, PayPal, or debit/credit card.

A Choice of Payment Method

When the membership registration form has been filled out, clicking the Register button sends the user to a page giving the user a choice of three payment methods, as shown in Figure 9-17.

Figure 9-17. *Giving the user a choice of payment method*

The display of PayPal logos has been deliberately duplicated on the page to show that you have a choice of either a vertical or horizontal logo. To avoid cluttering the page, you choose one only.The code for creating the page shown in Figure 9-17 is given in Listing 9-17.

Listing 9-17. Creating a Page for Alternative Methods of Payment (choose_pay.php)

The layout of the button elements can be tricky; therefore, in addition to a link to the main style sheet, an internal style is used to enable better control of the layout of the *Pay by Check* button.

```
<!doctype html>
<html lang=en>
<head>
<title>Choose pay. Alternative payment methods.</title>
<meta charset=utf-8>
<link rel="stylesheet" type="text/css" href="birds.css">
<style type="text/css">
#container { min-width:960px; max-width:1100px; }
#midcol { margin-left:150px; margin-right:150px; color:#003300; }
label {font-weight:bold; width:330px; float:left; text-align:right }
input, select { margin-bottom:5px; }
#submit { margin-left:330px; }
h2 { margin-bottom:0; margin-top:5px; color:#003300; }
h3.content { margin-top:0; color:#003300; }
.cntr { text-align:center; }
#mid-left-col { width:46%; float:left; height: 63px; }
#mid-right-col { width:46%; float:right; }
#content-button { position:absolute; left:-10px; top:-20px; margin:10px 30px 0 10px; ↵
width:180px; }
```

```
#content-button li { list-style-type:none; }
</style>
</head>
<body>
<div id="container">
<?php include("includes/header-thanks.php"); ?>
<?php include("includes/nav.php"); ?>
<?php include("includes/info-col-cards.php"); ?>
<div id="content"><!-- Start of the thank you page content. -->
<div id="midcol">
<h2>Thank you for registering</h2>
<h3>To complete your registration please pay the membership fee now. <br></h3>
<p class="cntr">When you have completed your registration you will be able to login ↵
to the member's only pages</p>
<p class="cntr">Membership classes: Standard 1 year: &pound;30, ↵
Standard 5years: &pound;125, Under 21: one year: &pound;2
</p>
<div id="mid-left-col">
<div id="content-button">
    <ul class="btn">
        <li class="btn"><a href="pay-with-check.php">Pay by Check</a></li>
    </ul>
</div>
</div>
<!--</div>-->
<div id="mid-right-col">
<!--insert the PayPal code next-->
<form action="https://www.paypal.com/cgi-bin/webscr" method="post">
    <input type="hidden" name="cmd" value="_s-xclick">
    <input type="hidden" name="hosted_button_id" value="XXXXXXXXXXXXX">
    <table>
    <tr>
    <td><input type="hidden" name="on0" value="Membership Class"><b>
    PayPal or Debit/credit card<br>Select the Membership Class</b></td>
    </tr>
    <tr>
    <td><select name="os0">
    <option value="Standard 1 Year &pound;30">Standard 1 Year &pound;30
    </option>
        <option value="Standard 5 Year &pound;125">Standard 5 Year &pound;125 &pound; ↵
        125.00 GBP
    </option>
    <option value="Under 21 1 Year &pound;2">Under 21 1 Year &pound;2 &pound;2.00 GBP
    </option>
    </select> </td>
    </tr>
    </table>
    <input type="hidden" name="currency_code" value="GBP">
        <input style="margin:10px 0 0 40px" type="image" ↵
        src="https://www.paypalobjects.com/en_US/GB/i/btn/btn_buynowCC_LG.gif" ↵
        name="submit" alt="PayPal  The safer, easier way to pay online."> ↵
```

```
        <img alt="" src="https://www.paypalobjects.com/en_GB/i/scr/pixel.gif" ↵
        width="1" height="1">
</form><!--end of the PayPal code-->
</div>
</div>
</div>
</div><br><br><br class="clear">
<!--End of the thankyou/payment page content-->
<?php include("includes/footer.php"); ?>
</body>
</html>
```

When the PayPal Pay Now button is clicked, the user is taken to the usual PayPal page for processing the payment.

The Check Payment

When users click the Pay by Check button, they will be taken to a page containing a printable form, as shown in Figure 9-18.

***Figure 9-18.** The printable form can be filled out on the screen except for the signature and date (pay-with-check.php)*

The code for creating the printable form is given in Listing 9-18.

Listing 9-18. Creating the Printable Form (pay-with-check.php)

The form is designed to be filled out on the screen and then printed.

```
<!doctype html>
<html lang=en>
<head>
<title>Pay with check</title>
<meta charset=utf-8>
<link rel="stylesheet" type="text/css" href="birds.css" media="screen">        #1
<link rel="stylesheet" type="text/css" href="print.css" media="print">         #2
<style type="text/css">                                                         #3
label { margin-bottom:5px; }
label { width:570px; float:left; text-align:right; }
#button { text-align:center; }
.cntr { width: 655px; }
.sign { font-weight:bold; margin-left:200px; }
#content { font-weight:bold; color:#003300; }
</style>
</head>
<body>
<div id='container'>
<?php include('includes/header.php'); ?>
<?php include('includes/nav.php'); ?>
<?php include('includes/info-col.php'); ?>
<div id='content'><!--Start of page content-->
<div id="midcol">
<h2>Complete your Registration by Paying with a Check</h2>
<h3>Thank you for registering online. Now please fill out this form.  Asterisks ⏎
indicate essential fields.<br>When you have filled out the form please print two ⏎
copies by clicking the "Print This Form" button. <br>Sign one copy and keep one for ⏎
reference. Sign a check payable to &quot;The Devon Bird Reserves&quot;. <br>Mail the ⏎
signed form and check to: <br>The Treasurer, The Devon Bird Reserves, 99 The Street, ⏎
The Village,  EX99 99ZZ </h3>
<form>
<div id="fields">
<label class="label" for="title">Title<span class="large-red">*</span>
<input id="title" name="title" size="35"></label>
<br><br><label class="label" for="firstname">First Name<span class="large-red">*</span>
<input id="firstname" name="Firstname" size="35"></label><br>
<br><label class="label" for="lastname">Last Name<span class="large-red">*</span>
<input id="firstname" name="lastname" size="35"></label><br>
<br><label class="label" for="useremail">Your Email Address<span class="large-red">*</span>
<input id="useremail" name="useremail" size="35"></label><br>
</div>
</form><br><br>
<p class="sign">
 Signed_____ Date_____</p>
 <br>
```

```
<div id="button">                                                        #4
<input type="button" value="Click to automatically print the form in black and ↵
white" onclick="window.print()" title="Print this Form"><br>
</div>
<!--End of content.--></div>
</div></div>
<?php include('includes/footer.php'); ?>
</body>
</html>
```

Explanation of the Code

```
<link rel="stylesheet" type="text/css" href="birds.css" media="screen">    #1
<link rel="stylesheet" type="text/css" href="print.css" media="print">     #2
```

It is impossible to print the form using PHP because PHP is a server-side script. However, the form is displayed by a browser and we can print from a screen displayed by a browser. We achieve this by means of a link to a separate conditional style sheet with the media attribute **media="print"**.

Line **#1** links to the main style sheet *birds.css* that displays the page on the screen using the media attribute **media="screen"**. Line **#2** links the page to the print version of the page. This is automatically invoked when the display is sent to a printer. The printed form does not need the header, menu, or footer. Also, using the CSS style sheet, we can cause it to print using only black ink so that the user does not have to use the more expensive color cartridge.

```
<style type="text/css">                                                   #3
        label { margin-bottom:5px; }
        label { width:570px; float:left; text-align:right; }
        #button { text-align:center; }
        .cntr { width: 655px; }
        .sign { font-weight:bold; margin-left:200px; }
        #content { font-weight:bold; color:#003300; }
</style>
```

The layout of the page is unique; therefore, an internal style is used to position the fields, the space for a signature, and the print button.

```
<div id="button">
<input type="button" value="Click to automatically print the form in black ↵    #4
and white" onclick="window.print()" title="Print this Form"><br>
</div>
```

This is the code for the button on the page that sends the browser display to the printer.

Printing Online Forms

The printed page is shown in Figure 9-19.

```
Pay with check                                              http://localhost/birds/pay-with-check.php

            Complete your Registration by Paying with a Check

        Thank you for registering online, now please fill out this form.  Asterisks indicate essential fields.
      When you have filled out the form please print two copies by clicking the "Print This Form" button.
        Sign one copy and keep one for reference, sign a check payable to "The Devon Bird Reserves".
                              Mail the signed form and check to:
          The Treasurer, The Devon Bird Reserves, 99 The Street, The Village,  EX99 99ZZ

                            Title* [Mr                         ]

                      First Name* [John                        ]

                      Last Name* [Doe                          ]

               Your Email Address* [jdoe@myisp.com             ]


              Signed_____ Date_____
```

Figure 9-19. *The top half of the printed page in black ink contains all the essential information*

To produce the printout shown in Figure 9-19, the form was filled out on the user's screen and then the print button was clicked. The result used minimal ink and no colored ink; however, it contained all that is necessary to become a member of the Devon Bird Reserves. The user signs the form and mails it together with the check. The user's address is entered into the database when he fills out the registration page; therefore, this does not need be repeated in the printed form.

The style sheet *print.css* is the key to producing the printable form. The code for this style sheet is shown in Listing 9-19.

Listing 9-19. Creating the Style Sheet for Printing Forms (print.css)

```
/*PRINT.CSS: style amendments for printing only. Set the font color to black only*/
body {color:black;}
/*SELECT ITEMS THAT YOU DO NOT WANT TO PRINT, e.g., header, menu, print-this-page ↵
button, and footer*/                                                            #1
#header, #nav, #leftcol, #button, #rightcol, #footer, #info-col, ul { display:none; }
input { border:1px black solid; }
h2 { font-size:16pt; color:black; text-align:center; }                          #2
h3 { text-align:center; font-size:11pt; color:black;}
/*REVEAL OUTGOING URL links on printed page*/                                    #3
a[href^="http://"]:after {content: "(" attr(href)")"; }
```

Explanation of the Code

```
/*SELECT ITEMS THAT YOU DO NOT WANT TO PRINT, e.g., header, menu, print-this-page
button, and footer*/                                                            #1
```

The CSS statement { `display:none;` } tells the printer which items should not be printed. To avoid wasting paper and ink when testing the appearance of the printed page, use the "Print preview" feature on the browser. Load the page into a browser, and click **File-->Print Preview** to see what the printable page will look like. If the printable page includes a page break, click the right-facing arrow at the bottom of the print preview screen to see subsequent pages.

Press the Esc key to switch out of the Print Preview mode.

```
h2 { font-size:16pt; text-align:center; }                              #2
h3 { text-align:center; font-size:11pt;}
```

To choose the correct font sizes for the printer, use point sizes (such as 16 pt. and 12 pt.), and use trial and error to optimize the sizes. You might have text within <p> </p> tags, so be sure to include a style for the paragraph font size.

```
/*REVEAL OUTGOING URL links on the printed page*/                      #3
a[href^="http://"]:after {content: "(" attr(href)")"; }
```

If the page contains a URL to your web site, you might wish this to appear on the printed page in a format that will be useful for the user (assuming that he prints and retains a copy of the form). Note the use of three types of brackets. In the form, the HTML would look like this:

```
<p>Click for
<a title="Click to visit the Devon Bird Reserves web site" ↵
href="http://www.the devonbirdreserves.co.uk">The Devon Bird Reserves</a></p>
```

The URL would be displayed in a browser as follows:
Click to visit the <u>Devon Bird Reserves</u> web site.
Using the code shown on line **#3**, the printed form would appear as follows:
Click to visit the Devon Bird Reserves web site (`http://www.devonbirdreserves.co.uk`).

■ **Caution**   Square check boxes are often used on HTML forms and printable forms. If you use Wingdings or Webdings for the check boxes, they might not display or print as boxes. However, practically every computer has the Unicode Lucida symbols. The check box entity *□* from the Unicode Lucida symbols will display correctly in all popular browsers. Use a font for the box that is much larger than the surrounding text.

Summary

In this chapter, I introduced the theory and practice of using multiple tables. You learned that such tables are virtual tables that are present only in the volatile memory of the server and that they can be viewed in a browser. The difference between various join methods was described. I then demonstrated that the virtual tables could be made visible on the screen by using SQL queries and PHP. A tutorial then showed you how to implement membership-fee payments by check. This was augmented by a demonstration of economical form printing, so that an application form and a check could be sent to the organization. In the next chapter, I will introduce you to an online message board.

CHAPTER 10

■ ■ ■

Creating a Message Board

A message board can be a stand-alone feature or an important component in a forum. A basic forum has at least four tables, one each for messages, membership registrations, threads, and replies. However, to save space, and deferring to the subtitle of this book, "A Simplified Approach," this chapter describes a simple message board with a table for messages and a table for members. My hope is that a grasp of the principles of this message board will inspire you to expand its features and explore more complex solutions. For your interest, at the end of this chapter I added a chart showing how you could enhance the message board to create a forum.

Message boards have fewer features than a forum; generally, they lack the ability to accept replies in a manner that allows them to be collected as threads. In a forum, the replies are connected to the original posting id and displayed in ascending date order. Although forums are used in many ways—for instance, for exchanging and providing technical information, help lines, and discussion groups—our message board is simply a means for collecting and displaying knowledge.

This chapter contains the following sections:

- The plan
- Create the message board database and tables
- Create the template for the message board
- Create the registration page
    - The Thank You page
- Register some members
- The login and logout pages
- Creating a gateway to the message board categories
- Posting quotations
- The home page
- Displaying the quotations
- Adding search facilities
- Searching for specific words or phrases
- Brief suggestions for enhancing the message board and for converting the message board into a basic forum

■ **Caution**   To prevent the display of unpleasant content, message boards require constant monitoring (moderating). Your potential clients should be warned about this before they commit themselves to a design contract with you.

The Plan

To simplify the message board in this chapter, users will not be able to view messages until they are registered and logged in. However, some of the messages will be shown on the home page to tempt users to register. In our example, the messages are quotations, and the aim is to build up a useful database of quotations. The login button on the home page will redirect registered users to a page where they will be able choose which of two types of quotation to view, either comical quotes or wise quotes.

When the message board is accessed, the registered member will be able to contribute a quote. Because the member is contributing quotations, I referred to threads as *quotations* in the tutorial. For further simplification, the number of columns in the tables is reduced to a practical minimum.

The user name for logging in will be a unique pseudonym chosen by the user because the great majority of message boards and forums insist that members remain anonymous. When members post a new quote, their pseudonym is the only name shown on the message board. However, when registering they might also be asked to provide their e-mail address so that the site administrator can contact them if necessary. Their e-mail address is never disclosed on the message board. If the e-mail address is not required when registering, the web site is unlikely to be subject to data-protection law because no personal information will be stored on the database. The registration form for this tutorial does include the e-mail address, but you can easily omit it. The plan outlined in the preceding text will be used for our message board tutorial.

We will now create the database and tables for the message board.

■ **Note**   Because the message board tutorial was extracted from a larger, more complex forum, some files and a table both retain the word *forum* instead of the words *message board*.

Create the Database

Download the files for this chapter from the book's page at *Apress.com*, and place them in a new folder named *msgboard* within the htdocs folder.

Start XAMPP, and in phpMyAdmin create the database named *msgboarddb*. Set the encoding to *utf8._general_ci*. This encoding is strongly recommended instead of the default collation because it can represent every Unicode character and is backwardly compatible with ASCII. Then select the *Databases* tab, select the box next to *msgboarddb*, and then click *privileges*. Add a new user with the following details:

> **User name:** brunel
>
> **Host:** localhost
>
> **Password:** trailblazer

Scroll down, and look for the words *Resource Limits*. These fields should all be zero, which is the default. Scroll down, and select *All privileges*. Click *Save* (or *Go* in some versions).

The database connection file *mysqli_connect.php* is included in the downloadable files. Be sure to add it to your htdocs folder. If you wish to create the file manually, use the following code:

```php
<?php
//Create a connection to the msgboarddb database.
// Set the access details as constants
DEFINE ('DB_USER', 'brunel');
DEFINE ('DB_PASSWORD', 'trailblazer');
DEFINE ('DB_HOST', 'localhost');
DEFINE ('DB_NAME', 'msgboarddb');
// Make the connection
$dbcon = @mysqli_connect (DB_HOST, DB_USER, DB_PASSWORD, DB_NAME) ←
OR die ('Could not connect to MySQL: ' . mysqli_connect_error() );
// Set the encoding
mysqli_set_charset($dbcon, 'utf8');
```

Create the Tables

Either import the tables using the downloadable *.sql* files, or create them manually. Before creating the tables, you need to decide whether you will require a full text search facility. You will need this if users would benefit from being able to search the message board for a particular quote; for example, he or she might search for the words "Mark Twain" to view a list of quotations by Mark Twain. If you do need a full text search facility, you must choose the MyISAM storage engine for the table that will be searched. However, if you have MySQL version 5.6.4 or later, the INNODB storage engine allows full text searches. For the latest information, see the MySQL web site http://dev.mysql.com/doc/refman/5.6/en/fulltext-search.html.

Unfortunately, at the time of writing, version 5.6 of MySQL was not available in the XAMPP download version 1.8.2. However, XAMPP 1.8.3 (for PHP 5.5 and above) now contains MySQL 5.6.4.

■ **Tip** If you wish to change a table's storage engine from INNODB to MYSQL or vice versa, this can be achieved by using phpMyAdmin. Instructions are given in the Appendix. As a precaution, before changing the storage engine, always back up your tables using phpMyAdmin's *Export* tab.

In the left panel of phpMyAdmin, click the *msgboarddb* database and then create two tables. First we will create the *members table* with six columns using the details shown in Table 10-1. Select the INNODB default storage engine.

Table 10-1. *The members table*

Columnname	Type	Length/value	Default	Attributes	NULL	Index	A_I
member_id	INT	8	None	UNSIGNED	☐	PRIMARY	☑
uname	VARCHAR	12	None		☐	UNIQUE	☐
email	VARCHAR	60	None		☐		☐
psword	CHAR	40	None		☐		☐
reg_date	DATETIME		None		☐		☐
member_level	TINYINT	2	None		☐		☐

The *member_id* is the PRIMARY key, and the *user_name* has a UNIQUE index to prevent duplicate entries.

You can import the *forum.sql* downloadable file or manually create the *forum* table with six columns. It contains a column named *post_id*, and this is configured as the PRIMARY KEY. After filling out the fields in phpMyAdmin, look below the columns and find the pull-down list of storage engines. Select the MyISAM storage engine if you are using an earlier version than XAMPP 1.8.3 (for PHP 5.5 and above) and MySQL versions earlier than version 5.6.4. This is because the tutorial will include full text searches. Give the message column a FULL TEXT index.

The table details are shown in Table 10-2.

***Table 10-2.** The attributes for the forum table*

Column name	Type	Length/value	Default	Attributes	NULL	Index	A_I
post_id	INT	8	None	UNSIGNED	☐	PRIMARY	☑
uname	VARCHAR	12	None		☐		☐
subject	VARCHAR	60	None		☐		☐
message	TEXT		None		☐	FULL TEXT	☐
post_date	DATETIME		None		☐		☐

Next we will examine some of the pages for the web site.

Create the Template for the Message Board Web Site

This step is not essential because the template will eventually be replaced by the home page. Most of the pages, including the index page, will be based on this template. On the home page, the body text in the template will eventually be replaced by some sample quotations to encourage users to register. The template for the pages is shown in Figure 10-1.

***Figure 10-1.** The basic template for the forum web site*

The code for producing the template is given in Listing 10-1a.

Listing 10-1a. Creating the Basic Template for the Forum's Web Site (template.php)

The page contains a link to the style sheet for the project.

```
<!doctype html>
<html lang=en>
<head>
<title>Forum template</title>
<meta charset=utf-8>
<link rel="stylesheet" type="text/css" href="msgboard.css">
<style type="text/css">
#header #tab-navigation ul { margin-left:58px; }
</style>
</head>
<body>
<div id='container'>
<?php include('includes/header.php'); ?>
<?php include('includes/info-col.php'); ?>
<div id='content'><!--Start of page content-->
<h2>This is the message board template</h2>
<p>The message board content. The message board content. The message board content. The message
board content. The message board content. <br>The message board content. The message board content.
The message board content. The message board content. <br>The message board content. The message
board content. <br>The message board content. The message board content. The message board content.
</p></div><!--End of the template content-->
</div>
<?php include('includes/footer.php'); ?>
</body>
</html>
```

The header uses a template that contains every horizontal menu button required by this chapter, but various buttons will be commented-out to suit each page; for instance, the registration page will have only a *home page* button; therefore, the other menu buttons will be commented-out for the registration page. You could, of course, have the same header for every page, but each page would then have several redundant buttons, something I dislike intensely.

The code for the template header is given in Listing 10-1b.

Listing 10-1b. Creating the Header for the Template (includes/header.php)

The menu choices that are commented-out for the template page are shown in bold type.

```
<div id="header">
<h1>Quick Quotes</h1>
<div id="tab-navigation">
    <ul>
        <li><a href="login.php">Login</a></li>
        <li><a href="logout.php">Logout</a></li>
        <li><a href="safer-register-page.php">Register</a></li>
        <!--<li><a href="post.php">Add a quote</a></li>-->
        <!--<li><a href="forum_c.php">Comical Quotes</a></li>-->
        <!--<li><a href="forum_w.php">Wise Quotes</a></li>-->
```

```
            <!--<li><a href="view_posts.php">View your Posts</a></li>-->
            <!--<li><a href="search.php">Search</a></li>-->
            <li><a href="index.php">Home page</a></li>
        </ul>
    </div>
</div>
```

The header uses a horizontal menu to provide the maximum amount of room on the page for members' postings and replies. The header menu block for all the pages is positioned absolutely (vertically), and the main style sheet displays the menu horizontally. However, the horizontal position of the menu block is eventually provided by an internal style in each page.

The CSS code for the main style sheet is given in Listing 10-1c.

Listing 10-1c. Creating the Main Style Sheet for the Message Board Pages (msgboard.css)

```
body {text-align:center; background-color:#D7FFEB; color:navy; font-family: ↵
"times new roman"; font-size: 100%; color: navy; margin: auto; }
h2 { font-size:150%; color:navy; text-align:center; margin-bottom:10px; }
h3 { font-size:110%; color:navy; text-align:center; margin-bottom:0; }
#container {position:relative; min-width:960px; max-width:1200px; margin:auto; ↵
text-align:left; }
#header, #header-members, #header-admin { margin:10px auto 0 auto; min-width:960px; ↵
max-width:1200px; height:175px; background-image: url('images/tile-pale.jpg'); ↵
color:white; background-repeat: repeat; padding:0; }
h1 {position:relative; top:40px; font-size:350%; color:white; margin:auto 0 auto 20px; ↵
width: 600px; }
#info-col { position:absolute; top:190px; right:10px; color:navy; width:135px; ↵
text-align:center; margin:5px 5px 0 0; }
#info-col h3 { width:130px; }
/* set general horizontal button styles */
li { list-style-type :none; margin-bottom: 3px; text-align: center; }
/* set general anchor styles */
li a { display: inline-block; color: white; font-weight: bold; text-decoration: none; }
/* specify state styles. */
/* mouseout (default) */
li a { background: #5B78BE; border: 4px outset #aabaff; }
/* mouseover */
li a:hover { display:inline-block; background: #0a4adf; border: 4px outset #8abaff; }
/* onmousedown */
li a:active { background:#aecbff; border: 4px inset #aecbff; }
#midcol {width:90%; margin:auto; }
#mid-left-col { width:48%; float:left; text-align:left; }
#mid-right-col {width:48%; float:right; text-align:left; }
#content { margin-left:150px; margin-right:150px; }
table { width:800px; border:1px navy solid; border-collapse:collapse; margin:auto; }
td { border:1px navy solid; padding:1px 0 1px 4px; text-align:left; }
form { margin-left:180px; }
#footer { margin:auto; text-align:center; clear:both; }
p.error { color:red; font-size:105%; font-weight:bold; text-align:center; }
.label { float:left; width:210px; text-align:right; clear:left; margin-right:5px; }
#submit { margin-left:215px; text-align:center; }
span.left { text-align:left; }
```

```
/*set the vertical position and an average horizontal position for the menu block*/
#tab-navigation ul { width:850px; position:absolute; top: 135px; left:310px; }
#tab-navigation li { height:25px; margin:5px; display:inline; }
#tab-navigation li a { height:25px; padding-left:10px; padding-right:10px; ↵
          display:inline; }
```

■ **Note**   At the moment, none of the Template Page buttons work because we have not yet created the other pages. This will be rectified later after we create some data to play with.

The code for the footer is given in Listing 10-1d.

Listing 10-1d. Creating the Footer (footer.php)

```
<div id="footer">
<p>Copyright &copy; Adrian West 2013 Designed by ↵
<a href="http://www.colycomputerhelp.co.uk/"> Adrian W West</a> </p>
</div>
```

The next step will be to create the registration page so that we can register some member's data.

Create the Registration Form

The registration form is a cut-down version of the form in Chapter 7. The form is shown in Figure 10-2.

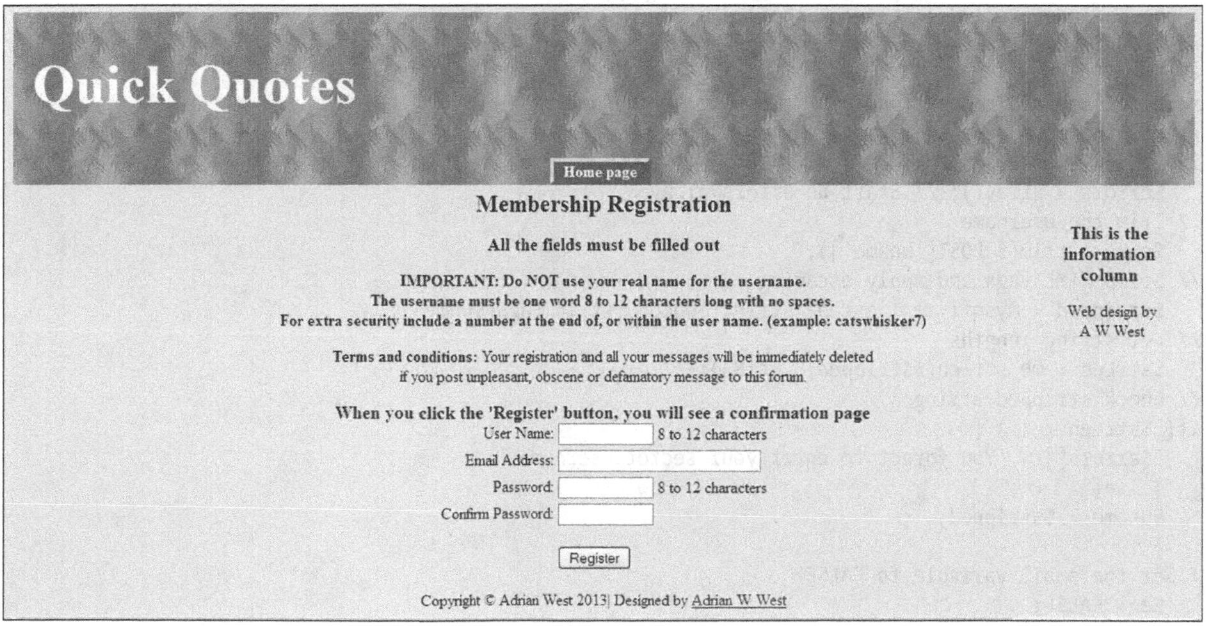

Figure 10-2. *The registration page*

As previously mentioned in the plan, the user name is not the actual name of the member, but a pseudonym for the purpose of logging in to the web site anonymously. In many forums, the e-mail field is omitted and only the user name and password are required for registration; those two items are usually sufficient for members to log in.

The code for the registration form is given in Listing 10-2.

Listing 10-2. Create the Registration Page (safer-register-page.php)

The following code inserts a record into the *members* table.

```php
<!doctype html>
<html lang=en>
<head>
<title>Registration page</title>
<meta charset=utf-8>
<link rel="stylesheet" type="text/css" href="msgboard.css">
<style type="text/css">
#midcol { width:98%; margin:auto; }
input, select { margin-bottom:5px; }
#tab-navigation ul { position:absolute; top: 135px; left:500px; }
p.warning { text-align:center; font-weight:bold; }
h2 { margin-bottom:0; margin-top:5px; }
h3.content { margin-top:0; }
.cntr { text-align:center; }
</style>
</head>
<body>
<div id="container">
<?php include("includes/header_register.php"); ?>
<?php include("includes/info-col.php");?>
<div id="content"><!--Start of the page-specific content-->
<?php
require ('mysqli_connect.php'); // Connect to the database
// Has the form been submitted?
if ($_SERVER['REQUEST_METHOD'] == 'POST') {
    $errors = array(); // Start an errors array
// Trim the username
    $unme = trim($_POST['uname']);
// Strip HTML tags and apply escaping
    $stripped = mysqli_real_escape_string($dbcon, strip_tags($unme));
// Get string lengths
    $strLen = mb_strlen($stripped, 'utf8');
// Check stripped string
if( $strLen < 1 ) {
    $errors[] = 'You forgot to enter your secret username.';
    }else{
    $uname = $stripped;
    }
//Set the email variable to FALSE
    $e = FALSE;
```

```php
// Check that an email address has been entered
if (empty($_POST['email'])) {
    $errors[] = 'You forgot to enter your email address.';
}
//remove spaces from beginning and end of the email address and validate it
if (filter_var((trim($_POST['email'])), FILTER_VALIDATE_EMAIL)) {
//A valid email address is then registered
    $e = mysqli_real_escape_string($dbcon, (trim($_POST['email'])));
    }else{
    $errors[] = 'Your email is not in the correct format.';
}
// Check that a password has been entered. If so, does it match the confirmed password?
if (empty($_POST['psword1'])){
    $errors[] ='Please enter a valid password';
    }
if(!preg_match('/^\w{8,12}$/', $_POST['psword1'])) {
    $errors[] = 'Invalid password, use 8 to 12 characters and no spaces.';
    }
if(preg_match('/^\w{8,12}$/', $_POST['psword1'])) {
    $psword1 = $_POST['psword1'];
    }
if($_POST['psword1'] == $_POST['psword2']) {
    $p = mysqli_real_escape_string($dbcon, trim($psword1));
    }else{
    $errors[] = 'Your two passwords do not match.';
    }
if (empty($errors)) { // If there are no errors, register the user in the database
// Make the query
$q = "INSERT INTO members (member_id, uname, email, psword, reg_date ) ↵
VALUES (' ', '$uname', '$e', SHA1('$p'), NOW()  )";
    $result = @mysqli_query ($dbcon, $q); // Run the query
if ($result) { // If the query ran OK
    header ("location: register_thanks.php");
    exit();
    } else { // If the query did not run OK
// Error message
    echo '<h2>System Error</h2>
    <p class="error">You could not be registered due to a system error. We apologize for any
inconvenience.</p>';
// Debugging message:
    echo '<p>' . mysqli_error($dbcon) . '<br><br>Query: ' . $q . '</p>';
    } // End of if ($result)
    mysqli_close($dbcon); // Close the database connection
// Include the footer and stop the script
    include ('includes/footer.php');
    exit();
    } else { // Display the errors
    echo '<h2>Error!</h2>
    <p class="error">The following error(s) occurred:<br>';
    foreach ($errors as $msg) { // Display each error
    echo " - $msg<br>\n";
    }
```

```
        echo '</p><h3>Please try again.</h3><p><br></p>';
        }// End of if (empty($errors))
            } // End of the main Submit conditionals
?>
<div id="midcol">
<h2>Membership Registration</h2>
    <h3>All the fields must be filled out</h3>
    <h3>IMPORTANT: Do NOT use your real name as the User name
        </h3>
<p class="cntr">Terms:Your registration and all your messages will be immediately ↵
cancelled<br>if you post unpleasant, obscene or defamatory messages to this forum.</p>
<h3 class="content">When you click the 'Register' button, you will see a confirmation ↵
page <br></h3>
<form action="safer-register-page.php" method="post">
<br><label class="label" for="email">Email Address:</label><input id="email" type="text" ↵
name="email" size="30" maxlength="60" value="<?php if (isset($_POST['email'])) ↵
echo $_POST['email']; ?>" >
<br><label class="label" for="psword1">Password:</label><input id="psword1" ↵
type="password" name="psword1" size="12" maxlength="12" value="<?php if ↵
(isset($_POST['psword1'])) echo $_POST['psword1']; ?>" > 8 to 12 characters
<br><label class="label" for="psword2">Confirm Password:</label>↵
<input id="psword2" type="password" name="psword2" size="12" ↵
maxlength="12" value="<?php if (isset($_POST['psword2'])) echo $_POST['psword2']; ?>" >
<br><label class="label" for="uname">User Name:</label><input id="uname" type="text" ↵
name="uname" size="12" maxlength="12" value="<?php if (isset($_POST['uname'])) ↵
echo $_POST['uname']; ?>"> 6 to 12 characters
<p><input id="submit" type="submit" name="submit" value="Register"></p>
</form>
</div></div></div><!-- End of the registration page content -->
<?php include ('includes/footer.php'); ?>
</body>
</html>
```

No explanation of the code is required because it is very similar to the registration form in Chapter 7.

■ **Note**   The included header file *header_register.php* is a copy of *header.php*. The redundant menu items are commented-out, leaving only the home page button. The *Register* button on the template's header will now work because it can link to our newly created registration page.

The Thank You Page

If the registration is successful, the Thank You page is displayed as shown in Figure 10-3.

Figure 10-3. *The Thank You page*

■ **Note** The included file *header_register.php* is re-used in the Thank You file. The code for the Thank You page is given in Listing 10-3.

Listing 10-3. Creating the Thank You Page (register_thanks.php)

```
<!doctype html>
<html lang=en>
<head>
<title>Registration thank you page</title>
<meta charset=utf-8>
<link rel="stylesheet" type="text/css" href="msgboard.css">
<style type="text/css">
p { text-align:center; }
#tab-navigation ul { position:absolute; top: 135px; left:500px;
}

</style>
</head>
<body>
<div id="container">
<?php include("includes/header_register.php"); ?>
<?php include("includes/info-col.php"); ?>
<div id="content"><!--Start of the thank you page content-->
<div id="midcol">
<h2>Thank you for registering</h2>
<h3>On the home page you will now be able to log in and add quotes to the message board.</h3>
</div>
</div></div><!--End of the thankyou page content-->
<?php include("includes/footer.php"); ?>
</body>
</html>
```

Register Some Members

Now that you have a registration form, you can use the register button in the template's header to register the members given in Table 10-3, or you can import the downloadable *members.sql* file.

Table 10-3. *Register some members*

User Name	E-mail address	Password
lilythepink	jsmith@myisp.co.uk	bumblebee6
giantstep12	ndean@myisp.co.uk	cartridge10
mechanic7	jdoe@myisp.co.uk	battery4car
skivvy	jsmith@outcook.com	dogsbody12
mythking	fincense@myisp.net	perfumed7

The members will automatically have the default *member_level* of zero. In this tutorial, the administrator's real name is Frank Incense. He is the last member on the preceding list. For maximum security, to log on as administrator, he also registered with the user name *skivvy*, the false e-mail address *jsmith@outcook.com*, and the password *dogsbody12*. He also has a *member_level* of 1. Although lack of space prevents the inclusion of a full administration facility in this tutorial, you might later wish to add full administration pages to the web site.

Now that we have some registered members, they can be allowed to log in.

The Login Page

The login page is shown in Figure 10-4.

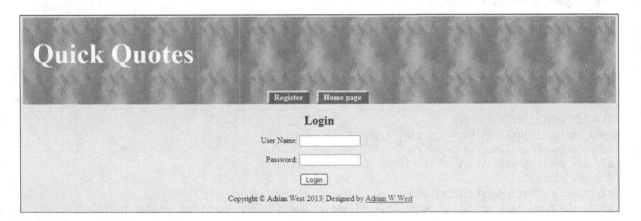

Figure 10-4. *The login page*

The code for the login page is given in Listing 10-4a.

Listing 10-4a. Creating the Login Page (login.php)

The header file *header_login.php* is a copy of *header.php* with the menu buttons commented-out except for *Register* and *Home page*. This code processes the submissions from the login form.

An internal style is used to position the form fields and to locate the menu buttons horizontally.

```
<!doctype html>
<html lang=en>
<head>
<title>login page </title>
<meta charset=utf-8>
<link rel="stylesheet" type="text/css" href="msgboard.css">
        <style type="text/css">
        h2 { color:navy; }
        #tab-navigation ul { margin-left:140px; }
        form { padding-left:295px; }
        .label { width:80px; float:left; text-align:right;}
        form p { width:250px; }
        p.submit {margin-left:86px; }
        </style>
</head>
<body>
<div id='container'>
<?php
include ( 'includes/header_login.php' ) ;
// Display any error messages if present
if ( isset( $errors ) && !empty( $errors ) )
{
 echo '<p id="err_msg">A problem occurred:<br>' ;
 foreach ( $errors as $msg ) { echo " - $msg<br>" ; }
 echo 'Please try again or <a href="safer-register-page.php">Register</a></p>' ;
}
?>
<!-- Display the login form fields -->
<h2>Login</h2>
<form action="process_login.php" method="post">                              #1
<p><label class="label" for="uname">User Name:</label><input id="uname" type="text"
name="uname" size="16" maxlength="16" value="<?php if (isset($_POST['uname']))
echo $_POST['uname']; ?>"></p>
<p><label class="label" for="psword">Password:</label><input id="psword"
type="password" name="psword" size="16" maxlength="16" value="<?php if
(isset($_POST['psword'])) echo $_POST['psword']; ?>" ></p>
<p class="submit"><input type="submit" value="Login" ></p>
</form>
<?php
include ( 'includes/footer.php' ) ;
?>
</div>
</body>
</html>
```

Explanation of the Code

You will have seen all the code before, but the line numbered **#1** refers to a file that needs explaining:

```
<form action="process_login.php" method="post">                                      #1
```

The file named *process_login.php* launches the login process. The code for this is given in Listing 10-4b. Using external files for processing variables is good practice and assists in establishing security because hackers have to probe the web site for the related files before they can cause mischief.

Processing the Login

Place this file in the *htdocs* folder.

Listing 10-4b. Creating the Code for Processing the Login (process_login.php)

```php
<?php
// Was the form submitted?
if ( $_SERVER[ 'REQUEST_METHOD' ] == 'POST' )
{
// Connect to the database
require ( 'mysqli_connect.php' ) ;
// Load the validation functions
require ( 'login_functions.php' ) ;                                      #1
// Check the login data
list ( $check, $data ) = validate ( $dbcon, $_POST[ 'uname' ], $_POST[ 'psword' ] ) ;
// If successful, set session data and display the forum.php page
if ( $check )
{
// Access the session details
        session_start();
        $_SESSION[ 'member_id' ] = $data[ 'member_id' ] ;
        $_SESSION[ 'uname' ] = $data[ 'uname' ] ;
        load ( 'forum.php' ) ;
        }
// If it fails, set the error messages
        else { $errors = $data; }
// Close the database connection
        mysqli_close( $dbcon ) ;
        }
// Because it failed, continue to display the login page
include ( 'login.php' ) ;
?>
```

Line **#1** refers to a file named *login_functions.php*. This file contains two functions; one processes the data entered by the user, and the second loads the appropriate page. The code for *login_functions.php* is given in Listing 10-4c.

Create the Functions for Logging In

Listing 10-4c. Creating the Functions Required for the Login Process (login_functions.php)

```php
<?php
// Create the function for loading the URL of the login page
function load( $page = 'login.php' )
{
// The code for setting the page URL
        $url = 'http://' . $_SERVER[ 'HTTP_HOST' ] . dirname( $_SERVER[ 'PHP_SELF' ] ) ;
// If the the URL has any trailing slashes, remove them and add a forward slash to the URL
        $url = rtrim( $url, '/\\' ) ;
        $url .= '/' . $page ;
//Redirect to the page and exit the script
        header( "Location: $url" ) ;
        exit() ;
}
// Create a function to check the user name and password
function validate( $dbcon, $uname = '', $p = '')
{
// Start an array to hold the error messages
        $errors = array() ;
// Has the user name been entered?
        if ( empty( $uname ) )
        { $errors[] = 'You forgot to enter your user name' ;
        }
        else  { $uname = mysqli_real_escape_string( $dbcon, trim( $uname ) ) ;
        }
// Has the password been entered
        if ( empty( $p ) )
        { $errors[] = 'Enter your password.' ;
        }
        else { $p = mysqli_real_escape_string( $dbcon, trim( $p ) ) ;
        }
// If everything is OK, select the member_id and the user name from the members' table
        if ( empty( $errors ) )
        {
$q = "SELECT member_id, uname FROM members WHERE uname='$uname' AND psword=SHA1('$p')" ;
        $result = mysqli_query ( $dbcon, $q ) ;
        if ( @mysqli_num_rows( $result ) == 1 )
        {
        $row = mysqli_fetch_array ( $result, MYSQLI_ASSOC ) ;
        return array( true, $row ) ;
        }
// Create an error message if the user name and password do not match the database record
        else { $errors[] = 'The user name and password do not match our records.' ;
        }
        }
// Retrieve the error messages
        return array( false, $errors ) ;
}
```

The first function *load()* loads a page that is specified in the brackets. The second function *validate()* validates the user name and password entered by the user. It displays error messages in the event of an unsuccessful login.

Logging Out

When the member logs out, the logout page appears as shown in Figure 10-5.

Figure 10-5. *The logout page*

Logging out is an important security feature. The code for the logout page is given in Listing 10-5.

Listing 10-5. Creating the Logout File (logout.php)

An internal style is used to position the menu button and the text.

```php
<?php
session_start() ;
// Redirect users if they are not logged in
        if ( !isset( $_SESSION[ 'member_id' ] ) )
        {
        require ( 'login_functions.php' ) ; load() ;
        }
?>
<!doctype html>
<html lang=en>
<head>
<title>Logout code</title>
<meta charset=utf-8>
<link rel="stylesheet" type="text/css" href="msgboard.css">
        <style type="text/css">
        #tab-navigation ul { margin-left:190px; }
        h3 { text-align:center; margin-top:-10px; }
        </style>
</head>
<body>
<div id='container'>
<?php
```

```
//Re-use the registration header that has only one menu button i.e. the Home Page button
        include ( 'includes/header_register.php' ) ;
// Remove the session variables from the session
        $_SESSION = array() ;
// Destroy the session
        session_destroy() ;
// Display the thank you message
        echo '<h2>Thank you for logging out!</h2>
        <br><h3>Logging out is a very important security measure</h3> ';
        include ( 'includes/footer.php' ) ;
?>
</div>
</body>
</html>
```

The login page described earlier, redirects registered users to the forums page, where they can choose which forum to view. This page is described next.

Creating a Gateway to the Two Categories of Quotes

The gateway page enables members to choose which category to view. It is shown in Figure 10-6.

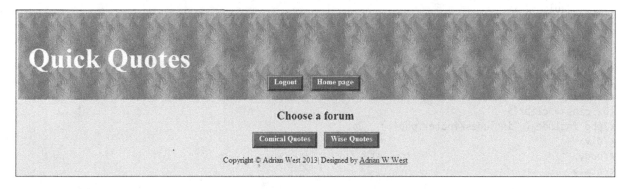

Figure 10-6. *The forums page allows the user to choose a quotes category*

I could have placed the two new buttons in the header, but I prefer to maximize their visibility by placing them in the body of the page.

The code for the gateway page is given in Listing 10-6.

Listing 10-6. Creating a Gateway to the Two Categories (forum.php)

The header file *header_forum_choice.php* is a copy of the header file with the menu buttons commented-out except for *Logout* and *Home page*.

An internal style is used to position the horizontal menu and the two new category buttons.

```php
<?php
session_start() ;
// Redirect the user if not logged in
if ( !isset( $_SESSION[ 'member_id' ] ) ) {
require ( 'login_functions.php' ) ; load() ; }
?>
<!doctype html>
<html lang=en>
<head>
<title>Forum page</title>
<meta charset=utf-8>
<link rel="stylesheet" type="text/css" href="msgboard.css">
<style type="text/css">
#forum_links { position:absolute; top:115px; left:115px; }
#header #tab-navigation ul { margin-left:185px; }
</style>
</head>
<body>
<div id='container'>
<?php include ( 'includes/header_forum_choice.php' ) ;?>
<h2>Choose a forum</h2>
<div id="forum_links">
<div id="tab-navigation">
        <ul>
        <li><a href="forum_c.php">Comical Quotes</a></li>
        <li><a href="forum_w.php">Wise Quotes</a></li>
    </ul>
</div>
</div>
<br><br>
<br class="clear">
<?php include ( 'includes/footer.php' ) ; ?>
</div>
</body>
</html>
```

Before we create the two forum pages, we need to have some quotations to display in the forums pages. We will now create a form so that we can enter some quotations.

The Form for Posting Quotations

The posting form is shown in Figure 10-7.

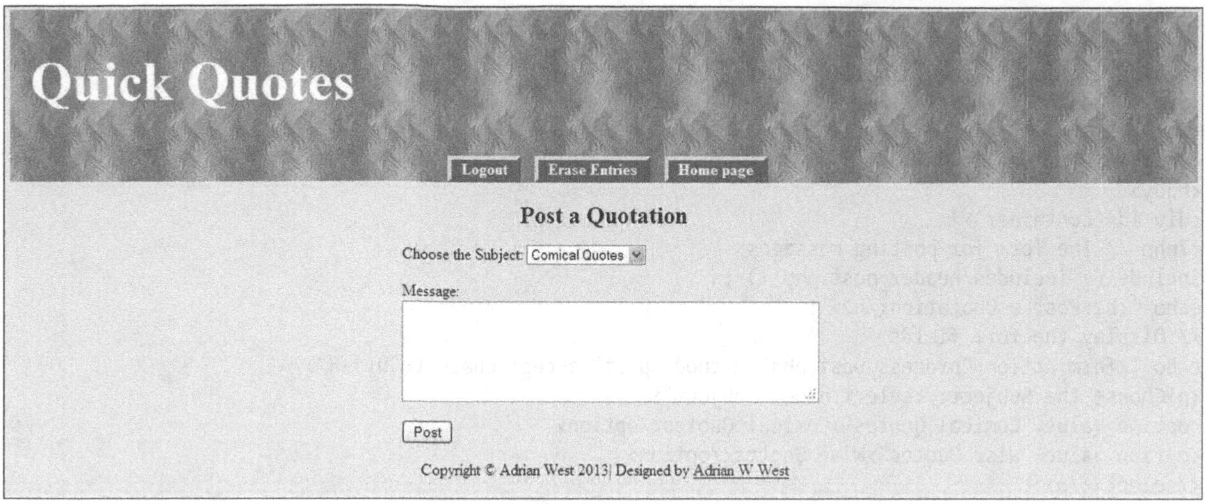

Figure 10-7. The form for posting quotations

You can use the word "Subject" as I have or, if you wish, you can replace it with "Category". In this tutorial, they are synonymous. A pull-down menu is used for the subject for two reasons:

- I assumed that the message-board owner wants to limit the number of subjects (categories) because the owner does not want members to create new subjects. Members will instead add new quotations to either the Comical Quotations subject or the Wise Quotations subject.

- The spelling needs to be consistent. A pull-down menu guarantees this. An owner can, of course, add new subjects (categories) to the pull-down menu.

The code for the posting page is given in Listing 10-7a.

Listing 10-7a. Creating the Form for Posting New Quotations (post.php)

The included file *header_post.php* is a copy of *header.php* with the buttons commented-out except for *Logout* and *Home Page*. The *Add a quote* button is replaced by an *Erase Entries* button as follows:

```
<li><a href="post.php">Erase Entries</a></li>
```

A session is used to ensure that only members are allowed to post new quotations. An internal style positions the form fields and the menu block.

```php
<?php
session_start() ;
// Redirect if not logged in.
if ( !isset( $_SESSION[ 'member_id' ] ) ) {
require ( 'login_functions.php' ) ; load() ; }
?>
<!doctype html>
<html lang=en>
<head>
<title>The form for posting subjects and messages</title>
<meta charset=utf-8>
```

```
<link rel="stylesheet" type="text/css" href="msgboard.css">
<style type="text/css">
#tab-navigation ul { margin-left:85px; }
form { padding-left:215px; }
</style>
</head>
<body>
<div id='container'>
<?php // The form for posting messages
include ( 'includes/header_post.php' ) ;
echo '<h2>Post a Quotation</h2>';
// Display the form fields
echo '<form action="process_post.php" method="post" accept-charset="utf-8">
<p>Choose the Subject: <select name="subject">
<option value="Comical Quotes">Comical Quotes</option>
<option value="Wise Quotes">Wise Quotes</option>
</select></p>
<p>Message:<br><textarea name="message" rows="5" cols="50"></textarea></p>
<p><input name="submit" type="submit" value="post"></p>
</form>';
include ( 'includes/footer.php' ) ; //posting an entry into the database table ↵
automatically sends a message to the forum moderator                                #1
// Assign the subject using a ternary operator
$subject = "Posting added to Quick Quotes message board";
$user = isset($_SESSION['uname']) ? $_SESSION['uname'] : "";
$body = "Posting added by " . $user;
mail("admin@myisp.co.uk", $subject, $body, "From:admin@myisp.co.uk\r\n");
?>
</div>
</body>
</html>
```

Explanation of the Code

```
//posting an entry into the database table automatically sends an e-mail message ↵
to the forum moderator                                                            #1
// Assign the subject using a ternary operator
$subject = "Posting added to Quick Quotes Forum";
$user = isset($_SESSION['uname']) ? $_SESSION['uname'] : "";
$body = "Posting added by " . $user;
mail("admin@myisp.co.uk", $subject, $body, "From:admin@myisp.co.uk\r\n");
?>
```

Naturally, you must replace the dummy e-mail addresses with your own. Note that the two e-mail addresses are the same when sending an e-mail to yourself.

The database can, of course, be moderated by an administrator who is familiar with phpMyAdmin; however, it would be good to create a user-friendly administration facility for someone who is not familiar with phpMyAdmin. (Review the previous Chapters, especially Chapter 3, for instructions on creating administration pages.) A user-friendly administration page allows the administrator to view a table of the latest posts. This table would have *Delete* and *Edit links* as described in Chapter 3.

The code beginning with line #1 sends an e-mail to the administrator's real e-mail address (not his dummy e-mail address) to notify him that a member has posted a message. He would then use his administration facility to view the message to decide whether it complies with the rules of the forum. The e-mail in this example is the simplest possible. The PHP function mail() has the following format:

```
mail(to, subject, body, from)
```

The *to* and *from* must be e-mail addresses. The variables can be basic, like *$subject* is in this example, or very complex. In Listing 10-7a, the *username* of the person posting the message is pulled from the session and then concatenated with some text to form the body of the e-mail. The items *subject*, *to*, and *from* create the header of the e-mail. The header is the top section of the e-mail, the body is the window below the header. The resulting e-mail will look like Table 10-4.

Table 10-4. *The appearance of the e-mail*

From:	admin@myisp.co.uk
Date:	02 August 2013 17:26
To:	admin@myisp.co.uk
Subject:	Posting added to Quick Quotes message board

Posting added by lilythepink

■ **Note** E-mails will not be sent and received using your computer unless you install and configure a program such as Mercury (bundled with XAMPP). Mercury is tricky, but Internet help is available. I prefer to test the e-mail by uploading the file to one of my web sites together with a minimal database. For Internet help with Mercury, try the videos on YouTube. Begin with http://www.youtube.com/watch?v=VU4PT7xMSOo, use the pause button when you want to take notes. On the same YouTube page, you will find several other tutorials. The tutorials are easier than written instructions. Two example scripts for e-mailing are provided in the Appendix.

Processing the Postings

The user input is tested by means of two external files, *process_post.php*, and *login_functions.php* that are used to redirect a user who has not logged in.

The code for *process_post.php* is given in Listing 10-7b.

Listing 10-7b. Creating the File for Processing the Postings (process_post.php)

```php
<?php
// Start the session
session_start();
// Include the login functions to check for errors
        require ( 'login_functions.php' ) ;
// If users are not logged in, redirect them
if ( !isset( $_SESSION[ 'member_id' ] ) ) { load() ; }
//Connect to the database
        require ( 'mysqli_connect.php' ) ;
```

```
// Has the form been submitted?
if ($_SERVER['REQUEST_METHOD'] == 'POST')
{
// Check that the user has entered a subject and a message                    #1
if ( empty($_POST['subject'] ) ) { echo '<p>You forgot to enter a subject.</p>'; }
if ( empty($_POST['message'] ) ) { echo '<p>You forgot to enter a message.</p>'; }
if ( !empty( $_POST['message']))
{
$message = mysqli_real_escape_string( $dbcon, strip_tags(trim( $_POST['message'] )) ) ; #2
}
// If successful, insert the post into the database table. This check is not essential, but it
// does ensure that the page has not been compromised by a hacker.
if( !empty($_POST['subject']) && !empty($_POST['message']) )
{
//Make the insert query                                                        #2
$q = "INSERT INTO forum(uname, subject, message, post_date)
VALUES ('{$_SESSION['uname']}', '{$_POST['subject']}','$message',NOW() )";
$result = mysqli_query ( $dbcon, $q ) ;
// If it fails, display an error message
if (mysqli_affected_rows($dbcon) != 1) { echo '<p>Error</p>'.mysqli_error($dbcon); }
else { load('forum.php'); }
// Close the database connection
mysqli_close( $dbcon ) ;
}
}
// Create a link back to the forum page
echo '<p><a href="forum.php">Forum</a>' ;
include ( 'includes/footer.php' ) ;
?>
```

Explanation of the Code

```
// Check that the user has entered a subject and a message                    #1
if ( empty($_POST['subject'] ) ) { echo '<p>You forgot to enter a subject.</p>'; }
```

This check is not essential, but it does ensure that the page has not been compromised by a hacker.

```
$message = mysqli_real_escape_string( $dbcon, strip_tags(trim( $_POST['message'] )) ) ; #2
}
// If successful, insert the posting into the database table.
if( !empty($_POST['subject']) && !empty($_POST['message']) )
{
```

The text area for messages is a magnet for malevolent persons wanting to insert dangerous scripts. Therefore, special security filters must be built into the code. The message in the textarea is cleaned by using three functions in line **#1**; note that the functions have been nested. The functions are as follows:

- *trim* removes spaces from the beginning and end of the message.

- *strip_tags* removes HTML tags because these might contain harmful scripts, for example:
  <script>*some JavaScript code*</script>.

- You have met `mysqli_real_escape_string` many times before. It will remove any unwanted characters, including apostrophes. For instance, if the user enters a message containing the words *one's* or *he's*, the apostrophe will be entered into the forum table correctly and an error message will be avoided.

```
//Make the insert query                                          #3
$q = "INSERT INTO forum(uname, subject, message, post_date)
VALUES ('{$_SESSION['uname']}', '{$_POST['subject']}','$message', NOW() )";
$result = mysqli_query ( $dbcon, $q ) ;
```

The query values are as follows:

- `'{$_SESSION['uname']}'`: The user name is provide by the user initiated session.

- `'{$_POST['subject']}'`: The subject is a global variable provided by the user's entry in *post.php*.

- `'$message'`: This is defined in the previous block of code beginning with line **#1**.

- `NOW()`: This is automatically provided by the DATETIME entry when the user posts a quotation.

Post Some Quotations

Now that we have a form for inserting postings into the forum table, we will post the quotations shown in Table 10-5. Or you could use phpMyAdmin to import the file *forum.sql* that you will find in the downloaded files for this chapter. As each quotation is posted, you will be redirected to the forum page with the two buttons for choosing either comical or wise quotes. However, you will not be able to view the quotations yet because we have not created the two pages for displaying them.

Table 10-5. Post some quotations

Login as...	Subject (a.k.a. Forum)	Message
lilythepink	Wise Quotes	"Adversity causes some men to break: others to break records." William Arthur Ward
mechanic7	Comical Quotes	"I love deadlines. I like the whooshing sound they make as they fly by." Douglas Adams
lilythepink	Comical Quotes	"Golf is a good walk spoiled." Mark Twain
lilythepink	Comical Quotes	"Life is one darned thing after another." Mark Twain
giantstep12	Comical Quotes	Jack Benny once said, "Give me golf clubs, fresh air and a beautiful partner and you can keep the golf clubs and fresh air."
mythking	Wise Quotes	"Nothing great was ever achieved without great enthusiasm." Ralph Waldo Emerson
mythking	Wise Quotes	"Wise sayings often fall on barren ground, but a kind word is never thrown away." Arthur Helps
mythking	Comical Quotes	"Many a small thing has been made large by the right kind of advertising." Mark Twain'

(continued)

Table 10-5. (*continued*)

Login as...	Subject (a.k.a. Forum)	Message
mythking	Wise Quotes	"To do two things at once is to do neither." Publilius Syrus
giantstep12	Wise Quotes	"Anyone who has never made a mistake has never tried anything new." Albert Einstein
giantstep12	Comical Quotes	"Experience is simply the name we give our mistakes." Oscar Wilde
giantstep12	Comical Quotes	"If you want to recapture your youth, just cut off his allowance." Al Bernstein
mechanic7	Comical Quotes	"Technological progress has merely provided us with a more efficient means for going backwards." Aldous Huxley
lilythepink	Wise Quotes	"Real knowledge is to know the extent of one's ignorance." Confucius
mechanic7	Wise Quotes	"It is amazing what you can accomplish if you do not care who gets the credit." Harry S. Truman

Remember: The date and time of the postings will be added automatically.

Now that we have some quotations to display, we will create the home page.

The Home Page

The home page will display a small selection of the quotations to tempt the user to register as a member of the message board. The home page is shown in Figure 10-8.

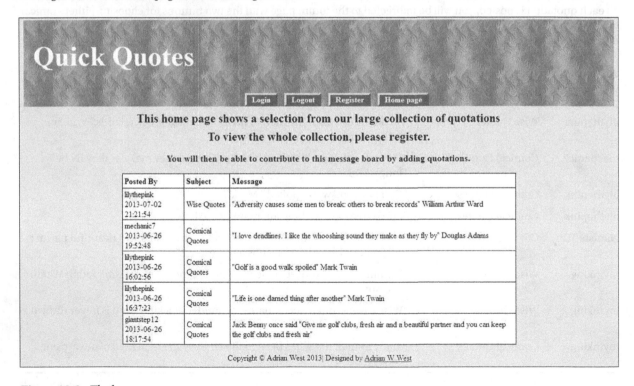

Figure 10-8. The home page

The code selects five quotations from the table named *forum*. The code for the home page is given in Listing 10-8.

Listing 10-8. Creating the Home Page (index.php)

An internal style is used to position the horizontal menu buttons. The header for the home page is the template header *header.php*.

```
<!doctype html>
<html lang=en>
<head>
<title>Home page</title>
<meta charset=utf-8>
<link rel="stylesheet" type="text/css" href="msgboard.css">
        <style type="text/css">
        table { background:white; color:black; }
        th {padding:4px; border:1px black solid; }
        #tab-navigation ul { margin-left:95px; }
        h2 { margin-bottom:0; margin-top:10px; }
        h3 {margin-bottom:0; margin-top:0; }
        </style>
</head>
<body>
<div id='container'>
<?php include ( 'includes/header.php' ) ;?>
<h2>This home page shows a selection from our large collection of quotations.</h2>
<h2>To view the whole collection, please register.</h2><br>
<h3>You will then be able to contribute to this forum by adding quotations.</h3>
<?php
// Connect to the database
require ( 'mysqli_connect.php' ) ;
// Make the query
$q = "SELECT uname,post_date, subject, message FROM forum LIMIT 5" ;          #1
$result = mysqli_query( $dbcon, $q ) ;
if ( mysqli_num_rows( $result ) > 0 )
{
echo '<br><table><tr><th>Posted By</th><th>Subject</th><th id="msg">Message</th></tr>';
while ( $row = mysqli_fetch_array( $result, MYSQLI_ASSOC ))
{
echo '<tr><td>' . $row['uname'].'<br>'.$row['post_date'].'</td>
<td>'.$row['subject'].'</td><td>' . $row['message'] . '</td> </tr>';
}
echo '</table>' ;
}
else { echo '<p>There are currently no messages.</p>' ; }
mysqli_close( $dbcon ) ;
include ( 'includes/footer.php' ) ;
?>
</div>
</body>
</html>
```

Explanation of the Code

The majority of the code you have seen before, but the query in line **#1** is a little different:

```
$q = "SELECT uname,post_date, subject, message FROM forum LIMIT 5" ;                    #1
```

The query selects items from the *forum* table for display, but the LIMIT keyword ensures that only five lines are shown.

We will now create two pages, one for each forum (subject).

The Comical Quotes Page

The comical quotes page is shown in Figure 10-9.

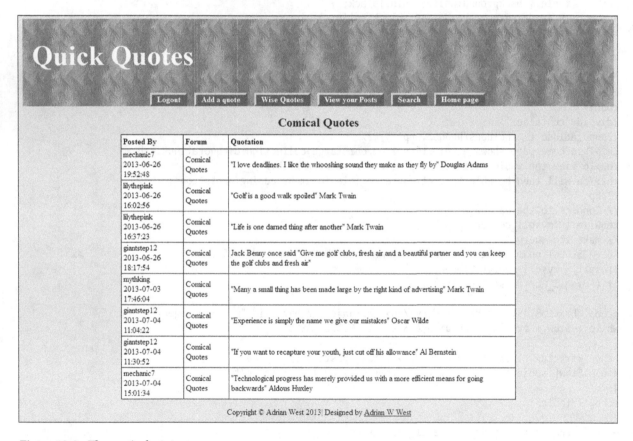

Figure 10-9. The comical quotes page

The code given in Listing 10-9 selects only the comical quotes from the database *forum* table.

Listing 10-9. Creating the Comical Quotes Page (forum_c.php)

An internal style is used to format the table and to position the table and menu buttons.

```php
<?php session_start() ;
// Redirect if not logged in
if ( !isset( $_SESSION[ 'member_id' ] ) ) { require ( 'login_functions.php' ) ; load() ; }
?>
<!doctype html>
<html lang=en>
<head>
<title>Comical quotes forum page</title>
<meta charset=utf-8>
<link rel="stylesheet" type="text/css" href="msgboard.css">
        <style type="text/css">
        table { background:white; color:black;  }
        th {padding:4px; border:1px black solid; }
        #tab-navigation ul { margin-left:-95px; }
        </style>
</head>
<body>
<div id='container'>
<?php
include ( 'includes/header_comical.php' ) ;
// Connect to the database
require ( 'mysqli_connect.php' ) ;
// Make the query                                                        #1
$q = "SELECT uname,post_date,subject,message FROM forum ↵
WHERE subject = 'Comical Quotes' ORDER BY 'post_date' ASC";
        $result = mysqli_query( $dbcon, $q ) ;
        if ( mysqli_num_rows( $result ) > 0 )
        {
        echo '<h2>Comical Quotes</h2>↵
        <table><tr><th>Posted By</th><th>Forum</th> <th id="msg">Quotation</th></tr>';
        while ( $row = mysqli_fetch_array( $result, MYSQLI_ASSOC ))
        {
        echo '<tr><td>' . $row['uname'].'<br>'.$row['post_date'].'</td>
        <td>'.$row['subject'].'</td><td>' . $row['message'] . '</td> </tr>';
        }
        echo '</table>' ;
        }
        else { echo '<p>There are currently no messages.</p>' ; }
//Close the database connection
mysqli_close( $dbcon ) ;
include ( 'includes/footer.php' ) ;
?>
</div>
</body>
</html>
```

Explanation of the Code

Most of the code in Listing 10-9 will be familiar, and there are plenty of comments in the Listing. We will now examine line **#1**:

```
// Make the query                                                    #1
$q = "SELECT uname,post_date,subject,message FROM forum ↵
WHERE subject = 'Comical Quotes' ORDER BY 'post_date' ASC";
```

The query selects only the comical quotes from the *forum* table. The quotes will be sorted in ascending order of posting—that is, oldest first.

To confirm that the file is satisfactory, log in and load the file into the address bar of a browser as `http://localhost/msgboard/forum_c.php`

The Header for the Comical Quotes Page

After viewing the comical quotes page, the user may also wish to view the *Wise Quotes* page. To enable the user to do this, the comment-out is removed from the *Wise Quotes* button in the comical quotes header *header_comical.php*. The comment-outs have also been removed from those menu buttons that enable members to search the database. For the moment, those two buttons will be inactive because we have not yet designed the relevant pages.

The buttons to be displayed are shown in bold type in the code snippet for the new header as follows:

```
<div id="header">
<h1>Quick Quotes</h1>
<div id="tab-navigation">
    <ul>
        <!--<li><a href="login.php">Login</a></li>-->
        <li><a href="logout.php">Logout</a></li>
        <!--<li><a href="safer-register-page.php">Register</a></li>-->
        <li><a href="post.php">Add a Quote</a></li>
        <!--<li><a href="forum_c.php">Comical Quotes</a></li>-->
        <li><a href="forum_w.php">Wise Quotes</a></li>
        <li><a href="view_posts.php">View your Posts</a></li>
        <li><a href="search.php">Search</a></li>
                <li><a href="index.php">Home page</a></li>
    </ul>
</div>
</div>
```

To confirm that the file is satisfactory, with XAMPP running, log in and load the file into the address bar of a browser as `http://localhost/msgboard/forum_c.php`.

The Wise Quotes Page

This page is almost the same as the *Comical Quotes* page except for the MySQL query. Also, the *Wise Quotes* button has been commented-out, and the *Comical Quotes* button is made active by removing its comment-out. Figure 10-10 shows the *Wise Quotes* page.

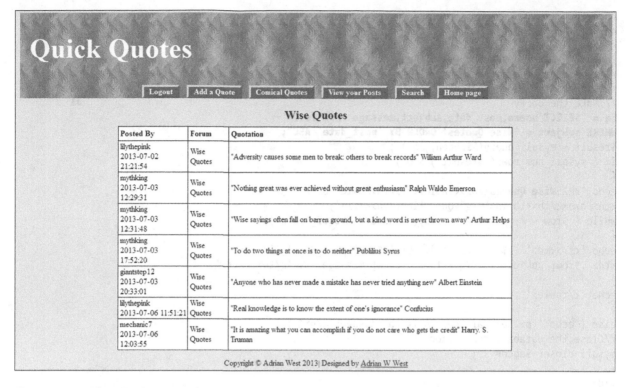

Figure 10-10. *The Wise Quotes page*

The page displays only the wise quotes. The code for the Wise Quotes page is given in Listing 10-10.

Listing 10-10. Creating the Wise Quotes Page (forum_w.php)

An internal style is used to position the table and the menu buttons.

```
<?php session_start() ;
// Redirect if not logged in
if ( !isset( $_SESSION[ 'member_id' ] ) ) { require ( 'login_functions.php' ) ; load() ; }
?>
<!doctype html>
<html lang=en>
<head>
<title>Wise quotes Forum page</title>
<meta charset=utf-8>
<link rel="stylesheet" type="text/css" href="msgboard.css">
        <style type="text/css">
        table { background:white; color:black; }
        th {padding:4px; border:1px black solid; }
        #tab-navigation ul { margin-left:-107px; }
        </style>
</head>
```

```
<body>
<div id='container'>
<?php
include ( 'includes/header_wise.php' ) ;
// Connect to the database
require ( 'mysqli_connect.php' ) ;
// Make the query                                                    #1
$q = "SELECT uname,post_date,subject,message FROM forum ↵
WHERE subject = 'Wise Quotes' ORDER BY 'post_date' ASC";
$result = mysqli_query( $dbcon, $q ) ;
if ( mysqli_num_rows( $result ) > 0 )
{
echo '<h2>Wise Quotes</h2><table><tr><th>Posted By</th> ↵
<th>Forum</th><th id="msg">Quotation</th></tr>';
while ( $row = mysqli_fetch_array( $result, MYSQLI_ASSOC ))
{
echo '<tr><td>' . $row['uname'].'<br>'.$row['post_date'].'</td>
<td>'.$row['subject'].'</td><td>' . $row['message'] . '</td> </tr>';
}
echo '</table>' ;
}
else { echo '<p>There are currently no messages.</p>' ; }
//Close the database connection
mysqli_close( $dbcon ) ;
?>
</div>
<?php include ( 'includes/footer.php' ) ; ?>
</body>
</html>
```

Explanation of the Code

The code is almost identical to the listing for the *Comical Quotes* forum page, except for the items shown in bold type in Listing 10-10:

```
// Make the query                                                    #1
$q = "SELECT uname,post_date,subject,message FROM forum ↵
WHERE subject = 'Wise Quotes' ORDER BY 'post_date' ASC";
```

The query selects only the records where the subject is "Wise Quotes." The quotes will be sorted in ascending order of posting—that is, oldest first.

As with the comical quotes page, a new header named *header_wise.php* will allow the user to redirect to the *Comical Quotes* page.

The Header for the Wise Quotes Page

The header code is identical to the header for the *Comical Quotes* page except that the *Wise Quotes* button is commented-out, and the comment-out is removed from the *Comical Quotes* button. Note that the *View your Posts* and

Search buttons will not work yet, because the relevant pages have not been created. The displayed buttons are shown in bold type in the code snippet for the header as follows:

```
<div id="header">
<h1>Quick Quotes</h1>
<div id="tab-navigation">
    <ul>
        <!--<li><a href="login.php">Login</a></li>-->
        <li><a href="logout.php">Logout</a></li>
        <!--<li><a href="safer-register-page.php">Register</a></li>-->
        <li><a href="post.php">Add a Quote</a></li>
        <li><a href="forum_c.php">Comical Quotes</a></li>
        <!--<li><a href="forum_w.php">Wise Quotes</a></li>- ->
        <li><a href="view_posts.php">View your Posts</a></li>
        <li><a href="search.php">Search</a></li>
        <li><a href="index.php">Home page</a></li>
    </ul>
</div>
</div>
```

Adding Search Facilities

The most likely reasons for searching are as follows:

- Members may want to view a list of their own postings.

- Members might wish to search the messages for particular words or phrases, or quotes by a particular author.

Before we can implement these searches, we must create the pages that will display the search results. Figure 10-11 shows the display for viewing an individual member's postings.

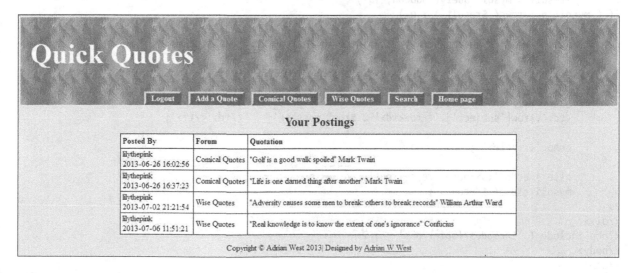

Figure 10-11. Displaying one member's postings

The code for the page displaying a member's posting is given in Listing 10-11.

Listing 10-11. Creating a Page to Display an Individual Member's Postings (view_posts.php)

An internal style positions the menu buttons and sets the table details.

```
<!doctype html>
<html lang=en>
<head>
<title>View a member's postings</title>
<meta charset=utf-8>
<link rel="stylesheet" type="text/css" href="msgboard.css">
<style type="text/css">
table { background:white; color:black; }
th {padding:4px; border:1px black solid; }
#tab-navigation ul { margin-left:-107px; }
</style>
</head>
<body>
<div id='container'>
<?php
// Start the session
session_start() ;
// Redirect if not logged in
if ( !isset( $_SESSION[ 'member_id' ] ) ) { require ( 'login_functions.php' ) ; load() ; }
        include ( 'includes/header_your_posts.php' ) ;
// Connect to the database
        require ( 'mysqli_connect.php' ) ;
// Make the query                                                         #1
        $q = "SELECT uname,post_date,subject,message FROM forum ⏎
        WHERE uname = '{$_SESSION['uname']}' ORDER BY post_date ASC";
        $result = mysqli_query( $dbcon, $q ) ;
if ( mysqli_num_rows( $result ) > 0 )
        {
        echo '<h2>Your Postings</h2><table><tr><th>Posted By</th><th>Forum</th>
        <th id="msg">Quotation</th></tr>';
        while ( $row = mysqli_fetch_array( $result, MYSQLI_ASSOC ))
        {
        echo '<tr><td>' . $row['uname'].'<br>'.$row['post_date'].'</td>
        <td>'.$row['subject'].'</td><td>' . $row['message'] . '</td> </tr>';
        }
        echo '</table>' ;
        }
        else { echo '<p>There are currently no messages.</p>' ; }
        mysqli_close( $dbcon ) ;
?>
</div>
<?php include ( 'includes/footer.php' ) ; ?>
</body>
</html>
```

Explanation of the Code

You will have seen most of the code before, but the query needs some explanation.

```
// Make the query                                              #1
$q = "SELECT uname,post_date,subject,message FROM forum ↩
WHERE uname = '{$_SESSION['uname']}' ORDER BY post_date ASC";
```

The query selects the items to be displayed and specifies two conditions: (i) show postings only for the user name specified in the session, (ii) order the table row display in ascending order of date of posting.

The Header for *View Posts.php*

The header menu will have six buttons. These are shown in bold type in the following snippet of code for *header_your_posts.php*.

```
<div id="header">
<h1>Quick Quotes</h1>
<div id="tab-navigation">
    <ul>
        <!--<li><a href="login.php">Login</a></li>-->
        <li><a href="logout.php">Logout</a></li>
        <!--<li><a href="safer-register-page.php">Register</a></li>-->
        <li><a href="post.php">Add a Quote</a></li>
        <li><a href="forum_c.php">Comical Quotes</a></li>
        <li><a href="forum_w.php">Wise Quotes</a></li>
        <!--<li><a href="view_posts.php">View your Posts</a></li>-->
        <li><a href="search.php">Search</a></li>
        <li><a href="index.php">Home page</a></li>
    </ul>
</div>
</div>
```

We will now enable the members to undertake full text searches.

Search for Specific Words or Phrases

Members might wish to see a table of quotes by Mark Twain, or a list of quotes about golf; the members would therefore be searching for particular words or phrases. This would require a *Search* button in the headers of both forum pages linked to a form for entering search criteria. As an alternative, the search field could be incorporated into the forum pages; however, in keeping with the book's subtitle, we will employ the simpler method using a button that links to a search form.

A full text search will search though every message to find the word(s). To achieve this, the forum table must use the MyISAM storage engine unless you are using later programs, such as XAMPP 1.8.3 with MySQL 5.6.4 and PHP 5+. The column named *messages* must be indexed.

Full text searches can be used on VARCHAR and TEXT columns. Full text searches are case insensitive and will ignore the following:

- Partial words. If you want to search for "spoiled," you have to search for the full word. Just searching for "spoil" won't return what you are looking for.

- Words containing less than four characters.

- Stop words. These are words that are extremely common, such as *the, a, an, as, by, his, her, with*, and *you*.

- A word or phrase that is included in more than 50% of the rows in the column being searched. The word or phrase in this case is treated as a stop word, and you will receive an error message saying "MATCH AGAINST returns zero rows." This can usually be avoided by having more records in a table.

Depending on which version of XAMPP you are using, you might have to change the type of storage engine. In any case, you will need to select FULL TEXT index and these steps are described next.

Preparing the Table for Full Text Searches

1. If you are using programs earlier than XAMPP 1.8.3, MySQL 5.6.4, and PHP 5+, the *forum* table should have been created to use the MyISAM storage engine. If you forgot to do this, use phpMyAdmin to change it. Full instructions are given in the Appendix. Alternatively, you could install the later version of XAMPP and MySQL.

2. In phpMyAdmin, click the *msgboarddb* database and then click the *forum* table. Click the *Structure* tab, select the box next to the *message* column, and then use the pull-down *More* menu to select a FULL TEXT index.

■ **Caution**   If you fail to select FULL TEXT index, you will see an error message when you run a search. Note that only one full text search index is allowed per table, although two columns can be combined with one full text index.

The Full Text Search Form

We will now create a form for searching specific words or phrases within messages (quotations).

The search form is shown in Figure 10-12.

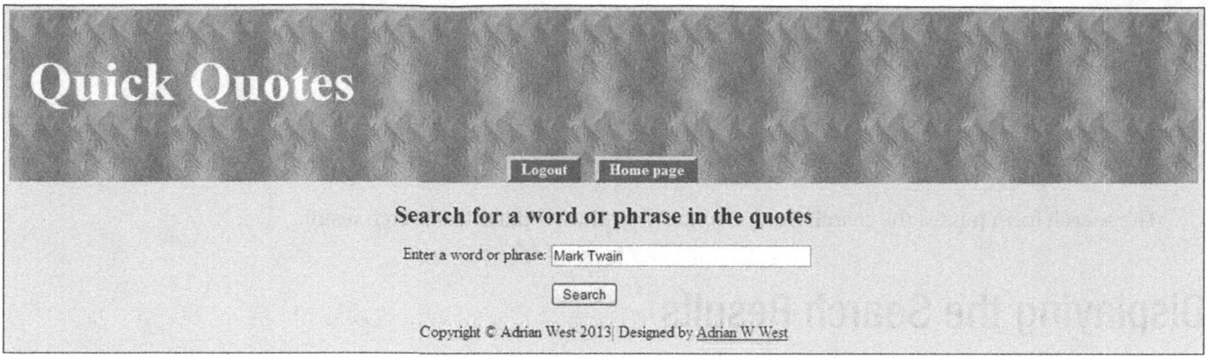

Figure 10-12. *The search form*

In Figure 10-12, the member has entered the search words "Mark Twain". The code for the search form is given in Listing 10-12.

Listing 10-12. Creating the Search Form (search.php)

An internal style positions the menu horizontally.

```
<!doctype html>
<html lang=en>
<head>
<title>Search form</title>
<meta charset=utf-8>
<link rel="stylesheet" type="text/css" href="msgboard.css">
<style type="text/css">
#tab-navigation ul { margin-left:145px; }
</style>
</head>
<body>
<div id="container">
<?php
// Start the session
session_start() ;
// Redirect if not logged in
if ( !isset( $_SESSION[ 'member_id' ] ) ) { require ( 'login_functions.php' ) ; load() ; }
// Use the same header as for forum.php
include("includes/header_forum_choice.php");
?>
<div id="content"><!-- Start of search page content. -->
<h2>Search for a word or phrase in the quotes</h2>
<form action="quotes_found.php" method="post">
    <p><label class="label" for="target">Enter a word or phrase: </label>
        <input id="target" type="text" name="trget" size="40" maxlength="60" ↵
        value="<?php if (isset($_POST['target'])) echo $_POST['target']; ?>"></p>
    <p><input id="submit" type="submit" name="submit" value="Search"></p>
</form>
```

```
<?php include ('includes/footer.php'); ?>
<!-- End of the search page content. -->
</div>
</div>
</body>
</html>
```

The search form passes the search word(s) to the page that displays the search results.

Displaying the Search Results

Figure 10-13 shows how the full text search displays the results.

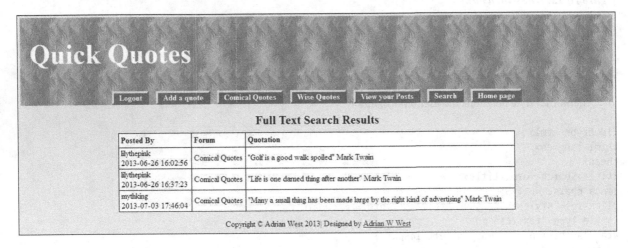

Figure 10-13. *The search results for quotations by Mark Twain are displayed*

Note that the number of quotations by Mark Twain is less than 50% of all the quotations contained in our *forum* table. If the number of quotes by Mark Twain had been more than 50% of the quotations, no results would have been displayed. In our example database table, there are 23 quotes. Mark Twain is cited for three quotes; he is therefore cited for 13% of the total. Because this is less than 50% of the total, he will be found and displayed. If the table contained only six quotes, Mark Twain would be cited for 50% of the total and therefore he would not be found and displayed in a search for "Mark Twain". In other words, the group of words "Mark Twain" would be treated as if it was a stop word such as *his*, *her*, *with*, and *you*. If you know that a word or phrase exists in the database table, but a full text search fails to find it, either you don't have enough quotes in the table or at least 50% of the quotes contain the search word or phrase. The code for the *quotes_found* page is given in Listing 10-13a.

Listing 10-13a. Creating the Search Results Page (quotes_found.php)

An internal style sheet positions the menu buttons horizontally.

```
<!doctype html>
<html lang=en>
<head>
<title>Quotes found</title>
<meta charset=utf-8>
```

```
<link rel="stylesheet" type="text/css" href="msgboard.css">
<style type="text/css">
table { background:white; color:black; }
th {padding:4px; border:1px black solid; }
#tab-navigation ul { margin-left:-167px; }
</style>
</head>
<body>
<div id='container'>
<?php include('includes/header_quotes_found.php'); ?>
<div id='content'><!--Start of the quotes found page content-->
<?php
// Start the session
session_start() ;
// Redirect if not logged in
if ( !isset( $_SESSION[ 'member_id' ] ) ) { require ( 'login_functions.php' ) ; load() ; }
// Connect to the database
require ( 'mysqli_connect.php' ) ;
//if POST is set                                                            #1
if($_SERVER['REQUEST_METHOD'] == 'POST' ) {
$target = $_POST['target'];//Set variable
}
// Make the full text query                                                 #2
$q = "SELECT uname,post_date,subject,message FROM forum WHERE MATCH (message) ↵
AGAINST ( '$target') ORDER BY post_date ASC";
$result = mysqli_query( $dbcon, $q ) ;
if ( mysqli_num_rows( $result ) > 0 )
{
echo '<h2>Full Text Search Results</h2>
<table><tr><th>Posted By</th><th>Forum</th><th id="msg">Quotation</th></tr>';
while ( $row = mysqli_fetch_array( $result, MYSQLI_ASSOC ))
{
echo '<tr><td>' . $row['uname'].'<br>'.$row['post_date'].'</td>
<td>'.$row['subject'].'</td><td>' . $row['message'] . '</td> </tr>';
}
echo '</table>' ;
}
else { echo '<p>There are currently no messages.</p>' ; }
mysqli_close( $dbcon ) ;
?>
</div><!--End of the quotes found page content.-->
</div>
<?php include('includes/footer.php'); ?>
</body>
</html>
```

■ **Note**   If you run this file and you see this error message, "Warning: mysqli_num_rows() expects parameter 1 to be mysqli_result, boolean given in…," you probably forgot to choose *Full Text Search* for the table.

Explanation of the Code

```
//if POST is set                                                    #1
if($_SERVER['REQUEST_METHOD'] == 'POST' ) {
$target = $_POST['target'];//Set variable
}
```

The search form sent the target word or phrase (in this example, it was Mark Twain) to this page, where it is assigned to the variable *$target*.

```
// Make the full text query                                         #2
$q = "SELECT uname,post_date,subject,message FROM forum WHERE MATCH (message) ↵
AGAINST ( '$target') ORDER BY post_date ASC";
$result = mysqli_query( $dbcon, $q ) ;
```

The full text query searches the *forum* table for messages (quotations) that contain the words "Mark Twain" as stored in the variable *$target*. Note the brackets, the commas, and the double and single quote marks; they are important. The format for a full text search query is as follows:

SELECT list of items FROM some table WHERE MATCH (the column) AGAINST(the search words) ;

The key words MATCH and AGAINST are the main differences between a standard SELECT query and a full text search query.

The Header for the *quotes_found* Page

The code for the header is given in Listing 10-13b.

Listing 10-13b. Creating the Header for the Quotes Found Page (header_quotes_found.php)

```
<div id="header">
<h1>Quick Quotes</h1>
<div id="tab-navigation">
    <ul>
        <!--<li><a href="login.php">Login</a></li>-->
        <li><a href="logout.php">Logout</a></li>
        <!--<li><a href="safer-register-page.php">Register</a></li>-->
        <li><a href="post.php">Add a quote</a></li>
        <li><a href="forum_c.php">Comical Quotes</a></li>
        <li><a href="forum_w.php">Wise Quotes</a></li>
        <li><a href="view_posts.php">View your Posts</a></li>
        <li><a href="search.php">Search</a></li>
        <li><a href="index.php">Home page</a></li>
    </ul>
</div>
</div>
```

Several enhancements can be added to the message board, but I only have space to mention them very briefly.

Enhancing the Message Board

The message board in this chapter was greatly simplified for the benefit of readers who are not familiar with databases. By using the knowledge you gained from previous chapters, it is possible to add enhancements as follows:

- The pages for displaying the two categories of quotes could display paginated results. (Review Chapters 5 and 8 for a reminder of how to do this.)

- Members may wish to change their passwords. (Review Chapter 3 for details.)

- Members may have forgotten their passwords; they can be sent a new password. This is covered in Chapter 11.

Converting the Message Board to a Forum

At the beginning of this chapter, I said that I would briefly describe a structure for converting the message board to a forum. A forum requires maximum *normalization* and *atomicity*. (See Chapter 9 to refresh your memory on the definition of those terms.) More tables are required, and several of these would be linked by queries containing the keyword JOIN.

A forum requires additional tables for threads and replies. With earlier versions of XAMPP, MySQL, and PHP, there is a mixture of storage engines for the tables. Some use INNODB, and others use MyISAM. Later versions use INNODB only.

The message board was moderated by the administrator as a result of an automatic e-mail containing the name of the poster and the date. When the quote was submitted, it was inserted immediately into the database table; a better solution is to create a temporary table for postings so that the quotes are not accessible to members until the moderator approves them.

It would be helpful if the administrator had facilities to delete or edit a quote without using phpMyAdmin. His admin page could display a table of recent posts that contained links for editing and deleting as described in Chapter 3.

The minimum number of tables required for a forum is four, as shown in Figure 10-14.

```
forums
---------------------------------
forum_id MEDIUMINT (6) primary
forum_name CHAR (60)
forum_descr CHAR (60)
```

```
replies
---------------------------------
reply_id MEDIUMINT (6) primary
reply_content TEXT
reply_date DATETIME
reply_thread MEDIUMINT (6) foreign
reply_by MEDIUMINT (6) foreign
```

```
members
---------------------------------
member_id MEDIUMINT (6) primary
email VARCHAR (60)
registration_date DATETIME
user_name CHAR (12)
psword CHAR (40)
member_level TINYINT (2)
```

```
threads
---------------------------------
thread_id MEDIUMINT(6) primary
thread_title VARCHAR (100)
thread_date DATETIME
thread_forum MEDIUMINT (6) foreign
thread_by (INT6) foreign
```

Figure 10-14. *The tables for a forum*

If you would like to experiment with a more complex forum similar to the one shown in Figure 10-14, you can download a tutorial and the code from the following web site:

```
http://net.tutsplus.com/tutorials/php/how-to-create-a-phpmysql-powered-forum-from-scratch/?search_index=36
```

Summary

In this chapter, we studied the plan and structure for a basic message board. We created a registration page and login form. We developed a gateway to two pages of quotes and then created those pages. We learned how to create a form for posting messages. We created two search forms: one enabled members to search for a list of their own postings, and another was designed to undertake full text searches. Some enhancements to the basic message board were suggested, and finally a brief outline of a basic forum was provided together with a resource for exploring it. The next chapter describes a basic e-commerce web site.

CHAPTER 11

■ ■ ■

E-Commerce: A Brief Introduction

E-commerce web sites accept payment in exchange for goods or services. A user orders from a range of goods or services displayed in the web site's catalog pages. The details of the user's orders are stored in the web site's database. Money passes from the user to the web-site owner. This is achieved by means of a payment system incorporated into the web site. Finally, the ordered items are delivered to the user. Users can track the progress of their orders, update their account details, and if necessary, contact a customer support department.

Some types of e-commerce web sites do not need a database management system—for instance, an online shop with a limited range of goods, and with no expectation of expanding the range, can operate successfully without a database. I provided two of my clients with that type of web site, and you can view one of them at www.annroejones-artist.co.uk.

Two types of e-commerce sites would benefit from using a database: (i) An online shop with an extensive range of goods or services, for instance Amazon, and (ii) an online shop with a limited range of goods, but the owner has every intention of expanding the range. The brief outline for an e-commerce site in this chapter is based on this type of shop.

This chapter describes two types of shopping carts: a PayPal shopping cart, and a custom shopping cart. These are presented in three parts as follows:

- Features common to both shopping carts

  - Security warning

  - The plan

  - The home page

  - Registering users

  - The Login page with a "forgotten password" link

  - The administration

  - Searching for products

- Features applicable only to the PayPal shopping cart

  - Integrating with the PayPal shopping cart

  - The art table for use with a PayPal shopping cart

  - Adding paintings for the PayPal shopping cart

  - The product display with PayPal Shopping cart buttons

- Features applicable to the custom shopping cart (demonstration files provided)

    - Add paintings to a table for a custom shopping cart

    - The database and tables

    - Displaying the products using the custom shopping cart links

    - Adding purchases to the custom cart

    - The checkout page

    - The additional administrative tasks

I left out several processes in order to fit this brief outline into one chapter, but the outline will provide you with a starting point for further study. This chapter is not a tutorial because the code alone for a tutorial would occupy around 50 pages. In fact, this chapter contains very little code because the web site described combines most of the code already shown and explained in the previous chapters.

For instance:

- The registration page is similar to the registration page described in Chapter 6.

- Most of the administration facilities were described in Chapters 3 and 8.

- Chapter 9 described the use of multiple tables.

Login and logout pages were covered fully in several previous chapters. However, the login page in this chapter contains a link to enable users to retrieve a forgotten password; the code is provided for this feature.

■ **Note** This chapter is a very brief introduction to an e-commerce web site. To deal fully with a practical example of an e-commerce web site with its payment gateway, stock control system, order tracking, security measures, invoicing and customer services would require a whole book. You will find a list of resources for designing and developing e-commerce web sites in the appendix.

My thanks go to Roger St. Barbe for providing the images of colored etchings. His method of producing the etchings is fascinating, a précis of the process can be found on his web site:

`http://www.dolphin-gallery.co.uk`

Although we state that each product is unique, Roger does actually produce a limited number of signed copies of each etching. For the sake of simplicity, in our example "The Dove Gallery" will stock only one copy. I own the other paintings used in this chapter. The artist James Kessell (now deceased) was a double Royal Academy artist (London and Birmingham UK).

■ **Note** In this outline description of an e-commerce web site, when code is provided, no attempt has been made to accommodate Internet Explorer 8. The downloadable files for the PayPal shopping cart section are included in a separate subfolder together with a Read Me file describing how to set up the PayPal database and tables. The main downloadable folder named *ecommerce* contains the custom shopping cart files.

Items Common to Both Shopping Carts

Most topics in this section apply to e-commerce web sites using a PayPal shopping cart or a custom cart. The two most important topics for both shopping carts are security and careful planning.

Security Warning

Database-driven e-commerce web sites can be extremely vulnerable; therefore, security is a primary concern. By heeding the following warnings, you can make an e-commerce web site reasonably secure:

- A developer should not attempt to launch an e-commerce web site until he or she has achieved a high level of expertise with PHP and MySQL.

- Knowledge of PHP *stored procedures* and *transactions* is essential for e-commerce. The Appendix contains resources for, and a brief outline of, these techniques.

- The developer must thoroughly understand the inherent security problems.

- Developers must be aware of and fully comply with the data protection laws for their territory, and with the laws governing online trading.

- The web site should never store customers' bank and credit card details unless a costly and efficient security scheme is in place.

- To avoid some of the worry associated with Internet financial transactions, always use a secure payment system such as PayPal, Stripe, Sage Pay, or Authorize.net. If you decide to use their shopping cart buttons, be sure to choose the encoded versions.

- An e-commerce database-driven web site must use an unshared secure server.

- Use *https* pages. These are protected by a secure socket layer (SSL).

■ **Note**   The login details for the two web sites are as follows:

For the custom shopping cart administrator, e-mail: `miker@myisp.com` Password: `willgates`

For the custom shopping cart registered user, e-mail: `rbush@myisp.co.uk` Password: `redblooms`

For the PayPal shopping cart administrator, e-mail: `ddruff@myisp.co.uk` Password: `epidermal`

We will now examine a plan for an e-commerce web site.

The Plan

As usual, the first design step for creating a database means discussing the web-site owner's requirements and then producing a plan to fulfill those requirements:

- The web site outlined in this chapter sells original paintings and colored etchings.

- An administrator will be able to add or delete paintings and artists from the database tables by means of a user-friendly interface.

- The basic e-commerce database would use a large number of tables, typically 12 or more, but we will discuss only five as follows:

  - *user*: The administrator and registered users. This will include the user's address. For brevity, it will not include an alternative delivery address.

  - *art*: This table contains a description of the paintings and will be used to display a catalog of the stock of paintings.

  - *artist*: Contains the name of the artist. To save space, it will not contain the traditional brief description of the artist.

  - *orders*: For information about the items ordered, the order date, and cost.

  - *order_contents*: Contains the order number and the dispatch date.

The database tables are described fully in the custom shopping cart section.

■ **Note**   During the planning stage, the owner and the developer decide whether users should be asked to register up front or at the checkout stage. If they think an up-front registration will deter users, the second solution should be adopted. The up-front solution can be made less daunting by providing radio buttons or a check box on the registration page to enable users to opt out of receiving e-mails announcing special offers. The custom shopping cart web site described in this chapter requires the prospective user to register up front and log in. In the PayPal shopping cart version, up-front registration is optional.

The Home Page

To encourage viewers to register, the home page displays tempting samples of the products. A suggested home page is shown in Figure 11-1.

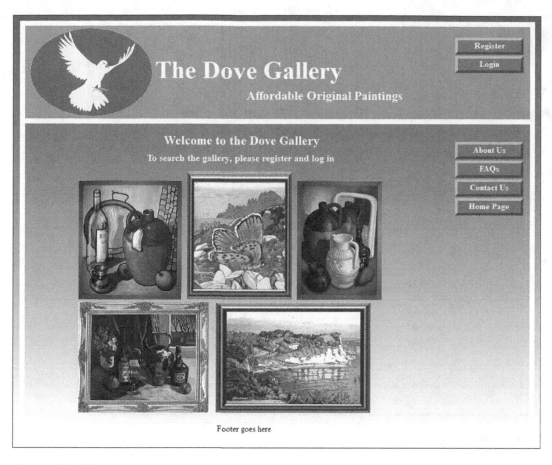

Figure 11-1. *The home page*

The code for the home page and its header are included in the downloadable files as *index.php* and *header_home*, respectively. Note the *Register* button and a *Login* button in the header. By displaying some of the products, you encourage users to register in order to see the full range. The home page for the PayPal Shopping cart has additional search capabilities. It can be found in the downloadable subfolder named *shopper*.

Registering Users

The registration page is shown in Figure 11-2.

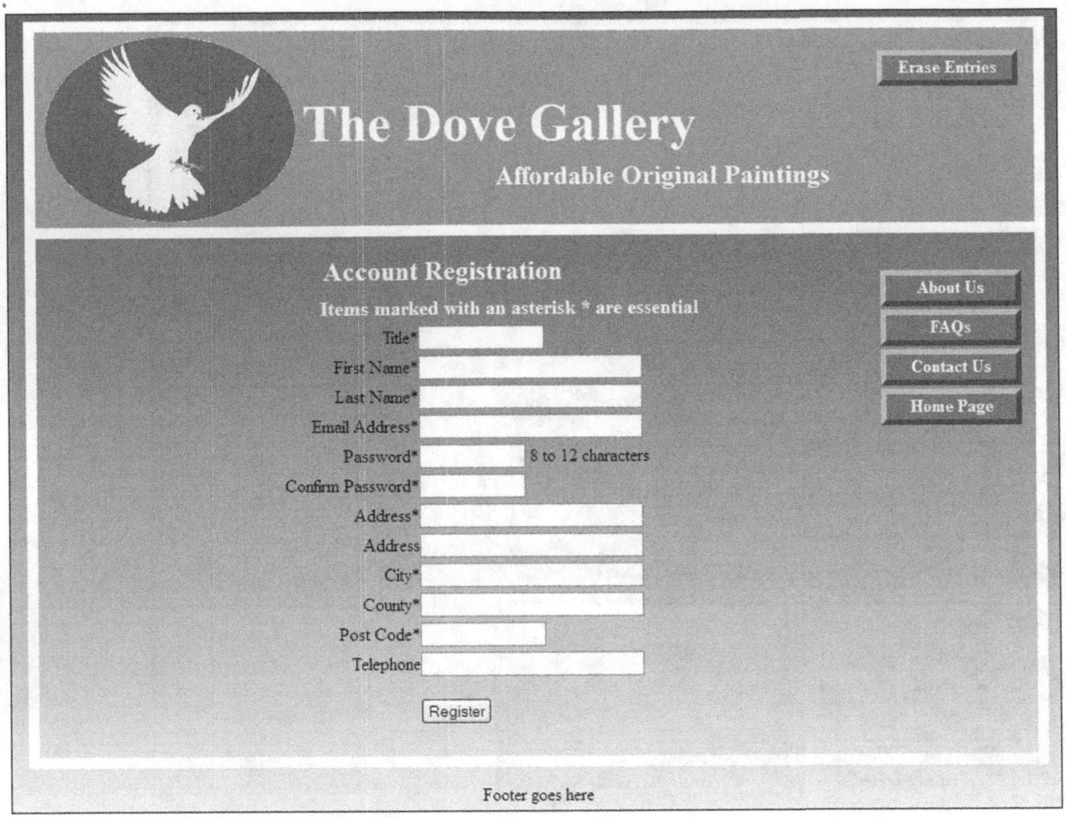

Figure 11-2. *The Registration page*

No listing is provided for this page because the code was described in Chapter 6. (The Dove Gallery styling is the only difference.) A single menu button in the header is adequate for the registration page because the user can escape to the home page using the main menu. A more comprehensive registration page would have fields for an alternative shipping address and a text area for delivery instructions. The page might also contain two radio buttons or a check box for opting out of an option to receive e-mails describing special offers. Radio buttons and check boxes were described in Chapter 7. The designer would need to create an extra column in the *users* table to contain the users' response to the option.

The administrator will register as a USER with her proper name, e-mail address and password. Then she will register as the ADMINISTRATOR by entering a fictitious name and e-mail address and a password so that she alone can log in to the administration pages.

Then phpMyAdmin is used to edit the administrator's *user_level* to a number greater than zero so that registered users and the administrator are directed to their appropriate pages when they log in.

The Header for the Registration Form

The header for the registration form requires only one menu button. This clears data from the registration fields if the user wishes to start again. No home page button is needed in the header menu because it is in the main menu. The snippet of code for the header is given in Listing 11-2.

Listing 11-2. Creating the Header for the Registration Page (header_reg.inc)

```
<div id="header-button">
<ul>
<li><a href="register.php">Erase Entries</a></li>
</ul>
</div>
<h1>The Dove Gallery</h1>
<h2>Affordable Original Paintings</h2>
```

After successfully registering, the user will see a *thank-you* page similar to those in previous chapters.

The Login Page with a *Forgotten-Password* Link

The login page is shown in Figure 11-3.

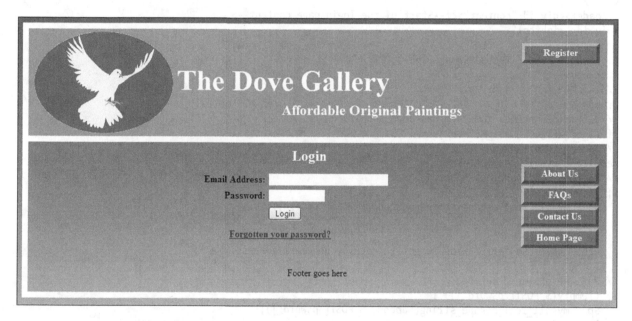

Figure 11-3. *The Login page*

The code for the login page is given in Listing 11-3

Listing 11-3. Creating the Login Page (login.php)

The form fields are positioned by means of an internal style.

```
<!doctype html>
<html lang=en>
<head>
<title>Login page</title>
<meta charset=utf-8>
<link rel="stylesheet" type="text/css" href="transparent.css">
```

```
        <style type="text/css">
        #content h2 { width:60px; margin-left:-40px; }
        p.error { color:red; font-size:105%; font-weight:bold; text-align:center;}
        form { margin-left:130px; }
        .submit { margin-left:215px; }
        .cntr { text-align:center; margin-left:20px; }
        </style>

</head>
<body>
<div id="container">
<header>
<?php include('includes/header_login.inc'); ?>
<div id="logo">
    <img alt="dove" height="170" src="images/dove-1.png" width="234">
</div>
</header><div id="content"><!--Start of the login page content-->
<div id="rightcol">
    <nav>
    <?php include('includes/menu.inc'); ?>
    </nav>
</div>
<?php
// Determine whether the form has been submitted
if ($_SERVER['REQUEST_METHOD'] == 'POST') {
//Connect to database
require ('mysqli_connect.php');
// Was the email address entered?
if (!empty($_POST['email'])) {
    $e = mysqli_real_escape_string($dbcon, $_POST['email']);
    } else {
    $e = FALSE;
    echo '<p class="error">You forgot to enter your email address.</p>';
    }
// Was the password entered?
if (!empty($_POST['psword'])) {
    $p = mysqli_real_escape_string($dbcon, $_POST['psword']);
    } else {
    $p = FALSE;
    echo '<p class="error">You forgot to enter your password.</p>';
    }
    if ($e && $p){//If no problem was encountered
// Select the user_id, first_name and user_level for that email/password combination
$q = "SELECT user_id, fname, user_level FROM users WHERE (email='$e' AND ↵
psword=SHA1('$p'))";
    $result = mysqli_query ($dbcon, $q);
// Check the result
if (@mysqli_num_rows($result) == 1) {//The user input matched the database record
// Start the session, fetch the record and insert the three values in an array
    session_start();
    $_SESSION = mysqli_fetch_array ($result, MYSQLI_ASSOC);
```

```
$_SESSION['user_level'] = (int) $_SESSION['user_level']; // Ensure the user level ↩
is an integer.
// The login page redirects the user either to the admin page or the user's search page
// Use a ternary operation to set the URL
$url = ($_SESSION['user_level'] === 51) ? 'admin_page.php' : 'users_search_page.php';
header('Location: ' . $url); // The user is directed to the appropriate page
exit(); // Cancel the rest of the script
    mysqli_free_result($result);
    mysqli_close($dbcon);
    } else { // If no match was found
echo '<p class="error">Your email address and password combination does not match our ↩
records.<br>Perhaps you need to register. Click the Register button on the header menu</p>';
    }
    } else { // If there was a problem
    echo '<p class="error">Please try again.</p>';
    }
    mysqli_close($dbcon);
    } // End of submit conditionals
?>
<!--Display the form fields-->
<div id="loginfields">
<?php include ('includes/login_page.inc.php'); ?>
</div>
<p> </p>
<p class="cntr"><a href="forgot.php"><b>Forgotten your password?</b></a></p>          #1
<footer>
<?php include ('includes/footer.inc'); ?>
</footer>
</div>
</div>
</body>
</html>
```

■ **Note**   The code for logging out is the same as in the previous chapters.

Explanation of the Login Code

The login and logout files are available in the download files for this chapter. The code for the login page is the same as the book's previous login files except for the page style and the inclusion of the following statement:

<p class="cntr"><a href="forgot.php"><b>Forgotten your password?</b></a></p>   #1

This is simply a link to the page named *forgot.php*. The code for this page is given in Listing 11-4.

Retrieving a Forgotten Password

You may have wondered why I left it for so late in the book to introduce a means of retrieving a forgotten password. My reasoning was as follows:

- I decided that the more complex PHP code required would be best introduced in a later chapter when you have become more proficient in the use of PHP.

- Password retrieval was not necessary in the earlier tutorials because you were not interacting with real users who might have forgotten their passwords.

- I assumed that the reader would not attempt to migrate a database-driven web site to an external host until he or she had at least reached Chapter 11. Password retrieval involves sending an e-mail to the user. This cannot be tested unless the reader either uploads the web site to a host or installs an e-mail-processing program on his or her computer.

■ **Caution** If you click the *Forgotten your password* link and then click the *Get a new password* button, you will cause a password to be changed. However, if you do this on a computer's server with no e-mail client, such as Mercury, you will not receive the e-mail; therefore, you will not know the new password. You will no longer be able to log in as that user. The *Get a new password* button works only if you upload the file to a server together with the database and tables. However, if you have a configured e-mail client such as Mercury installed on your computer, you would be able to test the file and receive an e-mail containing the new password.

Figure 11-4 shows the interface for retrieving a forgotten password.

Figure 11-4. *Retrieving a forgotten password*

The code for the forgotten password page is given in Listing 11-4.

Listing 11-4. Creating the Forgotten Password Page (forgot.php)

An internal style provides the layout of the form elements.

```html
<!doctype html>
<html lang=en>
<head>
<title>Forgotten password form</title>
<meta charset=utf-8>
<link rel="stylesheet" type="text/css" href="transparent.css">
        <style type="text/css">
        #content h2 { margin-left:-220px;}
        #content h2.main_title { margin-left:-100px; }
        #content h3 { margin-left:90px; }
        l { margin-top:0; }
        ul li {height:30px; }
        p { margin-bottom:-5px; }
        form { margin-left:180px; }
        #submit {margin-top:0; margin-left:215px; }
        p.error { color:red; font-size:105%; font-weight:bold; text-align:center;}
        footer { margin-left:-20px; }
        </style>
</head>
<body>
<div id="container">
<header>
<?php include('includes/header_forgot.inc'); ?>
<div id="logo">
<img alt="dove" height="170" src="images/dove-1.png" width="234">
</div>
</header>
<div id="content">
<?php
if ($_SERVER['REQUEST_METHOD'] == 'POST') {
require ('mysqli_connect.php');
// Assign the value FALSE to the variable $user_id
   $user_id = FALSE;
// If the email address has been entered, validate it
if(filter_var($_POST['email'],FILTER_VALIDATE_EMAIL)){
// Does that email address exist in the database?                              #1
$q = 'SELECT user_id FROM users WHERE email="'. mysqli_real_escape_string ↩
  ($dbcon, $_POST['email']) . '"';
$result = mysqli_query ($dbcon, $q) or trigger_error("Query: $q\n<br>↩
MySQL Error: " . mysqli_error($dbcon));
if (mysqli_num_rows($result) == 1) { // Retrieve the user's id
$row = mysqli_fetch_array($result,MYSQLI_NUM);
$user_id = $row[0];
} else { // If the users_id for that email address was not found
echo '<p class="error">That email address is not in our records</p>';
}
}
```

```
if ($user_id) { // If the user_id for the email address was found, create a random password
$p = substr ( md5(uniqid(rand(), true)), 5, 10);                                           #2
// Update the users database table with the new password
$q = "UPDATE users SET psword=SHA1('$p') WHERE user_id=$user_id LIMIT 1";
$result = mysqli_query ($dbcon, $q) or trigger_error("Query: $q\n<br>↵
MySQL Error: " . mysqli_error($dbcon));
if (mysqli_affected_rows($dbcon) == 1) { // If the password was updated successfully
// Send an email to the user
$body = "Your password has been changed to '$p'. Please log in as soon as possible ↵
using the new password. Then change it immediately. Otherwise, if a hacker has ↵
intercepted this email he will know your login details.";
mail($_POST['email'], 'Your new password.', $body, 'From: admin@thedovegallery.co.uk');   #3
// Echo a message and exit the code
echo '<h3>Your password has been changed. You will shortly receive the new temporary ↵
password by email.</h3>';
mysqli_close($dbcon);
include ('includes/footer.inc');
exit(); // Stop the script
} else { // If the query failed to run
echo '<p class="error">There was a system error, your password could not be changed. ↵
We apologize for any inconvenience.</p>';
}
}
mysqli_close($dbcon);
}
?>
<div id="rightcol">
<nav>
<?php include('includes/menu.inc'); ?>
</nav>
</div>
<h2 class="main_title">Forgotten Your Password?</h2>
<h3>When you apply, you will receive your new password in an email. Access that email↵
<br>within the next few minutes. Don't delay! For maximum security, immediately log in ↵
with your new password and then change the password as quickly as possible.<br></h3>
<form action="forgot.php" method="post">
<p><label class="label" for="email"><b>Your email adddress</b></label> ↵
<input id="email" type="text" name="email" size="30" maxlength="30" ↵
value="<?php if (isset($_POST['email'])) echo $_POST['email']; ?>"><br>
<p><input id="submit" type="submit" name="submit" value="Get a new password"></p>
</form>
<footer>
<?php include ('includes/footer.inc'); ?>
</footer><br></div>
<div></div></div>
</body>
</html>
```

Explanation of the Code

```
// Does that email address exist in the database?                              #1
$q = 'SELECT user_id FROM users WHERE email="'. mysqli_real_escape_string ↵
($dbcon, $_POST['email']) . '"';
$result = mysqli_query ($dbcon, $q) or trigger_error("Query: $q\n<br>↵
MySQL Error: " . mysqli_error($dbcon));
```

The first statement cleans the e-mail address before it is used in the SELECT statement. In the second statement, you will not have seen the *trigger error()* function before. This is a standard PHP function and a neat way of displaying error messages during development. The script will stop if an error is detected, and an informative error message will be displayed.

```
$p = substr ( md5(uniqid(rand(), true)), 5, 10);                               #2
// Update the users table with the new password
$q = "UPDATE users SET psword=SHA1('$p') WHERE user_id=$user_id LIMIT 1";
$result = mysqli_query ($dbcon, $q) or trigger_error("Query: $q\n<br>↵
MySQL Error: " . mysqli_error($dbcon));
if (mysqli_affected_rows($dbcon) == 1) { // If the password was updated successfully
// Send an email to the user
```

The first line creates a new randomly generated string. It is hashed using the slightly less secure md5 hashing method. The md5 string will be 32 characters long. Note the digits (5 and 10); they select a 10-digit portion of the string starting at the fifth digit. In the third line, the UPDATE query enters the shortened string into the *users* table using the more secure SHA1 hashing method.

The *trigger_error()* function is used again in the fourth line. The shortened and randomly generated string is the user's new temporary password. This is sent to the user in an e-mail (reference line **#3**).

A plan for the role of administrator will be described next.

Administration

The administrator should be able to do the following:

- Add or remove an artist.
- Add paintings to the catalog.
- Remove paintings from the catalog when they are sold.
- Update prices.
- View users' details.
- View the orders.
- Change his own password.

Due to space limitations, only the first two tasks are described in this chapter. Several other tasks are omitted; for instance, in a real-world e-commerce web site, the administrator's team would also be able to view the orders, process the orders, control the stock situation, and manage customer services. There are some downloadable administration files, but others (such as those enabling the administrator to edit and delete data in the database tables) are not provided because they are similar to the administration files shown previously in Chapters 2, 3, and 8.

The administration page will be described next.

347

Creating the Administration Page

When the administrator logs in, she will be taken straight to a dual-purpose administration page that will enable her to add an artist. Figure 11-5 shows the *administration/add an artist* page. Note the new header menu buttons.

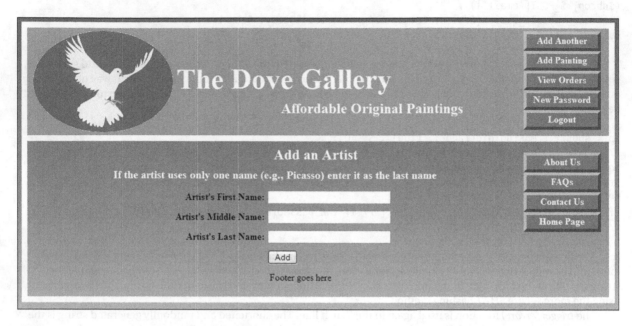

Figure 11-5. *The administration/"Add an Artist" page*

The administration page has several new header buttons, including a *New Password* button. For brevity the third and fourth menu buttons are not active. This avoids having to repeat the code from Chapters 2 and 3 in this already overcrowded chapter, but feel free to add the links and their pages if you wish. The administration page is also the *Add an Artist* page. The code starts with a session to ensure that only the administrator can access this page. The *admin_page.php* is a shortened version of the *add-a-house* page in Chapter 8. For brevity, the code will not be repeated here. The file *admin_page.php* is included in the downloadable files so that you can examine it. However, you should not attempt to add artists because file *artist.sql* is provided with the demonstration files for the custom shopping cart.

Add an Artist

For viewing the demonstration custom cart described later, three artists are included in the downloadable file *artists.sql*. They are listed in Table 11-1.

Table 11-1. *The Artists' Names*

First name	Middle name	Last name
Adrian	W	West
Roger	St.	Barbe
James		Kessell

Searching and Displaying Products

When registered users log in, they will be directed to the search page. The search criteria in this example are based on the type and price of paintings. Other fields could be added, such as size, medium, and an artist's name. In that case, all the fields would be given NULL attributes so that users can choose to limit their search criteria. For instance, they might wish to search for abstract oil paintings, at a certain maximum price, by a particular artist. Or they might wish to search for all the paintings by a particular artist. Our simplified minimal search page is shown in Figure 11-6.

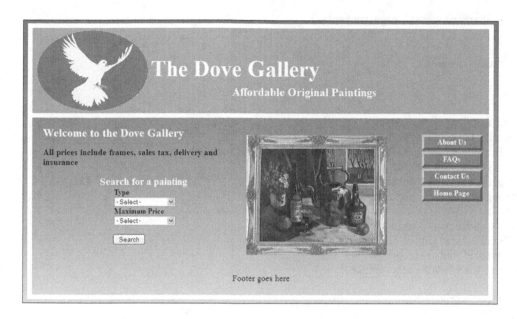

Figure 11-6. *The users' search page*

The page allows registered users to search for a particular type of painting (still-life, nature, or abstract) and to set the maximum price they are willing to pay. This page is also the home page in the PayPal version of the web site. In the PayPal version, the code does not begin with a session because users do not have to log in.

The code for the users' search page is given in Listing 11-6.

Listing 11-6. Creating the Users' Search Page (users_search_page.php)

```
The session and DOCTYPE go here
<title><title>The registered user's search page, custom cart version</title></title>
<meta charset=utf-8>
<link rel="stylesheet" type="text/css" href="transparent.css">
        <style type="text/css">
        p { font-size:110%; }
        #midcol h2 { width:400px; }
        #mid-left-col h3 {font-size:150%; text-align:left; }
        select { width:130px; }
        form { margin-left:150px; }
        .search { margin:0 0 0 120px; font-weight:bold; font-size:130%; color:white; }
        #submit { width:70px; position:absolute; left:190px; }
        </style>
</head>
```

```
<body>
<div id="container">
<header>
<?php include('includes/header_forgot.inc'); ?>
<div id="logo">
  <img alt="dove" height="170" src="images/dove-1.png" width="234">
</div>
</header>
<div id="content"><!--Start of users' page content-->
<div id="rightcol">
   <nav>
   <?php include('includes/menu.inc'); ?>
   </nav>
</div>
<div id="midcol">
<div id="mid-left-col">
   <h3><b>Welcome to the Dove Gallery</b></h3>
   <p><b>All prices include frames, sales tax, delivery and insurance</b></p>
   <p class="search"><strong>Search for a painting</strong></p>
<form action="found_pics_cart.php" method="post">                              #1
   <strong>Type</strong><br>
   <select name="type">
     <option value="">- Select -</option>
     <option value="still-life">Still Life</option>
     <option value="nature">Nature</option>
     <option value="abstract">Abstract</option>
   </select><br>
   <strong>Maximum Price</strong><br>
   <select name="price">
     <option value="">- Select -</option>
     <option value="40">&pound;40</option>
     <option value="80">&pound;80</option>
     <option value="800">&pound;800</option>
     </select><br>
   <p><input id="submit" type="submit" name="submit" value="Search"></p>
</form>
</div>
<div id="mid-right-col">
<p><img alt="Copper Kettle by James Kessell" height="254" width="300"↵
 src="images/k-copper-kettle-300.jpg"></p>
</div>
<br class="clear">
</div>
<footer>
<?php include ('includes/footer.inc'); ?>
</footer></div>
</div>
</body>
</html>
```

Explanation of the Code

```
<form action="found_pics_cart.php" method="post">
```
#1

The file *found_pics_cart.php* is one of the demonstration files for the custom cart described later.

Features Applicable Only to the PayPal Shopping Cart

In the downloadable files, there is a subfolder named *shopper* for demonstrating the PayPal version of the e-commerce web site; the subfolder contains instructions for setting up the PayPal shopping cart database and tables. In the subfolder, you will find a different version of the *admin_add_painting.php* interface that allows the administrator to insert the PayPal shopping cart code. This is described next.

■ **Note**   This example assumes the use of PayPal buttons downloaded from a PayPal account for processing the purchase of a painting. Guidance for downloading PayPal buttons is given later in this section. Note that PayPal can also be integrated with a custom shopping cart.

The tables for the custom shopping cart are shown later in the chapter. The *art* table for a PayPal shopping cart is slightly different from the custom shopping cart *art* table. Note that an extra column is used to hold the code for the PayPal shopping cart buttons, this is shown in Table 11-2. The *.sql* file can be found in the *shopper* subfolder.

Table 11-2. *The art Table for a PayPal Shopping Cart*

Columnname	Type	Length/values	Default	Attributes	NULL	Index	A_I
art_id	INT	8	None	UNSIGNED	☐	PRIMARY	☑
thumb	VARCHAR	50					
type	VARCHAR	50	None		☐		☐
price	DECIMAL	6,2	None	UNSIGNED	☐	INDEX	☐
medium	VARCHAR	50	None		☐		☐
artist_id	INT	8	None	UNSIGNED	☐		☐
description	VARCHAR	150	None		☐		☐
ppcode	TEXT	500	None		☐		☐

Different payment systems might require tables that match their particular process. In this chapter, we will only be covering a PayPal cart and a custom cart.

The administrator's interface for adding paintings and PayPal code is shown in Figure 11-7.

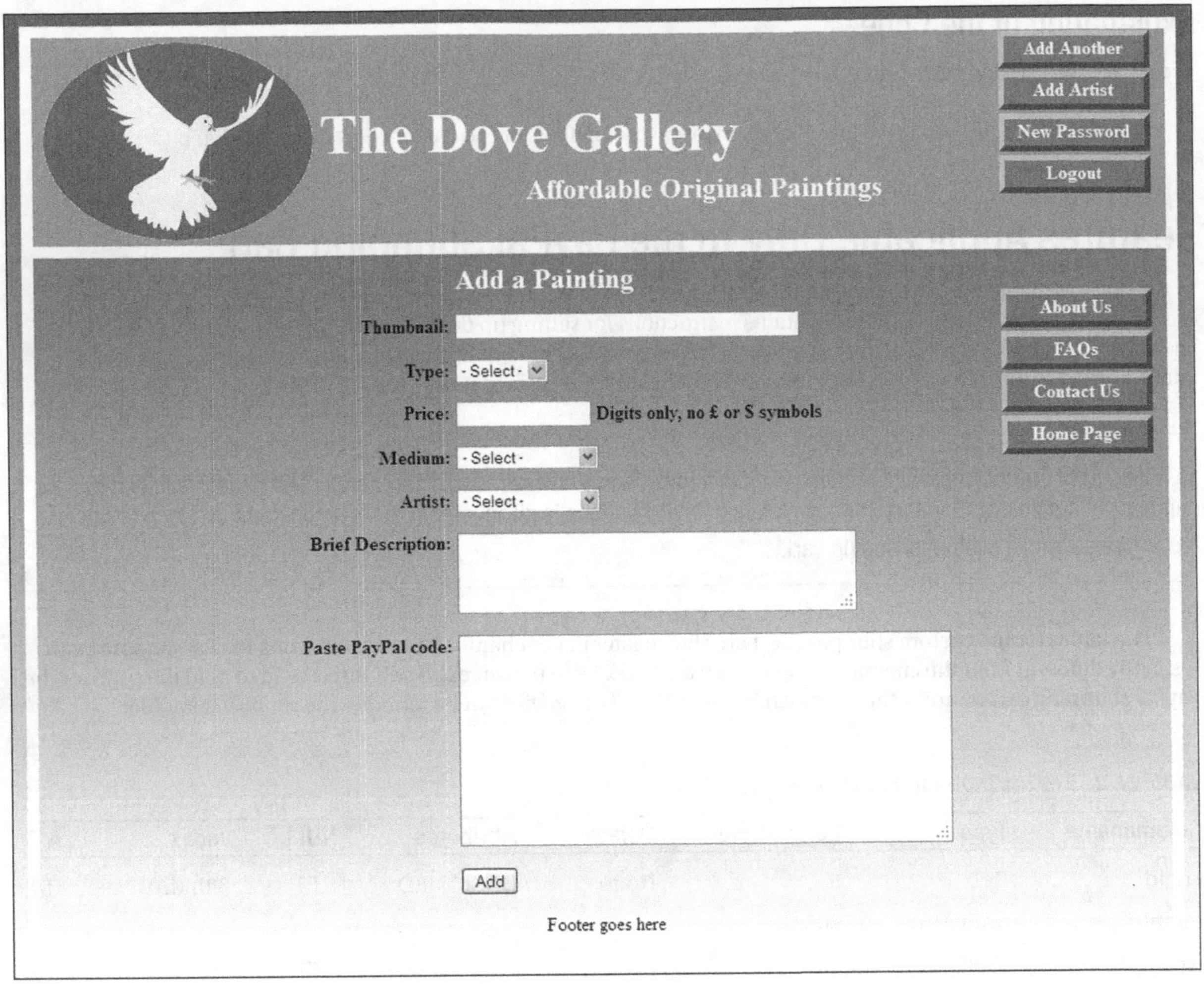

Figure 11-7. *The administrator's interface for adding paintings and PayPal "Add to Cart" buttons*

The code for this page must begin with a session so that it can be accessed only by the administrator. The page is similar to the *add-a-house page* in Chapter 8, and the procedure is exactly the same as the instructions in Chapter 8. However, in this example an additional text area is included for the PayPal code. The procedure for obtaining the PayPal code is described later. Part of the code for the page is given in Listing 11-7a, where the PayPal item is shown in bold type. The code for a pull-down menu for artists is also shown in bold type. The downloadable code is included in the subfolder named *shopper*.

Partial Listing 11-7a. Creating the Page for Adding a Painting (admin_add_painting.php)

```
The session and the DOCTYPE go here
<title>The admin_add_painting page with a PayPal code textarea)</title>
<meta charset=utf-8>
<link rel="stylesheet" type="text/css" href="transparent.css">
        <style type="text/css">
        #header-button { margin-top:-10px; }
        #content h2 { margin-left:-70px; }
```

```
        form { margin-left:140px; }
        p.error { color:red; font-size:105%; font-weight:bold; text-align:center;}
        #submit { margin-left:-170px; }
        </style>
</head>
<body>
<div id="container">
<header>
<?php include('includes/header_admin.inc'); ?>
<div id="logo">
    <img alt="dove" height="170" src="images/dove-1.png" width="234">
</div>
</header>
<div id="content"><!--Start of admin/add paintings content-->
<?php
// This code is a query that INSERTs a painting into the art table
// Confirm that the form has been submitted
if ($_SERVER['REQUEST_METHOD'] == 'POST') {
    $errors = array(); // Start an array to contain the error messages
// Check if a thumbnail url has been entered
    if (empty($_POST['thumb'])) {
    $errors[] = 'You forgot to enter the thumbnail url';
    }else{
    $thumb = ($_POST['thumb']);
    }
// Check for a type
    if (empty($_POST['type'])) {
    $errors[] = 'You forgot to select the type of painting';
    }else{
    $type = trim($_POST['type']);
    }
// Has a price been entered?
    if (empty($_POST['price'])){
    $errors[] ='You forgot to enter the price.' ;
    }
    elseif (!empty($_POST['price'])) {
//Remove unwanted characters and ensure that the remaining characters are digits
    $price = preg_replace('/\D+/', '', ($_POST['price']));
    }
// Has the medium been entered?
    if (empty($_POST['medium'])) {
    $errors[] = 'You forgot to select the medium';
    }else{
    $medium = ($_POST['medium']);
    }
// Has the artist been entered?
    if (empty($_POST['artist'])) {
    $errors[] = 'You forgot to select the artist';
    }else {
    $artist = ($_POST['artist']);
    }
```

```php
// Has a brief description been entered?
   if (empty($_POST['mini_descr'])) {
   $errors[] = 'You forgot to enter the brief description';
   }else{
   $mini_descr = strip_tags($_POST['mini_descr']);
    }
// Has the PayPal code been entered?                                      #1
   if (empty($_POST['ppcode'])) {
   $errors[] = 'You forgot to enter the PayPal code';
   }else{
   $ppcode = ($_POST['ppcode']);
   }
if (empty($errors)) { // If no errors were encountered, register the painting in the database
   require ('mysqli_connect.php'); // Connect to the database
// Make the query                                                         #2
$q = "INSERT INTO art (art_id, thumb, type, price, medium, artist, mini_descr, ppcode) ↵
VALUES (' ', '$thumb', '$type', '$price', '$medium', '$artist', '$mini_descr', '$ppcode' )";
   $result = @mysqli_query ($dbcon, $q); // Run the query.
   if ($result) { // If the query ran without a problem
   echo '<h2>The painting was successfully registered</h2><br>';
   } else { // If it was not registered, display an error message
   echo '<h2>System Error</h2>
<p class="error">The painting could not be added due to a system error. We apologize for ↵
any inconvenience.</p>';
// Debugging message
   echo '<p>' . mysqli_error($dbcon) . '<br><br>Query: ' . $q . '</p>';
} // End of the if ($result)
   mysqli_close($dbcon); // Close the database connection
   } else { // Display the errors messages
   echo '<h2>Error!</h2>
   <p class="error">The following error(s) occurred:<br>';
   foreach ($errors as $msg) { // Print each error.
   echo " - $msg<br>\n";
   }
   echo '</p><h3>Please try again.</h3><p><br></p>';
}// End of the if (empty($errors))
   } // End of the main submit conditionals
?>
<div id="rightcol">
<nav>
<?php include('includes/menu.inc'); ?>
</nav>
</div>
<h2>Add a Painting</h2>
<form  action="admin_page_pp.php" method="post">↵
<p><label class="label" for="thumb"><b>Thumbnail:</b></label>
<input id="thumb" type="text" name="thumb" size="45" maxlength="45"↵
value="<?php if (isset($_POST['thumb'])) echo $_POST['thumb']; ?>"></p>
<p><label class="label"><b>Type:</b></label>
```

```
<select name="type" >
    <option value="">- Select -</option>
    <option value="Still-life">Still Life</option>
    <option value="Nature">Nature</option>
    <option value="Abstract">Abstract</option>
</select><br>
<p><label class="label" for="price"><b>Price:</b></label>↵
<input id="price" type="text" name="price" size="15" maxlength="15" ↵
value="<?php if (isset($_POST['price'])) echo $_POST['price']; ?>"></p>
<p><label class="label"><b>Medium:</b></label>↵
<select name="medium" >
    <option value="">- Select -</option>
    <option value="Oil-painting">Oil Painting</option>
    <option value="Colored-etching">Colored Etching</option>
</select><br>
<p><label class="label"><b>Artist:</b></label>
<select name="artist" >                                          #3
    <option value="">- Select -</option
    <option value="Adrian-W-West">Adrian W West</option>
    <option value="Roger-St-Barbe">Roger St. Barbe</option>
    <option value="James-Kessell">James Kessell</option>
</select><br>
<p><label class="label"><b>Brief Description:</b></label>
<textarea name="mini_descr" rows="3" cols="40"></textarea></p>
<p><label class="label"><b>Paste PayPal code:</b></label>
//insert a text area for the PayPal code
<textarea name="ppcode" rows="10" cols="50"></textarea></p>       #4
    <div id="submit">
    <p><input id="submit" type="submit" name="submit" value="Add"></p>
    </div>
</form><!--End of the "add a painting content"-->
<div>
<footer>
<?php include ('includes/footer.inc'); ?>
</footer></div>
</div>
</div>
</body>
</html>
```

Explanation of the Code

Line numbers **#1**, **#2** and **#4** will process the PayPal code; line number **#3** starts the pull-down list of artists and this is explained next.

```
<select name="artist">                                          #3
    <option value="">- Select -</option
    <option value="Adrian-W-West">Adrian W West</option>
    <option value="Roger-St-Barbe">Roger St. Barbe</option>
    <option value="James-Kessell">James Kessell</option>
</select>
```

Because this example web site uses only three artists for brevity, the pull-down menu for the *artist* field is hard-coded. However, e-commerce web sites should be extensible in the hope that the business will grow. In our example, the owner hopes that the number of artists will increase, also, some names may be dropped and others will be added. To dynamically change the pull down list of artists to accommodate a larger number of artists, new artist, and discontinued artists, the pull-down list would preferably retrieve artists from the *artists* table.

This can be achieved by replacing the hard-coded section with the code given in Listing 11-7b. This code can be used in other types of database-driven web sites; therefore, it is included in the downloadable files for this chapter.

Listing 11-7b. Replacing the Pull-Down Hard Code So That It Pulls Data from the Artists Table (get_artists.php)

```
<select name="artist">
    <option>--Select the artist--</option>
<?php // Fetch all the artists from the artist table and insert them in the artist pull-↵
down menu
$q = "SELECT artist_id, CONCAT_WS(' ', first_name, middle_name, last_name) ↵
FROM artists ORDER BY last_name, first_name ASC";
    $result = mysqli_query ($dbcon, $q);
if (mysqli_num_rows($result) > 0) {
    while ($row = mysqli_fetch_array ($result, MYSQLI_NUM)) {
    echo "<option value=\"$row[0]\"";
// Ensure that the form names are sticky
if (isset($_POST['artist']) && ($_POST['artist'] == $row[0]) ) echo ' selected="selected"';
    echo ">$row[1]</option>\n";
    }
    } else {
    echo '<option>Please add a new artist</option>';
    }
    mysqli_close($dbcon); // Close the database connection.
    ?>
</select></p>
```

Integrating with the PayPal Shopping Cart

PayPal is secure and familiar to millions throughout the world. The PayPal payment buttons are encoded so that the prices cannot be manipulated by rogue customers. When a product is paid for, PayPal will send the administrator an e-mail containing the following information: the date and ID of the transaction, the amount paid, the e-mail address of the user, the user's delivery address, and a description of the purchased item.

■ **Note**   PayPal provides a safe, self-contained environment called *Sandbox*. This enables web-site developers to test PayPal transactions without paying real money.

The PayPal payment system will not be described in detail because this would need its own chapter (or two). A full description would probably become obsolete anyway, because PayPal frequently updates and simplifies the process. Instead of giving detailed instructions, I provided this overview so that you know what to look for on the PayPal web site. PayPal and other PayPal resources provide plenty of instructions on their web sites. Two helpful forums are listed in the appendix. They will help you learn about configuring PayPal and will solve problems you might meet when integrating the cart buttons with your web site.

To create a business account, access the PayPal web site for your territory (for example, www.paypal.com for the USA or www.paypal.co.uk for the UK). Registration is free and not difficult to set up. Then access your business account, click the business tab, and use the search field to locate the necessary buttons and logos.

Each product in the e-commerce catalog will require its unique *Add to Cart* button. These can be fully configured using your account on the PayPal web site. The code for each button can then be copied and pasted into the database's *art* table. In our example, this is achieved by pasting the code into the PayPal textarea of the page shown in Figure 11-7.

■ **Note**   The PayPal buttons will not be visible on the *search results* page unless you are online.

PayPal provides several credit/debit card logos. The logos inform users that payments can be made even if they do not have a PayPal account. Figure 11-8 shows two standard encoded PayPal buttons and a horizontal version of a credit/debit card logo.

Figure 11-8. *The appearance of the buttons and credit/debit card logo*

The dummy codes for the PayPal buttons are included in this chapter's downloadable subfolder named *shopper*. The code for real-world PayPal buttons will be unique and will apply only to products on your own e-commerce web site.

The code for an *Add to Cart* button will be similar to the example in Listing 11-8a. For security, the ID value for each product is given as XXXXXXX, but real-world buttons will have digits instead of Xs.

Listing 11-8a. Sample Code for a PayPal "Add to Cart" Button

```
<form target="paypal" action="https://www.paypal.com/cgi-bin/webscr" method="post">
<input name="cmd" value="_s-xclick" type="hidden">
<input name="hosted_button_id" value="XXXXXXX" type="hidden">
<p><input src="https://www.paypal.com/en_GB/i/btn/btn_cart_LG.gif" name="submit" ↵
alt="PayPal - The safer, easier way to pay online." style="float: left;" border="0" ↵
type="image"><img alt="" src="https://www.paypal.com/en_GB/i/scr/pixel.gif" border="0" ↵
height="1" width="1"></p>
</form>
```

You need to place a PayPal *View Cart* button in the header of the shop's *found_paintings* pages. The code for the *View Cart* button will be something like Listing 11-8b.

Listing 11-8b. The Code for a PayPal "View Cart" Button

The dummy e-mail address shown in bold type must be replaced by the PayPal account owner's e-mail address. When an order is checked out, PayPal will send the details in an e-mail to that address.

```
<form name="_xclick" target="paypal" ↵
action="https://www.paypal.com/uk/cgi-bin/webscr" method="post">
<input type="hidden" name="cmd" value="_cart"> ↵
<input type="hidden" name="business" value="me@mybusiness.co.uk"> ↵
<input type="image" src="https://www.paypal.com/en_GB/i/btn/view_cart.gif" border="0" ↵
name="submit" alt="Make payments with PayPal - it's fast, free and secure!"> ↵
<input type="hidden" name="display" value="1">
</form>
```

■ **Caution**   When configuring a unique PayPal button for each product in the shop, the configuration must include the price, the currency (US dollars or GB pounds), the name of the item being purchased, and the product identity number. Most importantly, ensure that you configure the PayPal buttons so that the user is prompted to enter a delivery address. The PayPal buttons will be automatically encoded.

Displaying the Result of a Search

Figure 11-9 shows the result of a search for nature paintings costing £40 each or less.

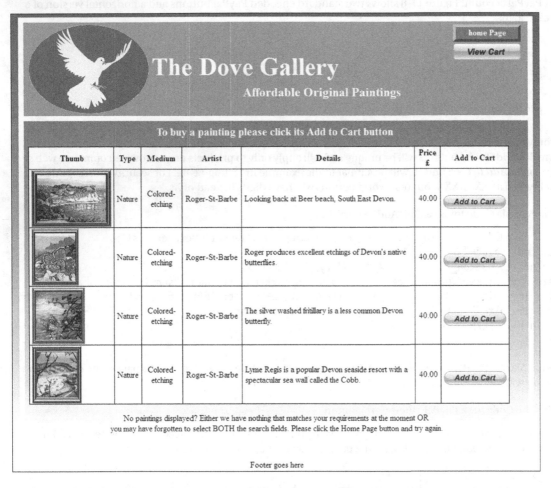

Figure 11-9. *The result of searching for nature paintings costing £40 or less*

The PayPal *Add to Cart* and *View Cart* buttons link directly to PayPal, so that when an *Add to Cart* button is clicked, the PayPal cart is actioned automatically. When the *View Cart* button is clicked, PayPal displays the cart information in the user's browser.

The file for Listing 11-9a is included in the downloadable subfolder *shopper*.

Listing 11-9a. Creating a Page for Displaying Search Results (found_paintings.php)

```
The session and the DOCTYPE go here.
<title>The page for displaying the found paintings</title>
<meta charset=utf-8>
<link rel="stylesheet" type="text/css" href="transparent.css">
        <style type="text/css">
        body { margin:auto; }
        p{ text-align:center; }
        table, td, th { width:930px; border-collapse:collapse; border:1px black solid; ↵
        background:white;}
        td, th { padding-left:5px; padding-right:5px; text-align:center; }
        td.narrow, th.narrow { width:45px;}
        td.descr { text-align:left; }
        td.medium, th.medium { width:100px;}
        td.artist, th.artist { width:210px;}
        td.thumb, th.thumb { width:125px; text-align:center;}
        #content h3 { text-align:center; font-size:130%; font-weight:bold;}
        img { display:block;}
        #header-button { margin-top:-5px;}
        </style>
</head>
<body>
<div id="container">
<header>
<?php include('includes/header_found_pics.inc'); ?>
<div id="logo">
   <img alt="dove" height="170" src="images/dove-1.png" width="234">
   </div>
</header>
<div id="content"><!--Start of table display content-->
<h3>To buy a painting please click its Add to Cart button</h3>
<p>
<?php
$type=$_POST['type'];
$price=$_POST['price'];
require ('mysqli_connect.php'); // Connect to the database
// Fetch the records that match the search criteria
$q = "SELECT art_id, thumb, type, price, medium, artist, mini_descr, ppcode ↵
FROM art WHERE type='$type' AND price <= '$price' ORDER BY price ASC ";
$result = @mysqli_query ($dbcon, $q);
if ($result) { // If the query encountered no problems, display the records
// Table header
echo '<table>
   <tr>
      <th class="thumb"><b>Thumb</b></th>
      <th class="narrow"><b>Type</b></th>
      <th class="medium"><b>Medium</b></th>
      <th class="artist"><b>Artist</b></th>
      <th class="descr"><b>Details</b></th>
```

#1

```
      <th class="narrow"><b>Price</b></th>
      <th class="medium"><b>Add to Cart</b></th>
   </tr>';
// Fetch and echo the matching records
while ($row = mysqli_fetch_array($result, MYSQLI_ASSOC)) {
echo '<tr>
      <td class="thumb"><img src='.$row['thumb'] . '></td>
      <td class="narrow">' . $row['type'] . '</td>
      <td class="medium">' . $row['medium'] . '</td>
      <td class="artist">' . $row['artist'] . '</td>
      <td class="descr">' . $row['mini_descr'] . '</td>
      <td class="narrow">' . $row['price'] . '</td>
      <td class="medium">' . $row['ppcode'] . '</td>
      </tr>';
      }
echo '</table>'; // Close the table
   mysqli_free_result ($result); // Free up the resources
   } else { // If the query encountered a problem
// Error message
   echo '<p class="error">The records could not be retrieved. We apologize for any ↵
inconvenience.</p>';
// Debugging error message:
   echo '<p>' . mysqli_error($dbcon) . '<br><br>Query: ' . $q . '</p>';
   } // End of if ($result)
mysqli_close($dbcon); // Close the database connection
?>
<p>No paintings displayed? Either we have nothing that matches your requirements ↵
at the moment OR<br>you may have forgotten to select BOTH the search fields. Please ↵
click the Home Page button and try again.</p>
</div><!--End of table display content-->
<?php include("includes/footer.inc"); ?>
</div>
</body>
</html>
```

Explanation of the Code

```
<tr>                                                                    #1
   <th class="thumb"><b>Thumb</b></th>
   <th class="narrow"><b>Type</b></th>
   <th class="medium"><b>Medium</b></th>
   <th class="artist"><b>Artist</b></th>
   <th class="descr"><b>Details</b></th>
   <th class="narrow"><b>Price</b></th>
   <th class="medium"><b>Add to Cart</b></th>
</tr>';
```

The words *thumb, narrow, medium, artist,* and *descr* set the width of the displayed columns. Refer to the internal style at the beginning of the listing to see the widths of these columns.

The code for the *found_pics* header is given in Listing 11-9b.

Listing 11-9b. Creating the User's Page Header (header_found_pics.inc)

```
<div id="header-button">
    <ul>
     <li><a href="index.php">home Page</a></li>
     <form name="_xclick" target="paypal"
      action="https://www.paypal.com/uk/cgi-bin/webscr" method="post">
      <input type="hidden" name="cmd" value="_cart">
      <input type="hidden" name="business" value="me@mybusiness.co.uk">
      <input type="image" src="https://www.paypal.com/en_GB/i/btn/view_cart.gif" border="0" ↵
      name="submit" alt="Make payments with PayPal - it's fast, free and secure!">
      <input type="hidden" name="display" value="1">
     </form>
...</ul>
</div>
<h1>The Dove Gallery</h1>
<h2>Affordable Original Paintings</h2>
```

That concludes the brief description of a PayPal shopping cart. I will now describe a demonstration custom shopping cart so that you can discover how a custom shopping cart works.

A Custom Shopping Cart

Many e-commerce web sites use their own custom shopping cart. By this, I mean a shopping cart designed by the web-site developer. This helps to maintain customer records and re-orders.

Custom carts can be linked to a payment system such as PayPal. The code for achieving the PayPal link is beyond the scope of this brief description, but resources for integrating PayPal with a custom cart are included in the Appendix. Custom shopping carts are complex and require several interactive pages to replace the online PayPal system. The process is best described by a flow chart such as the one shown in Figure 11-10.

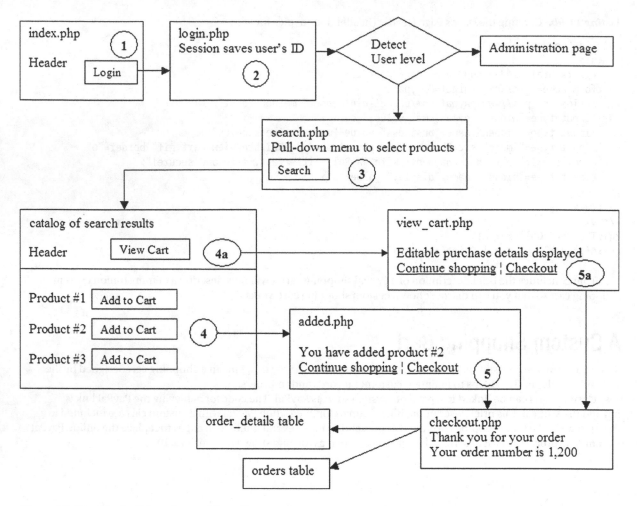

Figure 11-10. *A typical shopping cart flow diagram*

The numbered circles indicate the steps taken by a user. After logging in (step 2), the user's ID is saved in a session that passes to all the subsequent pages. The user level is detected, and the user is redirected to a search page (step 3); our example has pull-down menus containing search criteria. The user selects the search criteria and clicks the *Search* button. She is then redirected to a catalog of products that match her search criteria. If the user decides to buy a painting, she will click its *Add to Cart* button (step 4). This sends the product ID and the user ID to the cart; a message confirming the action is displayed (step 5). The display has a *Continue shopping* link and a link to the *Checkout* page. Clicking the *Continue shopping* link returns the user to the shop page (step 4) where the user can add more products. If the user clicks the *View Cart* button on the header menu, she will be shown a tabular display showing the products she has chosen and the cost. This tabular display allows the user to change the quantities or remove an item from the cart.

The Database and Tables

Downloadable images and files are provided only for demonstrating the custom shopping cart. The search page and the *search results* page are hard-coded so that you can instantly explore the workings of a custom shopping cart. To view the demonstration, follow these steps:

1. Create a folder in htdocs named *ecommerce*.

2. In phpMyAdmin, create a database named *shopdb* using the *user* and *password* given in the connection file listed next.

    The downloadable file for accessing the database is *mysqli_connect.php* and has the following code:

    ```php
    <?php
    $dbcon = @mysqli_connect ( 'localhost', 'turing', 'computerman', 'shopdb' )
    # If it fails
    OR die ( mysqli_connect_error() ) ;
    # Set the encoding
    mysqli_set_charset( $dbcon, 'utf8') ;
    ?>
    ```

3. Use phpMyAdmin to import the downloadable *.sql* files to create the already populated tables.

When you have complete steps 1 to 3, you can begin to explore the cart.

Exploring the Custom Shopping Cart

With XAMPP running, type **localhost/ecommerce/** in the address field of a modern browser (not Internet Explorer 8), and then follow these steps:

1. Log in as Rose Bush using the e-mail address *rbush@myisp.co.uk* and the password *redblooms*.

2. When the search results page appears, select any type of painting and any maximum price. The hard code will ignore what you select and send you directly to the page with *Add to Cart* links.

3. When the search results page appears, click any *Add to cart* link and then click the *View cart* button.

4. In the cart view, try changing the quantity from 1 to 2, and then click the *Update cart* link.

5. In the cart view, click the *Continue shopping* link and add another painting. Then click the *View Cart* button on the header menu.

6. To remove a painting from the cart view, change one of the quantities to zero and click the *Update cart* link.

The populated tables and the PHP files are in the downloads for the custom shopping cart demonstration. For your information, the five tables and the file listings are shown next.

The Tables

The minimal *artists* table has four columns, as shown in Table 11-3.

Table 11-3. *The artists Table*

Columnname	Type	Length/values	Default	Attributes	NULL	Index	A_I
artist_id	INT	8	None	UNSIGNED	☐	PRIMARY	☑
afname	VARCHAR	30	None		☑		☐
amname	VARCHAR	30	None		☑		☐
alname	VARCHAR	40	None		☐		☐

Because the user or administrator might wish to do a full text search for an artist, the MyISAM storage engine was selected for the *artists* table. With the latest versions of XAMPP, MySQL, and PHP, the INNODB storage engine also allows full text searches.

The details of the paintings are stored in a table named *art* with seven columns, as shown in Table 11-4.

Table 11-4. *The art Table*

Columnname	Type	Length/values	Default	Attributes	NULL	Index	A_I
art_id	INT	8	None	UNSIGNED	☐	PRIMARY	☑
thumb	VARCHAR	50	None		☐		☐
type	VARCHAR	30	None		☐		☐
medium	VARCHAR		None		☐		☐
artist_id	INT	8	None	UNSIGNED	☐		☐
mini_descr	VARCHAR	150	None		☐		☐
price	DECIMAL	6,2	None	UNSIGNED	☐	INDEX	☐

Again, this used the MyISAM storage engine to enable a full text search. With the latest versions of XAMPP, MySQL, and PHP, the INNODB storage engine also allows full text searches. The column named *thumb* is for storing the URLs for thumbnail images of the paintings. The description column contains the name of the painting, its size, some information about the picture, such as whether an oil painting was painted on canvas or board. A real-world *art* table might also include a column for the URLs of enlarged versions of the paintings. Note that the downloadable table has no column for PayPal shopping cart button code.

The minimal *orders* table has four columns, the order ID, the user ID, the price, and the order date. This is shown in Table 11-5.

Table 11-5. *The orders Table*

Columnname	Type	Length/Values	Default	Attributes	NULL	Index	A_I
order_id	INT	8	None	UNSIGNED	☐	PRIMARY	☑
user_id	INT	8	None	UNSIGNED	☐	INDEX	☐
total_price	DECIMAL	7,2	None		☐		☐
order_date	TIMESTAMP		None			INDEX	

The *orders* table needs to be able to join with other tables; therefore, the INNODB storage engine was used.

A table named *order_contents* with five columns contains various IDs, the price, the quantity ordered, and the dispatch date, as shown in Table 11-6.

Table 11-6. *A Minimal Order Contents Table*

Columnname	Type	Length/Values	Default	Attributes	NULL	Index	A_I
content_id	INT	8	None	UNSIGNED	☐	PRIMARY	☑
order_id	INT	8	None	UNSIGNED	☐	INDEX	☐
art_id	INT	8	None	UNSIGNED	☐	INDEX	☐
price	DECIMAL	5,2	None	UNSIGNED	☐	INDEX	☐
quantity	INT	4	None	UNSIGNED	☐		☐
dispatch_date	DATETIME	60	None		☐		☐

To link this table with other tables, the INNODB storage engine was chosen.

Normally, there would be a column for quantity, and this is shown for completeness in Table 11-6. However, if the paintings are originals (as in our example web site), only one of each exists—in which case, a quantity column is not required. If the shop sold prints or ink cartridges, a quantity column would be essential. Columns for the dispatch address and special delivery instructions would also be included.

The simplistic *order* and *order_contents* tables are presented only to make the statement that similar tables would be part of an e-commerce web site.

Finally, the *users* table for the e-commerce web-site has 14 columns, as shown in Table 11-7.

Table 11-7. *The Types and Attributes for a Minimal users Table*

Column name	Type	Length/Values	Default	Attributes	NULL	Index	A_I
user_id	MEDIUMINT	8	None	UNSIGNED	☐	PRIMARY	☑
title	VARCHAR	12	None		☐		☐
fname	VARCHAR	30	None		☐		☐
lname	VARCHAR	40	None		☐		☐
email	VARCHAR	50	None		☐		☐
psword	CHAR	40	None		☐		☐
reg_date	DATETIME		None		☐		☐
user_level	TINYINT	2	None	UNSIGNED	☐		☐
addr1	VARCHAR	50	None		☐		☐
addr2	VARCHAR	50	None		☑		☐
city	VARCHAR	50	None		☐		☐
county	VARCHAR	30	None		☐		☐
pcode	VARCHAR	10	None		☐		☐
phone	VARCHAR	15	None		☑		☐

An administrator might wish to carry out a full text search of the registered users' table; therefore, the MyISAM storage engine was used. With the latest versions of XAMPP, MySQL, and PHP, the INNODB storage engine also allows full text searches.

A *user_level* column is included to enable the login page to differentiate between a registered user and an administrator. The users have a *user_level* of zero, and the administrator has been given the user level 51.

The downloadable file *users.sql* contains two registrations, which are shown in Table 11-8. These users' details will be used when you explore the workings of the custom shopping cart later in the chapter.

Table 11-8. *The Data for Two People in the First Five Columns of the users Table (users.sql)*

	User	Administrator
Title	Mrs	Mr
First Name	Rose	Mike
Last Name	Bush	Rosoft
E-mail	rbush@myisp.co.uk	miker@myisp.com
Password	redblooms	willgates

To save space in the preceding table, I have not shown the addresses that are contained in the table's *.sql* file. I gave Mrs. Bush and Mr. Rosoft the same mailing address because they are actually the same person. The address details are not accessed again in this example e-commerce web site; therefore, they are not important. You will need to refer to the user's e-mail address and password when you explore the custom shopping cart demonstration.

When the administrator Mike Rosoft logs in, he will be directed to an admin page. This is described next.

Add Paintings to a Table for a Custom Shopping Cart

To add paintings to a database table intended for a custom shopping cart, the administration interface is almost the same as the one used for a PayPal cart, but the text area for the PayPal code is omitted. The new interface is shown in Figure 11-11.

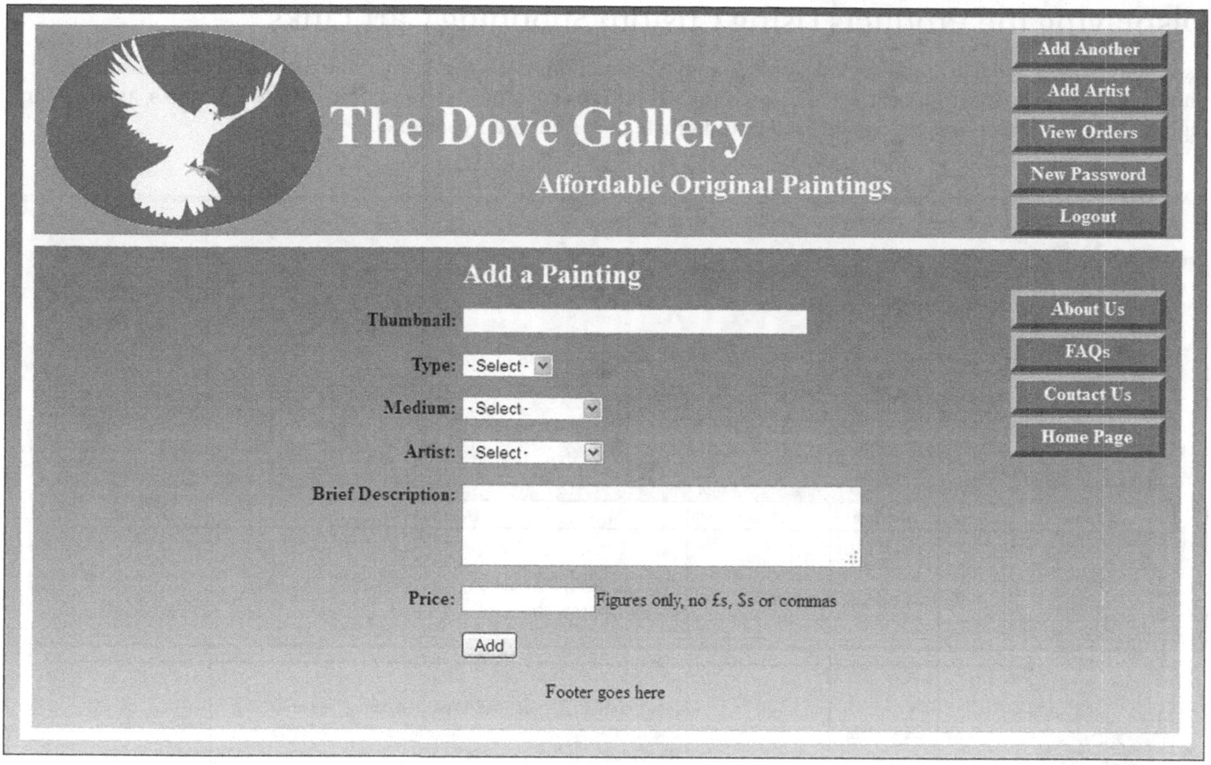

Figure 11-11. *The interface for adding paintings for the custom cart*

No listing is given for this interface because it is similar to Listing 11-7, except that the PayPal textarea is omitted. The file *admin_page.php* is included in the downloadable files so that you can examine it. However, you should not attempt to use it because all the thumbnail pictures have already been inserted in the file *art.sql* provided with the demonstration files for the custom shopping cart.

When registered users log in, they can search for paintings and purchase them. The search page was shown earlier in Figure 11-6.

■ **Note** Because I hard-coded the page that displays the paintings, a search will take you straight to the display shown in Figure 11-12 no matter what type of painting or what price you enter into the search fields. This is deliberate because the demonstration is designed to direct you instantly to the display of products with their *Add to Cart* links. You can then use the *Add to Cart* links to explore the features of the *View Cart* demonstration. A search page that is not hard-coded can be found in the subfolder for the PayPal shopping cart version.

We will now describe the result of the hard-coded search page using the custom shopping cart.

Displaying the Products Using Custom Shopping Cart Links

As in the earlier PayPal example, when a user searches for paintings, the result is a table displaying the chosen paintings. However, in this case, the PayPal *Add to Cart* buttons are replaced by custom *Add to Cart* links, as shown in Figure 11-12. Your own images can be used as links instead of standard hyperlinks.

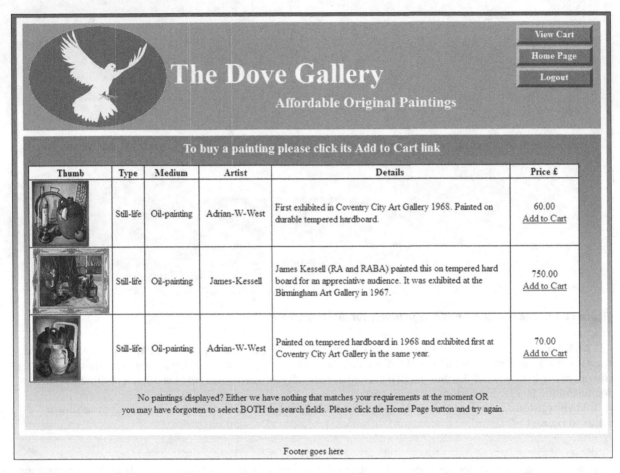

Figure 11-12. *The display of paintings with "Add to Cart" links*

In addition to swapping the PayPal buttons for *Add to Cart* links, the *prices* and *Add to Cart* links are located together in the last column.

■ **Note** The ability to show an enlarged version of a painting together with an expanded description would be a useful addition to this page of search results. Amazon provides a good example; by clicking the thumbnail image of a book, the image expands, and you can view a contents list and the book's introduction. You can even browse through a few of the book's pages. To achieve a similar display, the art table would require an additional column for the URL of the enlarged version as described in Chapter 8 for a real estate agent.

In Listing 11-12, the hard-coded query in the demonstration shopping cart display is shown in bold type.

Listing 11-12. Creating a Hard-Coded Page of Search Results for a Custom Cart (found_pics_cart.php)

```php
<?php
session_start();
if (!isset($_SESSION['user_id'])){
header('location:login.php');
exit();
}
?>
<!doctype html>
<html lang=en>
<head>
<title>The page for displaying the found paintings </title>
<meta charset=utf-8>
<link rel="stylesheet" type="text/css" href="transparent.css">
        <style type="text/css">
        body {  margin:auto; }
        p{ text-align:center; }
        table, td, th { width:930px; border-collapse:collapse; border:1px black solid;
        background:white;}
        td, th { padding-left:5px; padding-right:5px; text-align:center; }
        td.narrow, th.narrow { width:45px;}
        td.descr { text-align:left; }
        td.medium, th.medium { width:100px;}
        td.artist, th.artist { width:210px;}
        td.thumb, th.thumb { width:125px; text-align:center;}
        #content h3 { text-align:center; font-size:130%; font-weight:bold;}
        img { display:block;}
        #header-button { margin-top:-5px;}
        </style>
</head>
<body>
<div id="container">
<header>
<?php include('includes/header_found_pics_cart.inc'); ?>
<div id="logo">
...<img alt="dove" height="170" src="images/dove-1.png" width="234">
</div>
</header>
<div id="content"><!--Start of table displaying selected paintings-->
<h3>To buy a painting please click its Add to Cart link</h3>
<p>
<?php
//Connect to the database
require ( 'mysqli_connect.php' ) ;
// Apply some hard coding to retrieve three items from the art table
$q = "SELECT * FROM art LIMIT 3";
$result = mysqli_query( $dbcon, $q ) ;
```

#1

369

```php
if ( mysqli_num_rows( $result ) > 0 )
{
// Table header
echo '<table>
<tr>
<th class="thumb"><b>Thumb</b></th>
<th class="narrow"><b>Type</b></th>
<th class="medium"><b>Medium</b></th>
<th class="artist"><b>Artist</b></th>
<th class="descr"><b>Details</b></th>
<th class="narrow"><b>Price</b></th>
</tr>';
// Fetch the matching records and populate the table
while ($row = mysqli_fetch_array($result, MYSQLI_ASSOC)) {
   echo '<tr>
   <td class="thumb"><img src='.$row['thumb'] . '></td>
   <td class="narrow">' . $row['type'] . '</td>
   <td class="medium">' . $row['medium'] . '</td>
   <td class="artist">' . $row['artist'] . '</td>
   <td class="descr">' . $row['mini_descr'] . '</td>
   <td class="artist">' . $row['price'] .                                     #2
       '<br><a href="added.php?id=' . $row['art_id'] . '">Add to Cart</a></td>
   </tr>';
   }
   echo '</table>'; // End of table
// Close the database connection
  mysqli_close( $dbcon ) ;
}
// Or notify the user that no matching paintings were found
else { echo '<p>There are currently no items matching your search criteria.</p>' ; }
?>
<p>No paintings displayed? Either we have nothing that matches your requirements at the moment
OR<br>you may have forgotten to select BOTH the search fields. Please click the Home Page button and
try again.</p>
</div><!--End of table display content-->
<?php include("includes/footer.inc"); ?>
</div>
</body>
</html>
```

Explanation of the Code

```php
<?php                                                                          #1
//Connect to the database
require ( 'mysqli_connect.php' ) ;
// Apply some hard coding to retrieve three items from the art table
$q = "SELECT * FROM art LIMIT 3";
```

To save space, this SELECT statement was hard-coded to fetch all the records with a LIMIT of three results. This means that when you explore the demonstration files, you can quickly display a page containing custom cart links so that you can experiment with the *View Cart* files. A real-world SELECT statement would select all the paintings matching the user's search criteria. This can be demonstrated using the downloadable *shopper* subfolder files. To select all the files that match search criteria, the SELECT statement would be as follows:

```php
<?php
$type=$_POST['type'];
$price=$_POST['price'];
// Select all the records that match the search criteria
require ('mysqli_connect.php'); // Connect to the database.
$q = "SELECT art_id, thumb, type, medium, artist, mini_descr, price FROM art ↵
WHERE type='$type' AND price <= '$price' ORDER BY price DESC ";
    <td class="artist">' . $row['price'] .
    '<br><a href="added.php?id=' . $row['art_id'] . '">Add to Cart</a></td>        #2
```

This code combines the price of the each selected painting with an *Add to Cart* link and places both items in the last column of the displayed table. The line break <br> pushes the link below the price.

Adding Purchases to the Cart

When the user clicks one of the *Add to Cart* links, the details of the purchases are entered into the cart and the user will see one of two confirmation messages, as shown in Figures 11-13a and 11-13b.

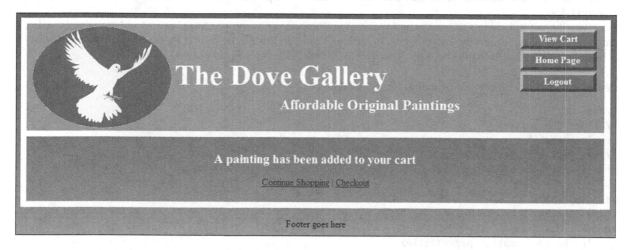

Figure 11-13a. *Confirmation of an addition to the cart*

Figure 11-13b. Confirmation that another of the same product has been added to the cart

The next figure is not really applicable to this example web site because the paintings are originals and you can't order more than one of each. However, the facility to add another identical painting is included here for completeness so that you can test this feature. If the user adds another of the same product, she will see the confirmation shown in Figure 11-13b.

Note the two links below the confirmation message. The user can continue shopping and add more items to the cart. She can choose to view the cart contents by clicking *View Cart* link on the header menu. She could also use the second link to go straight to the checkout. The code for the confirmation page is given in Listing 11-13.

Listing 11-13. Creating the Confirmation Page (added.php)

```php
<?php
// Start the session
session_start() ;
// Redirect the user if he is not logged in
if (!isset( $_SESSION['user_id'] ) ) {require ('login_tools.php') ; load() ; }
?>
<!doctype html>
<html lang=en>
<head>
<title>The confirmation page</title>
<meta charset=utf-8>
<link rel="stylesheet" type="text/css" href="transparent.css">
        <style type="text/css">
        body { margin:auto; }
        p{ text-align:center; }
        #content h3 { text-align:center; font-size:130%; font-weight:bold;}
        img { display:block;}
        #header-button { margin-top:-5px;}
        </style>
</head>
<body>
<div id="container">
<header>
```

```php
<?php include('includes/header_found_pics_cart.inc'); ?>
<div id="logo">
   <img alt="dove" height="170" src="images/dove-1.png" width="234">
</div>
</header>
<div id="content"><!--Start of the confirmation page-->
<p>
<?php
if ( isset( $_GET['id'] ) ) $id = $_GET['id'] ;
// Connect to the database
require ( 'mysqli_connect.php' ) ;
// Get selected painting data from the art table                          #1
$q = "SELECT * FROM art WHERE art_id = $id" ;
$result = mysqli_query( $dbcon, $q ) ;
if ( mysqli_num_rows( $result ) == 1 )
{
   $row = mysqli_fetch_array( $result, MYSQLI_ASSOC );
// Does the cart already contain one of that product id
   if ( isset( $_SESSION['cart'][$id] ) )
   {
// Add another one of those paintings
   $_SESSION['cart'][$id]['quantity']++;
    echo '<h3>Another one of those paintings has been added to your cart</h3>';
   }
   else
   {
// Add a different painting
   $_SESSION['cart'][$id]= array ( 'quantity' => 1, 'price' => $row['price'] ) ;
    echo '<h3>A painting has been added to your cart</h3>' ;
   }
}
// Close the database connection
mysqli_close($dbcon);
// Insert three links
echo '<p><a href="found_pics_cart.php">Continue Shopping</a> | <a href="cart.php">View Cart</a> ↵
| <a href="checkout.php">Checkout</a> | <a href="logout.php">Logout</a></p>' ;
?>
</div><!--End of confirmation page content-->
<?php include("includes/footer.inc"); ?>
</div>
</body>
</html>
```

Explanation of the Code

```
// Get selected painting data from the art table                          #1
```

Following this comment, the details of the selected paintings are checked to determine which of two messages to display, either *A painting has been added* or *Another of those paintings has been added*.

If the user chooses to view the cart, she will see the contents displayed as shown in Figure 11-14a.

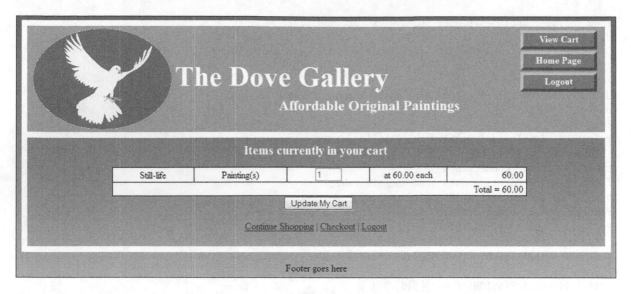

Figure 11-14a. *The cart content shows that the user added one painting costing £60*

The quantity in the third column of the table can be edited by the user. To remove a painting from the cart, the user will change the current figure to zero. After editing the quantity, the user must click the *Update My Cart* button to reveal the new subtotal (last column in the top row) and the revised total price.

If she clicks the *Continue Shopping* link, the page shown in Figure 11-12 reappears and she can click another *Add to Cart* link to add another painting. If she added a new painting worth £750 to the cart, and she viewed the cart, she would see the revised cart content as shown in Figure 11-14b.

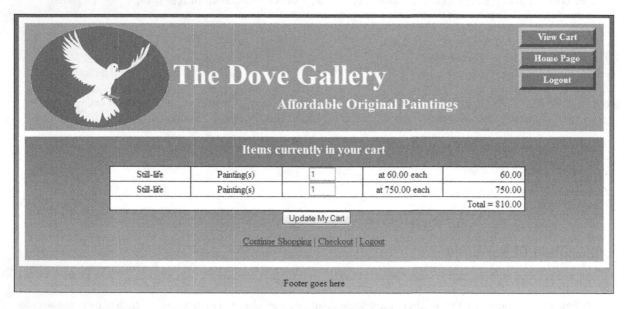

Figure 11-14b. *The contents of the cart after adding another painting costing £750*

The code for creating the *View Cart* page is given in Listing 11-14.

Listing 11-14. Creating the View Cart Page (cart.php)

```php
<?php
// Start the session
session_start();
// Redirect the user if he is not logged in
if ( !isset( $_SESSION[ 'user_id' ] ) ) { require ( 'login_tools.php' ) ; load() ; }
?>
<!doctype html>
<html lang=en>
<head>
<title>The view cart page</title>
<meta charset=utf-8>
<link rel="stylesheet" type="text/css" href="transparent.css">
        <style type="text/css">
        body { margin:auto; }
        p{ text-align:center; }
        table { width:700px; border-collapse:collapse; border:1px black solid; ↵
        background:white; margin-left:135px;}
        td, th { padding-left:5px; padding-right:5px; text-align:center; }
        #content h3 { text-align:center; font-size:130%; font-weight:bold;}
        #header-button { margin-top:-5px;}
        #submit { margin-left: 425px;
        }
        </style>
</head>
<body>
<div id="container">
<header>
<?php include('includes/header_found_pics_cart.inc'); ?>
<div id="logo">
   <img alt="dove" height="170" src="images/dove-1.png" width="234">
   </div>
</header>
<div id="content"><!--Start of table of cart contents-->
   <h3>Items currently in your cart</h3>
<p>
<?php
if ( $_SERVER['REQUEST_METHOD'] == 'POST' )
{
// If the user changes the quantity, update the cart
   foreach ( $_POST['qty'] as $art_id => $item_qty )                          #1
   {
// Ensure that the id and the quantity are integers
   $id = (int) $art_id;
   $qty = (int) $item_qty;
// If the quantity is set to zero, clear the session or else store the changed quantity
```

375

```php
    if ( $qty == 0 ) { unset ($_SESSION['cart'][$id]); }
    elseif ( $qty > 0 ) { $_SESSION['cart'][$id]['quantity'] = $qty; }
    }
}
// Set the initial variable for the total cost
    $total = 0;
// Display the cart contents
    if (!empty($_SESSION['cart']))
{
// Connect to the database
    require ('mysqli_connect.php');
// Get the items from the shop table and insert them into the cart
    $q = "SELECT * FROM art WHERE art_id IN (";                              #2
    foreach ($_SESSION['cart'] as $id => $value) { $q .= $id . ','; }
    $q = substr( $q, 0, -1 ) . ') ORDER BY art_id ASC';
    $result = mysqli_query ($dbcon, $q);
// create a form and a table
    echo '<form action="cart.php" method="post">
<table><tr>';
    while ($row = mysqli_fetch_array ($result, MYSQLI_ASSOC))
    {
// Calculate the subtotals and the grand total                              #3
    $subtotal = $_SESSION['cart'][$row['art_id']]['quantity'] * ↵
    $_SESSION['cart'][$row['art_id']]['price'];
    $total += $subtotal;
// Display the table
    echo "<tr> <td>{$row['type']}</td><td>Painting(s)</td>
    <td><input type=\"text\" size=\"3\" name=\"qty[{$row['art_id']}]\" ↵
value=\"{$_SESSION['cart'][$row['art_id']]['quantity']}\"></td>
    <td>at {$row['price']} each </td> <td style=\"text-align:right\">".↵
number_format ($subtotal, 2)."</td></tr>";
    }
// Close the connection to the database
    mysqli_close($dbcon);
// Display the total
    echo ' <tr><td colspan="5" style="text-align:right">↵
    Total = '.number_format($total,2).'</td></tr>
</table>
    <input id="submit" type="submit" name="submit" value="Update My Cart"></form>';
    }
    else
// Or display a message
    { echo '<p>Your cart is currently empty.</p>' ; }
// Create some links
    echo '<p><a href="found_pics_cart.php">Continue Shopping</a> | ↵
    <a href="checkout.php">Checkout</a></p>' ;
?>
</div><!--End of the view cart content page-->
<?php include("includes/footer.inc"); ?>
</div>
</body>
</html>
```

Explanation of the Code

The comments within the listing explain the steps used to populate a cart. However, some items need a little more explanation as follows:

```
foreach ( $_POST['qty'] as $art_id => $item_qty )
```
#1

The *View Cart* process relies on sessions and also some complex arrays. The function foreach is a special loop that works with arrays. In line **#1**, the item $_POST['qty'] is an array containing the quantity of a particular product. The symbol => does not mean equal to or greater than; it is an array operator that associates the item qty with the $art_id of the product.

```
$q = "SELECT * FROM art WHERE art_id IN (";
foreach ($_SESSION['cart'] as $id => $value) { $q .= $id . ','; }
$q = substr( $q, 0, -1 ) . ') ORDER BY art_id ASC';
```
#2

Values are added to a session array named cart shown in bold type.

```
// Calculate the subtotals and the grand total
    $subtotal = $_SESSION['cart'][$row['art_id']]['quantity'] * ←
    $_SESSION['cart'][$row['art_id']]['price'];
    $total += $subtotal;
// Display the table
    echo "<tr> <td>{$row['type']}</td><td>Painting(s)</td>
    <td><input type=\"text\" size=\"3\" name=\"qty[{$row['art_id']}]\" ←
value=\"{$_SESSION['cart'][$row['art_id']]['quantity']}\"></td>
    <td>at {$row['price']} each </td> <td style=\"text-align:right\">".←
number_format ($subtotal, 2)."</td></tr>";
    }
```
#3

The session arrays are used to insert values into the cells of the *View Cart* table. Note that in the code that formats the table, the double quotes are escaped by using backslashes.

■ **Note**   In a real-world web site, to achieve the necessary standard of security, two techniques would be used: *prepared statements* and *transactions*. These advanced concepts are beyond the scope of this book, but you can learn about them using the resources provided in the Appendix.

We will briefly mention the checkout page.

The Checkout Page

When the checkout link is clicked, four things happen:

- A *Thank You* page appears, which also states the order number.

- The order details are posted to the *order_contents* table.

- The order is entered into the *orders* table.

- The shopping cart is emptied and is ready for the next purchases.

The *Thank You* page is shown in Figure 11-15.

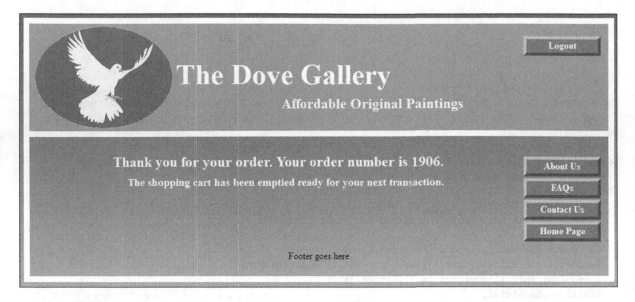

Figure 11-15. *The Thank You page*

The checkout page is included in the downloadable files as *checkout.php*, but it is hard-coded to produce the display shown in Figure 11-15. Because of this, its function is limited so that checking out has no effect on the *orders* and *order_contents* tables.

Additional Administrative Tasks

The process for adding artists and paintings was described earlier in the chapter, but an administrator must perform several other tasks. Editing and deleting artists and paintings can be achieved by the techniques described in Chapter 3. Other tasks are usually undertaken by an administration team. These duties include order processing, shipping, stock control, financial control, and customer support. All these activities would be recorded in the appropriate database tables.

Summary

In this chapter, two useful techniques were included: retrieving a forgotten password and dynamically loading a pull-down menu. You learned about some of the many elements required for an e-commerce web site. However, the need for brevity meant that the number of elements discussed was limited. Because a practical e-commerce web site needs an enormous number of files, the chapter described the main displays as seen by a user. The chapter was not a tutorial, but a description of an e-commerce web site followed by a hard-coded demonstration of a shopping cart. The hard-coded files allowed you to quickly explore the custom shopping cart.

PayPal shopping cart files in the subfolder *shopper* allowed you to explore features such as a search file that was not hard-coded and the administration file for inserting PayPal code into a table.

I hope you were able to appreciate the fact that e-commerce webs sites are very complex and that the need for very tight security is paramount. I also hope the chapter has inspired you to explore some of the e-commerce resources given in the appendix.

CHAPTER 12

■ ■ ■

Troubleshooting Your Database-Driven Web Site

As you worked through the chapters, you will have encountered many error messages. This is normal; even seasoned programmers see error messages as they develop new projects. If you can't immediately locate where a mistake was made, walk away and return later when your frustration has subsided. I sometimes leave the problem for a day and continue with some other part of the project.

This chapter lists some of the problems, the error messages, and their solutions. If your problem is not in the list, try entering the error message into a search engine.

■ **Tip** I usually make a copy of a faulty page and save it with a new name. I can then experiment by changing the code on the copy rather than mess up the original page.

Humans can infer a meaning from poorly written or spoken grammar. For instance, despite the double negative, we know that "I ain't got no money" means the man is broke. When listening to a hesitant speaker, we mentally omit the "ums," "ers," and "you knows" from each sentence so that we can understand what the speaker means. Computers are unable to apply common sense to code containing mistakes or extraneous characters. However, computers can provide very helpful error messages, and they are usually right, *so read them carefully*.

Although error messages can be frustrating, they are an extremely valuable tool because we learn better and faster from our mistakes, and the messages usually explain the mistakes in plain English. A small number of messages might seem cryptic, but familiarity will eventually help you to understand them.

■ **Tip** Don't try random changes to fix a problem. Take time to think it through carefully. Then try one change at a time by commenting out and replacing the line(s) of code. If that change does not work, delete the new line and remove the comment-out characters to restore the original code. Comment-out the sections where you think the error occurred, but be very careful that your comment-outs do not cause a mismatch of curly brackets. Place the comment-outs around the code *between* a pair of existing curly brackets.

HTML Code Errors

Most WYSIWYG web editors have built-in error checking. For instance, Microsoft Expression Web 4 (now free) has an excellent error checker. The errors are highlighted in yellow, and pressing the F9 key in code view reveals and explains the errors step by step.

Browser Quirks

In the event of a display fault, don't investigate the code until you try the page in a different browser. For example, if the page display is unsatisfactory in Internet Explorer, it might be fine in Mozilla Firefox or vice versa. In such a case, the code contains no errors, but you will need to use a conditional style sheet for the browser that gives a poor display. A conditional style sheet for Internet Explorer 8 was provided in some of the earlier chapters in this book. Many conditional style sheets are available at the following location:

`http://quirksmode.org/dom/tests/stylesheets.html`

Install the five main browsers in your computer: Internet Explorer, Mozilla Firefox, Safari, Chrome and Opera. Put their icons on the desktop, and test your pages in each browser as you work. You might find one of the following browser emulators to be helpful:

- IE Tester from: `http://www.my-debugbar.com/wiki/IETester/HomePage`

- Net Renderer from `http://netrenderer.com`

- `https://browserlab.adobe,com/en-us/features.html`

A Style Change Has No Effect

It's particularly frustrating to make a style change and find that it has no effect. This is due to a style in some file that is taking precedence over the style you are trying to change. The rogue style is probably lurking in one of the included files. Remove styles from all included files, and place them in the main style sheet. Avoid inline styles and, wherever possible, remove internal styles from the <head></head> section of a page and place them in external style sheets. Reduce the number of external style sheets to an absolute minimum.

Most modern browsers have development tools that make it easy to see which styles are being applied to each element so that you can track and fix the rogue style.

A Page Fails to Validate

Always validate each page of a web-site code using the W3C validator available at `http://validator.w3.org`. Remember that PHP is run in the background and produces HTML. The validator scans the HTML and not the PHP script.

Validating with the W3C validator is an important form of troubleshooting. It ensures that your pages are correctly coded so that browsers do not produce odd results. Also, search engines will not be blocked by your minor coding errors when pages are valid. By using validated pages, visually impaired users will be able to access your pages; otherwise, small coding errors can baffle an automated screen reader. Mobile devices use cut-down versions of browsers, and they cannot cope with the errors in nonvalidated sites.

If you put styling instructions in an included file, the W3C validator will display a failure message in a red font like this: "Element style not allowed as child of element div." To solve this problem, remove the style instruction from the included file and put the style in the main style sheet.

A PayPal Pull-Down Menu Does Not Work

Judging by the cries for help on the Internet, this is an occasional but frustrating problem. If using a pull-down menu results in a PayPal error message, you would normally check the code carefully to see if you can spot the problem. This usually fails to produce a solution. If you upload the code to a forum for analysis, the forum normally confirms your own analysis—that is, that the code is correct. At the time of this writing, if you send an e-mail to PayPal you will receive only a list of FAQs. Very rarely are the FAQs related to your problem.

To save yourself time and frustration, don't fiddle with the PayPal code; instead, simply log in to your PayPal account, set up a new pull-down menu, and copy the code. Then replace the faulty code with the new code. When setting up the pull-down menu, omit the currency symbols, such as £, because these will display as a square box or some other symbol. If you try to replace the currency symbols with an entity, the code will usually fail.

PHP Script Errors

The three main error levels are as follows:

- **Errors:** These errors halt the script, and the fault must be corrected.

- **Warnings:** The script can recover from this error level, but the error should be found and corrected.

- **Notices:** Minor errors in the script that need correcting. Often this is caused by a misspelled variable name.

Included Items Missing from the Display

"Includes" will appear only when you view the page using a URL. Check that XAMPP has been started and that Apache and MySQL are running. Also, check that the included files are actually in the folder specified in the PHP code.

Call to an Undefined Function

Either you called a function that you forgot to define, or there is a spelling error in the function call. You might have called what you thought was a standard PHP function that does not actually exist.

Cannot Redeclare Function

You have created a function and declared it twice; remove one of the declarations.

Undefined Index or Undefined Variable

Check the spelling of the index or variable, paying attention to the case of each letter. Check that the variable has been assigned a value. Perhaps you forgot to initiate the variable before you called it. A missing dollar sign (or an upper case S instead of a dollar sign) at the beginning of a variable will also cause this error to appear.

Empty Variable Value

This error is caused by forgetting the initial dollar sign or misspelling a variable. Check the case of each letter in a variable.

General Variable Errors

Echo statements provide a simple way to track down variable errors in a long script. Taking a registration script as an example, beneath *each* validation check add an echo statement.

For instance, where the e-mail variable is validated, add the echo statement as shown in bold type:

```
// Check for an email address
if (empty($_POST['email'])) {
$errors[] = 'You forgot to enter your email address.';
} else {
$e = trim($_POST['email']);
echo "<p>\$e is $e</p>\n";
}
```

To test the script, deliberately cause it to stop running by omitting an entry in one of the fields. You will see the error message saying you forgot to enter data in one of the fields, and you will also see a list of variables and their content. You might see a variable that does not have the content you expected.

Headers Already Sent

Perhaps you called a header function after you sent some HTML (or even a space) to the browser. The following piece of code will fail because the header statement is preceded by some HTML:

```
<html>
<?php
header("location:somefile.php");
?>
```

This statement will work:

```
<?php
header("location:somefile.php");
?>
<html>
```

If you put a space before the <?php tag, the error message will reappear.

Blank Screen

This can be caused by the same fault that produces the "headers already sent" message.

If you are expecting a display produced by a looping array and nothing appears, you probably forgot that arrays start at zero and you started the loop at 1.

Some incorrect HTML or PHP can produce a blank screen. The fault can also result from an error that has halted the script.

Unexpected End of File in Line *xxx*

This is a common PHP error, and it refers to the last line in the file. It usually means you have a mismatched number of curly brackets or normal brackets. For instance, you might have 20 opening curly brackets but only 19 closing brackets. To find the missing bracket, try indenting the PHP code so that the brackets can be counted more easily. To find the error in a large file, print a hard copy of the code and then number all the left brackets with a red pen and all the right brackets with a green pen. The number of red brackets must equal the number of green brackets. Often, this error is caused by using a normal bracket instead of a curly bracket or vice versa. Free tools such as Notepad++ and Microsoft Expression Web Version 4 show helpful line numbers. Some HTML editors highlight tags that do not have a matching opening or closing tag.

Common PHP Parse Errors

Almost all parse errors are caused by missing items and unmatched items in PHP statements. Opening curly brackets or normal brackets might not have matching closing brackets. Opening quotation marks might not have a closing quotation mark. Perhaps the quotes don't match—for instance, opening with a single quote and closing with a double quote or vice versa. If you forget to escape a quotation mark in a string, you will see a parse error. Following are some typical parse error messages.

You will see something like "unexpected (/)" or "unexpected (,)". These are the easiest PHP parsing errors to spot because the PHP parser directs you to the line and column in the code where the error is located.

```
Parse error: expecting (,) or (;) in /somefile.php on line 10
```

Often, this means that you forgot to close the statement with a semicolon.
A missing normal bracket ")" or quote mark can also trigger this error.
If you see an error message like this:

```
Parse error: unexpected T_echo, expecting (,) or (;) on /somefile.php on line 10
```

again, you omitted a closing semicolon, but this time it applies to the statement before line 10.

The incorrect nesting of quote marks can result in the "unexpected" type of error messages and a display you did not expect.

The following code will produce a parse error:

```
$some_variable =  "table width="960px">";
```

The parser reads the first double quote and assumes that the double quote following the equal sign signals the end of the statement.

Use a pair of single quotes around the 960px to prevent this, as follows:

```
$some_variable =  "table width='960px'>";
```

If you omit the final double quote, the parser will continue to read the code until it finds another double quote. This could be several lines down, so the error message refers to that line rather than the line where the error is located. If you can't find the error on the line stated in the error message, move back through the lines until you find the mistake.

Unexpected T_STRING

The usual causes are a missing semicolon, missing quote, or missing double quote. An example of a missing quote follows:

```
$somevariable = 'fname ;
```

It should have been

```
$somevariable = 'fname' ;
```

Unexpected T_ELSE

Often this error results from having an extraneous semicolon after an if clause as follows:

```
If (some condition exists);
    {
    $result = "that condition exists" ;
    }
```

Remove the semicolon from the *if* clause to solve the problem. The error message can also appear if you have omitted one or more curly brackets, or you have more than one *else* clause in block of code. If you have more than one *else* clause, change the earlier one(s) to *elseif* so that you have only one *else* clause in a block of code.

Wrong Equals Sign

Check your code to see where you used the wrong equals sign. The rules for equal signs are as follows:

- A single equals sign is used to assign a value to a variable.

- If an item is to be equal to another item, you must use a double equals sign (==).

- If an item is to be absolutely identical to another item, you must use three equals signs (===).

Failed to Open Stream

This message indicates the server cannot find a file or an included file. Either the file being called is not in the correct folder or the file name has a spelling error. Sometimes we can forget to give the correct path for the file. The error message can be the result of the following statement:

```
<?php include(header.php) ?>;
```

Instead, the statement should have been the following:

```
<?php include(includes/header.php) ?>;
```

Warning: Division by Zero

Neither PHP nor mathematics allow division by zero. The message will indicate the location of the error so that you can correct it.

Display Is Not What Was Expected

Although many errors are the result of omitting characters, extraneous characters can display something you did not intend; for instance, the following code seems fine at first glance:

```
for ( $var = 0; $var =5; $var++ ) ;
{ echo 'display something' <br>;
}
```

The code was intended to loop through and display a variable five times. Unfortunately, it displayed the variable only once. This is because there should not be a semicolon after the *for* statement. The extraneous semicolon halts the loop so that only one item is displayed by the echo command. This extraneous semicolon is the PHP equivalent of the spoken "er" or "um." Humans can disregard them, but the PHP parser cannot.

MySQL Errors

Most MySQL and database errors are caused by the following:

- Listing the clauses in a query in the wrong order
- Misspellings
- Unbalanced brackets or quotes
- Unescaped apostrophes
- With INSERT queries, the columns names don't match the VALUES.

Table Displays Headings Only

When a table displays only the headings, it means that either (i) the item being searched does not exist in the database table or (ii) you know that the data exists, but the search criteria does not match the data in the database table. A typical case is shown in Figure 12-1.

Figure 12-1. *A table may display only the headings*

If you are sure that the data exists in the table being searched, the problem is that the SELECT query contains one or more incorrect items. A typical query is as follows:

```
$q = "SELECT ref_num, loctn, thumb, price, type, mini_descr, b_rooms, status FROM houses
WHERE loctn='$loctn' AND (price <= '$price') AND type='$type' AND b_rooms='$b_rooms'
ORDER BY ref_num ASC ";
```

Make a hard copy of the query so that you can refer to it and roll back the code if you mess up. Then, in your text editor, look for items that have a corresponding item in the WHERE clause. Delete one matching pair at a time, and test after each deletion.

If a populated table is then displayed, you know that the deleted item is the cause of the faulty display. You might find that the three pages involved in the process have differing entries. For instance, in the search page you might have the *location* items entered with hyphens such as South-Devon, Mid-Devon, and North-Devon; whereas in the administrator's add-a-house page, you might have underscores, such as South_Devon, Mid_Devon, and North_Devon.

Access Denied

The "access denied" error message looks something like this:

```
"Access denied for user 'root'@'localhost' <using password: YES>"
```

The YES means that a password was entered by the user; it does not mean that the user entered YES as the password. If the user failed to enter a password, you would see NO instead of YES.

The error message means that one or more of the items in your database connection file does not match the database details. It could be a misspelling in the connection file of any of the following items: user, password, host, or database name.

Syntax Errors

SQL syntax errors produce an error message like this:

```
Error 1064 (42000): You have an error in your SQL syntax
```

Fortunately, the message usually gives a clue to the whereabouts and cause of the error. It will say something like this: "near * FROM members at line 6". This means that line 6 contains an asterisk, and near that asterisk you will find the error.

Reference to a Primary Key Could Not be Created

If you try to set a foreign key in one table that links to a primary key in another table, ensure that both keys have exactly the same type and length. Otherwise, you will see an error message stating that the reference to the primary key could not be created.

Summary

This chapter described some error messages, and appropriate solutions were suggested. No doubt, you encountered many error messages as you worked through this book. In fact, you will always have to deal with error messages unless you are superhuman. I recommend that you recognize messages that are not mentioned in this chapter, make a note of them, and record the solutions.

We have come to the end of the instructional chapters, and you should now have an understanding of PHP and the basic principles for designing practical databases for web sites. I hope you will regard this book as a starting point for further study of PHP, MySQL and, in particular, security. This simplified approach to database design omitted such topics as PDO, Object Oriented Programming (OOP), Ajax, and Frameworks; none of them is essential. They are alternatives to the techniques employed in this book. The Appendix will help you locate resources for further study. You would also learn more by combining techniques from the chapters in this book.

■ ■ ■

Appendix

This Appendix contains details of four new downloadable files for arrays and PHP e-mailing. It has the following sections:

- PHP quick reference
    - Downloadable files for arrays
    - Downloadable files for e-mailing
- MySQL and phpMyAdmin quick reference
- What next?
- Resources (books and Internet help, including a forum tutorial, PayPal tutorials, PayPal forums, e-commerce resources)

PHP Quick Reference

The PHP references are in alphabetical order for rapid searching.

Arrays

Arrays are variables that store multiple values. The registration forms in previous chapters used an array to store all the error messages. The name of the array indicates a category, such as cars, error_messages, or cereals. In an array named cereals, the multiple values might be oats, barley, corn, and wheat. The array can be created using the following code:

```
$cereals = array();
```

The values can be inserted as follows (note that the key for the first value is zero):

```php
<?php
$cereals = array();
$cereals[0] = "oats";
$cereals[1] = "barley";
$cereals[2] = "corn";
$cereals[3] = "wheat";
?>
```

The number inside the square brackets is known as the *key*. Every *key* has a *value* paired with it. The first *key* in our example has a *value* oats. The following code will display the contents of the cereals array. The file is available in the downloadable files for the Appendix as *simple_array.php*.

```
<!doctype html>
<html lang=en>
<head>
<title>The simple array page</title>
<meta charset=utf-8>
<style type="text/css">
.cntr {text-align:center; }
</style>
</head>
<body>
<h2 class="cntr">This is the Array page</h2>
<p class="cntr">
<?php
$cereals = array();
$cereals[0] = "oats";
$cereals[1] = "barley";
$cereals[2] = "corn";
$cereals[3] = "wheat";
echo ("$cereals[0] " . "$cereals[1] " . "$cereals[2] " . $cereals[3]);
?>
</p>
</body>
</html>
```

The display would appear as follows:

Oats barley corn wheat

Note that the same array can also be initiated as follows:

```
$cereals = array("oats","barley","corn","wheat");
```

Associative Arrays

Associative arrays allow you to use strings called *keys* instead of reference numbers. This can provide more explicit code. Associative arrays use the array operator symbol =>. (Note that the symbol does not mean "equal to or greater than"). In the example given next, the => symbol indicates that the key Monday has the value "Clean car". The key is case sensitive; "Monday" is not the same as "monday".

■ **Caution**   In associative arrays, pay particular attention to the punctuation and quotes. Especially remember not to add a comma after the final array value (Church in our next example).

Let's look at an example with seven key/value pairs in an array that we will call $events. This file, named *assoc_array.php*, is available in the downloadable files for the Appendix.

```html
<!doctype html>
<html lang=en>
<head>
<title>The associative array page</title>
<meta charset=utf-8>
<style type="text/css">
h2 { margin-left:150px; }
p {margin-left:250px; text-align:left; }
</style>
</head>
<body>
<h2 class="cntr">This is the associative array page</h2>
<?php
$events = array(
'Monday' => 'Clean car',
'Tuesday' => 'Dental appointment',
'Wednesday' => 'Shopping',
'Thursday' => 'Gardening',
'Friday' => 'Fishing',
'Saturday' => 'Football match',
'Sunday' => 'Church'
);
foreach($events as $day => $event) {
echo "<p>$day: $event</p>\n";
}
?>
</body>
</html>
```

The code produces the following display:
This is the associative array page

Monday: Clean car

Tuesday: Dental appointment

Wednesday: Shopping

Thursday: Gardening

Friday: Fishing

Saturday: Football match

Sunday: Church

The downloadable files for the Appendix include *simple_array.php* and *assoc_array.php*.

Comments

PHP accepts three symbols to indicate a comment as follows:

```
//A single line comment
#A single line comment
/*A multiple line comment
    some text
    some text
    some text*/
```

Concatenation

Concatenating strings means joining them together by using a period. See the $full_name, for example:

```php
<?php
$first_name = 'Annie';
$last_name = 'Versary';
$full_name =$first_name . $last_name;
echo $full_name;
?>
```

The display would be as follows;

Annie Versary

Constants

Items that never change are stored as *constants* using the function define(). The function takes two parameters: the name of the constant and its fixed value. Because I have no intention of changing my first name, I could define it as a constant as follows:

```php
<?php
define('MY_FNAME', 'Adrian');
echo = 'Hello';
echo = MY_FNAME;
?>
```

The display would be:

Hello Adrian

■ **Note**   *Constants* do not use a dollar sign because they are not *variables*.

E-mailing with PHP

PHP provides an easy method for sending e-mails using the mail() function. The format is as follows:

```
mail($to,$subject,$message,$headers);
```

You can confirm that your hosting company's e-mail server will respond to PHP instructions. Create a PHP file named *simple_email.php*, or use the downloadable file. Then insert your own e-mail address in place of the two dummy addresses *me@myisp.co.uk*:

```
<!doctype html>
<html lang=en>
<head>
<title>Testing a simple email</title>
<meta charset=utf-8>
</head>
<body>
<?php
mail("me@myisp.co.uk", "This is a subject", "This is the body of the email", ↵
"From:me@myisp.co.uk\r\n");
?>
</body>
</html>
```

Upload the file *simple_email.php* to the host, and then access the file from a browser. You will see a blank page, but you should receive an e-mail via your usual e-mail client, such as Windows Live Mail or a web mail client.

Note that \n stands for a new line and \r stands for a carriage return or Enter. Together they drop down one line and start a new line from the beginning—that is, from the left side of that line.

A more practical version, *multiple_email.php*, includes multiple recipients and uses variables instead of hard coding. As a first test, I used my alternative e-mail address to replace recipient-1. The e-mail addresses of cooperative friends or colleagues were used for recipient-3 and recipient-4. The code for *multiple_email.php* shown next is provided in the downloadable files for the Appendix.

```
<!doctype html>
<html lang=en>
<head>
<title>An email for multiple recipients</title>
<meta charset=utf-8>
</head>
<body>
<?php
$to = " me@myisp.co.uk, recipient-2@someisp.co.uk ";
$subject = "My email test.";
$message = "This is the body of the email";
$headers = "From: me@myisp.co.uk\r\n";
$headers .= "Reply-To: me@myisp.co.uk\r\n";
$headers .= "CC: recipient-3@someisp.co.uk\r\n";
$headers .= "BCC: recipient-4@someisp.com\r\n";
mail($to,$subject,$message,$headers);
if ( mail($to,$subject,$message,$headers) ) {          #1
   echo "The email has been sent!";
   } else {
   echo "The email has failed!";
   }
?>
</body>
</html>
```

The elements To:, CC:, and BCC: can consist of several recipients. You accomplish this by using a comma-separated list as shown in the line beginning with $to. To use the file with fewer recipients, simply delete the unwanted items. Save the file as *multiple_email.php*, and upload the file to a host. Then access the file from a browser. You should receive the e-mail(s) via your usual e-mail client, such as Windows Live Mail or web mail.

Explanation of the Code

The top section of an e-mail is the header. The variables called $headers supply the header with its content. The $headers are concatenated using a dot and an equals sign (.=), and each one is moved down a line by the code (\r\n).

```
if ( mail($to,$subject,$message,$headers) ) {                              #1
    echo "The email has been sent!";
    } else {
    echo "The email has failed!";
    }
```

This block of code is optional and can be deleted. It will let you know whether the e-mail was sent or not, but it will not tell you whether it was received.

Functions

A *function* is a self-contained piece of reusable code that performs a task when called. PHP has over a thousand built-in functions. In this book, you have been using several built-in functions, for instance: array(), mysqli_real_escape_string(), include(), require(), strip_tags(), count(), and mysqli_connect().

A function name can contain letters, digits, and underscores but not hyphens. The name must not begin with a digit, and function names are not case sensitive. A function can be created by the web designer using the following format:

```
function function_name()
{ task to be performed; }
```

For example:

```
function greeting()
        { echo "Hello user!" ; }
```

The function can be called from within a script as follows:

```
<?php
    greeting();
?>
```

This would display as "Hello user!"

include( ) vs. require( )

Both functions pull a file into an HTML page. The difference is that if include() fails to retrieve the file, the script will display an error message and continue to run; if require() encounters the same problem, it will stop the script. Use include() for including most files, but use require() for vital items, such as accessing the database connection file. If the connection fails, it is pointless to continue.

if, else, and elseif

A series of PHP conditional statements can take the following pattern:

if something is true
Do this
elseif something else is true
Do that
else
Do something different from the previous two instructions.

You can use as many *elseif* statements as you like, but only one *else* is permitted and it must be the last item in the list of conditionals.

When students look at my code for a registration page, they ask why several *else* clauses appear one after another when there should be only one. Some code that prompts the question is as follows:

```php
if (empty($errors)) { // If no problems occurred in the user's input
    //Determine whether the email address has already been registered for a user
    $q = "SELECT user_id FROM users WHERE email = '$e' ";
    $result=mysqli_query ($dbcon, $q) ;
if (mysqli_num_rows($result) == 0){//The email address was not already registered ↵
therefore register the user in the users table
    // Make the query
    $q = "INSERT INTO users (user_id, title, fname, lname, email, psword, registration_date,↵
     uname, class, addr1, addr2, city, county, pcode, phone, paid) VALUES (' ', '$title', ↵
     '$fn', '$ln', '$e', SHA1('$p'), NOW(), '$uname','$class', '$ad1', '$ad2', '$cty', ↵
     '$cnty', '$pcode', '$ph', '$pd')";
    $result = @mysqli_query ($dbcon, $q); // Run the query
if ($result) { // If the query ran without a problem
    header ("location: register-thanks.php");
    exit();
} else { // If the query failed to run
// Error message
    echo '<h2>System Error</h2>
<p class="error">You could not be registered due to a system error. We apologize for ↵
the inconvenience.</p>';
// Debugging message
    echo '<p>' . mysqli_error($dbcon) . '<br><br>Query: ' . $q . '</p>';
} // End of if ($result)
    mysqli_close($dbcon); // Close the database connection.
// Include the footer and stop the script
    include ('includes/footer.php');
    exit();
}else{//The email address is already registered
    echo '<p class="error">The email address is not acceptable because it is ↵
already registered</p>';
    }
}else{ // Display the errors
```

Explanation of the Code

The *ifs* and *elses* are shown in bold type There are three *ifs* and three *elses*. The three *elses* appear to be following each other, but in fact the *ifs* and *elses* are nested; they are each complete in themselves, as you will see from the formatted summary that follows:

```
if (empty($errors)) { //If no problems occur in the user's input, run the query
    if (mysqli_num_rows($result) == 0) { //The email address is not already registered, ↵
        so continue to run the query
        if ($result) { //If the query ran without a problem, continue to run the script
        }else{ //If the query fails to run, display an error message
    }else{ //The email address is already registered, display that information to the user
}else{ //If errors are detected, display the errors
```

Loops

A *loop* is a device that searches through an array or a file item by item. It functions by executing a block of code as long as a condition is true.

The *while* Loop

The *while* loop is used when the number of items that might be retrieved is unknown. The format for a while loop is:

```
while (condition is true)
{
do something
}
```

We used *while* loops in pages that retrieved the results of search queries. The code looped through the data in a database table and displayed records if they existed. This use of the *while* loop was as follows:

```
// Fetch and print all the records
while ($row = mysqli_fetch_array($result, MYSQLI_ASSOC)) {
    echo '<tr>...
```

While records were found, the rows were retrieved and displayed in a table.

The *for* Loop

The *for* loop and the *foreach* loop are used when the number of items is known. The *for* loop has the following format:

```
for (start value, last value, expression) {
do something
}
```

The *for* loop used in the next example is restricted to a known number of iterations (in this case, 3):

```
<!doctype html>
<html lang=en>
<body>
<?php
for($x=0; $x<=3; $x++)
{
echo "Iteration: $x<br>";
}
?>
</body>
</html>
```

The display would be:

> Iteration: 1
>
> Iteration: 2
>
> Iteration: 3

The *foreach* Loop

This loop is used with arrays with a known number of elements. If an array holds the three primary colors, you know there are three items; therefore, use *foreach*. The *foreach* loop has the following format:

```
foreach ($array as $value)
{
code to be executed
}
```

Take the example of an array holding the three primary colors:

```
<!doctype html>
<html lang=en>
<body>
<?php
$primaries = array("red","yellow","blue");
foreach ($primaries as $value) {
echo "value <br>";
}
?>
</body>
</html>
```

The display would be as follows:

> red
>
> yellow
>
> blue

foreach is used in the next snippet of code, which was extracted from the registration pages in this book. Because the loop followed some code that detected a number of error messages (or no messages) in the *$errors* array, the number of messages is known to be either zero or a known amount.

```php
} else { // Display the errors
  echo '<h2>Error!</h2>
  <p class="error">The following error(s) occurred:<br>';
  foreach ($errors as $msg) { // Display each error
    echo " - $msg<br>\n";
  }
  echo '</p><h3>Please try again.</h3><p><br></p>';
}
```

The *do while* Loop

The *do while* loop executes the piece of code once, and then it will check the result. If the result is not equal to a predetermined amount, it will continue to loop until the result is equal to the predetermined amount. The *do* and the *while* are separated by the code that executes some task, as follows:

```php
An initial variable;
do
{code to be executed;
}
while (condition is true);

body text first
        <?php
        $x=1;
        do
        (
        echo "Number: $x <br>";
        }
        while ($x<=3)
        ?>
```

The display would be:

Number: 1

Number: 2

Number: 3

Numbers

Here are some examples of valid numbers for use in PHP scripts:

Valid integers: 4 and –4

Valid floating point numbers: 4.0 or –4.0 or 40.44

Invalid numbers: ¾ or 3a or 04.01.14

The operators for numbers are: add +, subtract –, multiply *, divide /

Here's an example:

```php
<?php
  $price = 100;
  $sales_tax = 0.2;
  $total_price = $price + ($price * $sales_tax);
  echo $total_price;
?>
```

The total price displayed would be 120.

Quotation Marks

Items enclosed within single quotes are treated literally. Items within double quotes are replaced by their values, as shown in the following example:

```php
<?php
$fname = 'Adrian';
   echo 'Single quotes will display $fname. ';
   echo "Double quotes will display $fname";
?>
```

The display would be:

Single quotes will display $fname. Double quotes will display Adrian

Note that numbers do not require quotes.

Sessions

The period of uninterrupted time that a user spends viewing a web site is a *session*. By using a PHP built-in array named $_SESSION, a user's data can be stored in a session as she moves from page to page. This is achieved by assigning the user's data to a session as follows:

```php
if (isset($_POST['id']))
{
$id = $_POST['id'];
}
session_start()
$_SESSION['id'] = $id
do some action
```

The function session_start() must appear on every page where a session will be used. The function will then either start a session or access an existing session. The function must appear in the page code before anything is sent to the browser. It will not tolerate even a preceding space or empty line.

Logging In with a Session

We have used sessions in most chapters, and the login pages provide a typical example, as shown in the following snippet:

```php
<?php
// Check if the login form on the login page has been submitted
if ($_SERVER['REQUEST_METHOD'] == 'POST') {
    require ('mysqli_connect.php'); //connect to database
//Insert your email validation code here and assign email alias as $e
// Insert your password validate code here and assign password alias as $p
if ($e && $p){//if no problems were encountered
// Fetch the user_id, first_name and user_level for that email/password combination:
$q = "SELECT user_id, fname, user_level FROM users WHERE (email='$e' AND psword=SHA1('$p'))";
    $result = mysqli_query ($dbcon, $q);
// Was there a record that matched the email/password combination
if (@mysqli_num_rows($result) == 1) {//if a database record matched the user's input
// Fetch the record and set the session data
    session_start();                                                          #1
    $_SESSION = mysqli_fetch_array ($result, MYSQLI_ASSOC);
$_SESSION['user_level'] = (int) $_SESSION['user_level']; // Ensure user level is an integer
// Use a ternary operation to set the URL                                     #2
$url = ($_SESSION['user_level'] === 1) ? 'admin-page.php' : 'members-page.php';
header('Location: ' . $url); // Make the browser load either the members' or the admin page
exit(); // Stop the script.
    mysqli_free_result($result);
    mysqli_close($dbcon);
    } else { // No match was made
echo '<p class="error">The email address and password entered do not match our records.</p>'
    }
    } else { // If there was a system problem
    echo '<p class="error">Please try again.</p>';
    }
    mysqli_close($dbcon);
    } // End of submit conditional
?>
<!-- Display the form fields-->                                               #3
<div id="loginfields">
<?php include ('login_page.inc.php'); ?>
</div>
```

Note that the *session_start*() function (line **#1**) is not preceded by anything that is sent to the browser. It is followed by code that takes the data from the found record and assigns the data to the session. A ternary operator (line **#2**) then uses the data stored in the session to make the browser load either the members' or the admin page. After the PHP code is processed, the code finally sends some information to the browser (line **#3**).

Logging Out Destroys a Session

Sessions are located in the memory of the server for security; closing the browser will end the session. However, if the user wishes to log out and then browse the web site's public pages, for security she can log out and the code in the logout page shown next will destroy the session.

```php
<?php
session_start();//access the current session
// If no session id variable exists, redirect the user
if (!isset($_SESSION['user_id'])) {
header("location:index.php");
exit();
}else{ //Destroy the session
    $_SESSION = array(); // Destroy the variables stored in the session
    session_destroy();    // Destroy the session itself
    setcookie (session_name(), '', time()-3600);
    setcookie('PHPSESSID', time()-3600,'/', 0, 0);//Destroy the cookie
header("location:index.php");
exit();
}
```

Ternary Operator

The ternary operator is a very concise way of setting a conditional. The ternary operation uses the symbols ? and the colon : The example is taken from Chapter 3 of this book.

```php
// Use a ternary operation to set a page URL
$url = ($_SESSION['user_level'] === 1) ? 'admin-page.php' : 'members-page.php';
header('Location: ' . $url); // Make the browser load either the members' or ↵
the admin page
exit(); // Stop the script
```

The first part (enclosed in brackets) takes the user_level in the session array and asks if it is identical to 1. The three equal signs mean *identical to*. The item after the question mark is stating that if the user_level is identical to 1, then assign the *admin-page.php* to the variable named $url. The colon is the equivalent of else; therefore, if *user_level* is not identical to 1, $url is set so that it directs the user to the *members-page.php*. (Registered members have a *user_level* of 0.) The variable *$url*, therefore, is set to a particular page, and the user is redirected to that page using the *header()* function.

```php
header('Location: ' . $url); // Make the browser load either the members' or the admin page
exit(); // Quit the script
```

The long-hand equivalent of the preceding ternary statement is

```php
if ($_SESSION['user_level'] === 1) {
header('location: admin-page.php');
exit();
}else{
header('location: members-page.php');
exit();
}
```

Validation and Sanitization Filters

The following script validates an e-mail address using the *filter_var()* function:

```
//If the email address is present, trim it
   if (isset($_POST['email'])) {
   $etrim = trim($_POST['email']);
//Validate the trimmed address
   $validated_etrim = (filter_var($etrim, FILTER_VALIDATE_EMAIL));
   $e = mysqli_real_escape_string($dbcon, $validated_etrim);
   }else{
$errors[] = 'Your email address is invalid or you forgot to enter your email address.';
}
```

Malicious user input can be sanitized by means of the filter_var function. If a user inputs script into a registration form variable named $last_name, any HTML or JavaScript tags can be removed as follows:

```
$last_name ='<script>alert('some_alert');</script>';
echo filter_var($last_name, FILTER_SANITIZE_STRING);
```

The <script></script> tags will be removed, leaving a harmless string as follows:

```
$sanitized_input = alert('some_alert');
```

Resources listing the filter_var functions are given later in this Appendix.

Variables

Variables store values and can be accessed only on the page on which they are created. If you click a link to switch to another page, the next page knows nothing about that variable. However, there are ways of passing the variable's value to another page. Variables begin with a dollar sign ($). Following the dollar sign, the variable's name can be text (uppercase or lowercase), hyphens, or underscores. The name can include numbers but must not start with a number.

Example: $first_name

Variables are case sensitive, $Firstname is not the same as $firstname.

Variables: Predefined (aka Built-in Variables or Global Variables)

You have used PHP predefined variables in most of the chapters. They allowed us to transfer data from a form to a handler, or from one HTML page to another. Predefined variables always begin with a dollar sign and an underscore, as shown in the following four examples:

```
$_SERVER,      $_POST['fname']    $_GET(fname},    $_SESSION['fname'],
```

In our tutorials, the predefined variables $_POST['fname' were assigned to shorter variables like this:

```
$fname = $_POST['fname']
```

Variables: String

String variables are groups of characters enclosed in single or double quotes—for example:

```
$my_pet = 'cat';    $animal = "dog";    $birthday = 'March 10th, 1952';
```

If the string contains an apostrophe, it must be escaped—for example: $last_name = "O\'Brien"

MySQL and phpMyAdmin Quick Reference

INSERT

When using the **INSERT** query to insert data into a table, the query has two parts: the column names and the VALUES, as shown in the following example:

```
$q = "INSERT INTO users (user_id, title, fname, lname, email, psword, registration_date) ↵
VALUES (' ', '$title', '$fn', '$ln', '$e', SHA1('$p'), NOW())";
```

The number and order of the *column names* must exactly match number and order of the *values*.

SELECT

The elements of a **SELECT** query must be in the following order:

SELECT (column or expression) **AS** (set an alias) **FROM** (table) **WHERE** (condition) **ORDER BY** (column)

AS and **ORDER BY** are optional and can be omitted. **ORDER BY** can be followed by the keywords ASC or DESC to specify how the selected items are to be ordered. The number of records selected can be specified by putting LIMIT and an *integer* at the end of the query.

UPDATE

Let's say Rose Bush has a new e-mail address. Use the **UPDATE** query to change it as follows:

```
$q = UPDATE users SET email ='rbush@mynewisp.co.uk' WHERE user_id = 15 LIMIT 1
```

Storage Engines and phpMyAdmin

Before creating a table, you need to decide whether you will require a full text search facility for searching through text in a database table. A user might wish to search for a particular topic. For example, he or she might search for the words "Mark Twain" to view a list of quotations by Mark Twain. If you need this facility, choose the MyISAM storage engine for your tables. However, if you have MySQL version 5.6.4 or later, the INNODB storage engine allows full text searches. For the latest information, see the MySQL web site:

```
http://dev.mysql.com/doc/refman/5.6/en/fulltext-search.html
```

Unfortunately, at the time of writing, the new version of MySQL was not available in the XAMPP download version 1.8.2. However, it is included in XAMPP version 1.8.3.

In phpMyAdmin, you can choose the type of storage engine. On the screen for creating the columns, a pull-down menu allows you to select the storage engine. This is shown circled in Figure App-1.

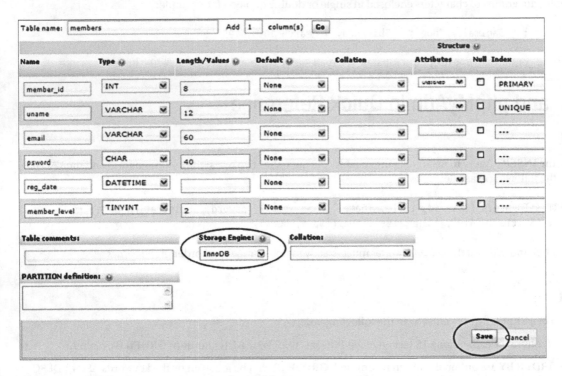

Figure App-1. *Selecting a storage engine for a table*

Changing the Storage Engine on an Existing Populated Table

If you wish to change an existing table's storage engine from INNODB to MyISAM, or vice versa, this is quite easily accomplished in phpMyAdmin as long as you have not changed collations or decreased the column size. As a precaution, before changing the engine, always back up your table using the phpMyAdmin *Export* facility. After changing the engine, check that all is well with the web site and then back up the table again.

The items referred to in the steps that follow are shown circled in Figure App-2.

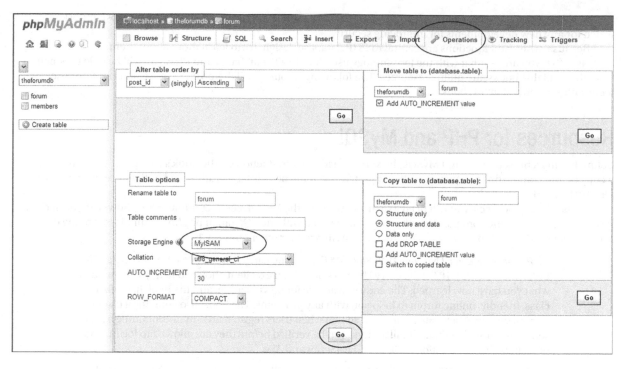

Figure App-2. *Changing the type of storage engine*

1. In phpMyAdmin, click the name of your database in the left panel.

2. In the left panel, click the table you wish to change.

3. Click the *Operations* tab.

4. Use the storage engine's pull-down menu to select the engine.

5. Click Go.

What Next?

I hope the simplified approach in this book has inspired you to explore more advanced PHP techniques for developing databases. For increased security, you will need to learn about prepared statements and transactions. Prepared statements are analogous to *include* statements. The variable content of a query is taken out of the main code, and that content is the prepared statement (named *stmt*). The content is then pulled into the query by means of a *bind* statement. Separating the components of a query is a strong security measure.

Transactions ensure that items such as orders are truly completed before inserting them into the database table. Transactions allow the user to roll back to amend the order details or even cancel the order.

You might wish to examine the merits of procedural PHP vs. Object Oriented PHP (OOP); both will produce the same outcome, but OOP can be advantageous for maintaining very large web sites. This book used procedural PHP throughout. OO P is a recent addition to PHP and will be more familiar to programmers who are acquainted with Perl or C++.

JavaScript, Ajax, and jQuery can add enhancements to a database-driven web site. Help on these topics is provided in the resources listed next.

Use the resources to keep abreast of improvements and modifications in PHP and MYSQL. Most importantly, watch for any new developments for improving security.

Because arrays and functions are central to PHP database design, try to learn more about them.

Now that you are familiar with the terminology used for MySQL databases and PHP, you will be able to benefit from the available books and online resources. The following resources will help you to move on from the basic techniques described in this book.

Resources for PHP and MySQL

Before buying a book on PHP and MySQL, be sure to read the introduction on the book's web page. If possible, borrow a copy before committing to a purchase. You might find that the book is far too advanced or that it covers what you already learned.

To use these resources, you will need to learn how to use the MySQL client command line; however, you should now be able to adapt the commands so that they can be used with the *SQL* tab in phpMyAdmin. Here are the books I recommend (My opinion only, check the reviews on Amazon for other opinions):

- *PHP and MySQL for Dynamic Web Sites (4th Edition)* by Larry Ullman (Peachpit Press, 2012). ISBN-13:978-0-321-784-07-0. Larry Ullman's book is an excellent choice to help you expand on what you have now learned. The code is available for downloading, and the book has a first-class, friendly, online forum to help you with any problems. The book also contains a useful section on how to activate an account so that when users register, an e-mail containing a link is sent to them so that their e-mail address can be verified before they are allowed to log in. The book includes information on JQuery, JavaScript and Ajax.

- *PHP 6 and MySQL 5 for Dynamic Web Sites* by Larry Ullman (Peachpit Press, 2008). Visual QuickStart Guide. ISBN-13:978-0-321-52599-4. This book is a little out of date in a few minor instances and it may be out of print but still available from some sources. It is partly a sequel to the first book in this list. The first few chapters overlap the previous book but the practical examples are different and more advanced. Although PHP 6 has yet to be released, the various new versions of PHP 5 adopt many of the proposed PHP 6 features.

- *PHP and MySQL Web Development (4th Edition)* by Luke Welling and Laura Thomson (Pearson Education, Inc., 2009). ISBN-13:978-0-672-32916-6. The book has a CD containing all the code.

- *PHP for the Web (3rd edition)* by Larry Ullman (Peachpit Press, 2009). Visual QuickStart Guide. ISBN-13:978-0-321-44249-9. This book is also a little out of date in a few minor instances, but otherwise it's an excellent PHP resource. It is very practical and easy to follow. I frequently refer to it.

HTML and PHP Editing Software

Dreamweaver CC is the most comprehensive WYSIWYG editor. It is now part of Adobe's Creative Cloud package that you can pay for monthly as and when you need it. See `http://www.adobe.com`.

I have always used the full-featured WYSIWYG tool Microsoft Expression Web. Now Microsoft has discontinued it (incorporating the features into Visual Studio), but the good news is that Microsoft now provides the last version, Expression Web 4, as a free download, which you can download at `http://www.microsoft.com/en-us/download/details.aspx?id=36179`.

The free Notepad++ version 6.5.1 is an extremely useful non-WYSIWYG text editor that supports several programming languages. It is available from `http://notepad-plus-plus.org`.

PHP and MySQL Internet Resources

Here are some online resources you can refer to for further guidance:

- `http://www.htmlite.com/`: This site is great for practical PHP scripts and MySQL.
- If you own a book by Larry Ullman, be sure to try his superb forum at `http://larryullman.com/forums`.
- `http://www.phpbuilder.com`: This site has many PHP tutorials and a forum.
- `http://www.homeandlearn.co.uk/php/php.html`: This site contains PHP for beginners with some good example scripts.
- `http://www.w3schools.com/php/`: Here you'll find a good selection of PHP scripts.
- `http://www.zend.com`: This site offers tutorials and a forum from the brains behind the PHP core.
- `http://www.php.net`: Keep up to date by visiting this site, which was the original PHP web site.
- `http://net.tutsplus.com/tutorials/php/getting-clean-with-php/`: This site has good examples of the use of *filter_var()* for validating and sanitizing user input.

Resource for Creating a Forum

Try the following web site for a tutorials on creating a forum:

`http://net.tutsplus.com/tutorials/php/how-to-create-a-phpmysql-powered-forum-from-scratch/?search_index=36`

E-Commerce Resources

The first two book resources previously listed contain some information on e-commerce web sites. The CD provided with the book by Luke Welling and Laura Thomson has a good example of a custom shopping cart.

For resources dealing specifically with e-commerce, try the following:

- *Effortless E-Commerce with PHP and MySQL* by Larry Ullman (New Riders). ISBN-13: 978-0-321-65622-3. At the time of this writing, Larry Ullman was working on a second edition of his manual.

Online Tutorials

One online tutorial gives instructions using 20 videos averaging 15 minutes each. View this at `http://www.youtube.com/playlist?list=PL442E340A42191003`.

Of course, you won't be able to create an e-commerce web site by viewing videos, you would also need a great deal of documentation so that you can study the code and adapt it. However, the videos give an excellent outline of the enormous amount of work that would be required to create a fully operational e-commerce web site.

A good tutorial for an e-commerce database with downloadable files can be found at: `http://www.webassist.com/community/tutorials/view_tutorial.php?tid=101`.

Integrating PayPal with a Custom Shopping Cart

Check out the following web sites for information related to custom shopping carts:

```
https://www.paypal.com/us/cgi-bin/webscr?cmd=_shoppingcart-intro-outside
https://www.paypal.com/cgi-bin/webscr?cmd=p/xcl/rec/sc-techview_outside
https://www.paypal.com/cgi-bin/webscr?cmd=_pdn_howto_checkout_outside
https://developer.paypal.com/webapps/developer/docs/classic/paypal-payments-↵
standard/integration-guide/cart_upload/
```

The third web site in the preceding list has some useful coded examples. The fourth web site has extra information and some helpful screen shots.

PayPal Forums

For the USA, check out the following web site: `https://www.paypal-community.com/t5/US-PayPal-Community/ct-p/US`. For the UK, check out the following web site: `https://www.paypal-community.com/t5/UK-Community/ct-p/UK`.

Third-Party Shopping Carts

Third-party shopping carts are available from the following resources:

- **Click Cart:** I have seen very good reports of *Click Cart Pro* software. Apparently, it makes easy work of integrating payment systems into a web site. It supports the world's most popular payment systems, including PayPal, Authorize.net, and Sage Pay. The cost at the time of writing was $199, and upgrades are $99. As e-commerce database web sites can be developed only by firms with deep pockets, the price is small compared to the annual budgets of most companies. For more details visit the following web site: `http://www.kryptronic.com/`.

- **Stripe:** This is the latest payment gateway for PHP-based web sites. Charges are low for successful transactions, and it operates by means of users' credit/debit cards. Your web-site development team needs to have a good knowledge of JavaScript because the gateway depends on the application of JavaScript and jQuery. For more information visit `https://stripe.com`. For the U.K version, visit `https://stripe.com/gb`.

- **Authorize.net:** This is a USA and Canadian payment gateway that accepts credit/debit cards. It requires a setup fee of $99 and $20 monthly payments. Details can be found at `http://www.authorize.net`.

Summary

The Appendix provided an alphabetical list of the main PHP code required for creating interactive web sites and databases. This was followed by a brief reference for MySQL and phpMyAdmin. The question *"What next?"* was posed, and some suggestions offered. To help you to progress beyond the basic instruction given in this book, a list of resources was provided.

Index

■ X, Y, Z

Get the eBook for only $10!

> Now you can take the weightless companion with you anywhere, anytime. Your purchase of this book entitles you to 3 electronic versions for only $10.

This Apress title will prove so indispensible that you'll want to carry it with you everywhere, which is why we are offering the eBook in 3 formats for only $10 if you have already purchased the print book.

Convenient and fully searchable, the PDF version enables you to easily find and copy code—or perform examples by quickly toggling between instructions and applications. The MOBI format is ideal for your Kindle, while the ePUB can be utilized on a variety of mobile devices.

Go to www.apress.com/promo/tendollars to purchase your companion eBook.